school law
cases and concepts

Second edition

MICHAEL W. LA MORTE

University of Georgia

Prentice-Hall, Inc., Englewood Cliffs, New Jersey 07632

Library of Congress Cataloging-in-Publication Data

La Morte, Michael W.
  School law.

  I. Educational law and legislation—United States—
Cases. I. Title.
KF4118.L25 1987   344.73'07   86-12255
                      347.3047
ISBN 0-13-793720-2

Editorial/production supervision and interior design: Virginia Cavanagh Neri
Manufacturing buyer: Barbara Kelly Kittle

Printed in the United States of America

10 9 8 7 6 5 4 3 2 1

ISBN 0-13-793720-2   01

Prentice-Hall International (UK) Limited, *London*
Prentice-Hall of Australia Pty. Limited, *Sydney*
Prentice-Hall of Canada Inc., *Toronto*
Prentice-Hall Hispanoamericana, S.A., *Mexico*
Prentice-Hall of India Private Limited, *New Delhi*
Prentice-hall of Japan, Inc., *Tokyo*
Prentice-Hall of Southeast Asia Pte. Ltd., *Singapore*
Editora Prentice-Hall do Brasil, Ltda., *Rio de Janeiro*

contents

2   SCHOOLS AND THE STATE   20

3   STUDENTS AND THE LAW   80

4   TEACHERS AND THE LAW   188

5 SCHOOL DESEGREGATION 285

6   SCHOOL FINANCE REFORM   343

7   EDUCATOR AND SCHOOL DISTRICT LIABILITY   369

table of cases*

*Edited cases are indicated by *italics*

preface

Those in public education are well aware that courts, over the last several decades, have played a significant role in establishing educational policy. Decisions in such areas as desegregation, prayer, and Bible reading, public school financing, student rights, and personnel issues attest to the extent and magnitude of judicial influence. Foremost among the many reasons for the increased court involvement has been the perception, especially of those holding minority views, that the judiciary was a receptive and efficacious branch of government. Although this contention is no longer as strongly held as it once was the judiciary continues to be viewed as an institution willing to address issues other branches of government refused to address or were reluctant even to recognize.

The resultant judicial activity has produced a sizable body of school law with which educators should be familiar if they wish to conduct themselves in a legally defensible manner. Those educators who "fly by the seat of their pants" or who act on the basis of what they think the law "should be" may be in difficulty if sufficient thought is not given to the legal implications and ramifications of their policies or conduct. Consequently, this text provides introductory material for those educators and lay persons interested in K-12 educational issues who have little or no knowledge of, or background in, school law. This would include such groups as teachers, school administrators, school board members, preservice teachers, and public school students and their families.

It would be difficult for a one-volume work to cover all of the significant topics in school law. Therefore, this text attempts to address important issues in school law with an emphasis on those having an impact at the school-building level. Additionally, material is presented to enable the reader to better understand the sources of law under which educational policy is developed and carried out and a brief description of the dual judicial system. Also included are several appendices containing sections on how to analyze a court decision, how to research school law issues, an edited federal constitution, and edited statutory material. A glossary is included to provide the definitions of commonly used legal terminology.

Chapter 1 offers sufficient background to facilitate comprehension of succeeding chapters. Included in this chapter is a discussion of areas of underlying importance with which educators may be unfamiliar: the legal significance of the sources of law under which educators operate; federal and state constitutions; federal and state statutes; state school board policy; attorney general's opinions; local school board policy and local school policy; the significance of the Fourteenth Amendment's due process and equal protection provisions as a basis for many school lawsuits; the importance of case law in establishing educational policy; and the organization of the American dual court system.

Chapter 2 examines the extent of the state's and local school system's authority when individuals disagree with educational policy. A reading of the court decisions in this chapter reveals the judiciary's attempt to establish a balance between the legitimate demands or objections of individuals toward education policy and school authorities' perception of their responsibility to the greater population. School law issues selected to illuminate this area include compulsory school attendance; religion in the schools; use of facilities; aid to nonpublic schools; school fees; and immunization.

This writer has found that issues pertaining to students and teachers are of particular interest to school law students; therefore, Chapters 3 and 4, which address these topics, comprise a major portion of the text. Chapter 3 presents material pertinent to student interests, such as freedom of expression; suspension and expulsion; corporal punishment; search; dress and grooming; pregnancy, parenthood, and marriage; education of handicapped students; participation in extracurricular activities; and school punishment for out-of-school offenses. Chapter 4 examines such teacher-related issues as freedom of expression; academic freedom; nonrenewal and dismissal; dress and grooming; bargaining; discrimination based on sex, race, age, and handicap; and political activities of teachers.

Chapters 5 and 6 provide a historical legal perspective to the issues of school desegregation and the legal attacks on the adequacy of state school finance plans. Although a 1954 United States Supreme Court decision held de jure public school segregation to be unconstitutional, racial segregation in the schools—the subject of chapter 5—continues to be an issue in many school systems across the country. Chapter 6 examines the issue of wealth disparity within a state as a factor in challenging a state's school-financing plan. This issue emerged as a legal one in the early 1970s and continues to be an issue in many states. A knowledge of the complexities of school finance is not necessary for an understanding of the material in this chapter.

Chapter 7 addresses the extent, if any, of educator and school district liability for damages as a result of their official action or inaction. Since the law in this area varies considerably among the states, emphasis is given to such general concepts as duty and standard of care, school district immunity, duties of supervision, and malpractice. Tort law is a highly specialized branch of law that is exceedingly complicated; therefore, this chapter makes the reader aware of the potential of liability for damages resulting form improper behavior.

Appendices provide additional information enabling the reader to gain a broader perspective. Appendices A and B are designed to be primers for the reader who wishes to become more adept at analyzing court decisions or engaging in school-related legal research. Appendix B is designed to provide rudimentary legal-research methodology and information on primary and secondary legal resources available to those interested in legal research. Appendix C contains sections of the United States Constitution and amendments that are most relevant for educators. Appendix D contains edited federal statues and implementing regulations having significance for educators. A glossary of often-used legal terminology is included for the reader's convenience in better understanding the edited court decisions.

Edited verbatim decisions constitute a substantial portion of this book. Such decisions provide a rich source of information, enabling a reader to gain an insight and understanding of school law that cannot be obtained through secondary analysis. The reading of a judge's or justice's written opinion—majority, concurring, or dissenting—provides valuable philosophical underpinnings for a thorough understanding of judicial rationale. It also enables the reader to relate a court's legal rationale to a specific factual context. Emphasis is on substantive school law issues. Deleted from the edited cases is material not related to the issue being examined, material pertaining to technical legal matters, and procedural legal issues that are of primary interest to attorneys.

Inclusion of a particular decision was based on several factors. These included selecting the case decided by the highest level court that had addressed the specific school law issue under consideration, thereby providing the widest applicability; the case that best represented the majority of cases in areas where the law was not well settled; or the case that best illustrated the historic evolvement of the case law under consideration.

Notes and questions follow many of the edited decisions. The notes are designed to provide helpful information to the reader, such as background material; additional citations for those interested in pursuing further the issue under consideration; the extent to which the law is well settled; or other views if the law is not well settled. Provocative questions are included to illuminate the topic and foster discussion.

This book has not been written with the intention of expressing opinions for or against views espoused by school administrators, teachers, or students, nor to contend that the judiciary is a meddlesome instutution thwarting the efforts of educators. Rather, the book's purpose is to provide those who are involved in public education with a rudimentary knowledge base for making educationally sound decisions within the legal framework. Having such knowledge may reduce the tendency to act on the basis of what the law should be rather than what it is. In that sense, this book stresses the descriptive, not the prescriptive. The author assumes that public school students learn best about law and order through its observance by knowledgeable teachers, school administrators, and school board members. And since an important aspect of public school education is the inculcation in students of the notion that we are a "nation of laws and not of men," educators must be familiar with the school law to abide by it. This is of considerable concern to the author because of his experience as a youth under Adolph Hitler in Nazi Germany. It was observed that one strategy a dictator such as Hitler used to strengthen and solidify his power was the systematic breakdown of law in Germany. As the law was increasingly disregarded, the power of the Nazis increased, and the country became a "nation of men and not of laws." It was a delight to have the opportunity of revising the first edition of this text, as the examination of school law issues continues to be, for me, an exciting and rewarding enterprise.

Finally, a book such as this does not serve as a substitute for competent legal advice should it be needed. However, in addition to a knowledge of school law, an understanding of the material in this book should help to foster a more fruitful exchange with an attorney when that is necessary.

In acknowledgement, students in my school law classes over the years deserve a special word of thanks not only for their scintillating and penetrating questions but also for sharing with me what school law topics they deemed important as they carried out their school-related responsibilities. Several students—Robert Meadows, Betty Hull, Jeffrey Williams, and Lauren Anderson—have made valuable contributions, and they have my gratitude. Pat McCollum and Neil McIntyre deserve special recognition for their assistance in checking sources and persistence in dealing with administrative details. Of course, any failure of omission or commission in this book is the sole responsibility of the author.

educational governance: sources of law and the courts

Introduction

Governance in America is based on the notion that we are "a nation of laws and not of men." Consequently, those involved in making and enforcing public school policy should ensure that their actions are lawful. Educational policy may not be enforced arbitrarily or capriciously but must be based on such appropriate legal authority as federal or state constitutional or statutory provisions, state board of education or state department of education regulations, case law, or local school board policy.

Several forces are operating, however, that at times make it difficult for those who administer public schools to function in a lawful manner. These forces include a federal system of government composed of several levels and corresponding branches that bear on the educational enterprise, changing and sometimes conflicting laws or policies, and a climate of uncertainty regarding case law due to the frequent involvement of the judiciary in establishing educational policy.

Under the federal system, the three levels of government—federal, state, and local—all have a voice in educational matters, although not necessarily in unison. Difficulties develop, since some areas of educational governance overlap considerably in responsibility among the three levels of government and their corresponding branches. These difficulties are exacerbated not only by the unclear delineation of authority but also by the uncertainty of determining which authority is supreme when irreconcilable conflicts exist.

Although education is not specifically mentioned in the federal Constitution, the federal government has had an historic involvement in it. Programs under various federal laws pertaining to education in recent years have made up approximately 6 percent of the total amount of money expended for public elementary and secondary education. Perhaps of greater importance is the pervasive and significant force of the federal judiciary in influencing educational policy. Controversial education issues such as racial segregation in schools, financing of schools, due process for both students and teachers, the role of religion in the schools, and the extent to which students and teachers may engage in freedom of expression have all been addressed by the federal judiciary.

State government has plenary power over public education, and this power is carried out by constitutional and statutory provisions, executive acts, state board of education policies, and actions of chief state school officers. The roles of governmental participants vary among the state governments. The extent of state authority over local school systems is also not uniform; however, it is generally considered to be directly proportional to the state's financial contribution to public education.

The degree of authority that local school systems have over educational matters depends on a state's constitutional and statutory provisions. These local powers may be delegated or implied. Although it is the prevailing belief that public schools are controlled locally, many students of educational governance suggest that a so-called myth of local control may be operating. They argue that in many instances the state has more meaningful power over education policy than the local school system does.

Since each level of government is inextricably intertwined in public educational governance, problems often arise for building-level educators—for instance, when one level or branch of government does not agree with policies or decisions made by another level or branch. Misunderstanding on the part of educators may also exist regarding the legitimate role of each of the levels of governance. Examples of these conflicts abound: a local school system not wishing to desegregate but forced to by a federal court order; "wealthy" local school systems barred, as a result of a state supreme court decision, from appreciably supplementing the state-financed program; and local school systems having to accept an amount of disruption by students wishing to express themselves on political, social or economic matters, protected by a United States Supreme Court decision.

The difficulty of attempting to administer schools in a lawful manner is compounded when educators, unfamiliar with the nuances of the legal system, perceive seeming inconsistencies and occasionally acrimonious disagreement among judges in certain court decisions. Such a situation occurs when a decision is changed one or more times as an educational issue winds its way through the appellate process. Occasionally, this process reveals sharp philosophical differences among judges. The lack of consistency in court decisions regarding certain issues is also troubling to some educators. They often find it difficult to understand why an educational practice has court approval in one state or area of federal jurisdiction and not in another. The legitimacy of a federal court overruling a state court's decision is also not always completely understood, especially when such a ruling increases the difficulty of administering schools because of strong local, state, or regional disagreement with such a ruling.

School administrators often view themselves as working in a climate of uncertainty as to the legality of their administrative decisions. This may be due to an insufficient knowledge of constitutional law as it pertains to educational matters or an inadequate knowledge of recent court decisions. Relying on what is perceived as sound educational practice in making administrative decisions is helpful, but it is not always a guarantee that the practice will avoid conflict with case law.

One remedy for ensuring lawful administrative conduct and reducing conflict and misunderstanding among educators is a systematic study of the sources of law under which educators operate. Such a study follows and is designed to illuminate the legitimate role of the various levels of government and their component branches. Although sources of law may be examined in various ways, a particularly fruitful method is to analyze those sources that spring from each level of government.

I. Sources of Law

A. Federal Level

At the federal level, the Constitution and its amendments, statutes, rules and regulations of administrative agencies, case law, presidential executive orders, and attorney general's opinions all constitute sources of law under which educators operate.

1. Constitution and Amendments

Although the federal Constitution does not contain the word education, constitutional interpretation by the judiciary has had unquestionable impact on educational policymaking. Particularly significant is the judiciary's interpretation of the Fourteenth Amendment to the Constitution. A brief examination of this amendment may be helpful, on the basis both of its historical origins and of its requirements for due process and equal protection of the law as they pertain to educational matters.

a. Historical Perspective   Prior to the adoption of the Fourteenth Amendment in 1868, Americans, under the federal system of government, had a particular kind of dual relationship with state and national governments regarding their civil rights. This came about largely as a result of skepticism, if not an outright distrust, of central government that existed after the Revolutionary War as a consequence of experiences under British rule. To ensure that a central government would not again run roughshod over an individual's civil rights, a Bill of Rights was added to the Constitution shortly after that document was ratified. Protections afforded those early Americans under the Bill of Rights included: freedoms regarding religion, speech, press, peaceable assembly, and petitioning for a redress of grievances; a right to bear arms; protection against unreasonable searches and seizures; guarantee of a grand jury indictment in capital offenses; protection against being subject to double jeopardy or self-incrimination; the right of due process; the right to own property; the right to have a speedy trial by an impartial jury; and protection against excessive bail and cruel and unusual punishments. These protections, however, were those Americans had against their *central* government. They did not automatically have these rights against their state government as a result of the inclusion of the rights in the federal Constitution.

Protection of civil rights against state action was provided by state constitutions, and every state, as it was accepted into the Union, provided for a Bill of Rights similar to that found in the federal Constitution. It should be noted, however, that prior to the adoption of the Fourteenth Amendment, if a state's constitution did not contain a provision for guaranteeing, for instance, freedom of speech or religion, an American did not necessarily have those protections against his or her state. Although state constitutions may have contained language that afforded individuals their civil rights, as a practical matter, state-guaranteed civil rights protections were not always uniformly applied.

In the years prior to the Civil War, another factor influenced the dual relationship Americans had with their state and federal governments. For the most part, Americans, during that time, thought of themselves primarily as citizens of the state within which they resided and citizens of the United States secondarily. An individual considered himself a Virginian or New Yorker first, for instance, and an American citizen second. Although we have no way of knowing with any exactitude, it is entirely conceivable that regional allegiance, too, ran higher than national allegiance on the part of many (the South, before the Civil War, may be a prime example of this).

This dual relationship with state and central governments and the historic primary allegiance to one's state was significantly altered by the adoption of the Fourteenth Amendment to the Constitution in 1868. This amendment provided, in part, that

All persons born or naturalized in the United States and subject to the jurisdiction thereof, are citizens of the United States and of the State wherein they reside. No State shall make or enforce any law which shall abridge the privileges or immunities of citizens of the United States. Nor shall any State deprive any person of life, liberty or property, without due process of law, nor deny to any person within its jurisdiction the equal protection of the laws.

From a constitutional standpoint, the juxtaposition of the words "are citizens of the United States and of the State wherein they reside" is most revealing, since the United States is mentioned first. The legal significance of this juxtaposition and subsequent language of the amendment have been interpreted as establishing national citizenship as being primary where certain questions dealing with individual rights are concerned.

This amendment, which was intended initially to guarantee rights to newly freed slaves, has also provided protection for the individual from various forms of arbitrary or capricious state action. Since the amendment affords national citizenship primacy regarding constitutional rights, an individual is shielded against state action that may run counter to guarantees he or she has as a citizen of the United States. Under this concept, the state cannot deprive a person of rights he or she has as an American. As a result of United States Supreme Court action, for instance, a state may not condone de jure racially segregated school systems. Neither may students be deprived of their freedoms pertaining to religion by school board policy that allows Bible reading or prayers during normal school hours. These are the kinds of rights individuals have as United States citizens, and no state action, local administrative conduct, or local school board policy may violate them.

Under the Fourteenth Amendment, a state and those operating under its auspices must honor those rights, guaranteed by the Constitution, federal statutes, and case law, that a person has as a result of being an American. From a constitutional standpoint, these rights must be observed by the state and those operating under the color of the state, and they may not be infringed upon as a result of a state or local election, state or local administrative action, or state court action.

Proponents of a "state's rights theory" for American government have reluctantly accepted certain court decisions based on the Fourteenth Amendment and have adamantly refused to abide by others. Objection to the amendment by such groups is often based on the method used to gain its ratification. Ratification of the amendment was a required step for readmittance to the Union after the Civil War.

b. Due Process and Equal Protection   In addition to establishing the primacy of national citizenship with the protection of certain individual rights, the Fourteenth Amendment also provides for due process and equal protection of the law. These two concepts stem from an ideal of fairness in applying the law, and they are not necessarily mutually exclusive. In cases dealing with educational matters where the Fourteenth Amendment is cited, it is generally alleged that either (or both) due process or equal protection of the law has been denied. Although extremely complex in a legal sense, these concepts may best be understood by keeping in mind that they require government officials, which of couse includes educators, to be fair as they conduct governmental business. This necessitates reasonable and noncapricious action, in addition to abiding by statute and case law, on the part of public school officials when dealing with clients or personnel.

[1] Due Process

In the broadest sense, a person has received due process of law under the Fourteenth Amendment when he or she has been treated essentially the same by state action or local government action as another person has under similar circumstances when he or she is subject to deprivation of life, liberty, or property. Under this concept, governmental action may not be unreasonable or capricious, and when clients are not treated alike there must be a sound basis for dissimilar treatment.

Although the line between substance and procedure is often quite hazy, some have drawn a distinction between so-called procedural and substantive due process of law. According to this view, procedural due process, in the larger sense, deals with the question of whether or not a person has been accorded fair and proper treatment or procedure when apprehended or tried in a court. Accused persons must be given twelve jurors, for instance, if everyone else in their circumstances is given twelve jurors. Evidence to be presented against them must have been obtained properly, and their trials must be conducted according to established procedures. Questions dealing with procedural due process in the educational arena have received increasing attention, particularly in the area of suspension and expulsion from school. Substantive due process essentially deals with the question of fair treatment of persons by those acting under the color of the state and also with the question of the fairness and reasonableness of laws, regulations, and policies in the light of our constitutional heritage. The Fifth Amendment also contains a due process clause, and although there are similarities with the Fourteenth Amendment provision, the Fifth Amendment is considered exclusively to be protection against the federal government.

As is the case with many concepts, due process resists definition in the dictionary sense. It is a dynamic rather than a static concept. The definition in each instance depends largely on a combination of the specific facts in a situation, the law governing the situation, the particular

time in history in which judgment is being rendered, and the predilections of the individual judge(s) rendering the decision. The Supreme
Court, for instance, has never unanimously agreed on a standard for due
process. Yet it is the body that renders the ultimate and final decision
regarding whether or not due process has been denied. This point, in
addition to a discussion of the question of due process, was asserted by
Justice Frankfurter in *Sweezy* v. *New Hampshire*, 354 U.S. 234 (1957):

> To be sure, this is a conclusion based on a judicial judgment in balancing
> two contending principles—the right of the citizen to political privacy, as
> protected by the Fourteenth Amendment, and the right of the State to
> self-protection. And striking the balance implies the exercise of judgment.
> This is the inescapable judicial task in giving substantive content, legally
> enforced, to the Due Process Clause, and it is a task ultimately committed to
> this Court. It must not be an exercise of whim or will. It must be an overrid-
> ing judgment founded on something much deeper and more justifiable than
> personal preference. As far as it lies within human limitations, it must be an
> impersonal judgment. It must rest on fundamental presuppositions rooted
> in history to which widespread acceptance may be fairly attributed. Such a
> judgment must be arrived at in a spirit of humility when it counters the
> judgment of the State's highest court. But, in the end, judgment cannot be
> escaped—the judgment of this Court. (Pp. 266–67)

A basic issue—the balance between an individual's rights and the
necessity to protect the larger society—is addressed by courts when deprivation of due process is alleged. Courts must determine whether or not a
regulation, policy, law, lower-court decision, or action on the part of
someone who had a duty to perform was warranted in either limiting or
condoning a person's actions. A review of decisions involving educational
matters reveals that courts consider many factors when examining alleged
deprivation of due process by school officials. Foremost among these
factors is whether, overall, the school official's judgment was educationally
sound. Additionally, courts examine whether an official's actions were
guided primarily by administrative convenience or represented the spirit
of a conformity-minded, arrogant majority when there should have been
a willingness on the part of the majority to accept a degree of nondisruptive deviance.

A brief discussion of social contract theory may amplify the genesis
of the due process idea. Although the theory was discussed as early as
Plato, its more familiar philosophical underpinnings were advanced by
political philosophers several centuries ago, notably, Thomas Hobbes (*Le-
viathan*), John Locke (*Two Treatises of Government*), and Jean Jacques Rous-
seau (*The Social Contract*). Locke, whose social contract theory is probably
the one most familiar in the English-speaking world, attacked the divine
right of kings theory. He contended that societies were organized and
ruled by the consent of the governed and not by one who had potential

for becoming autocratic. Furthermore, he asserted that individuals by their nature had certain rights, which included life, liberty, and property. When by their own volition individuals left the primitive state of nature and agreed to be governed, they made a social contract with government that protected these natural rights. The justification for the state's existence, according to Locke, was based on its ability to protect these rights better than individuals could on their own. The price individuals paid for governmental protection was a relinquishment of the freedom they had in the state of nature. This was a limited type of "freedom," however, since it existed in an environment where there was greater potential for the "law of the jungle" and "might makes right" to prevail.

Many modern-day political theorists agree that the original thoughts of Locke and others regarding the social contract have come to stand for several propositions concerning the individual's relationship to government. These propositions include the notion that government rests on the consent of the governed; persons willingly yielded the freedom they had in the state of nature because they thought the state could offer them certain protections they could not provide for themselves; and although persons relinquished the freedom they had in the state of nature, their entering into a social contract with government included the government's guarantee against an arbitrary, capricious, and unreasonable denial of their rights of life, liberty, and property when they and the government interacted.

These propositions have considerable implications for educators. In accordance with social contract theory, school authorities have not only a legitimate but a mandatory role to play in protecting health and safety and in maintaining order. Students violating legitimate school rules may be subject to appropriate punitive action. Yet school authorities may not act arbitrarily, capriciously, or unreasonably toward individuals when protecting the majority, and due process must be provided when a liberty or property interest is involved.

[2] Equal Protection

Constitutional authorities contend that the equal-protection clause was inserted in the Fourteenth Amendment to ensure that blacks would be provided the same civil protections as white Americans. Under this notion, Negroes would not only have their civil rights protected, but they would also have the benefit of applicable laws. Although originally intended to ameliorate the transition from slavery to free status, the equal protection provision has had a dramatic effect in influencing policy in American public education.

From an educational standpoint, the equal protection clause represents the legal basis for prohibiting unreasonable classifications. Although some type of classification is often necessary in laws, rules, or policies, arbitrariness may not play a part. Methods of classifying students in public schools have often been based on such factors as sex, age, intelligence, marital status, parents' residence, race, pregnancy or motherhood, conduct, test scores, and wealth of their community. For these methods of classification to conform with equal protection guarantees, a reasonable relationship must exist between the objective to be accomplished and the type of classification employed. Also, if the state renders a benefit to one person within a class, all within that class must receive the benefit equally; and if one person within a class is deprived of a benefit by the state, all within that class must be deprived equally. This concept was expressed many years ago by the United States Supreme Court in *Barbier* v. *Connolly*, 113 U.S. 27 (1885), when it stated:

> Class legislation, discriminating against some and favoring others, is prohibited, but legislation which, in carrying out a public purpose, is limited in its application, if within the sphere of its operation it affects alike all persons similarly situated, is not within the amendment. (P. 32)

The principal idea inherent in equal protection, as in due process, is the concept of fairness. And as is the case with due process, whether or not equal protection has been granted or denied depends upon a balancing of several elements. These include sociological and psychological factors, sound educational policy, the benefit of a larger good to society as a result of the classification, contemporary customs and mores, and the protection of the individual's rights in the light of these considerations.

Courts have often employed a two-level test for measuring classifications against the equal protection clause. One is a "rational basis" test, which is employed when a "fundamental interest" is not involved. Under this test, there must be a sound reason for the classification, and all those classified alike must be treated as uniformly as possible. Additionally, the burden of proof is on the complainant to demonstrate that a challenged law or policy has no rational basis to achieve a legitimate state objective. By using this test, the United States Supreme Court has commonly exercised restraint in holding legislation in violation of the equal-protection provision of the Fourteenth Amendment.

A strict-scrutiny test is applied when a "fundamental interest" or "suspect classification" is involved. A presumption of constitutional validity disappears when a classification is "suspect." Examples of such classification include race, national origin, alienage, indigency, and illegitimacy. At this time sex is not considered a suspect classification. The strict-scrutiny test was discussed by the United States Supreme Court in *Plyler* v. *Doe*, 457 U.S. 202 (1982). The Court explained that some classifications are more likely than others to reflect deep-seated prejudice rather than legislative rationality in pursuit of some legitimate objective. It also stated that certain groups have historically experienced "political powerlessness" and thus have needed special protection from the majority. In situations where a suspect class or fundamental right is involved, the Court indicated that it is appropriate to enforce the mandate of equal protection by requiring the state to demonstrate that its classification has been precisely tailored to serve a compelling governmental interest. Although the complainant has the burden of proof when the rational-basis test is used, under the strict-scrutiny test the burden of proof is placed upon the state to show that the law or policy in question is necessary to accomplish a compelling state interest.

2. Statutes

Congress has enacted many statutes that provide educators with sources of law. The legal basis for this congressional involvement derives from the so-called general welfare clause in Article I of the United States Constitution. Some of the areas the national legislature has dealt with in recent years include: vocational education (Vocational Education Act of 1963—P.L. 88-210); building construction and operating expenses for schools affected by federal activities (School Facilities, Areas Affected by Federal Activities—P.L. 81-815 and Educational Agencies, Areas Affected by Federal Activities, Financial Aid—P.L. 81-874); defense (National Defense Education Act of 1958—P.L. 85-864); elementary and secondary education (Elementary and Secondary Education Act of 1965—P.L. 89-10); civil rights (Civil Rights Act of 1964—P.L. 88-352 and its various amendments); protecting information concerning students (Family Educational Rights and Privacy Act of 1974—P.L. 93-380*); sex discrimination (Title IX of the Education Amendments of 1972—P.L. 92-318*); handicapped children (Section 504 of the Rehabilitation Act of 1973—P.L. 93-112* and the Education for all Handicapped Children Act of 1975—P.L. 94-142 as amended by P.L. 98—199); bilingual education (Bilingual Education Act of 1968—Section 701 of P.L. 89-10 and Title VII of E.S.E.A. of 1965 as added by P.L. 90-247 and P.L. 93-380); and pregnancy bias (Pregnancy Discrimination Act of 1978—P.L. 95-555*).

Although local and federal educational agencies may occasionally disagree over the purpose and administration of federal statutes, compliance at the local level with controversial federal legislation has often been attained by the threat of a lawsuit, the lure of federal money, or a threat of a cutoff of federal funds already being received.

3. Case Law

Case law refers to principles of law established by courts. It is largely based on legal precedents declared in earlier court decisions in which

*See appendix D for material pertaining to this legislation.

there were similar factual situations. It is believed that following precedent affords a greater likelihood that citizens will be treated equally, and it has the added advantage of allowing a degree of predictability in future disputes. Although generally guided by precedent, courts are not bound by it in reaching a decision. A court may decide that the factual situation in the case being decided is not sufficiently similar to the one offering precedent or that the legal or philosophical rationale in the precedent-setting case no longer applies.

Federal courts, especially in the last several decades, have established a sizable body of case law. As a result, federal case law has been an influential, if not dominant, force in educational policymaking in recent years. Federal courts have addressed such issues as racial segregation, questions of equity in state methods for financing education, separation of church and state, due process and equal-protection considerations involving both students and teachers, the extent of freedom of expression for students and teachers, and dress and grooming standards for students and teachers. Precedent established by the federal judiciary in these areas provides educators with a significant source of law. Unfortunately, the case law is not always well settled, and conflicting opinions may occur among the federal district courts and courts of appeals. In this event educators must follow the case law established for their particular jurisdiction; however, vigilance must be exercised to ascertain appellate or Supreme Court actions that may reverse or modify existing case law. Consequently, it is vital that educators have a thorough understanding of cases where the law is well settled and be familiar with those relating to areas where it is not.

Although not always clearly understood by educators, a decision of the United States Supreme Court has the force of law and may be altered or modified only by another High Court decision or an amendment to the Constitution.* High Court decisions are not always observed by local school systems. Desegregation decisions and those dealing with Bible reading and recitation of sectarian prayers during school hours are prime examples. Since the Court does not have an enforcement arm, compliance with a decision must often be gained by continued court action, which may include requesting writs of injunction or mandamus.

4. Executive Orders and Attorney General Opinions

The president of the United States may issue an executive order that applies to education. Once issued, it would be a source of law for educators.

The attorney general of the United States may be asked to provide an official opinion pertaining to a constitutional or statutory educational

---

*Article III of the Constitution provides that the Supreme Court has appellate jurisdiction "with such exceptions, and under such regulations as the Congress shall make." Therefore, congressional action could conceivably restrict the Court's jurisdiction.

provision or a controversial educational practice. Such an opinion may be thought of as advisory and does not represent as compelling a source of law as case law.

B. State Level

Major state-level sources of law include the state's constitution, statutes, case law, state board of education policy, state department of education directives, rules and regulations of administrative agencies, executive orders, and attorney general opinions. As discussed previously, these state-level sources of law may not deprive individuals of the due process or equal protection of the laws they have as persons under the Fourteenth Amendment.

1. State Constitutions

Most state constitutions contain language committing the state to a responsibility for providing education. Although the constitutional terminology varies, it often takes the form of requiring that the legislature ensure the establishment and maintenance of a thorough and uniform or efficient system of schools. Such broad language is recognized as the ultimate authority within a state for furnishing education. Constitutional provisions may designate constitutional offices for education officials, such as state superintendent of schools and state board members. Constitutional provisions may also specify the creation of local school systems, method of selection and number of members for local school boards, qualifications and selection of local school superintendents, and authority and possibly limitations for local taxation for school purposes. A review of constitutional provisions pertaining to educational matters among the states reveals a wide range of format, from a few general designations in some states to a large number that are rather specific in other states.

Many states also have due process and/or equal protection of the law requirements similar to those found in the amendments to the federal Constitution. Consequently, state courts are often asked to interpret these in an educational context.

2. State Statutes

State statutes represent a significant source of law for educators. They are often more explicit than state constitutional provisions, and their purpose is to bring a more specific outline to broad constitutional directives or to codify case law. Statutes may regulate governmental functions such as the method of selection, terms and responsibility of state-level education officials. They may also stipulate the type of local or regional school systems; the method of selection, responsibilities, and terms of local school officials; and the powers of local education units.

State statutes generally deal with financing of the public schools, tax instruments, and the degree to which these instruments may be employed to raise local revenue. Often teacher-pupil ratios are specified, as are the teaching of certain subjects, minimum and maximum ages for subjection to compulsory education laws, length of school day and year, and rules regarding suspension and expulsion of students.

State statutes may also address areas dealing with personnel, such as tenure, retirement, collective bargaining or professional negotiation, meet-and-confer provisions, and fair dismissal procedures. Details pertaining to teaching certificates may be written into law, although this area is usually covered by state board of education policies.

3. Case Law

State court decisions can greatly aid educators in sensitive areas where there is no policy direction from statute, the constitution, or the state board of education. A decision by one state's highest court does not serve as binding precedent in another state. However, it does provide educators within the state with a significant source of law by enabling them to determine the rationale or philosophy of another state's highest legal body regarding an area of conflict.

For instance, building-level administrators are regularly faced with the dilemma of whether to search a student suspected of drug possession. This problem may be compounded by the absence of authoritative state directives and conflicting case law in other states. Consequently, a decision by a state's highest court on such an issue can aid building-level administrators as they attempt to discharge their duties in providing students with a drug-free environment.

There are notable exceptions, but in general, state courts historically have been reluctant to overturn existing school policies in the absence of clearly unreasonable, capricious, or arbitrary conduct on the part of school officials. Consequently, plaintiffs, when possible, have often opted to have their day in federal court instead of a state court.

4. State Board of Education, Chief State School Officer, and State Department of Education

The specific roles of the state board of education, the chief state board school officer, and the state department of education vary considerably among the states; yet these offices collectively and individually provide an important source of law for educators. Functional diversity among these offices in the various states often stems from different constitutional or statutory provisions and the political dynamism of the individuals associated with these offices. The formal relationship among the state board of education, the chief state school officer, and the state department of education is rarely detailed in state legislation. Therefore, in practice, the relationship often depends on the people involved. Occasionally, educators at the local level are not sufficiently familiar with the differences in authority among the three divisions. Consequently, pronouncements from one of these authorities may be viewed mistakenly as agreed-upon policy emanating from the state level.

Although the duties and responsibilities of state boards of education also vary, their primary function is to adopt the necessary policies, rules, and regulations to implement legislation and constitutional requirements. When not in conflict with constitutional decrees, these policies, rules, and regulations have the force of law.

The chief state school officer's role does not have uniformity among the states. This person administers the state department of education, the agency that deals directly with the local school systems. The department is the bureaucratic mechanism through which state policy is transmitted to local systems.

5. Attorney General Opinions

As the state's legal counsel, the attorney general may be asked for an opinion regarding an educational question when a constitutional or statutory provision is not clear or when case law does not serve as a distinct precedent. Such attorney general opinions serve as useful guides for the educator, but they do not represent the same degree of authority as a decision by a state's courts or by a federal court in whose jurisdiction the state lies.

C. Local Level

Sources of law with which educators in a local school system are most familiar are the local school board policies, rules, or regulations and their individual school's rules or regulations. Such local sources of law, among school systems, are widely dissimilar in regard to their length, comprehensiveness, and compliance with federal and/or state constitutional or statutory provisions. In many instances building-level administrators rely on this authority in dealing with such issues as administering corporal punishment, suspending a student, searching a student, censorship of the school newspaper or yearbook, student or teacher refusal to participate in patriotic exercises, use of a school building by members of the community, and dress and grooming standards for both students and teachers.

II. The American Judicial System

A dual judicial system composed of state and federal courts exists in the United States. The federal court system has its basis in the United States Constitution, which may be limited by acts of Congress or rulings of the United States Supreme Court. State court systems have their basis in state constitutional provisions or statutory enactments.

In some instances state and federal courts have concurrent jurisdiction, which presents a unique interplay between the two legal systems. This provides a prospective litigant with a choice in selecting the judicial system in which he or she wishes to initiate court action. Federal courts may be used, however, only if it can be shown that a federal question exists, and they may not interfere with state court proceedings unless a federal question is present, such as an alleged abridgement of a constitutional right.

When concurrent jurisdiction exists, plaintiffs will naturally select the court system perceived to be most sympathetic to their cause of action. In recent years plaintiffs have often viewed the federal judiciary in this light; therefore, an increasing number of cases that heretofore had been brough to state courts have been brought to the federal courts.

Prior to instituting court action, with few exceptions, one must exhaust all local and state administrative remedies before seeking a redress of grievances through court litigation. Failure to exhaust these administrative remedies by the plaintiff may result in a court's refusal to grant standing required for a hearing before the court.

Proceedings in school law often involve suits dealing with questions of due process and equal protection of the law brought in a branch of civil law termed equity law. The regular court system usually administers equity law, as separate courts do not normally exist to deal with it. However, in this type of action there is generally no jury, and the judge(s) is the sole determiner of what constitutes due process or equal protection, subject only to review by a higher court. Equity judgments regarding due process and equal protection are generally made on the basis of many variables, such as a close examination of the particular facts of a case, decisions in previous cases, and possibly the introduction of social science findings. If arbitrary or capricious conduct on the part of a governmental official can be demonstrated, the likelihood increases that either due process or equal protection has been denied. On the other hand, if educationally sound reasons are offered by the educator in attempting to explain the actions or conduct in dispute, the likelihood increases that due process or equal protection has been afforded. Ultimately, however, the judge(s) must determine—given a particular factual situation, present societal mores, actual or possible inconvenience or danger to society, and constitutional and other rights—where the balance lies between providing an individual with his or her constitutional rights and the legitimate demands of the larger society.

A. State Court Systems

Each state has the responsibility of establishing its own judicial system. Although this has resulted in the creation of fifty independent state court systems, certain basic similarities exist among them. Common to most states' judicial system is a court of original jurisdiction and some sort of appellate structure.

In most instances cases dealing with educational matters are initiated in the state's appropriate court of original jurisdiction. These courts are called circuit courts, district courts, courts of common pleas, or supreme courts (New York only), but in many states they are referred to as superior courts. Most litigation is settled in these courts, and they serve as the sole determiner of the facts in most cases.

Intermediate appellate courts constitute a second level of many state court systems. Approximately half of the states have established intermediate appellate courts, and they are called courts of appeals, appellate divisions or departments of the superior courts, appellate divisions of the supreme court (New York only), or appeals courts. Where present, these appellate level courts provide a tribunal between the trial court and the state's highest court of last resort. Unlike courts of original jurisdiction, state appellate courts do not engage in factual inquiries; rather these courts determine questions of law. Opinions are based on a written record provided by the court of original jurisdiction.

A state's highest level court is generally called the supreme court; however, it may be called the court of appeals, supreme judicial court, or the supreme court of appeals. Most state supreme courts rarely have original jurisdiction except under specific conditions mandated by state law. Their basic function is to review lower-court decisions on appeal. Purely state matters may not be appealed beyond a state's supreme court; however, if a federal question is involved an appeal may be made to the United States Supreme Court.

B. Federal Court System

By constitutional design, the federal judiciary was established as a separate and independent branch of the United States government. Subsequent federal legislation has provided for a federal judicial system, which presently includes district courts, courts of appeals, and the United States Supreme Court. A litigant must raise a federal question to have standing in a federal court. When dealing with educational issues this may be accomplished by alleging violation of a federal statute, such as 42 U.S.C. § 1983, or of amendments to the Constitution, such as the Fourteenth, First, Fourth, or Fifth.

1. District Courts

The district court, of which there are over ninety, is the court of original jurisdiction in the federal judicial system. Each state has at least one district court, and many states have between two and four districts. A district may be divided into divisions, and cases may be heard in different locations within those divisions.

UNITED STATES COURTS OF APPEALS and UNITED STATES DISTRICT COURTS

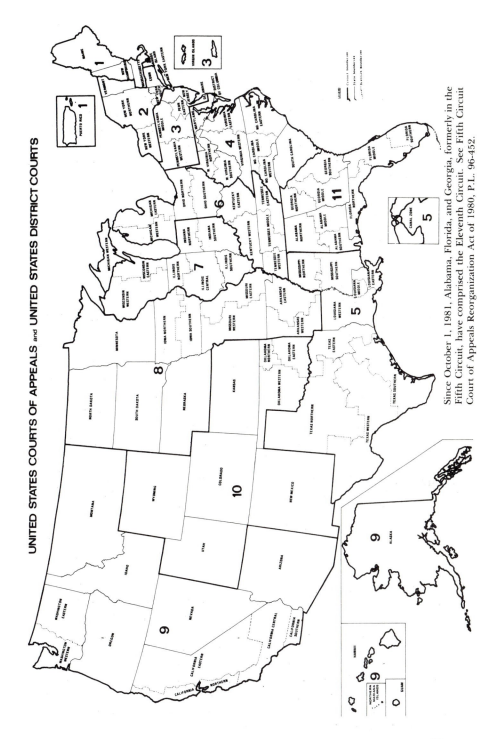

Since October 1, 1981, Alabama, Florida, and Georgia, formerly in the Fifth Circuit, have comprised the Eleventh Circuit. See Fifth Circuit Court of Appeals Reorganization Act of 1980, P.L. 96-452.

2. Court of Appeals

Courts of appeals represent the intermediate appellate level of the federal court system. Their primary function is to review appeals from district courts within the circuit, and decisions by a court of appeals are binding on the lower federal courts in the circuit. A decision by one court of appeals may stand as a persuasive decision for other courts of appeals, but it does not stand as binding authority. Courts of appeals base their decisions on the trial court's proceedings and any briefs filed by concerned parties. A case may be remanded to a lower court for further proceeding when the appellate court finds that the facts presented in the written record are insufficient to render a decision. The nation is divided into twelve federal judicial circuits, comprising eleven geographic regions and a twelfth circuit encompassing the District of Columbia (see map on page 17).

3. Supreme Court

The Supreme Court is the highest-level court in the federal judicial system, and there is no appeal from a decision rendered by this Court. When ruling on the constitutionality of a federal statute or practices within a state or local subdivision, such a ruling can be overturned only by an amendment to the Constitution or by a subsequent ruling by the Court. Nine justices including one chief justice make up the Court. As with other federal judges, their appointment is for life, and their compensation cannot be reduced during their tenure.

Most cases reach the Supreme Court by means of a writ of certiorari. Under this method an unsuccessful litigant in a lower-court decision petitions the Court to review the case, setting forth reasons why the case should be granted a writ. A case is accepted for review only if four justices vote to grant certiorari. Acceptance for review under this "rule of four" indicates that at least four members of the Court consider the case to have sufficient merit to be considered by the entire Court. Denial of certiorari leaves the decision of the lower court undisturbed but does not have the force of a written decision.

The Court's term begins on the first Monday in October and usually lasts for nine months. The number of cases docketed during a term has increased significantly. More than 5,000 cases have been docketed in recent years, while 2,313 cases were docketed in 1960 and 1,460 in 1945. Although the Court decides between 200 and 250 cases in a term, formal written opinions are rendered in approximately half of these decisions.

Court decisions dealing with educational matters have had a significant impact on educational policy in the last several decades. Many difficult decisions have had to be made by the Court because other branches or levels of government were unable to agree or were unwilling to make them. This has prompted some observers to suggest that the United States Supreme Court may have become the modern-day American oracle.

Some educators have doubts about the authority under which the Supreme Court determines questions of constitutionality. Although this right of judicial review is not explicitly provided for in the United States Constitution, many scholars agree that the framers of the Constitution expected the Court to assume this function. This notion was addressed by Alexander Hamilton in *Federalist Paper Number 78*, in which he asserted:

> ... the courts were designed to be an intermediate body between the people and the legislature ... to keep the latter within the limits assigned to their authority. The interpretation of the laws is the proper and peculiar province of the courts. ... It therefore belongs to them to ascertain its meaning, as well as the meaning of any particular act proceeding from the legislative body. ...

The Court's role as the final authority on interpreting the Constitution was established in its landmark decision, *Marbury* v. *Madison,* 1 Cranch 137 (1803), and it has continued to engage in judicial review since that time.

schools
and the state

INTRODUCTION

Public education is a governmental enterprise that receives enormous resources from the citizenry and with which most persons have direct contact for fairly extended periods of time. Consequently, since we live in a democratic society that allows for the close scrutiny of such public institutions, honest differences often arise concerning public school policies. This chapter's purpose is to examine the extent of the state's and local school system's authority when individuals disagree with educational policy involving such issues as compulsory attendance, religion in the schools, use of facilities, aid to nonpublic schools, school fees, and immunization. The thread woven throughout many of the court decisions dealing with these issues is the attempt by the courts to establish a balance between the legitimate demands or objections of individuals toward educational policy and school authorities' perception of their responsibility to the greater population.

I. Compulsory Attendance

A. Satisfied by Parochial, Private, or Home School Attendance

Every state has some form of compulsory education law. These laws generally provide that children between certain ages must attend a public, private, or home school, and failure to comply may be a criminal violation. Central to the legal disputes pertaining to compulsory attendance laws is the balancing of the state's interest in ensuring that students receive an appropriate education and the rights of parents to decide when and where their child attends school.

Pierce v. *Society of Sisters,* a landmark United States Supreme Court decision, affirmed the doctrine of compulsory school attendance. It also established the role of parochial and private schools in satisfying the state's demand that children receive schooling.

Pierce v. Society of Sisters

Supreme Court of the United States, 1925
268 U.S. 510

MR. JUSTICE MC REYNOLDS delivered the opinion of the Court.

These appeals are from decrees, based upon undenied allegations, which granted preliminary orders restraining appellants from threatening or attempting to enforce the Compulsory Education Act adopted November 7, 1922, under the initiative provision of her Constitution by the voters of Oregon.   *   *   *

The challenged Act, effective September 1, 1926, requires every parent, guardian or other person having control or charge or custody of a child between eight and sixteen years to send him "to a public school for the period of time a public school shall be held during the current year" in the district where the child resides; and failure to do so is declared a misdemeanor.   *   *   *   The manifest purpose is to compel general attendance at public schools by normal children, between eight and sixteen, who have not completed the eighth grade. And without doubt enforcement of the statute would seriously impair, perhaps destroy, the profitable features of appellees' business and greatly diminish the value of their property.

Appellee, the Society of Sisters, is an Oregon corporation, organized in 1880, with power to care for orphans, educate and instruct the youth, establish and maintain academies or schools, and acquire necessary real and personal property. It has long devoted its property and effort to the secular and religious education and care of children, and has acquired the valuable good will of many parents and guardians. It conducts interdependent primary and high schools and junior colleges, and maintains orphanages for the custody and control of children between eight and sixteen. In its primary schools many children between those ages are taught the subjects usually pursued in Oregon public schools during the first eight years. Systematic religious instruction and moral training according to the tenets of the Roman Catholic Church are also regularly provided. All courses of study, both temporal and religious, comtemplate continuity of training under the appellee's charge; the primary schools are essential to the system and the most profitable. It owns valuable buildings, especially constructed and equipped for school purposes. The business is remunerative—the annual income from primary schools exceeds thirty thousand dollars—and the successful conduct of this requires long time contracts with teachers and parents. The Compulsory Education Act of 1922 has already caused the withdrawal from its schools of children who would otherwise continue, and their income has steadily declined. The appellants, public officers, have proclaimed their purpose strictly to enforce the statute.

After setting out the above facts the Society's bill alleges that the enactment conflicts with the right of parents to choose schools where their children will receive appropriate mental and religious training, the right of the child to influence the parents' choice of a school, the right of schools and teachers therein to engage in a useful business or profession, and is accordingly repugnant to the Constitution and void. And, further, that unless enforcement of the measure is enjoined the corporation's business and property will suffer irreparable injury.

Appellee, Hill Military Academy, is a private corporation organized in 1908 under the laws of Oregon, engaged in owning, operating and conducting for profit an elementary, college preparatory and military training school for boys between the ages of five and twenty-one years. * * * It owns considerable real and personal property, some useful only for school purposes. The business and incident good will are very valuable. In order to conduct its affairs long time contracts must be made for supplies, equipment, teachers and pupils. Appellants, law officers of the State and County, have publicly announced that the Act of November 7, 1922, is valid and have declared their intention to enforce it. By reason of the statute and threat of enforcement appellee's business is being destroyed and its property depreciated; parents and guardians are refusing to make contracts for the future instruction of their sons, and some are being withdrawn.

The Academy's bill states the foregoing facts and then alleges that the challenged Act contravenes the corporation's rights guaranteed by the Fourteenth Amendment and that unless appellants are restrained from proclaiming its validity and threatening to enforce it irreparable injury will result. The prayer is for an appropriate injunction.

No answer was interposed in either cause, and after proper notices they were heard by three judges   *   *   *   on motions for preliminary injunctions upon the specifically alleged facts. The court ruled that the Fourteenth Amendment guaranteed appellees against the deprivation of their property without due process of law consequent upon the unlawful interference by appellants with the free choice of patrons, present and prospective. It declared the right to conduct schools was property and that parents and guardians, as part of their liberty, might direct the education of children by selecting reputable teachers and places. Also, that these schools were not unfit or harmful to the public, and that enforcement of the challenged statute would unlawfully deprive them of patronage and thereby destroy their owners' business and property. Finally, that the threats to enforce the Act would continue to cause irreparable injury; and the suits were not premature.

No question is raised concerning the power of the State reasonably to regulate all schools, to inspect, supervise and examine them, their teachers and pupils; to require that all children of proper age attend some school, that teachers shall be of good moral character and patriotic disposition, that certain studies plainly essential to good citizenship must be taught, and that nothing be taught which is manifestly inimical to the public welfare.

The inevitable practical result of enforcing the Act under consideration would be destruction of appellees' primary schools, and perhaps all other private primary schools for normal children within the State of Oregon. These parties are engaged in a kind of undertaking not inherently harmful, but long regarded as useful and meritorious. Certainly there is nothing in the present records to indicate that they have failed to discharge their obligations to patrons, students or the State.   *   *   *

*   *   *   [We] think it entirely plain that the Act of 1922 unreasonably interferes with the liberty of parents and guardians to direct the upbringing and education of children under their control. As often heretofore pointed out, rights guaranteed by the Constitution may not be abridged by legislation which has no reasonable relation to some purpose within the competency of the State. The fundamental theory of liberty upon which all governments in this Union repose excludes any general power of the State to standardize its children by forcing them to accept instruction from public teachers only. The child is not the mere creature of the State; those who nurture him and direct his destiny have the right,

coupled with the high duty, to recognize and prepare him for additional obligations.

* * *

Generally it is entirely true, as urged by counsel, that no person in any business has such an interest in possible customers as to enable him to restrain exercise of proper power of the State upon the ground that he will be deprived of patronage. But the injunctions here sought are not against the exercise of any *proper* power. Plaintiffs asked protection against arbitrary, unreasonable and unlawful interference with their pa-trons and the consequent distribution of their business and property. Their interest is clear and immediate.   * * *

The suits were not premature. The injury to appellees was present and very real, not a mere possibility in the remote future. If no relief had been possible prior to the effective date of the Act, the injury would have become irreparable. Prevention of impending injury by unlawful action is a well recognized function of courts of equity.

The decrees below are

Affirmed.

Notes and Questions

Does the Court's decision in **Pierce** reveal a bias in favor of the individual parent to have access to a pluralistic educational system by not allowing the state to have a monopoly over education?

The challenged Oregon law in **Pierce** had been promoted primarily by members of the Ku Klux Klan and the Oregon Scottish Rite Masons. Their actions were evidence of a xenophobic response on the part of some Americans after World War I to ensure that children would be properly socialized in the tenets of Americanism. The strong feelings against many foreigners and Catholics in particular at that time prompted a leading klansman to state: "Somehow these mongrel hordes must be Americanized; failing that, deportation is the only remedy." An attempt was made to picture Catholics as members of an organization that con-ducted its worship services in a foreign language, was controlled by a foreigner called a Pope, and practiced secret rituals.

An Amish group contested Wisconsin's compulsory attendance law, which required attendance at a public or private school until age sixteen. The Amish did not want their children to attend either a public or private high school after the eighth grade, because they considered such schools to be "worldly." A Supreme Court decision upheld the Amish position on several grounds. The Court contended that enforcing the state law would gravely endanger, if not destroy, the free exercise of Amish religious beliefs. Additionally, the Court's decision was influenced not only by the group's nearly three hundred years of existence but also by the perception that, although perhaps unconventional, the Amish had evidenced a highly successful social unit characterized by members who were productive, law abiding, and unwilling to accept welfare in any of its usual modern forms. See *Wisconsin v. Yoder*, 406 U.S. 205 (1972). Would the Court's rationale prevail if the group contesting a compulsory attendance law were the Black Muslims or the Ku Klux Klan rather than the Amish? Should students have a voice in this issue? Justice Douglas's opinion in *Yoder*, in which he dissents in part, suggests that students should have such a voice.

A Pentecostal parent who objected to sending his children to public schools was not upheld. The court ruled that the state's interest in compulsory attendance overrides the parent's interest in avoiding exposure to the unisex movement, secular humanism, and medical care. See *Duro v. District Attorney, Second Judicial District of North Carolina*, 712 F.2d 96 (4th Cir. 1983), cert. denied, 465 U.S. 1006 (1984). Parents were also not upheld when they refused to send their children to public school because those schools did not teach Indian heritage and culture. See *Matter of McMillan*, 30 N.C. App. 235, 226 S.E.2d 693 (1976).

The Supreme Court decisions in **Pierce** had immediate applicability only to the contested Oregon Compulsory Education Act and the issues arising from its attempted implementation. It did not automatically affect similar laws in other states. Individual state legislative action would be necessary to revoke similar laws in those states, and the absence of such legislative action would require a law suit to gain compliance with the **Pierce** rationale. Given the **Pierce** precedent, such a suit would undoubtedly be successful.

Some school districts have instituted policies under which a student is denied academic credit when a specified number of "unexcused" absences are incurred during a quarter or semester. Under these policies, unexcused absences may include tardies, truancies, suspension days, and other absences that school policy deems to be illegitimate. Such a policy was held to be invalid in *Gutierrez v. School District R-1*, 41 Colo. App. 411, 585 P.2d 935 (1978), because it was inconsistent with applicable statutory provisions. Other courts have held similarly to *Gutierrez*. See *Blackman v. Brown*, 100 Misc.2d 566, 419 N.Y.S.2d 796 (1978) and *Katzman v. Cumberland Valley School District*, 479 A.2d 671 (Pa. Comm. 1984). However, academic sanctions for unexcused absences were upheld in *Williams v. Board of Education for Marianna School District*, 274 Ark. 538, 626 S.W.2d 361 (1982) and *Campbell v. Board of Education of Town of New Milford*, 193 Conn. 93, 475 A.2d 289 (1984). Several courts have made a distinction between unexcused absences based on truancy and those resulting from disciplinary action. See *Dorsey v. Bale*, 521 S.W.2d 76 (Ky. 1975), and *Jones*

v. *Latexo Independent School District,* 499 F. Supp. 223 (Tex. 1980), in which academic sanctions resulting from suspensions were not upheld. In *New Braunfels Independent School District* v. *Armke,* 658 S.W.2d 330 (Tex. App. 1983), however, a school's use of academic sanctions for disciplinary purposes was upheld.

In the absence of statutory or case law prohibition, school systems having such policies should ensure that accurate attendance records are maintained, that the policy does not adversely have a disproportionate impact on any discrete group of students, such as minorities or the economically disadvantaged, and that exceptions to the policy are not made disproportionately, favoring a discrete group.

What are the provisons of the compulsory attendance law in your state?

B. Regulation of Nonpublic Schools

Once *Pierce* established the doctrine that private school attendance could satisfy a state's compulsory attendance requirements, the question arose as to the extent to which a state could regulate the private schools within its jurisdiction. The United States Supreme Court addressed this issue, one year after its **Pierce** decision, in *Farrington* v. *Tokushige,* 273 U.S. 284 (1926).

Farrington resulted from a state attempt to Americanize students: in this case Hawaii's attempt to regulate the predominately-Japanese foreign language schools on the islands. The contested regulations required teachers in these schools to possess "ideals of democracy," knowledge of American history, and fluency in English. Additionally they restricted hours of operation, established entrance requirements, and prescribed textbooks. These regulations, the Court held, served no demonstrable public interest, but instead amounted to a deliberate plan of strict governmental control, infringing on the rights of both parents and school owners.

Both **Pierce** and *Farrington,* therefore, reflect a philosophy that parents should have freedom of choice in the education of their children. Moreover, in sanctioning what many people feared was subversive, these decisions affirm a faith in the sustaining power of American tolerance.

Regulation of private schools varies among the states. Some states require that the quality of education provided by the private school be essentially equivalent to that provided in the public schools. This may include a requirement for certified teachers and certain course offerings. Other states merely have regulations dealing primarily with health, safety, and sanitation. Since attendance at a private school satisfies a state's compulsory attendance law, it is a legitimate state function to require attendance information from private schools.

State regulation of religious private schools has received court attention in recent years. These schools generally allege that their First Amendment religious freedom is being restricted. Courts have tended to reject these challenges to minimal instructional programs and requirements that teachers have baccalaureate degrees. See *Nebraska v. Faith Baptist Church,* 207 Neb. 802, 301 N.W.2d 571 (1981), appeal dismissed, 454 U.S. 803 (1981), *Bangor Baptist Church v. Maine,* 549 F. Supp. 1208 (Me. 1982), *North Dakota v. Shaver,* 294 N.W.2d 883 (N.D. 1981) and *North Dakota v. Rivinius,* 328 N.W.2d 220 (N.D. 1982), cert. denied, 460 U.S. 1070 (1983).

A parochial school in Puerto Rico refused a request from the Department of Consumer Affairs to divulge such matters as annual budgets, numbers of students, salaries of teachers, and cost of books and uniforms. In reversing the lower court, the First Circuit Court of Appeals held that the gathering of such information would encroach on the school's First Amendment rights. See *Surinach v. Pesquera de Busquets,* 604 F.2d 73 (1st Cir. 1979).

What is the status of private school regulation in your state? In addition to reviewing court decisions, you may wish to consult your state constitution, statutes, state school board policies, and attorney general opinions.

C. Home Instruction

Parents dissatisfied with both public and private schools frequently elect to instruct their children at home. Although some states do not have statutory provisions pertaining specifically to home instruction, those states that do often require the home program to be essentially "equivalent" to that offered in the public schools. Several courts have held that the absence of social contact tends to vitiate a home-instruction program. Some states require that the parent(s) providing the home instruction must be a qualified teacher.

Grigg v. Virginia

Supreme Court of Virginia, 1982
224 Va. 356, 297 S.E.2d 799

CARRICO, Chief Justice.

At the time this case arose, Code § 22–275.1 (now §22.1–254), part of the compulsory school attendance law, provided in part that parents shall send their school-age children to "a public school, or to a private, denominational or parochial school, or have such . . . children taught [in a home] by a tutor or teacher of qualifications prescribed by the State Board of Education and approved by the division superintendent. . . ." The principal question in this case is whether parents, not approved as tutors or teachers pursuant to the Code section, may qualify for the private school exemption by teaching their children at home.

The case originated in juvenile and domestic relations district court when the chief attendance officer for the City of Chesapeake school system filed separate petitions against Robert Grigg and Vickie Grigg, husband and wife, and their daughters, Stephanie and Nicole. The petitions against the parents alleged that the attendance officer had investigated and found "no valid reason" for the non-enrollment of the children in the public schools; the petitions prayed for entry of an order compelling the parents to enroll the children in the public schools or to make "other proper arrangements" for their education. * * *

Following adverse decisions by the juvenile court on the four petitions, the Griggs appealed. The circuit court ordered the petitions against Mr. and Mrs. Grigg merged with those against the children. After a hearing, the court found that Stephanie and Nicole were children in need of services. The court placed the children on unsupervised probation for a period of twelve months on condition that they "regularly attend a private, public, denominational or parochial school, or . . . be taught at home by a tutor or teacher of qualifications prescribed by the State Board of Education and approved by the Superintendent of Schools." The court also ordered the parents to send the children to one of the designated types of schools or to arrange for their instruction at home by an approved tutor or teacher.

It was stipulated below that Stephanie and Nicole, aged fourteen and eleven years, respectively, formerly attended public school in Chesapeake. They were withdrawn by their parents on January 2, 1980, in order that they might be "taught at home" by their mother.

The superintendent of schools gave the parents notice pursuant to Code § 22–275.—10 (now §22.1–261), requiring the children's attendance at school within three days, but neither child was re-enrolled. The parents sent a letter to the superintendent in March stating that the children were being instructed in a private school named "Ark II," which the parents had established in their home.

The parties stipulated also that Mrs. Grigg was the children's instructor and that she had not sought or received approval by state or local school authorities as a qualified tutor or teacher. The stipulation stated further that teachers in private, denominational, or parochial schools in Virginia are not required to meet the qualifications prescribed by the State Board of Education for tutors or teachers.

Mr. and Mrs. Grigg both testified below. Mr. Grigg said that he taught the children part of the time, but that Mrs. Grigg was the principal instructor. He is a high school graduate with the equivalent of an Associate's Degree in Industrial Technology; she obtained her high school diploma from a correspondence school. He stated the children were withdrawn from public school because he did not believe they were receiving an adequate education, because he did not approve of the language and violence present in the schools, and because he deplored the lack of morality in the public school setting. Mrs. Grigg echoed her husband's testimony in these respects.

In their instruction of the children, the parents employed the "Calvert School" program, using teaching manuals included in the materials furnished with the "Calvert Home Courses." The children received instruction daily from 8:00 a.m. to 4:00 or 5:00 p.m. during the school week; they were taught "everything that they had on a daily basis in the public schools [and] some extra things." Although she admitted it was "difficult," Mrs. Grigg stated she was able to cope "[j]ust fine" in caring for her two younger children, aged three and two years, while she taught Stephanie and Nicole.

* * *

The Griggs argue that the school attendance law is penal in nature and must be strictly construed, with every reasonable doubt regarding its interpretation resolved in their favor. They maintain that the term "private school" is undefined in the statute and that, unlike public schools, private schools are unregulated by the Commonwealth, even to the point that teachers in such schools need not be certified; hence, the term "private school" must be accorded a broad interpretation.

* * *

The Griggs attack Code §22–275.1 as void for vagueness. The Griggs assert the axiom that, to be valid, a statute must specify with reasonable certainty and definiteness the conduct which is commanded or prohibited; the enactment passes constitutional muster only if the average person may read it and understand whether he or she will incur a penalty for his or her actions. The statute in question fails this test, the Griggs maintain, for its lack of definition of the term "private school."

We do not believe that, as applied to the Griggs, the statute in question lacks specificity. The Griggs' argument concerning the alleged vagueness of the term "private school" misses its mark and only tends to divert attention from what should be the true focus of this inquiry, viz, that portion of Code § 22–275.1 which deals with home instruction. The

Griggs were engaged in home instruction, nothing more and nothing less; whether the term "private school" is sufficiently clear is irrelevant to the question whether the statute adequately informs the average person what conduct is permitted or prohibited with respect to home instruction. We think it beyond question that average parents reading §22–275.1 would know they could not instruct their children at home as an alternative to public instruction unless they were qualified as tutors or teachers according to the statute's requirements.

The Griggs' final contention is that the Commonwealth failed in its assumed burden of proving beyond a reasonable doubt that Stephanie and Nicole were children in need of services, as that term is defined in Code § 16.1–228. In pertinent part, this statute reads:

F. *"Child in Need of Services"* means:

1. A child who while subject to compulsory school attendance is habitually and without justification absent from school. . . .

*   *   *   *   *   *

Provided, however, to find that a child falls within [class] 1 . . . above . . . the child or his or her family must be in need of treatment, rehabilitation or services not presently being received and . . . the intervention of the court must be essential to provide the treatment, rehabilitation or services needed by the child or his or her family.

We believe that the Commonwealth carried its assumed burden of proof. It is undisputed in this case that the Grigg children were deliberately withdrawn from public school by their parents, that they were taught at home by persons who were not qualified as tutors or teachers, and that this unlawful practice would have continued indefinitely had the court not intervened and ordered the parents to comply with the school attendance law. The only justification advanced for these actions was the parents' belief that the instruction and training the children received at home were equal to or better than the services provided in public school. This excuse, though obviously sincere, was legally insufficient. Hence, the Commonwealth showed with almost conclusive effect all the elements listed in Code § 16.1–228 as necessary to a finding that the children were in need of services.

For the reasons assigned, the judgment of the trial court will be affirmed.

Affirmed.

Notes and Questions

When challenged by local school authorities and law enforcement officials, parents engaged in home instruction are generally brought to trial in a criminal action for failure to comply with a state's compulsory education law. Although there are exceptions, in most states the burden of demonstrating that the home instruction is substantially "equivalent" to that offered in the public schools is on the parents. See *New Jersey* v. *Massa*, 95 N.J. Super. 382, 231 A.2d 252 (1967), in which the court held that equivalent education elsewhere than at school requires only a showing of academic equivalence.

Does your state or local system have any provisions concerning home instruction for those unwilling to attend either public or private schools?

D. Admission Issues

Compulsory-attendance laws often state a minimum age at which formal education must begin. Disputes may arise when a child's birthday is a few days or perhaps weeks after a designated date or when parents believe their child is emotionally and intellectually ready to begin school at an earlier age. Parents who have changed their state of residence may also question restrictions prohibiting a child who has completed kindergarten in one state from enrolling in first grade in another state.

In the absence of state statutes or constitutional provisions establishing the age for entrance to school, local boards of education have an implied authority to establish them. See *Zweifel* v. *Joint District No. 1*, 76 Wis.2d 648, 251 N.W.2d 822 (1977).

The United States Supreme Court addressed the issue of public school admission of illegal aliens in *Plyler* v. *Doe*, 457 U.S. 202 (1981). The Court held that funding for the education of these children could not be withheld from local school districts, nor could local school districts deny enrollment to children not legally admitted to the country. This decision emphasized both the importance of public education in maintaining basic civic institutions and the lasting impact of educational deprivation on the life of a child.

Does your state or local school system have any provisions concerning a minimum age for school entry? If so, is there a provision for early admission or transfer from other states?

II. Religion in the Schools

Although the United States Supreme Court and lower federal court decisions have been consistent in declaring Bible reading for sectarian purposes and prayer in the public schools during normal school hours to be unconstitutional, this issue and others dealing with religious activities at public schools remain highly charged and emotional ones. Consequently, these issues have provided a persistent stream of litigation focusing on church-state relations.

In an effort to ensure a separation of church and state, the framers of the Constitution included the following language in the First Amendment: "Congress shall make no law respecting an establishment of religion, or prohibiting the free exercise thereof." On the basis of these words courts must determine the constitutionality of such questions as prayer and Bible reading in the public schools during normal school hours, baccalaureate services, Bible study or other religious clubs, dissemination of Gideon Bibles or other religious tracts, or observance of religious holidays.

Courts have not erected an unassailably high wall between the church and the state that would absolutely restrict governmental involvement with religion. Rather, a review of court decisions dealing with these issues reveals that the thread woven throughout the decisions is the attempt by courts to determine the height of the wall, given a particular factual situation.

A. School-Sponsored Prayer and Bible Reading

Two United States Supreme Court decisions in the early 1960s dramatically established the case law pertaining to prayer and Bible reading in the public schools. In *Engel* v. *Vitale* the Court, with one dissent, held that recitation of a prayer composed by the New York State Board of Regents, which was to be said in the presence of a teacher at the beginning of school each day, was unconstitutional and in violation of the establishment clause.

In *School District of Abington* v. *Schempp,* a lengthy decision of 117 pages, which included a majority opinion, three concurring opinions, and one dissent, the Court held that reading the Bible and reciting the Lord's Prayer in public schools during normal hours were unconstitutional. However, the Court asserted that the Bible could be read as literature in an appropriate class and that the history of religion or comparative religion could be taught.

Prayer in some public schools did not stop as a result of these decisions. The issue has remained a highly controversial one that has been interjected into local, state, and national political debate. Although litigation involving the issue continued uninterrupted in the lower courts, the United State Supreme Court did not directly address the issue again until *Wallace v. Jaffree* in 1985. In discussing the issue of prayer in the public schools the six-to-three decision in *Jaffree* held that the setting aside of classroom time for silent prayer was unconstitutional.

1. Recitation of a State Prayer

Engel v. Vitale

Supreme Court of the United States, 1962
370 U.S. 421

MR. JUSTICE BLACK delivered the opinion of the Court.

The respondent Board of Education of Union Free School District No. 9, New Hyde Park, New York, acting in its official capacity under state law, directed the School District's principal to cause the following prayer to be said aloud by each class in the presence of a teacher at the beginning of each school day:

> "Almighty God, we acknowledge our dependence upon Thee, and we beg Thy blessings upon us, our parents, our teachers and our Country."

This daily procedure was adopted on the recommendation of the State Board of Regents, a governmental agency created by the State Constitution to which the New York Legislature has granted broad supervisory, executive, and legislative powers over the State's public school system. These state officials composed the prayer which they recommended and published as part of their "Statement on Moral and Spiritual Training in the Schools," saying: "We believe that this Statement will be subscribed to by all men and women of good will, and we call upon all of them to aid in giving life to our program."

Shortly after the practice of reciting the Regents' prayer was adopted by the School District, the parents of ten pupils brought this action in a New York State Court insisting that use of this official prayer in the public schools was contrary to the beliefs, religions, or religious practices of both themselves and their children. Among other things, these parents challenged the constitutionality of both the state law authorizing the School District to direct the use of prayer in public schools and the School District's regulation ordering the recitation of this particular prayer on the ground that these actions of official governmental agencies violate that part of the First Amendment of the Federal Constitution which commands that "Congress shall make no law respecting an establishment of religion"—a command which was "made applicable to the State of New York by the Fourteenth Amendment of the said Constitution." The New York Court of Appeals * * * sustained an order of the lower state courts which had upheld the power of New York to use the Regents' prayer as a part of the daily procedures of its public schools so long as the schools did not compel any pupil to join in the prayer over his or her parents' objection. We granted certiorari to review this important decision involving the rights protected by the First and Fourteenth Amendments.

We think that by using its public school system to encourage recitation of the Regents' prayer, the State of New York has adopted a practice wholly inconsistent with the Establishment Clause. There can, of course, be no doubt that New York's program of daily classroom invocation of God's blessings as prescribed in the Regents' prayer is a religious activity. It is a solemn avowal of divine faith and supplication for the blessings of the Almighty. The nature of such a prayer has always been religious, none of the respondents has denied this and the trial court expressly so found. * * *

The petitioners contend among other things that the state laws requiring or permitting use of the Regents' prayer must be struck down as a violation of the Establishment Clause because that prayer was composed by government officials as a part of a governmental program to further religious beliefs. For this reason, petitioners argue, the State's use of the Regents' prayer in its public school system breaches the constitutional wall of separation between Church and State. We agree with that contention since we think that the constitutional prohibition against laws respecting an establishment of religion must at least mean that in this country it is no part of the business of government to compose official prayers for any group of the American people to recite as a part of a religious program carried on by government.

It is a matter of history that this very practice of establishing governmentally composed prayers for religious services was one of the reasons which caused many of our early colonists to leave England and seek religious freedom in America. The Book of Common Prayer, which was created under governmental direction and which was approved by Acts of Parliament in 1548 and 1549, set out in minute detail the accepted form and content of prayer and other religious ceremonies to be used in the established, tax-supported Church of England. The controversies over the Book and what should be its content repeatedly threatened to disrupt the peace of that country as the accepted forms of prayer in the established church changed with the views of the particular ruler that happened to be in control at the time. Powerful groups representing some of the varying religious views of the people struggled among themselves to impress their particular views upon the Government and obtain amendments of the Book more suitable to their respective notions of how religious services should be conducted in order that the official religious establishment would advance their particular beliefs. Other groups, lacking the necessary political power to influence the Government on the matter, decided to leave England and its established church and seek freedom in America from England's governmentally ordained and supported religion.

It is an unfortunate fact of history that when some of the very groups which had most strenuously opposed the established Church of England found themselves sufficiently in control of colonial governments in this country to write their own prayers into law, they passed laws making their own religion the official religion of their respective colonies. Indeed, as late as the time of the Revolutionary War, there were established churches in at least eight of the thirteen former colonies and established religions in at least four of the other five. But the successful Revolution against English political domination was shortly followed by intense opposition to the practice of establishing religion by law. * * *

By the time of the adoption of the Constitution, our history shows that there was a widespread awareness among many Americans of the dangers of a union of Church and State. These people knew, some of them from bitter personal experience, that one of the greatest dangers to the freedom of the individual to worship in his own way lay in the Government's placing its official stamp of approval upon one particular kind of prayer or one particular form of religious services. They knew the anguish, hardship and bitter strife that could come when zealous religious groups struggled with one another to obtain the Government's stamp of approval from each King, Queen, or Protector that came to temporary power. The Constitution was intended to avert a part of this danger by leaving the government of this country in the hands of the people rather than in the hands of any monarch. But this safeguard was not enough. Our Founders were no more willing to let the content of their prayers and their privilege of praying whenever they pleased be influenced by the ballot box than they were to let these vital matters of personal conscience depend upon the succession of monarchs. The First Amendment was added to the Constitution to stand as a guarantee that neither the power nor the prestige of the Federal Government would be used to control, support or influence the kinds of prayer the American people can say— that the people's religions must not be subjected to the pressures of government for change each time a new political administration is elected to office. Under that Amendment's prohibition against governmental establishment of religion, as reinforced by the provisions of the Fourteenth Amendment, government in this country, be it state or federal, is without power to prescribe by law any particular form of prayer which is to be used as an official prayer in carrying on any program of governmentally sponsored religious activity.

There can be no doubt that New York's state prayer program officially establishes the religious beliefs embodied in the Regents' prayer. The respondents' argument to the contrary, which is largely based upon the contention that the Regents' prayer is "non-denominational" and the fact that the program, as modified and approved by state courts, does not require all pupils to recite the prayer but permits those who wish to do so to remain silent or be excused from the room, ignores the essential nature of the program's constitutional defects. Neither the fact that the prayer may be denominationally neutral nor the fact that its observance on the part of the students is voluntary can serve to free it from the limitations of the Establishment Clause, as it might from the Free Exercise Clause, of the First Amendment, both of which are operative against the States by virtue of the Fourteenth Amendment. Although these two clauses may in certain instances overlap, they forbid two quite different kinds of governmental encroachment upon religious freedom. The Establishment Clause, unlike the Free Excercise Clause, does not depend upon any showing of direct governmental compulsion and is violated by the enactment of laws which establish an official religion whether those laws operate directly to coerce nonobserving individuals or not. This is not to say, of course, that laws officially prescribing a particular form of religious worship do not involve coercion of such individuals. When the power, prestige and financial support of the government is placed behind a particular religious belief, the indirect coercive pressure upon religious minorities to conform to the prevailing officially approved religion is plain. But the purposes underlying the Establishment Clause go much further than that. Its first and most immediate purpose rested on the belief that a union of government and religion tends to destroy government and to degrade religion. The history of governmentally established religion, both in England and in this country, showed that whenever government had allied itself with one particular form of religion, the inevitable result had been that it had incurred the hatred, disrespect and even contempt of those who held contrary beliefs. That same history showed that many people had lost their respect for any religion that had relied upon the support of government to spread its faith. The Establishment Clause thus stands as an expression of principle on the part of the Founders of our Constitution that religion is too personal, too sacred, too holy, to permit its "unhallowed perversion" by a civil magistrate. Another purpose of the Establishment Clause rested upon an awareness of the historical fact that governmentally established religions and religious persecutions go hand in hand. The Founders knew that only a few years after the Book of Common Prayer became the only accepted form of religious services in the established Church of England, an Act of Uniformity was passed to compel all the Englishmen to attend those services and to make it a criminal offense to conduct or attend religious gatherings of any kind—a law which was consistently flouted by dissenting religious groups in England and which contributed to widespread persecutions of people like John Bunyan who persisted in holding "unlawful [religious] meetings . . . to the great disturbance and distraction of the good subjects of this kingdom. . . ." And they knew that similar persecutions had received the sanction of law in several of the colonies in this country soon after the establishment of official religions in those colonies. It was in large part to get completely away from this sort of systematic religious persecution that the Founders brought into being our Nation, our Constitution, and our Bill of Rights with its prohibition against any governmental establishment of religion. The New York laws officially prescribing the Regents' prayer are inconsistent both with the purposes of the Establishment Clause and with the Establishment Clause itself.

It has been argued that to apply the Constitution in such a way as to prohibit state laws respecting an establishment of religious services in public schools is to indicate a hostility toward religion or toward prayer. Nothing, of course, could be more wrong. The history of man is inseparable from the history of religion. And perhaps it is not too much to say that since the beginning of that history many people have devoutly believed that "More things are wrought with prayer than this world dreams of." It was doubtless largely due to men who believed this that there grew up a sentiment that caused men to leave the cross-currents of officially established state religions and religious persecution in Europe and come to this country filled with the hope that they could find a place in which they could pray when they pleased to the God of their faith in the language they chose. And there were men of this same faith in the power of prayer who led the fight for adoption of our Constitution and also for our Bill of Rights with the very guarantees of religious freedom that forbid the sort of governmental activity which New York has attempted here. These men knew that the First Amendment, which tried to put an end to governmental control of religion and of prayer, was not written to destroy either. They knew rather that it was written to quiet well-justified fears which nearly all of them felt arising out of an awareness that governments of the past had shackled men's tongues to make them speak only the religious thoughts that government wanted them to speak and to pray only to the God that government wanted them to pray to. It is neither sacrilegious nor antireligious to say that each separate government in this country should stay out of the business of writing or sanctioning official prayers and leave that purely religious function to the people themselves and to those the people choose to look to for religious guidance.

It is true that New York's establishment of its Regents' prayer as an officially approved religious doctrine of that State does not amount to a total establishment of one particular religious sect to the exclusion of all others—that, indeed, the government endorsement of that prayer seems relatively insignificant when compared to the governmental encroachments upon religion which were commonplace 200 years ago. To those who may subscribe to the view that because the Regents' official prayer is so brief and general there can be no danger to religious freedom in its governmental establishment, however, it may be appropriate to say in the words of James Madison, the author of the First Amendment:

"[I]t is proper to take alarm at the first experiment on our liberties. . . . Who does not see that the same authority which can establish Christianity, in exclusion of all other Religions, may establish with the same ease any particular sect of Christians, in exclusion of all other Sects? That the same authority which can force a citizen to contribute three pence only of his property for the support of any one establishment, may force him to conform to any other establishment in all cases whatsoever?"

The judgment of the Court of Appeals of New York is reversed and the cause remanded for further proceedings not inconsistent with this opinion.

Reversed and remanded.

2. Prayer and Bible Reading

School District of Abington Township v. Schempp
Murray v. Curlett

Supreme Court of the United States, 1963
374 U.S. 203

MR. JUSTICE CLARK delivered the opinion of the Court.

    * * * These companion cases present the issues in the context of state action requiring that schools begin each day with readings from the Bible. While raising the basic questions under slightly different factual situations, the cases permit of joint treatment. In light of the history of the First Amendment and of our cases interpreting and applying its requirements, we hold that the practices at issue and the laws requiring them are unconstitutional under the Establishment Clause, as applied to the States through the Fourteenth Amendment.

    * * * The Commonwealth of Pennsylvania by law * * * requires that "At least ten verses from the Holy Bible shall be read, without comment, at the opening of each public school on each school day. Any child shall be excluded from such Bible reading, or attending such Bible reading, upon the written request of his parent or guardian." The Schempp family, husband and wife and two of their three children, brought suit to enjoin enforcement of the statute * * * . A three-judge statutory District Court for the Eastern District of Pennsylvania held that the statute is violative of the Establishment Clause of the First Amendment as applied to the States by the Due Process Clause of the Fourteenth Amendment and directed that appropriate injunctive relief issue. * * *

The appellees Edward Lewis Schempp, his wife Sidney, and their children, Roger and Donna, are of the Unitarian faith and are members of the Unitarian Church in Germantown, Philadelphia, Pennsylvania, where they * * * regularly attend religious services. * * *

On each school day at the Abington Senior High School between 8:15 and 8:30 a.m., while the pupils are attending their home rooms or advisory sections, opening exercises are conducted pursuant to the statute. The exercises are broadcast into each room in the school building through an intercommunications system and are conducted under the supervision of a teacher by students attending the school's radio and television workshop. Selected students from this course gather each morning in the school's workshop studio for the exercises, which include readings by one of the students of 10 verses of the Holy Bible, broadcast to each room in the building. This is followed by the recitation of the Lord's Prayer, likewise over the intercommunications system, but also by the students in the various classrooms, who are asked to stand and join in repeating the prayer in unison. The exercises are closed with the flag salute and such pertinent announcements as are of interest to the students. Participation in the opening exercises, as directed by the statute, is voluntary. The student reading the verses from the Bible may select the passages and read from any version he chooses, although the only copies furnished by the school are the King James version, copies of which are circulated to each teacher by the school district. During the period in which the exercises have been conducted the King James, the Douay and the Revised Standard versions of the Bible have been used, as well as the Jewish Holy Scriptures. There are no prefatory statements, no questions asked or solicited, no comments or explanations made and no interpretations given at or during the exercises. The students and parents are advised that the student may absent himself from the classroom or, should he elect to remain, not participate in the exercises.

* * *

At the first trial Edward Schempp and the children testified as to specific religious doctrines purveyed by a literal reading of the Bible "which are contrary to the religious beliefs which they held and to their familial teaching." * * * The children testified that all of the doctrines to which they referred were read to them at various times as part of the exercises. Edward Schempp testified at the second trial that he had considered having Roger and Donna excused from attendance at the exercise but decided against it for several reasons, including his belief that the children's relationships with their teachers and classmates would be adversely affected.

* * *

In 1905 the Board of School Commissioners of Baltimore City adopted a rule * * * . The rule provided for the holding of opening exercises in the schools of the city, consisting primarily of the "reading, without comment, of a chapter in the Holy Bible and/or the use of the Lord's Prayer." The petitioners, Mrs. Madalyn Murray and her son, William J. Murray III, are both professed atheists. Following unsuccessful attempts to have the respondent school board rescind the rule, this suit was filed for mandamus to compel its recission and cancellation. It was alleged that William was a student in a public school of the city and Mrs. Murray, his mother, was a taxpayer therein; that it was the practice under the rule to have a reading on each school morning from the King James version of the Bible; that at petitioners' insistence the rule was amended to permit children to be excused from the exercise on request of the parent and that William had been excused pursuant thereto; that nevertheless the rule as amended was in violation of the petitioners' rights to "freedom of religion under the First and Fourteenth Amendments" and in violation of "the principle of separation between church and state, contained therein. . . ." The petition particularized the petitioners' atheistic beliefs and stated that the rule, as practiced, violated their rights

> "in that it threatens their religious liberty by placing a premium on belief as against non-belief and subjects their freedom of conscience to the rule of the majority; it pronounces belief in God as the source of all moral and spiritual values, equating these values with religious values, and thereby renders sinister, alien and suspect the beliefs and ideals of your Petitioners, promoting doubt and question of their morality, good citizenship and good faith."

 * * * The Maryland Court of Appeals affirmed, the majority of four justices holding the exercise not in violation of the First and Fourteenth Amendments, with three justices dissenting. * * *

 * * *

The wholesome "neutrality" of which this Court's cases speak * * * stems from a recognition of the teachings of history that powerful sects or groups might bring about a fusion of governmental and religious functions or a concert of dependency of one upon the other to the end that official support of the State or Federal Government would be placed behind the tenets of one or of all orthodoxies. This the Establishment Clause prohibits. And a further reason for neutrality is found in the Free Exercise Clause, which recognizes the value of religious training, teaching and observance and, more particularly, the right of every person to freely choose his own course with reference thereto, free of any compulsion from the state. This the Free Exercise Clause guarantees. Thus, as we have seen, the two clauses may overlap. As we have indicated, the Establishment Clause has been directly considered by this Court eight times in the past score of years and, with only one Justice dissenting on the point, it has consistently held that the clause withdrew all legislative power respecting religious belief or the expression thereof. The test may be stated as follows: what are the purpose and the primary effect of the enactment? If either is the advancement or inhibition of religion then the enactment exceeds the scope of legislative power as circumscribed by the Constitution. That is to say that to withstand the strictures of the Establishment Clause there must be a secular legislative purpose and a primary effect that neither advances nor inhibits religion. * * *

Applying the Establishment Clause principles to the cases at bar we find that the States are requiring the selection and reading at the opening of the school day of verses from the Holy Bible and the recitation of the Lord's Prayer by the students in unison. These exercises are prescribed as part of the curricular activities of students who are required by law to attend school. They are held in the school buildings under the supervision and with the participation of teachers employed in those schools. * * * The trial court * * * has found that such an opening exercise is a religious ceremony and was intended by the State to be so. We agree with the trial court's finding as to the religious character of the exercises. Given that finding, the exercises and the law requiring them are in violation of the Establishment Clause.

*   *   *

It is insisted that unless these religious exercises are permitted a "religion of secularism" is established in the schools. We agree of course that the State may not establish a "religion of secularism" in the sense of affirmatively opposing or showing hostility to religion, thus "preferring those who believe in no religion over those who do believe." * * * We do not agree, however, that this decision in any sense has that effect. In addition, it might well be said that one's education is not complete without a study of comparative religion or the history of religion and its relationship to the advancement of civilization. It certainly may be said that the Bible is worthy of study for its literary and historic qualities. Nothing we have said here indicates that such study of the Bible or of religion, when presented objectively as part of a secular program of education, may not be effected consistently with the First Amendment. But the exercises here do not fall into those categories. They are religious exercises, required by the States in violation of the command of the First Amendment that the Government maintain strict neutrality, neither aiding nor opposing religion.

*   *   *

The place of religion in our society is an exalted one, achieved through a long tradition of reliance on the home, the church and the inviolable citadel of the individual heart and mind. We have come to recognize through bitter experience that it is not within the power of government to invade that citadel, whether its purpose or effect be to aid or oppose, to advance or retard. In the relationship between man and religion, the State is firmly committed to a position of neutrality. Though the application of that rule requires interpretation of a delicate sort, the rule itself is clearly and concisely stated in the words of the First Amendment. * * *

3. Silent Prayer, Meditation, and Voluntary Prayer

Wallace v. Jaffree

Supreme Court of the United States, 1985
472 U.S. ___, 105 S.Ct. 2479

JUSTICE STEVENS delivered the opinion of the Court.

At an early stage of this litigation, the constitutionality of three Alabama statutes was questioned: (1) §16–1–20, enacted in 1978, which authorized a one-minute period of silence in all public schools "for meditation," (2) §16–1–20.1, enacted in 1981, which authorized a period of silence "for meditation or voluntary prayer," and (3) § 16–1–20.2, enacted in 1982, which authorized teachers to lead "willing students" in a prescribed prayer to "Almighty God . . . the Creator and Supreme Judge of the world."

* * *

Appellee Ishmael Jaffree is a resident of Mobile County, Alabama. On May 28, 1982, he filed a complaint on behalf of three of his minor children; two of them were second-grade students and the third was then in kindergarten. The complaint named members of the Mobile County School Board, various school officials, and the minor plaintiffs' three teachers as defendants. The complaint alleged that the appellees brought the action "seeking principally a declaratory judgment and an injunction restraining the Defendants and each of them from maintaining or allowing the maintenance of regular religious prayer services or other forms of religious observances in the Mobile County Public Schools in violation of the First Amendment as made applicable to states by the Fourteenth Amendment to the United States Constitution." The complaint further alleged that two of the children had been subjected to various acts of religious indoctrination "from the beginning of the school year in September, 1981"; that the defendant teachers had "on a daily basis" led their classes in saying certain prayers in unison; that the minor children were exposed to ostracism from their peer group class members if they did not participate, and that Ishmael Jaffree had repeatedly but unsuccessfully requested that the devotional services be stopped. * * *

* * *

In its lengthy conclusions of law, the District Court viewed a number of opinions of this Court interpreting the Establishment Clause of the First Amendment, and then embarked on a fresh examination of the question whether the First Amendment imposes any barrier to the establishment of an official religion by the State of Alabama. After reviewing at length what it perceived to be newly discovered historical evidence, the District Court concluded that "the establishment clause of the first amendment to the United States Constitution does not prohibit the state from establishing a religion." In a separate opinion, the District Court dismissed appellees' challenge to the three Alabama statutes because of a failure to state any claim for which relief could be granted. The court's dismissal of this challenge was also based on its conclusion that the Establishment Clause did not bar the States from establishing a religion.

The Court of Appeals consolidated the two cases; not surprisingly, it reversed. The Court of Appeals noted that this Court had considered and had rejected the historical arguments that the District Court found persuasive, and that the District Court had misapplied the doctrine of *stare decisis.* The Court of Appeals then held that the teachers' religious activities violated the Establishment Clause of the First Amendment. With respect to §16–1–20.1 and §16–1–20.2, the Court of Appeals stated that "both statutes advance and encourage religious activities." The Court of Appeals then quoted with approval the District Court's finding that §16–1–20.1, and §16–1–20.2, were efforts "to encourage a religious activity. Even though these statutes are permissive in form, it is nevertheless state involvement respecting an establishment of religion." Thus, the Court of Appeals concluded that both statutes were "specifically the type which the Supreme Court addressed in *Engle* [v. *Vitale,* 370 U.S. 421 (1962)]." * * *

* * *

Our unanimous affirmance of the Court of Appeals' judgment concerning §16–1–20.2 makes it unnecessary to comment at length on the District Court's remarkable conclusion that the Federal Constitution imposes no obstacle to Alabama's establishment of a state religion. Before analyzing the precise issue that is presented to us, it is nevertheless appropriate to recall how firmly embedded in our constitutional jurisprudence is the proposition that the several States have no greater power to restrain the individual freedoms protected by the First Amendment than does the Congress of the United States.

* * *

Just as the right to speak and the right to refrain from speaking are complementary components of a broader concept of individual freedom of mind, so also the individual's freedom to choose his own creed is the counterpart of his right to refrain from accepting the creed established by the majority. At one time it was thought that this right merely proscribed the preference of one Christian sect over another, but would not require equal respect for the conscience of the infidel, the atheist, or the adherent of a non-Christian faith such as Mohammedism or Judaism. But when the underlying principle has been examined in the crucible of litigation, the Court has unambiguously concluded that the individual freedom of conscience protected by the First Amendment embraces the right to select any religious faith or none at all. This conclusion derives support not only from the interest in respecting the individual's freedom of conscience, but also from the conviction that religious beliefs worthy of respect are the product of free and voluntary choice by the faithful, and from recognition of the fact that the political interest in forestalling intolerance extends beyond intolerance among Christian sects—or even intolerance among "religions"—to encompass intolerance of the disbeliever and the uncertain. * * *

* * *

The legislative intent to return prayer to the public schools is, of course, quite different from merely protecting every student's right to engage in voluntary prayer during an appropriate moment of silence during the school day. The 1978 statute already protected that right, containing nothing that prevented any student from engaging in voluntary prayer during a silent minute of meditation. Appellants have not identified any secular purpose that was not fully served by §16–1–20 before the enactment of §16–1–20.1. Thus, only two conclusions are consistent with the text of §16–1–20.1: (1) the statute was enacted to convey a message of State endorsement and promotion of prayer; or (2) the statute was enacted for no purpose. No one suggests that the statute was nothing but a meaningless or irrational act.

We must, therefore, conclude that the Alabama Legislature intended to change existing law and that it was motivated by the same purposes that the Governor's Answer to the Second Amended Complaint expressly admitted; that the statement inserted in the legislative history revealed; and that Senator Holmes' testimony frankly described. The Legislature enacted §16–1–20.1 despite the existence of §16–1–20 for the sole purpose of expressing the State's endorsement of prayer activities for one minute at the beginning of each school day. The addition of "or voluntary prayer" indicates that the State intended to characterize prayer as a favored practice. Such an endorsement is not consistent with the established principle that the Government must pursue a course of complete neutrality toward religion.

The importance of that principle does not permit us to treat this as an inconsequential case involving nothing more than a few words of symbolic speech on behalf of the political majority. For whenever the State itself speaks on a religious subject, one of the questions that we must ask is "whether the Government intends to convey a message of endorsement or disapproval of religion." The well-supported concurrent findings of the District Court and the Court of Appeals—that §16–1–20.1 was intended to convey a message of State-approval of prayer activities in the public schools—make it unnecessary, and indeed inappropriate, to evaluate the practical significance of the addition of the words "or voluntary prayer" to the statute. Keeping in mind, as we must, "both the fundamental place held by the Establishment Clause in our constitutional scheme and the myriad, subtle ways in which Establishment Clause values can be eroded," we conclude that § 16–1–20.1 violates the First Amendment.

The judgment of the Court of Appeals is affirmed.

It is so ordered.

* * *

JUSTICE O'CONNOR, concurring in the judgment

* * *

It once appeared that the Court had developed a workable standard by which to identify impermissible government establishments of religion. See *Lemon* v. *Kurtzman*, 403 U.S. 602 (1971). Under the now familiar *Lemon* test, statutes must have both a secular legislative purpose and a principal or primary effect that neither advances nor inhibits religion, and in addition they must not foster excessive government entanglement with religion. * * * Despite its initial promise, the *Lemon* test has proven problematic. The required inquiry into "entanglement" has been modified and questioned, * * * and in one case we have upheld state action against an Establishment Clause challenge without applying the *Lemon* test at all. *Marsh* v. *Chambers*, 463 U.S. 783 (1983). * * *

JUSTICE REHNQUIST today suggests that we abandon *Lemon* entirely, and in the process limit the reach of the Establishment Clause to state discrimination between sects and government designation of a particular church as a "state" or "national" one. * * *

Perhaps because I am new to the struggle, I am not ready to abandon all aspects of the *Lemon* test. I do believe, however, that the standards announced in *Lemon* should be reexamined and refined in order to make them more useful in achieving the underlying purpose of the First Amendment. We must strive to do more than erect a constitutional "signpost," * * * , to be followed or ignored in a particular case as our predilections may dictate. Instead, our goal should be "to frame a principle for constitutional adjudication that is not only grounded in the history and language of the first amendment, but one that is also capable of consistent application to the relevant problems." * * * Last Term, I proposed a refinement of the *Lemon* test with this goal in mind. *Lynch* v. *Donnelly*, 465 U.S., at —— (concurring opinion).

The *Lynch* concurrence suggested that the religious liberty protected by the Establishment Clause is infringed when the government makes adherence to religion relevant to a person's standing in the political community. Direct government action endorsing religion or a particular religious practice is invalid under this approach because it "sends a message to nonadherents that they are outsiders, not full members of the political community, and an accompanying message to adherents that they are insiders, favored members of the political community." * * * Under this view, *Lemon's* inquiry as to the purpose and effect of a statute requires courts to examine whether government's purpose is to endorse religion and whether the statute actually conveys a message of endorsement.

The endorsement test is useful because of the analytic content it gives to the *Lemon*-mandated inquiry into legislative purpose and effect: In this country, church and state must necessarily operate within the same community. Because of this coexistence, it is inevitable that the secular interests of Government and the religious interests of various sects and their adherents will frequently intersect, conflict, and combine. A statute that ostensibly promotes a secular interest often has an incidental or even a primary effect of helping or hindering a sectarian belief. Chaos would ensue if every such statute were invalid under the Establishment Clause. For example, the State could not criminalize murder for fear that it would thereby promote the Biblical command against such killing. The task for the Court is to sort out those statutes and government practices whose purpose and effect go against the grain of religious liberty protected by the First Amendment.

The endorsement test does not preclude government from acknowledging religion or from taking religion into account in making law and policy. It does preclude government from conveying or attempting to convey a message that religion or a particular religious belief is favored or preferred. Such an endorsement infringes the religious liberty of the non-adherent, for "[w]hen the power, prestige and financial support of government is placed behind a particular religious belief, the indirect coercive pressure upon religious minorities to conform to the prevailing officially approved religion is plain." * * * At issue today is whether state moment of silence statutes in general, and Alabama's moment of silence statute in particular, embody an impermissible endorsement of prayer in public schools.

Twenty-five states permit or require public school teachers to have students observe a moment of silence in their classrooms.[1] A few statutes provide that the moment of silence is for the purpose of meditation alone. * * * The typical statute, however, calls for a moment of silence at the beginning of the school day during which students may meditate, pray, or reflect on activities of the day.

* * *

By mandating a moment of silence, a State does not necessarily endorse any activity that might occur during the period. * * * Even if a statute specifies that a student may choose to pray silently during a quiet moment, the State has not thereby encouraged prayer over other specified alternatives. Nonetheless, it is also possible that a moment of silence statute, either as drafted or as actually implemented, could effectively favor the child who prays over the child who does not. For example, the message of endorsement would seem inescapable if the teacher exhorts children to use the designated time to pray. Similarly, the face of the statute or its legislative history may clearly establish that it seeks to encourage or promote voluntary prayer over other alternatives, rather than merely provide a quiet moment that may be dedicated to prayer by those so inclined. The crucial question is whether the State has conveyed or attempted to convey the message that children should use the moment of silence for prayer. This question cannot be answered in the abstract, but instead requires courts to examine the history, language, and administration of a particular statute to determine whether it operates as an endorsement of religion. * * *

* * *

The Court does not hold that the Establishment Clause is so hostile to religion that it precludes the State from affording schoolchildren an opportunity for voluntary silent prayer. To the contrary, the moment of

[1]See Ala. Code §§16–1–20, 16–1–20.1 (Supp. 1984): Ariz. Rev. Stat. Ann. §15–522 (1984); Ark. Stat. Ann. § 80–1607.1 (1980); Conn. Gen Stat. §10–16a (1983); Del. Code Ann., Tit. 14, § 4101 (1981) (as interpreted in Del. Op. Atty. Gen. 79–1011 (1979)); Fla. Stat. § 233.062 (1983); Ga. Code Ann. § 20–2–1050 (1982); Ill. Rev. Stat., ch. 122, ¶771 (1983); Ind. Code § 20–10.1–7–11 (1982); Kan. Stat. Ann § 72.5308a (1980); La. Rev. Stat. Ann § 17:2115(A) (West 1982); Me. Rev. Stat. Ann., Tit. 20–A, § 4805 (1983); Md. Educ. Code Ann. § 7–104 (1985); Mass. Gen. Laws Ann., ch. 71, §1A (1982); Mich. Comp. Laws Ann. § 380.1565 (Supp. 1984–1985); N.J. Stat. Ann. § 18A:36–4 (West Supp. 1984–1985); N.M. Stat. Ann. § 22–5–4.1 (1981); N.Y. Educ. Law § 3029–a (McKinney 1981); N.D. Cent. Code § 15–47–30.1 (1981); Ohio Rev. Code Ann. § 3313.60.1 (1980); Pa. Stat. Ann., Tit. 24, § 15.1516.1 (Purdon Supp. 1984–1985); R.I. Gen. Laws § 16–12–3.1 (1981); Tenn. Code Ann. § 49–6–1004 (1983); Va. Code § 22.1–203 (1980); W.Va. Const., Art. III, § 15–a.

silence statutes of many States should satisfy the Establishment Clause standard we have here applied. The Court holds only that Alabama has intentionally crossed the line between creating a quiet moment during which those so inclined may pray, and affirmatively endorsing the particular religious practice of prayer. This line may be a fine one, but our precedents and the principles of religious liberty require that we draw it. In my view, the judgment of the Court of Appeals must be affirmed.

* * *

Notes and Questions

Sandra Day O'Connor, who wrote a concurring opinion in *Jaffree,* is the first woman Supreme Court justice. Prior to her appointment by President Reagan she was an assistant attorney general and a legislator in Arizona.

Although the Court struck down the practice of school-sponsored silent prayer, which was authorized in sixteen states at the time of the decision, a careful reading of the decision suggests that allowing for a moment of silence, which was authorized in nine states, may be constitutional.

Is the issue of non-school-sponsored silent prayer really a nonissue since students cannot be prevented from silently praying during the course of a school day?

Suppose every child in a public school classroom voted to begin each class with a prayer and Bible reading. Would this lift any constitutional infirmity?

Prayer issues dealing with governmental agencies other than public schools have also appeared before the judiciary. See *Marsh* v. *Chambers,* 463 U.S. 783 (1983), which upheld the Nebraska legislative practice of opening the day with prayer. An earlier decision by the New Jersey Supreme Court upheld the practice of opening a municipality's public meetings with invocation, prayer, or silent prayer. See *Marsa* v. *Wernick,* 86 N.J. 232, 430 A.2d 888 (1981), cert. dismissed, 454 U.S. 958 (1981).

North Dakota's Ten Commandments Law, which required the display of a placard containing the Ten Commandments of the Christian and Jewish religions in a conspicuous place in every classroom, was held to violate the Establishment Clause of the First Amendment. See *Ring* v. *Grand Forks School District No. 1,* 483 F. Supp. 272 (N.D. 1980). Although a state law that required the posting of the Ten Commandments in public classrooms was upheld by a tie vote of the Kentucky Supreme Court, *Stone* v. *Graham,* 599 S.W.2d 157 (Ky. 1980), this provision was struck down by a five-to-four decision of the United States Supreme Court in 449 U.S. 1104 (1981).

Some states provide penalties for noncompliance with statutory provisions prohibiting Bible reading or prayer. In Arizona, a "teacher . . . who conducts . . . any religious exercises in school is guilty of unprofessional conduct and his certificate shall be revoked." In Alaska and Nevada school funds may be withheld if noncompliance with statutory provisions exists.

May the singing of Christmas carols with religious significance be prohibited as part of a school program? See *Muka* v. *Sturgis,* 53 App. Div.2d 716, 383 N.Y.S.2d 933 (1976), which upheld such a prohibition. But see *Citizens Concerned for Separation of Church and State* v. *City and County of Denver,* 508 F. Supp. 823 (Col. 1981) upholding a city's observance of a holiday with religious music, and *Florey* v. *Sioux Falls School District 49-5,* 619 F.2d 1311 (8th Cir. 1980), cert. denied, 449 U.S. 987 (1980), which upheld the presentation of holiday assemblies that contained religious art, literature, and music, as long as such materials were not presented in an attempt to advance or inhibit religion. The decision held that

> Only holidays with both religious and secular bases may be observed; music, art, literature and drama may be included in the curriculum only if presented in a prudent and objective manner and only as part of the cultural and religious heritage of the holiday; and religious symbols may be used only as a teaching aid or resource and only if they are displayed as part of the cultural and religious heritage of the holiday and are temporary in nature. Since all programs and materials authorized by the rules must deal with the secular or cultural basis or heritage of the holidays and since the materials must be presented in a prudent and objective manner and symbols used as a teaching aid, the advancement of a "secular program of education," and not of religion, is the primary effect of the rules. (P. 1317)

However, this court stated that a kindergarten program that was primarily religious in content was unconstitutional.

In reference to holiday displays, the United States Supreme Court upheld in a five-to-four decision a forty-year practice of having a nativity scene in a park owned by a nonprofit organization. See *Lynch* v. *Donnelly,* 465 U.S. 668 (1984).

May public schools conduct baccalaureate services? *Chamberlin* v. *Dade County Board of Public Instruction,* 377 U.S. 402 (1964) and 171 So.2d 535 (Fla. 1965), and *Goodwin* v. *Cross County School District No. 7,* 394 F.Supp. 417 (Ark. 1973), address this question but do not provide a definitive answer. Decisions allowing school-sponsored baccalaureate services generally stress the voluntary nature of such services. Would the same reasoning hold for prayers offered at an athletic contest?

May prayers be offered at a public school graduation exercise? Courts have generally agreed that this practice does not violate the First Amendment. See *Grossberg* v. *Deusebio,* 380 F. Supp. 285 (Va. 1974); *Wiest* v. *Mt. Lebanon School District,* 457 Pa. 166, 320 A.2d 362 (1974), cert.

denied, 419 U.S. 967 (1974); and *Stein* v. *Plainwell Community Schools*, 610 F.Supp. 43 (Mich. 1985). Opinions in these decisions also stressed the voluntary nature of graduation exercises. However, a federal district court has held that inclusion of religious invocation and benediction led by a Christian minister in a public high school's graduation ceremony violates the establishment clause. See *Graham* v. *Central Community School District of Decatur County*, 608 F. Supp. 531 (Iowa 1985).

Permitting prayers at student assemblies held on public school property, although voluntary, violates the prohibition against governmental establishment of religion according to *Collins* v. *Chandler Unified School District*, 644 F.2d 759 (9th Cir. 1981), cert. denied, 454 U.S. 863 (1981). Morning devotional readings over a school's public address system were also judged to be unconstitutional. See *Hall* v. *Board of School Commissioners of Conecuh County*, 656 F.2d 999 (5th Cir. 1981).

Many public schools have Bible or other religious study groups that meet on school grounds before, during, or after school. In some instances they have been recognized as official student-body organizations and have often advertised their activities on bulletin boards or through the school newspaper. Occasionally, such groups meet during an "activity period." This has been a much-litigated issue, and courts have generally held against such meetings. See *Brandon* v. *Board of Education of Guilderland Central School District*, 635 F.2d 971 (2d Cir. 1980), cert. denied, 454 U.S. 1123 (1981), *Lubbock Civil Liberties Union* v. *Lubbock Independent School District*, 669 F.2d 1038 (5th Cir. 1982), and *Bender* v. *Williamsport Area School District*, 741 F.2d 538 (3rd Cir. 1984). However, in 1984 the United States Congress passed the Equal Access Act, P.L. 98-377, permitting such religious meetings.* The constitutionality of this act may be assessed by the Supreme Court since certiorari was granted in *Bender*.

Teachers' use of school facilities for religious meetings has also come under judicial purview. An Indiana school-district policy that banned religious meetings of teachers on school property, before the teachers were to report for duty, was upheld. See *May* v. *Evansville-Vanderburgh School Corporation*, 615 F. Supp. 761 (Ind. 1985).

Most states have laws similar to a 1964 federal civil rights law requiring employers to allow workers a day off for their Sabbath if that does not cause "undue hardship" to the business. However, the Supreme Court struck down a Connecticut statute that allowed employees to absent themselves from work on any day that they claimed as their sabbath. The court maintained that the statute imposed on employers the absolute duty to conform their business practices to the religious practices of their employees. It would allow no exceptions, for example, in the event of a teacher's claiming a Friday sabbath. The court contended that the statute's primary

*See appendix D for edited provisions of the Equal Access Act, P.L. 98-377.

effect was the advancement of a particular religious practice. See *Estate of Thornton* v. *Caldor, Inc*, 472 U.S. ___, 105 S.Ct. 2914 (1985).

A religiously-oriented private school risks losing its tax-exempt status if it pursues racially discriminatory practices. Loss of tax-exempt status due to such practices was upheld in *Bob Jones University* v. *United States,* 461 U.S. 574 (1983). The university was devoted to the teaching and propagation of fundamentalist religious beliefs, which included that God intends segregation of the races and that scriptures forbid interracial dating and marriage. Students were expelled if they did not follow these prohibitions.

Does your state or local school system have provisions for school-sponsored Bible reading or prayer, silent prayer, meditation, voluntary prayer, observance of religious holidays, or religious study groups? Will noncompliance with statutory provisions prohibiting Bible reading or prayer result in any penalties in your state?

B. Distribution of Religious Literature

A controversy arising in Florida, decided by the Fifth Circuit Court of Appeals in **Meltzer v. Board of Public Instruction,** reveals the persistence of litigation involving church-state issues. The court, en banc, held that a local school board's resolution requiring daily Bible reading and prayer in the public schools is unconstitutional. However, an equally divided court upheld both the guidelines for the distribution of religious literature in the public schools and Florida's "Christian virtue" statute.

Meltzer v. Board of Public Instruction of Orange County

United States Court of Appeals, Fifth Circuit, 1978
577 F.2d 311, cert. denied, 439 U.S. 1089 (1979)

PER CURIAM:
 * * *   The Court en banc considered the following issues: (1) whether the District Court correctly denied relief on the constitutional challenge to the Orange County school board's resolution requiring daily morning devotionals of Bible reading and prayer in the public schools; (2) whether the District Court correctly denied relief on the constitutional challenge to the Orange County school board's guidelines for the distribution of religious literature at designated locations on the school premises; (3) whether the District Court's denial of relief on the constitutional challenge to Fla. Stat. § 231.09(2) (the "Christian virtue" statute which requires teachers to inculcate Christian virtues in their students) presents a case or controversy. The Court en banc adopts the portion of the panel

opinion which reverses the District Court on issue (1) and which holds the morning devotional unconstitutional. The Court en banc affirms by an equally divided vote the District Court's holding on issues (2) and (3).
REVERSED IN PART: AFFIRMED IN PART.

JOHN R. BROWN, Chief Judge, with whom TUTTLE, GOLD-BERG, GODBOLD and LEWIS R. MORGAN, Circuit Judges join, dissenting in part:

For reasons set out in the panel's decision and amplified here, I must respectfully dissent as to issues (2) and (3).

With its equally divided vote affirming the District Court the en banc Court today reaches an extraordinary result and countenances activity which harms the principles of religious liberty embodied in the Constitution and rooted firmly in our Nation's heritage. The distribution of religious literature, particularly massive quantities of one faith's sacred scripture, through the public schools to impressionable children advances religion and encourages excessive government entanglement with religion in contravention of the Establishment Clause. Similarly, Fla. Stat. § 231.09(2) which in mandatory terms directs teachers to inculcate "Christian virtues" in their young pupils is unconstitutional. * * *

A brief summary of the facts of this case reveals that the equally divided en banc Court's decision is plainly at odds with the First Amendment's principles of religious freedom. On August 24, 1970, the Orange County Board of Public Instruction held a meeting at which a member of the Gideon Camp asked permission to distribute Gideon Bibles to the students at the public schools. The request was approved. At this meeting the Board also adopted a resolution calling for a five to seven minute morning exercise in every school to consist of prayer and Bible reading. At the next meeting of the Board, on September 15, 1970, the eventual plaintiffs in this case complained to the Board that the morning exercise devotional and the distribution of Gideon Bibles violated their religious rights.

At a third meeting of the Board, counsel for the Board gave his opinion that the morning exercises were not unlawful. * * * The Board thereupon refused to modify its policy regarding opening day exercises. The morning exercise program was found to be unconstitutional by the panel and this result is affirmed by the en banc Court. Notwithstanding this affirmance of the panel, the unconstitutional morning devotional is relevant here to the extent it implicates the Florida "Christian virtue" statute and to the extent it reflects the general predilection of the Board to encourage an institutionalized form of religion in the public schools.

Following this third meeting, on October 7, 1970, the Board did issue guidelines for the distribution of Bibles or other religious literature. Prior to the issuance of the guidelines, groups of Gideons would go from classroom to classroom walking up and down the aisles distributing Bibles to those students who indicated they would like one. In this fashion 15,000 Bibles were distributed to the school children during class.

The October 7th guidelines were designed ostensibly to quell the religious minorities' cries of protest. Under the guidelines a location within the school facilities would be designated for the distribution of religious literature supplied by outside groups. The guidelines, however, applied only to religious literature, and permitted the periodic announcement to the pupils that the literature was available. No similar invitation was issued to other pressure interest groups such as the United States Chamber of Commerce, N.A.A.C.P., AFL-CIO, Ripon Society, Americans for Democratic Action or others who have a legitimate interest in advancing their causes through the capture of young minds. The guidelines were adopted nine days before the lawsuit was filed.

Although the guidelines might appear as a concession to the religious minorities by allowing all religions to distribute literature, as applied only the Gideons took advantage of the arrangement. More importantly, they took advantage of the guidelines to the tune of 33,000 additional Bibles distributed after adoption of the guidelines. Apparently the distribution was made at locations highly visible to the students, such as cafeterias, by the Gideons themselves. * * *

* * *

Our decision today permits young, impressionable students to receive influential dosages of one group's beliefs through repeated and massive distribution of the Bible. The children cannot help but view the school system's formal tolerance of such distribution as the placement of the community's imprimatur on this particular movement and all that it embodies. This is precisely what the Establishment Clause prohibits. One does not need to be a prophet to realize that after this Court's holding today some children in Florida schools will be coerced, pressured, or influenced into accepting one faith over others not as fortunate to receive state approval.

* * *

Each state effort to promote or accommodate religion is measured against a three-tiered Establishment Clause standard. To pass muster under the Constitution the state action in question must reflect a clearly secular purpose, have a primary effect that neither advances nor inhibits religion, and avoid excessive government entanglement with religion. * * * The Supreme Court views these criteria as "guidelines with which to identify instances in which the objectives of the Religion Clauses have been impaired." * * *

An examination of the record reveals that the Bible distribution guidelines fail to reflect a secular purpose. First, on their face the guidelines, entitled "Religious Books and Literature," apply solely to the distribution of *religious* literature, and expressly do not apply to the distribution of secular literature.

* * *

Considered as a whole the record portrays a pattern of conduct which manifests the Board's predilection to encourage particular religions and in doing so to promote most particularly the aims of the Gideon movement. In the face of rulings by both the Florida state court and the federal District Court which indicated the likely constitutional infirmity of a Bible distribution scheme, the Board's conduct exhibits a sectarian commitment to Bible distribution, sectarian in the sense that the Board thought availability of Bibles was for religious values, not, say as instruments of good literature. * * *

* * *

Our equally divided vote on the issue of the constitutionality of the "Christian virtue" statute * * * reflects a concern that the claim is imaginary, speculative, and of insufficient immediacy to warrant the issuance of a declaratory judgment. I have no difficulty in concluding that the "Christian virtue" statute is sufficiently implicated in the activities of the Board to wholly justify declaratory relief. First, the Board sustained its policy permitting Bible distributions, and Bible reading and prayer by relying in part upon the statute. Moreover, this policy is still in effect. Finally, the statute is in mandatory terms—it imposes an affirmative duty on the state's instructional personnel to inculcate Christian virtues. Although no one has been disciplined recently for noncompliance with the statute, this reflects primarily the teacher's, principal's, and Board's acceptance of the statute and its aim—the inculcation of Christianity.

* * * Although our research has not disclosed any illuminating legislative history which would shed light on our task, we think it of particular significance that the Florida legislature passed a statute only a few years prior to its passage of the Christian virtue statute, which made Bible reading mandatory in the public schools of Florida. This statute, which immediately preceded the Christian virtue statute in the Florida statutes, remained in effect until repealed in 1965. We think it not unreasonable to suppose that the Christian virtue statute, which was made an additional subsection to the same statute as the compulsory Bible reading statute, was meant to be complementary to that statute. * * *

* * * The evidence below is very persuasive that the phrase, "Christian virtue" suggest a very particular type of virtue—a virtue that is tied particularly to one religion, and a type of virtue that is or may be at odds with other, minority, religions' concepts of virtue. Furthermore, common sense tells us that this is so. If this statute had required the inculcation of "Jewish virtue," or "Moslem virtue," we have no doubt that the unconstitutionality of the statute would be conceded by all. We can see no forthright, honest distinction when the word "Christian" is substituted for "Jewish" or for "Moslem" in our hypothetical. We therefore conclude that the "Christian virtue" statute has as one of its major purposes the advancement of a particular religion. * * *

* * *

We emphasize that the downfall of this statute is its use of the word "Christian" and the effect the inclusion of that word has had on the practices of the Board of Public Instruction of Orange County and the area public schools. If the statute read exactly the same, except that the word "Christian" was excised, we would probably hold the statute constitutional. As it stands now, we have measured it against the standards set by the Supreme Court for measuring whether a statute passes muster under the First Amendment, and we have found it wanting. * * *

* * *

Notes and Questions

Distribution of Gideon Bibles was litigated more than three decades earlier. See *Tudor* v. *Board of Education of Borough of Rutherford,* 14 N.J. 31, 100 A.2d 857 (1953), cert. denied, 348 U.S. 816 (1954), where distribution of the Bibles was prohibited.

Under the guidelines discussed in **Meltzer,** religious groups such as Hare Krishnas, Buddhists, Muslims, or Jews could have their literature distributed at a public school. Would it be a restriction of the right of freedom of religion if no religious literature were allowed to be distributed?

Will the rationale of the evenly divided Fifth Circuit Court of Appeals regarding distribution of religious literature and the inculcation of Christian virtues be adopted by other federal courts of appeal?

Does your state or local school system have any policies pertaining to the distribution of religious literature?

C. Released and Shared Time
and Religious Instruction

Two significant United States Supreme Court decisions have addressed the questions of releasing public school students during normal school hours and thereby enabling them to receive religious instruction. In one of the decisions, *McCollum* v. *Board of Education of School District No. 71,*

333 U.S. 203 (1948), the Court invalidated a plan under which separate Protestant, Catholic, and Jewish religious classes were taught in the public school buildings. The Court contended that the use of tax-supported property for religious instruction, the close cooperation between school authorities and religious officials, and the use of the state's compulsory-education system all tended to promote religious education, and, therefore, violated the First Amendment. In another decision, *Zorach* v. *Clauson*, 343 U.S. 306 (1952), the Court upheld a plan whereby students were released during public school hours to attend religious instruction classes off the school premises. The Court stated:

> The government must be neutral when it comes to competition between sects. It may not thrust any sect on any person. It may not make a religious observance compulsory. It may not coerce anyone to attend church, to observe a religious holiday, or to take religious instruction. But it can close its doors or suspend its operations as to those who want to repair to their religious sanctuary for worship or instruction. No more than that is undertaken here. (P. 314)

A federal district court, in *Lanner* v. *Wimmer*, 463 F.Supp. 867 (Utah 1978), has held that academic credit could not be given in a released-time seminary program for courses in the Old Testament and New Testament. The Tenth Circuit Court of Appeals modified this decision in 662 F.2d 1349 (10th Cir. 1981). The court ruled that the process of gathering attendance slips and the necessity of judging whether the courses were mainly denominational violated the First Amendment. The court held that neither the released-time program itself nor the granting of credit toward participation in extracurricular activities offended the establishment and Free Exercise Clauses.

Several cases have addressed the issue of shared time. In one case a public school would not enroll a parochial school student in a band course at the public school. The public school had a policy of allowing attendance in its schools only by fulltime students. See *Snyder* v. *Charlotte Public School District*, 421 Mich. 517, 365 N.W.2d 151 (1984), in which the Michigan Supreme Court ruled that public schools must open "nonessential elective courses" such as band, art, and advanced mathematics to private school students.

A shared-time and a community-education program conducted by public school teachers within participating non-public school facilities were struck down by the United States Supreme Court in *Grand Rapids School District* v. *Ball*, 473 U.S. __, 105 S.Ct. 3216 (1985). In this case public school teachers taught remedial math and reading, art, music, and physical education in parochial schools during the school day. Public school teachers also taught gymnastics, home economics, Spanish, and drama after school.

Is it permissible for a public school system to offer Bible study courses? See *Wiley* v. *Franklin,* 474 F. Supp. 525 (Tenn. 1979), which held that such courses could not be offered unless they were (1) secular in nature, intent, and purpose; (2) neither advancing nor inhibiting religion, and (3) offered in a manner that avoided excessive entanglement between government and religion. See *Crockett* v. *Sorenson,* 568 F. Supp. 1422 (Va. 1983) for a similar view. A course entitled Science of Creative Intelligence—Transcendental Meditation, which involved religious activity, was held to constitute establishment of religion proscribed by the First Amendment. See *Malnak* v. *Yogi,* 592 F.2d 197 (3rd Cir. 1979).

A state supreme court upheld the nonrenewal of a teacher who devoted excessive time to creationism and religion in his biology class and who failed to cover basic biology principles. The school board had established guidelines that allowed the teacher a specified amount of time to teach the theories of evolution or creation. See *Dale* v. *Board of Education, Lemmon Independent School District,* 316 N.W.2d 108 (N.D. 1982). Additionally statutes in Arkansas and Louisiana requiring balanced treatment to the teaching of creation science and evolution science were held to violate the Constitution. See *McLean* v. *Arkansas Board of Education,* 529 F. Supp. 1255 (Ark. 1982), and *Aguillard* v. *Edwards,* 765 F.2d 1251 (5th Cir. 1985).

III. Use of Facilities

Another issue that often arises at the local school level has to do with the extent, if any, that school buildings may be used during noninstructional hours. In most instances the local school board has either implied or specific authority to promulgate reasonable rules for the use of school buildings when they are not being used for school purposes or when their use does not interfere with normal school operations. Controversies often arise when the use of school facilities is requested by a group whose purpose or speaker may be offensive to some in the community, that represents certain religious organizations, or that is primarily interested in using the facility for commercial gain.

A general rule that has evolved concerning the use of school facilities suggests that if facilities are to be leased to one type of group, they must be available to all within the group. However, such use may be denied if (1) the user fails or refuses to abide by reasonable rules and regulations pertaining to the use, (2) there is a demonstrated danger of violence or disruption associated with meetings of this particular group, and (3) the meeting violates a local ordinance or either state or federal constitutional provisions or law. It should be noted that in the absence of a state statute mandating their use, local systems are not obligated to make school buildings available for public activities.

Those denied use of a school facility often allege that their right of freedom of expression has been denied. The United States Supreme Court addressed this notion in *Police Department of the City of Chicago* v. *Mosley*, 408 U.S. 92 (1972), when it stated:

> Necessarily, then, under the Equal Protection Clause, not to mention the First Amendment itself, government may not grant the use of a forum to people whose views it finds acceptable, but deny use to those wishing to express less favored or more controversial views. And it may not select which issues are worth discussing or debating in public facilities. There is an "equality of status in the field of ideas," and government must afford all points of view an equal opportunity to be heard. Once a forum is opened up to assembly or speaking by some groups, government may not prohibit others from assembling or speaking on the basis of what they intend to say. Selective exclusions from a public forum may not be based on content alone, and may not be justified by reference to content alone. (P. 96)

Country Hills Christian Church v. Unified School District No. 512

United States District Court, District of Kansas, 1983
560 F. Supp. 1207

SAFFELS, District Judge.

* * *

Defendants have made available their school buildings and facilities to non-school community organizations at a reasonable rent. Groups as diverse as the Democratic Party and the Y.M.C.A. make use of defendants' buildings. Community groups use these buildings for singing songs, cooking group suppers, staging theatrical productions, playing basketball and airing their political and moral views. For example, the court heard testimony about the Voice of Reason meeting at night on December 7, 1982, at Indian Hills Junior High School, at which meeting school prayer, sex education and abortion were discussed.

The traditional public forum is a park or a public street. The First Amendment, through the Fourteenth, prohibits a state from abridging or denying use of a street or park for purposes of assembly, communication and discussion of public questions. * * * Use of the streets or parks may be subject to reasonable time, place and manner restrictions * * * , but only to the extent necessary to avoid a threat to public safety, peace or order. * * *

Streets and parks are not the only public places subject to the protection of the First Amendment. A public library may be a public forum, and, in some cases, a local government must allow its library to be used as a stage for political expression. * * * A railroad station is a public forum * * * , and a municipal bus terminal is a public forum * * * , while a city-owned bus is not. * * * A municipally-owned theater is a public forum. * * * Even a privately-owned shopping center can be a public forum. * * *

A public school is a public forum for its students and teachers. * * * If it is opened to the school district community for meetings and discussions during non-school hours, then it becomes a public forum for the community. * * *

Defendants, by and through their Policies Nos. 2000 and 2020, have created a public forum for the exercise of First Amendment rights. The forum is open to "recognized community groups." The dedication of school district facilities as a public forum for community groups makes the school buildings virtually the same, in concept, as streets and parks as far as the First Amendment is concerned.

This does not mean, however, that school buildings cannot be regulated to a greater degree than parks and streets. The nature of the school building, its function in the community and the activities normally conducted there, dictate that reasonable regulations of time, place and manner of use by community organizations may be imposed. * * * Defendants allege that if the court allows the Country Hills Christian Church to use Mill Creek Elementary School on Easter Sunday, the floodgates will be opened and the court must also order them to allow into their buildings snake cults, groups that practice animal sacrifices, groups that wear odd clothes, and groups that smoke and use fire in their worship services.

That is a bridge the court does not have to cross at this time. From the evidence, the court finds that plaintiffs conduct worship services of a more tame variety. Nevertheless, if defendants find that the handling of poisonous reptiles, fire and smoke, or the use of alcoholic beverages in a religious service conducted in a school building are activities which should be regulated, the First Amendment should pose no obstacle so long as the regulations are reasonable.

Religious worship and discussion are "forms of speech and association protected by the First Amendment." * * *

Once a forum is opened to assembly or speaking by some groups, a school district may not prohibit other groups from assembling or speaking on the basis of what they intend to say. Selective exclusions from a public forum may not be based on content alone, and may not be justified by reference to content. * * * The First Amendment prohibits excluding groups from a public forum based on the content of the group's intended speech even where the government was not required to create the forum in the first place. * * *

Defendants review requests to use School District facilities to determine whether or not each group will be engaging in religious worship. If the group is deemed to be making a request to use the School District facilities for a non-religious use, then the group's request is granted. If defendants determine the group will make religious use of the building, permission is denied. Plaintiffs fall into the latter group. Defendants have denied plaintiffs access to a public forum solely because of the content of plaintiff's proposed speech. This is a violation of the First Amendment. * * *

Defendants' primary function, that of educating children, does not exempt them from the provisions of the First Amendment. The First Amendment extends to public schools * * * , and unconstitutional exclusion of those who wish to use school buildings cannot be rationalized by reference to the school setting. "School desks and blackboards, like trees [in a park] or street lights [on a street], are but the trappings of the forum; what imports is the meeting of minds and not the meeting place." * * *

Defendants argue that children are impressionable and easily confused. They argue that children who attend Sunday school in the same building as their public school classes will come to feel that the School District endorses their church. Defendants argue that a child who attends Sunday school at a church may feel that the School District disapproves of his church because another sect is permitted to rent the child's school building during non-school hours. Defendants further argue that children will acquire an irreconcilable conflict between an apparently school-district-approved sect and their family's religion and church. This may or may not be true. There is no evidence in the record to support these contentions. Dr. Cormack, School District Psychologist, testified that he believed these contentions to be true, but he admitted that no empirical evidence existed in support of his theories and that no studies had been done to verify them. The court finds his testimony to be speculative and declines to give it any weight. * * *

* * *

The Establishment Clause requires the School District to be neutral in its relations with groups of religious believers, but does not require the School District to be an adversary to religious groups. The court finds the School District may not close their doors to groups who wish to rent School District facilities for purposes of religious worship during non-school hours, and that the Establishment Clause provides no defense to this action.

* * *

The present policy presents an unacceptable degree of entanglement with religion by the School District because of enforcement of its policy of exclusion of religious worship. The School District must determine in every questionable case what words and conduct constitute religious use or religious worship. Of course, this is "an impossible task in an age where many and various beliefs meet the constitutional definition of religion." * * * An open access policy would eliminate the need for the School District to determine what uses are religious and what uses are not religious.

"Entanglement" refers not only to the day-to-day interaction between government and religion; it also refers to the effect of government policies toward religion. In the end, the test for entanglement is one of degree. The question is whether or not government policy calls for "official or continuing surveillance" or excessive government involvement in religious organizations. * * *

"Entanglement" refers to either a governmentally-established religion or governmental interference with religion. Avoiding excessive entanglement does not require "perfect or absolute separation" of church and state * * * : there is "room for play in the joints productive of a benevolent neutrality which will permit religious exercise to exist without sponsorship" by the government. * * * A school district does not engage in excessive entanglement if it maintains a "kind of benevolent neutrality toward churches and religious exercise generally." * * * An open access policy would, at most foster such a benevolent neutrality, but would not subject defendants to an unconstitutional level of entanglement.

The court concludes that by allowing their facilities to be used during non-school hours by non-school community groups, defendants have created a public forum. Having created a public forum, defendants cannot exclude plaintiffs from the forum because of the religious content of plaintiff's intended speech unless such exclusion is justified under applicable constitutional case law. Defendants have not and cannot justify their policy of exclusion. The Establishment Clause does not justify excluding plaintiffs' religious services from School District buildings, and there is no evidence either that children will be harmed or that defendants risk placing an imprimatur of approval on religious sects which rent School District facilities.

Notes and Questions

In upholding the use of school property for religious services during nonschool hours, the New Jersey Supreme Court contended that a rental schedule should include the actual costs of utilities and administrative and janitorial services. Five years was considered "approaching the outer bounds of reasonable time and nearing the point of prohibited entanglement." See *Resnick* v. *East Brunswick Township Board of Education*, 77 N.J. 88, 389 A.2d 944 (1978).

In addressing the issue of conditioning the off-time use of public school facilities on the political or ideological views of the applicant, on its membership policies, or on its attendance restrictions, a federal appellate court declared that the school system was not responsible for the views expressed or for the composition of the group that expressed them. The court also stated that "merely permitting the occasional and temporary use of state facilities by racially discriminatory groups along with all others does not constitute significant state involvement in their practices." See *Knights of the Ku Klux Klan* v. *East Baton Rouge Parish School Board*, 578 F.2d 1122 (5th Cir. 1978). Also see *National Socialist White People's Party* v. *Ringers*, 473 F.2d 1010 (4th Cir. 1973).

California has a statute establishing a "civic center" at "each and every public school building and grounds within the state." Although the local board may adopt reasonable rules and regulations pertaining to the statute, community groups may use the facilities without charge to discuss subjects that "appertain to the educational, political, economic, artistic, and moral interests of the citizens."

California also has a law that provides for the leasing of surplus school facilities for private use. A California court of appeals held that a denial to a private school of the right to bid for the lease of surplus public school facilities was a denial of the private school's constitutional rights. See *Binet-Montessori, Inc.* v. *San Francisco Unified School District*, 98 Cal. App. 3d 991, 160 Cal. Rptr. 38 (1979).

Local businesspeople are often concerned that allowing the use of school facilities, which have been constructed at public expense, is a form of competition against them. This view was not upheld in *Hall* v. *Shelby County Board of Education*, 472 S.W. 2d 489 (Ky. 1971), where a local civic group organized and charged admission to musical programs. All profits were used for civic activities.

Although a school board delegated authority over most permit applications to its building-level administrators, it retained the authority to consider, with advice of counsel, the applications of religious groups for non-social or non-recreational meetings. In upholding this practice a federal appellate court contended that the school board's need to assess the complex issues concerning the Establishment Clause was sufficient justification for the minor inconvenience caused by the policy. See *Salinas* v. *School District of Kansas City*, 751 F.2d 288 (8th Cir. 1984).

Assume a local school board had a policy of allowing school facilities to be used by local groups. Would the school board be on sound constitutional footing if they barred any of the following local groups: a gay liberation league? a group wishing to legalize the use of marijuana, cocaine, or heroin? American Nazis? Save the Whales? Friends of Fidel Castro? Impeach the President Committee? Committee to recall local school board members? Devil worshippers? Nudists? Communists? What is the basis for your response in each of these instances?

Does your state have legislation pertaining to the use of public school facilities when they are not being used by the school system? Does your public school system have policies regulating the use of facilities?

IV. Aid to Nonpublic Schools

Approximately 10 percent of American students attend nonpublic schools. About 70 percent of those students are enrolled in Catholic schools, and approximately 15 percent of nonpublic school students attend non-church-related schools. Legislatures in several states having large numbers of nonpublic school students have passed measures which have attempted to financially assist the non-public school sector. Since these measures have raised serious questions pertaining to the proper separation of church and state under the First Amendment, their constitutionality has been examined by the United States Supreme Court.

Over the years, three tests have been developed by the Court to determine whether or not the Establishment Clause of the First Amendment has been violated. By employing these tests, the Court has attempted to determine whether or not a challenged statute (1) has a clearly secular purpose, (2) has a principle or primary effect that neither advances nor inhibits religion, and (3) does not foster an excessive government entanglement with religion.

In *Lemon* v. *Kurtzman,* 403 U.S. 602 (1971) the Court struck down both an attempt by the Rhode Island legislature to provide a 15 percent salary supplement to be paid to those teachers dealing with secular subjects in nonpublic schools and a Pennsylvania statute that provided financial support to nonpublic elementary and secondary schools by way of reimbursement for the cost of teachers' salaries, textbooks, and instructional materials in specified secular subjects. The Court held that the "cumulative impact of the entire relationship arising under the statutes in each state involves excessive entanglement between government and religion." Furthermore, the Court reasoned that these state programs had a divisive political potential that would be a threat to the normal political process. Since candidates would be forced to declare their position on amounts of money to be expended in such programs, political division along religious lines would develop. The Court contended that this was a principal evil that the First Amendment was intended to protect against.

A New York statute was struck down by the Court in *Levitt* v. *Committee for Public Education and Religious Liberty,* 413 U.S. 472 (1973). Under this statute nonpublic schools would have been reimbursed for expenses incurred in administering, grading, compiling, and reporting test results; maintaining pupil attendance and health records; recording qualifications and characteristics of personnel; and preparing and submitting various reports to the state. The Court ruled that such aid would have the primary purpose or effect of advancing religion or religious education and that it would lead to excessive entanglement between church and state. However, in *Committee for Public Education and Religious Liberty* v. *Regan,* 442 U.S. 928 (1980), a five-to-four opinion, the Court upheld a revised version of the law that had been declared unconstitutional in *Levitt.* The revised law allowed the state to reimburse private schools, including sectarian schools, for the expenses connected with keeping official attendance and other records, for administering three state tests, and for grading two of the tests.

Another New York law was invalidated, in *Committee for Public Education and Religious Liberty* v. *Nyquist,* 413 U.S. 756 (1973), which provided for the maintenance and repair of nonpublic school facilities, tuition reimbursement for parents of nonpublic school students, and tax relief for those not qualifying for tuition reimbursement. And a Pennsylvania law providing for parent reimbursement for nonpublic school students was also invalidated in *Sloan* v. *Lemon,* 413 U.S. 825 (1973). The majority opinion declared that there was no constitutionally significant difference between Pennsylvania's tuition-grant scheme and New York's tuition-reimbursement program, which was held violative of the establishment clause in *Nyquist.*

In *Meek* v. *Pittenger,* 421 U.S. 349 (1975), the Court was asked to rule on a Pennsylvania statute that provided for auxiliary services for exceptional, remedial, or educationally disadvantaged nonpublic school students; for lending instructional materials and equipment to nonpublic schools; and for lending textbooks to nonpublic school students. The Court invalidated all but the textbook-loan provision of the Pennsylvania law. It held that the act had the unconstitutional primary effect of advancing religion because of the predominantly religious character of the benefiting schools. Additionally, the Court stated that the act provided excessive opportunities for political fragmentation and division along religious lines. Expanding on this theme, the Court declared:

> This potential for political entanglement, together with the administrative entanglement which would be necessary to ensure that auxiliary-services personnel remain strictly neutral and nonideological when functioning in church-related schools . . . violates the constitutional prohibition against laws "respecting an establishment of religion." (P. 372)

In another decision, **Wolman v. Walter,** the Court addressed the constitutionality of an Ohio statute that had attempted to conform to the *Meek* ruling. The decision, which revealed wide disagreement among the justices, held that the provisions providing nonpublic students with books, standardized testing and scoring, diagnostic services, and therapeutic and remedial services were constitutional. However, provisions relating to instructional materials and equipment and field trip services were held to be unconstitutional.

Wolman v. Walter

Supreme Court of the United States, 1977
433 U.S. 229

MR. JUSTICE BLACKMUN delivered the opinion of the Court (Parts I, V, VI, VII, and VIII), together with an opinion (Parts II, III, and IV), in which THE CHIEF JUSTICE, MR. JUSTICE STEWART and MR. JUSTICE POWELL joined.

This is still another case presenting the recurrent issue of the limitations imposed by the Establishment Clause of the First Amendment, made applicable to the States by the Fourteenth Amendment, * * * on state aid to pupils in church-related elementary and secondary schools. * * *

I

Section 3317.06 was enacted after this Court's May 1975 decision in *Meek* v. *Pittenger,* * * * and obviously is an attempt to conform to the teachings of that decision. * * * In broad outline, the statute authorizes the State to provide nonpublic school pupils with books, instructional materials and equipment, standardized testing and scoring, diagnostic services, therapeutic services, and field trip transportation.

The initial biennial appropriation by the Ohio Legislature for implementation of the statute was the sum of $88,800,000. * * * Funds so appropriated are paid to the State's public school districts and are then expended by them. All disbursements made with respect to nonpublic schools have their equivalents in disbursements for public schools, and the amount expended per pupil in nonpublic schools may not exceed the amount expended per pupil in the public schools.

The parties stipulated that during the 1974–1975 school year there were 720 chartered nonpublic schools in Ohio. Of these, all but 29 were sectarian. More than 96% of the nonpublic enrollment attended sectarian schools, and more than 92% attended Catholic schools. * * * All such schools teach the secular subjects required to meet the State's minimum standards. The state-mandated five-hour day is expanded to include, usually, one-half hour of religious instruction. Pupils who are not members of the Catholic faith are not required to attend religion classes or to participate in religious exercises or activities, and no teacher is required to teach religious doctrine as a part of the secular courses taught in the schools. * * *

* * *

II

The mode of analysis for Establishment Clause questions is defined by the three-part test that has emerged from the Court's decisions. In order to pass muster, a statute must have a secular legislative purpose, must have a principal or primary effect that neither advances nor inhibits religion, and must not foster an excessive government entanglement with religion. * * *

In the present case we have no difficulty with the first prong of this three-part test. We are satisfied that the challenged statute reflects Ohio's legitimate interest in protecting the health of its youth and in providing a fertile educational environment for all the schoolchildren of the State. As is usual in our cases, the analytical difficulty has to do with the effect and entanglement criteria.

* * * We have acknowledged before, and we do so again here, that the walls of separation that must be maintained between the church and state "is a blurred, indistinct, and variable barrier depending on all the circumstances of a particular relationship." * * *

III
Textbooks

Section 3317.06 authorizes the expenditure of funds:

"(A) To purchase such secular books as have been approved by the superintendent of public instruction for use in public schools in the state and to loan such textbook to pupils attending nonpublic schools within the district or to their parents. Such loans shall be based upon individual requests submitted by such nonpublic school pupils or parents. Such requests shall be submitted to the local public school district in which the nonpublic school is located. Such individual requests for the loan of textbooks shall, for administrative convenience be submitted by the nonpublic school pupil or his parent to the nonpublic school which shall prepare and submit collective summaries of the individual requests to the local public school district. As used in this section, "textbook" means any book or book substitute which a pupil uses as a text or text substitute in a particular class or program in the school he regularly attends."

* * *

* * * [W]e conclude that § 3317.06(A) is constitutional.

IV
Testing and Scoring

Section 3317.06 authorizes expenditure of funds:

"(J) To supply for use by pupils attending nonpublic schools within the district such standardized tests and scoring devices as are in use in the public schools of the state."

These tests "are used to measure the progress of students in secular subjects." * * * Nonpublic school personnel are not involved in either the drafting or scoring of the tests. * * * The statute does not authorize any payment to nonpublic school personnel for the costs of administering the tests.

* * *

There is no question that the State has a substantial and legitimate interest in insuring that its youth receive an adequate secular education. * * * The State may require that schools that are utilized to fulfill the State's compulsory-education requirement meet certain standards of instruction, * * * and may examine both teachers and pupils to ensure that the State's legitimate interest is being fulfilled. * * * Under the section at issue, the State provides both the schools and the school district with the means of ensuring that the minimum standards are met. The nonpublic school does not control the content of the test or its result. This serves to prevent the use of the test as a part of religious teaching * * * . Similarly, the inability of the school to control the test eliminates the need for the supervision that gives rise to excessive entanglement. We therefore agree with the District Court's conclusion that § 3317.06(J) is constitutional.

V
Diagnostic Services

Section 3317.06 authorizes expenditures of funds:

"(D) To provide speech and hearing diagnostic services to pupils attending nonpublic schools within the district. Such service shall be provided in the nonpublic school attended by the pupil receiving the service.

"(F) To provide diagnostic psychological services to pupils attending nonpublic schools within the district. Such services shall be provided in the school attended by the pupil receiving the service."

It will be observed that these speech and hearing and psychological diagnostic services are to be provided within the nonpublic school. It is stipulated, however, that the personnel (with the exception of physicians) who perform the services are employees of the local board of education; that physicians may be hired on a contract basis; that the purpose of these services is to determine the pupil's deficiency or need of assistance; and that treatment of any defect so found would take place off the nonpublic school premises. * * *

Appellants * * * argue that the speech and hearing staff might engage in unrestricted conversation with the pupil and, on occasion, might fail to separate religious instruction from secular responsibilities. They further assert that the communication between the psychological diagnostician and the pupil will provide an impermissible opportunity for the intrusion of religious influence.

The District Court found these dangers so insubstantial as not to render the statute unconstitutional. * * * We agree. This Court's decisions contain a common thread to the effect that the provision of health services to all schoolchildren—public and nonpublic—does not have the primary effect of aiding religion. * * *

* * *

We conclude that providing diagnostic services on the nonpublic school premises will not create an impermissible risk of the fostering of ideological views. It follows that there is no need for excessive surveillance, and there will not be impermissible entanglement. We therefore hold that § § 3317.06 (D) and (F) are constitutional.

VI
Therapeutic Services

Sections 3317.06 (G), (H), (I), and (K) authorize expenditures of funds for certain therapeutic, guidance, and remedial services for students who have been identified as having a need for specialized attention. Personnel providing the services must be employees of the local board of education or under contract with the State Department of Health. The services are to be performed only in public schools, in public centers, or in mobile units located off the nonpublic school premises. * * *

Appellants concede that the provision of remedial, therapeutic, and guidance services in public schools, public centers, or mobile units is constitutional if both public and nonpublic school students are served simultaneously. * * * Appellants express particular concern over mobile units because they perceive a danger that such a unit might operate merely as an annex of the school or schools it services.

* * *

Accordingly, we hold that providing therapeutic and remedial services at a neutral site off the premises of the nonpublic schools will not have the impermissible effect of advancing religion. Neither will there be any excessive entanglement arising from supervision of public employees to insure that they maintain a neutral stance. It can hardly be said that the supervision of public employees performing public functions on public property creates an excessive entanglement between church and state. Sections 3317.06 (G), (H), (I), and (K) are constitutional.

VII
Instructional Materials and Equipment

Sections 3317.06 (B) and (C) authorize expenditures of funds for the purchase and loan to pupils or their parents upon individual request of instructional materials and instructional equipment of the kind in use in the public schools within the district and which is "incapable of diversion to religious use." Section 3317.06 also provides that the materials and equipment may be stored on the premises of a nonpublic school and that publicly hired personnel who administer the lending program may perform their services upon the nonpublic school premises when necessary "for efficient implementation of the lending program."

Although the exact nature of the material and equipment is not clearly revealed, the parties have stipulated: "It is expected that materials and equipment loaned to pupils or parents under the new law will be similar to such former materials and equipment except that to the extent that the law required that materials and equipment capable of diversion to religious issues will not be supplied." * * * Equipment provided under the predecessor statute * * * included projectors, tape recorders, record players, maps and globes, science kits, weather forecasting charts and the like. The District Court * * * found the new statute, as now limited, constitutional because the court could not distinguish the loan of material and equipment from the textbook provisions * * * .

In *Meek* * * * the Court considered the constitutional validity of a direct loan to nonpublic schools of instructional material and equipment, and, despite the apparent secular nature of the goods, held the loan impermissible. * * *

* * * Despite the technical change in legal bailee, the program in substance is the same as before: The equipment is substantially the same; it will receive the same use by the students; and it may still be stored and distributed on the nonpublic school premises. In view of the impossibility of separating the secular education function from the sectarian, the state aid inevitably flows in part in support of the religious role of the schools. * * * [W]e hold § § 3317.06 (B) and (C) to be unconstitutional.

VIII
Fields Trips

Section 3317.06 also authorizes expenditures of funds:

"(L) To provide such field trip transportation and services to nonpublic school students as are provided to public school students in the district. School districts may contract with commercial transportation companies for such transportation service if school district busses are unavailable."

There is no restriction on the timing of field trips; the only restriction on number lies in the parallel the statute draws to field trips provided to public school students in the district. The parties have stipulated that the trips "would consist of visits to governmental, industrial, cultural, and scientific centers designed to enrich the secular studies of students." * * * The choice of destination, however, will be made by the nonpublic school teacher from a wide range of locations.

The District Court * * * held this feature to be constitutionally indistinguishable from that with which the Court was concerned in *Everson* v. *Board of Education*, 330 U.S. 1 (1947). We do not agree. * * *
* * * First, the nonpublic school controls the timing of the trips and, within a certain range, their frequency and destinations. Thus, the school, rather than the children, truly are the recipients of the service and, as this Court has recognized, this fact alone may be sufficient to invalidate the program as impermissible direct aid. * * * Second, although a trip may be a location that would be of interest to those in public schools, it is the individual teacher who makes a field trip meaningful. The experience begins with the study and discussion of the place to be visited; it continues on location with the teacher pointing out items of interest and stimulating the imagination; and it ends with a discussion of the experience. The field trips are an integral part of the educational experience, and where the teacher works within and for a sectarian institution, an unacceptable risk of fostering religion is an inevitable byproduct. * * * Funding of field trips, therefore, must be treated as was the funding of maps and charts * * * , the funding of buildings and tuition, * * * and the funding of teacher-prepared tests * * * ; it must be declared an impermissible direct aid to sectarian education.

Moreover, the public school authorities will be unable adequately to insure secular use of the field trip funds without close supervision of the nonpublic teachers. This would create excessive entanglement. * * * We hold § 3317.06 (L) to be unconstitutional.

IX

In summary, we hold constitutional those portions of the Ohio statute authorizing the State to provide nonpublic school pupils with books, standardized testing and scoring, diagnostic services, and therapeutic and remedial services. We hold unconstitutional those portions relating to instructional materials and equipment and field trip services.

The judgment of the District Court is therefore affirmed in part and reversed in part.

It is so ordered.

Notes and Questions

In a five-to-four decision, *Mueller* v. *Allen*, 463 U.S. 388 (1983), the Court upheld a Minnesota law permitting taxpayers to claim a deduction from gross income on their state income tax returns for expenses incurred for "tuition, textbooks and transportation" not exceeding $500 for dependents in grades K–6 and $700 for dependents in grades 7–12. A distinction between this decision and the Court's 1973 *Nyquist* ruling appears to be that *Nyquist* rejected a tax *credit* for parents whose children attended nonpublic school, while *Mueller* allowed a tax *deduction* for all parents, including those whose children attended public schools. The tax deduction, the *Mueller* majority reasoned, was simply part of the state's tax law permitting deductions for a number of things. The dissenters argued that the difference between a tax credit and a deduction was "a distinction without a difference," and that 90 percent of private school students were in sectarian schools.

A New Jersey statute was held to be unconstitutional that provided taxpayers with a $1,000 tax deduction for each child attending nonpublic schools. See *Public Funds for Public Schools of New Jersey* v. *Byrne*, 590 F.2d 514 (3rd Cir. 1979), aff'd, 442 U.S. 907 (1979).

The United State Supreme Court, in a five-to-four decision, upheld the constitutionality of providing transportation to parochial school students in *Everson* v. *Board of Education of Township of Ewing*, 330 U.S. 1 (1947). Demonstrating that it continues to be an issue, a Rhode Island statute providing for the busing of students to nonpublic schools was held not to violate state or federal constitutional provisions. See *Members of the Jamestown School Committee* v. *Schmidt*, 405 A.2d 16 (R.I. 1979).

The Court struck down the use of federal education funds under Chapter I (formerly Title I of the Elementary and Secondary Education Act) to pay public school teachers who taught in programs aimed at helping low-income, educationally deprived students in parochial schools. See *Aguilar* v. *Felton,* 473 U.S. __, 105 S.Ct. 3232 (1985).

Does your state have any provisions for aid to nonpublic schools?

V. School Fees

Disputes often arise in regard to the charging of fees by public school systems for supplies, materials, extracurricular activities, and texts. Whether or not fees may be legitimately charged depends upon statutory provisions or the interpretation of a state's constitution. Although decisions in several states have denied the charging of fees for textbooks and/or supplies, decisions in other states have taken an opposite view.

The California Supreme Court considered the issue of charging fees for extracurricular activities in *Hartzell* v. *Connell.*

Hartzell v. Connell

Supreme Court of California, 1984
35 Cal.3d 899, 201 Cal. Rptr. 601

BIRD, Chief Justice.

May a public high school district charge fees for educational programs simply because they have been denominated "extracurricular"?

The Santa Barbara High School District (District) offers a wide variety of extracurricular activities, ranging from cheerleading to madrigal singing, and from archery to football. Many of these activities are of relatively recent origin. For example, in 1956, Santa Barbara High School fielded six athletic teams while today there are thirty-eight.

Prior to the 1980–1981 school year, any student could participate in these activities free of charge. The programs were financed by a combination of District contributions (mostly state aid and local tax revenues), ticket sales, and fundraising activities conducted by the constituent high schools.

In the spring of 1980, the District school board (Board) decided to cut its budget by $1.1 million. This decision reflected a drop in revenues due to the combined effects of inflation, declining enrollment, and the adoption of Proposition 13. Among the items to be reduced was the District's contribution to the high school extracurricular programs.

The Board considered two plans for adapting the programs to fit its reduced budget. The first plan called for a major cut in interscholastic athletic competition, including the reduction of the high school program from over 30 teams to only 8 and the elimination of interscholastic competition at the ninth grade level. Under this plan, the surviving programs were to remain open to all students free of charge.

The second plan provided for a less extensive cut in athletic competition—elimination of the ninth grade program only. To make up the difference, it proposed to raise money by charging students fees for participation in dramatic productions, musical performances, and athletic competition.

The Board chose the second option. Under the plan finally adopted, students are required to pay $25 for *each* athletic team in which they wish to participate, and $25 per category for any or all activities in *each* of the following four categories: (1) dramatic productions (e.g., plays, dance performances and musicals); (2) vocal music groups (e.g., choir and madrigal groups); (3) instrumental groups (e.g., orchestra, marching band, and related groups such as the drill team and flag twirlers); and (4) cheerleading groups.

* * *

In an attempt to ensure that the fees would not prevent any students from participating, the District has implemented a fee-waiver program. Upon showing a financial need, a student may obtain a "scholarship" to participate without paying the fee. The standard of need is similar to that of the free lunch program.

The fee-waiver policy has been supplemented with an outreach program. Teachers and coaches are asked to inform their principals of any students who, though expected to participate in an activity, do not do so. These students are then interviewed by the principal to determine whether the fee prevented them from participating.

* * *

The trial court rejected all of the plaintiffs' claims, primarily on the ground that none of the activities covered by the fee program are "integral" to credit courses.

The California Constitution requires the Legislature to "provide for a system of common schools by which a *free school* shall be kept up and supported in each district. . . ." (Cal. Const., art. IX, § 5, emphasis added.) This provision entitles "the youth of the State . . . to be educated at the public expense." * * *

Plaintiffs assert that the imposition of fees for educational extracurricular activities violates the free school guarantee. They are correct.

* * *

Accordingly, this court holds that all educational activities—curricular or "extracurricular"—offered to students by school districts fall within the free school guarantee of article IX, section 5. Since it is not disputed that the programs involved in this case are "educational" in character, they fall within that guarantee.

Defendants argue, however, that the fee-waiver policy for needy students satisfies the requirement of the free school guarantee. They suggest that the right "to be educated at the public expense" * * * amounts merely to a right *not to be financially prevented* from enjoying educational opportunities. This argument contradicts the plain language of the Constitution.

In guaranteeing "free" public schools, article IX, section 5 fixes the precise extent of the financial burden which may be imposed on the right to an education—none. * * * A school which conditions a student's participation in educational activities upon the payment of a fee clearly is *not* a "free school."

The free school guarantee reflects the people's judgment that a child's public education is too important to be left to the budgetary circumstances and decisions of individual families. It makes no distinction between needy and nonneedy families. Individual families, needy or not, may value education more or less depending upon conflicting budget priorities. * * *

The free school guarantee lifts budgetary decisions concerning public education out of the individual family setting and requires that such decisions be made by the community as a whole. Once the community has decided that a particular educational program is important enough to be offered by its public schools, a student's participation in that program cannot be made to depend upon his or her family's decision to pay a fee or buy a toaster.

Nor may a student's participation be conditioned upon application for a special waiver. The stigma that results from recording some students as needy was recognized early in the struggle for free schools. * * *

Finally, defendants warn that, if the fees are invalidated, many school districts may be forced to drop some extracurricular activities. They argue that invalidation would—in the name of the free school guarantee—produce the anomalous result of reducing the number of educational opportunities available to students.

This court recognizes that, due to legal limitations on taxation and spending * * * , school districts do indeed operate under difficult financial constraints. However, financial hardship is no defense to a violation of the free school guarantee. * * *

Perhaps, in the view of some, public education could be more efficiently financed by peddling it on the open market. Under the California Constitution, however, access to public education is a right enjoyed by all—not a commodity for sale. Educational opportunities must be provided to all students without regard to their families' ability or willingness to pay fees or request special waivers. This fundamental feature of public education is not contingent upon the inevitably fluctuating financial health of local school districts. A solution to those financial difficulties must be found elsewhere—for example, through the political process.

In conclusion, this court holds that the imposition of fees for educational activities offered by public high school districts violates the free school guarantee. The constitutional defect in such fees can neither be corrected by providing waivers to indigent students, nor justified by pleading financial hardship.

Plaintiffs also argue that the fee requirement violates title 5, section 350 of the California Administrative Code (hereafter title 5, section 350). That section provides: "A pupil enrolled in a school shall not be required to pay *any* fee, deposit, or other charge not specifically authorized by law." * * *

* * *

In conclusion, the imposition of fees as a precondition for participation in educational programs offered by public high schools on a noncredit basis violates the free school guarantee of the California Constitution and the prohibition agianst school fees contained in title 5, section 350 of the California Administrative Code.

The judgment is reversed.

* * *

Notes and Questions

A short survey of states' constitutional provisions and case law concerning the issue of school fees is discussed in *Cardiff* v. *Bismarck Public School District,* 263 N.W.2d 105 (N.D. 1978). May a student's transcript be withheld for failure to pay school fees? See *Paulson* v. *Minidoka County School District No. 331,* 93 Ida. 469, 463 P.2d 935 (1970) where the court stated that "free common schools" were not being provided when access to official reports of students' records depended upon payment of a $25 unconstitutional school fee. May a transcript of grades be withheld for failure to pay a legitimate fee?

Incidental fees for attendance at athletic or literary events and the use of the library have generally been upheld even when there is a constitutional requirement for providing free public schools. What determines whether or not a school may charge an "incidental" fee but not other fees?

Does your state constitution or statute address the issue of school fees? What is the practice or policy regarding fees in your school system?

VI. Immunization

State statutes authorizing or requiring vaccination or immunization as a condition of school attendance have been upheld in every instance where they have been challenged. Such statutes often contain an exemption for those who are members of religious organizations that do not permit inoculation or that rely on spiritual means or prayer for healing.

Brown v. Stone

Supreme Court of Mississippi, 1980
378 So.2d 218, cert. denied,
449 U.S. 887 (1980)

SMITH, Presiding Justice, for the Court.

This is an appeal by Charles H. Brown, father and next friend of Chad Allan Brown, a six-year-old boy, from a decree of the Chancery Court of Chickasaw County sustaining a demurrer filed to his bill which sought an injunction to compel the Board of Trustees of the Houston Municipal Separate School District to admit his son as a student without compliance with the immunization requirements of Mississippi Code Annotated section 41–23–37 (1972 Supp.) This statute provides, (among other things):

> Except as provided hereinafter, it shall be unlawful for any child to attend any school, kindergarten or similar type of facility intended for the instruction of children (hereinafter called "schools"), either public or private, unless they shall first have been vaccinated against those diseases specified by the State Health Officer.

> A certificate of exemption from vaccination for medical reasons may be offered on behalf of a child by a duly licensed physician and may be accepted by the local health officer when, in his opinion, such exemption will not cause undue risk to the community. A certificate of religious exemption may be offered on behalf of a child by an officer of a church of a recognized denomination. This certificate shall certify that parents or guardians of the child are bona fide members of a recognized denomination whose religious teachings require reliance on prayer or spiritual means of healing.

There was filed with the bill the following certificate, signed by a minister of the Church of Christ:

Be it known that the church of Christ as a religious body does not teach against the use of medecines, [sic] immunizations or vaccinations as prescribed by a duly [sic] physician. However, Dr. Charles Brown, our local chiropractor, who is a member of the North Jackson Street Church of Christ in Houston, Mississippi does have strong convictions against the use of any kind of medications and we respect his views.

/s/ *Charles E. Bland*
Charles E. Bland
Minister

* * *

If the religious exemption from immunizations is to be granted only to members of certain recognized sects or denominations whose doctrines forbit it, and, as contended by appellants, to individuals whose private or personal religious beliefs will not allow them to permit immunization of their children, to this extent the highly desirable and paramount public purpose of the Act, that is, the protection of school children generally comprising the school community, is defeated.

* * *

It is a matter of common knowledge that prior to the development of protection against smallpox by vaccination, the disease, on occasion, ran rampant and caused great suffering and sickness throughout the world. According to the great weight of authority, it is within the police power of the State to require that school children be vaccinated against smallpox, and that such requirement does not violate the constitutional rights of anyone, on religious grounds or otherwise. In fact, this principle is so firmly settled that no extensive discussion is required.

* * *

After a thoughtful consideration of the facts and the arguments advanced by the appellants, we have concluded that the statute in question, requiring immunization against certain crippling and deadly diseases particularly dangerous to children before they may be admitted to school, serves an overriding and compelling public interest, and that such interest extends to the exclusion of a child until such immunization has been effected, not only as a protection of that child but as a protection of the large number of other children comprising the school community and with whom he will be daily in close contact in the school room. The relationship of parent and child is one in which the law concerns itself more with parental duties than with parental rights. The relationship carries with it a duty resting upon the parent to provide the child with food, clothing and shelter and to protect the child from preventable exposure to danger, disease and immorality. It must not be forgotten that a child is indeed himself an individual, although under certain disabilities until majority, with rights in his own person which must be respected and may be enforced. Where its safety, morals and health are involved, it becomes a legitimate concern of the state.

The protection of the great body of school children attending the public schools of Mississippi against the horrors of crippling and death resulting from poliomyelitis or smallpox or from one of the other diseases against which means of immunization are known and have long been practiced successfully, demand that children who have not been immunized should be excluded from the school community until immunization has been accomplished. That is the obvious overriding and compelling public purpose of Senate Bill No. 2650. To the extent that it may conflict with the religious beliefs of a parent, however sincerely entertained, the interests of the school children must prevail. Senate Bill No. 2650 is a reasonable and constitutional exercise of the police power of the state insofar as it provides for the immunization of children before they are permitted to enter school.

The exception, which would provide for the exemption of children of parents whose religious beliefs conflict with the immunization requirements, would discriminate against the great majority of children whose parents have no such religious convictions. To give it effect would result in a violation of the Fourteenth Amendment to the United States Constitution which provides that no state shall make any laws denying to any person within its jurisdiction the equal protection of the laws, in that it would require the great body of school children to be vaccinated and at the same time expose them to the hazard of associating in school with children exempted under the religious exemption who had not been immunized as required by the statute.

* * *

We have no difficulty here in deciding that the statute is "complete in itself" without the provision for religious exemption and that it serves a compelling state interest in the protection of school children. Therefore, we hold that the provision providing an exception from the operation of the statute because of religious belief is in violation of the Fourteenth Amendment to the United States Constitution and therefore is void.
* * *
We find that all of the other provisions of the statute are valid and constitutional and embody a reasonable exercise of the police power of the state.

The decree appealed from will, therefore, be affirmed.

Affirmed.

* * *

Note

Exemption may not be provided for students receiving a note of medical exemption from a chiropractor. See *Heard* v. *Payne,* 281 Ark. 485, 665 S.W.2d 865 (1984).

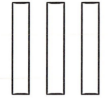

students
and the law

INTRODUCTION

Countless interactions between students and school officials occur during a day in the public schools. Students' or their parents' disagreement or unhappiness with a school official's actions or with school policy may result from such interaction. The vast majority of such disputes are not litigable, however, unless school authorities have violated a student's constitutional rights or have acted in a flagrantly unreasonable, arbitrary, or capricious manner.

Historically, courts have generally upheld school authorities if these authorities could demonstrate that they had acted in a reasonable manner. Although courts, for the most part, continue to assume this posture for nonconstitutional questions, beginning in the 1960s many court decisions provided students with equal protection benefits and due process protections which they had not previously enjoyed. The result has been an increasing tendency for courts to uphold the student's position when it could be shown that liberty or property interests were implicated and that the student had not received the requisite due process or equal protection under the law. As we saw in chapter 1, the Fourteenth Amendment to the

Constitution establishes that a person must receive due process when the state or those acting under the color of the state attempt to deprive or restrict that person's liberty or property interests. As we shall see, the United States Supreme Court has extended First Amendment rights to students and held that students do not "shed their constitutional rights to freedom of speech or expression at the schoolhouse gate." A large number of cases have discussed students' constitutional rights of freedom of speech or expression in such contexts as the wearing of buttons or symbols in political protests, refusal to engage in a patriotic exercise, publishing of so-called underground newspapers, and censorship of official school newspapers. However, such conduct as hurling an obscenity at a teacher in a math class under the guise of freedom of expression is not protected by the Constitution.

Court decisions reveal a strong concern that school officials uphold the rights of students in both fact and spirit. And often without actually stating it as such, court decisions indicate that school officials should be models of constitutional propriety as they engage in the political socialization process with students. Although court decisions do not always specifically mention the public school's role in the political socialization process, it is apparent that the courts consider the school's role a vital one, especially in the area of freedom of expression. As we shall see, courts consider the place of freedom of expression so important in the hierarchy of individual rights that they are willing to uphold a student's right of freedom of expression even if it creates disruption.

In addition to issues involving students' rights of free expression, this chapter will address issues dealing with suspension, expulsion, or involuntary transfer from school; corporal punishment; search of students and their lockers; dress and grooming; pregnancy, parenthood, and marriage; handicapped students; participation in extracurricular activities; and school punishment for out-of-school offenses.

I. Freedom of Expression

A. Speech and Symbolic Speech

Students were not recognized as having the First Amendment right of freedom of speech when the United States Supreme Court addressed the question in *Tinker* v. *Des Moines Independent Community School District.* Although the decision did not address the question of "pure speech," since the issue before the Court involved the wearing of armbands by students, the Court's decision in *Tinker* provided the public school community with a clear message that a student had the right of freedom of expression.

The *Tinker* decision ushered in a period when students challenged school authorities in other areas, such as restrictions pertaining to the publication and distribution of underground newspapers, requirements of prior school approval for material in the official school newspaper, and punishment for refusing to participate in patriotic exercises.

Tinker v. Des Moines Independent Community School District

Supreme Court of the United States, 1969
393 U.S. 503

MR. JUSTICE FORTAS delivered the opinion of the Court.

Petitioner John F. Tinker, 15 years old, and petitioner Christopher Eckhardt, 16 years old, attended high schools in Des Moines, Iowa. Petitioner Mary Beth Tinker, John's sister, was a 13-year-old student in junior high school.

In December 1965, a group of adults and students in Des Moines held a meeting at the Eckhardt home. The group determined to publicize their objections to the hostilities in Vietnam and their support for a truce by wearing black armbands during the holiday season and by fasting on December 16 and New Year's Eve. Petitioners and their parents had previously engaged in similar activities, and they decided to participate in the program.

The principals of the Des Moines schools became aware of the plan to wear armbands. On December 14, 1965, they met and adopted a policy that any student wearing an armband to school would be asked to remove it, and if he refused he would be suspended until he returned without the armband. Petitioners were aware of the regulation that the school authorities adopted.

On December 16, Mary Beth and Christopher wore black armbands to their schools. John Tinker wore his armband the next day. They were all sent home and suspended from school until they would come back without their armbands. They did not return to school until after the planned period for wearing armbands had expired—that is, until after New Year's Day.

This complaint was filed in the United States District Court by petitioners, through their fathers, under §1983 of Title 42 of the United States Code. It prayed for an injunction restraining the respondent school officials and the respondent members of the board of directors of the school district from disciplining the petitioners, and it sought nominal damages. After an evidentiary hearing the District Court dismissed the complaint. It upheld the constitutionality of the school authorities' action on the ground that it was reasonable in order to prevent disturbance of school discipline. * * * The court referred to but expressly declined to follow the Fifth Circuit's holding in a similar case that the wearing of symbols like the armbands cannot be prohibited unless it "materially and substantially interfere[s] with the requirements of appropriate discipline in the operation of the school." * * *

On appeal, the Court of Appeals for the Eighth Circuit considered the case *en banc*. The court was equally divided, and the District Court's decision was accordingly affirmed, without opinion. * * * We granted certiorari. * * *

The District Court recognized that the wearing of an armband for the purpose of expressing certain views is the type of symbolic act that is within the Free Speech Clause of the First Amendment. * * * As we shall discuss, the wearing of armbands in the circumstances of this case was entirely divorced from actually or potentially disruptive conduct by those participating in it. It was closely akin to "pure speech" which, we have repeatedly held, is entitled to comprehensive protection under the First Amendment. * * *

First Amendment rights, applied in light of the special characteristics of the school environment, are available to teachers and students. It can hardly be argued that either students or teachers shed their constitutional rights to freedom of speech or expression at the schoolhouse gate. This has been the unmistakable holding of this Court for almost 50 years. * * *

* * * On the other hand, the Court has repeatedly emphasized the need for affirming the comprehensive authority of the States and of school officials, consistent with fundamental constitutional safeguards, to prescribe and control conduct in the schools. * * * Our problem lies in the area where students in the exercise of First Amendment rights collide with the rules of the school authorities.

The problem posed by the present case does not relate to regulation of the length of skirts or the type of clothing, to hair style, or deportment. * * * It does not concern agressive, disruptive action or even group demonstrations. Our problem involves direct, primary First Amendment rights akin to "pure speech."

The school officials banned and sought to punish petitioners for a silent, passive expression of opinion, unaccompanied by any disorder or disturbance on the part of petitioners. There is no evidence whatever of petitioners' interference, actual or nascent, with the schools' work or of collision with the rights of other students to be secure and to be let alone. Accordingly, this case does not concern speech or action that intrudes upon the work of the schools or the rights of other students.

Only a few of the 18,000 students in the school system wore the black armbands. Only five students were suspended for wearing them.

There is no indication that the work of the schools or any class was disrupted. Outside the classrooms, a few students made hostile remarks to the children wearing armbands, but there were no threats or acts of violence on school premises.

The District Court concluded that the action of the school authorities was reasonable because it was based upon their fear of a disturbance from the wearing of the armbands. But, in our system, undifferentiated fear or apprehension of disturbance is not enough to overcome the right of freedom of expression. Any departure from absolute regimentation may cause trouble. Any variation from the majority's opinion may inspire fear. Any word spoken, in class, in the lunchroom, or on the campus, that deviates from the views of another person may start an argument or cause a disturbance. But our Constitution says we must take this risk, * * * ; and our history says that it is this sort of hazardous freedom—this kind of openness—that is the basis of our national strength and of the independence and vigor of Americans who grow up and live in this relatively permissive, often disputatious, society.

In order for the State in the person of school officials to justify prohibition of a particular expression of opinion, it must be able to show that its action was caused by something more than a mere desire to avoid the discomfort and unpleasantness that always accompany an unpopular viewpoint. Certainly where there is no finding and no showing that engaging in the forbidden conduct would "materially and substantially interfere with the requirements of appropriate discipline in the operation of the school," the prohibition cannot be sustained. * * *

In the present case, the District Court made no such finding, and our independent examination of the record fails to yield evidence that the school authorities had reason to anticipate that the wearing of the armbands would substantially interfere with the work of the school or impinge upon the rights of other students. Even an official memorandum prepared after the suspension that listed the reasons for the ban on wearing the armbands made no reference to the anticipation of such disruption.

On the contrary, the action of the school authorities appears to have been based upon an urgent wish to avoid the controversy which might result from the expression, even by the silent symbol of armbands, of opposition to this Nation's part in the conflagration in Vietnam. It is revealing, in this respect, that the meeting at which the school principals decided to issue the contested regulation was called in response to a student's statement to the journalism teacher in one of the schools that he wanted to write an article on Vietnam and have it published in the school paper. (The student was dissuaded.)

It is also relevant that the school authorities did not purport to prohibit the wearing of all symbols of political or controversial significance. The record shows that students in some of the schools wore buttons relating to national political campaigns and some even wore the Iron Cross, traditionally a symbol of Nazism. The order prohibiting the wearing of armbands did not extend to these. Instead, a particular symbol—black armbands worn to exhibit opposition to this Nation's involvement in Vietnam—was singled out for prohibition. Clearly, the prohibition of expression of one particular opinion, at least without evidence that it is necessary to avoid material and substantial interference with schoolwork or discipline, is not constitutionally permissible.

In our system, state-operated schools may not be enclaves of totalitarianism. School officials do not possess absolute authority over their students. Students in school as well as out of school are "persons" under our Constitution. They are possessed of fundamental rights which the State must respect, just as they themselves must respect their obligations to the State. In our system, students may not be regarded as closed-circuit recipients of only that which the State chooses to communicate. They may not be confined to the expression of those sentiments that are officially approved. In the absence of a specific showing of constitutionally valid reasons to regulate their speech, students are entitled to freedom of expression of their views. * * *

* * *

* * * The principal use to which the schools are dedicated is to accommodate students during prescribed hours for the purpose of certain types of activities. Among those activities is personal intercommunication among the students. This is not only an inevitable part of the process of attending school; it is also an important part of the educational process. A student's rights, therefore, do not embrace merely the classroom hours. When he is in the cafeteria, or on the playing field, or on the campus during the authorized hours, he may express his opinions, even on controversial subjects like the conflict in Vietnam, if he does so without "materially and substantially interfer[ing] with the requirements of appropriate discipline in the operation of the school" and without colliding with the rights of others. * * * But conduct by the student, in class or out of it, which for any reason—whether it stems from time, place, or type of behavior—materially disrupts classwork or involves substantial disorder or invasion of the rights of others is, of course, not immunized by the constitutional guarantee of freedom of speech. * * *

Under our constitution, free speech is not a right that is given only to be so circumscribed that it exists in principle but not in fact. Freedom of expression would not truly exist if the right could be exercised only in an area that a benevolent government has provided as a safe haven for crackpots. The Constitution says that Congress (and the States) may not abridge the right to free speech. This provision means what it says. We properly read it to permit reasonable regulation of speech-connected activities in carefully restricted circumstances. But we do not confine the permissible exercise of First Amendment rights to a telephone booth or the four corners of a pamphlet, or to supervised and ordained discussion in a school classroom.

If a regulation were adopted by school officials forbidding discussion of the Vietnam conflict, or the expression by any student of opposition to it anywhere on school property except as part of a prescribed classroom exercise, it would be obvious that the regulation would violate the constitutional rights of students, at least if it could not be justified by a showing that the students' activities would materially and substantially disrupt the work and discipline of the school. * * * In the circumstances of the present case, the prohibition of the silent passive "witness of the armbands," as one of the children called it, is no less offensive to the Constitution's guarantees.

As we have discussed, the record does not demonstrate any facts which might reasonably have led school authorities to forecast substantial disruption of or material interference with school activities, and no disturbances or disorders on the school premises in fact occurred. These petitioners merely went about their ordained rounds in school. Their deviation consisted only in wearing on their sleeve a band of black cloth, not more than two inches wide. They wore it to exhibit their disapproval of the Vietnam hostilities and their advocacy of a truce, to make their views known, and, by their example, to influence others to adopt them. They neither interrupted school activities nor sought to intrude in the school affairs or the lives of others. They caused discussion outside of the classrooms, but no interference with work and no disorder. In the circumstances, our Constitution does not permit officials of the State to deny their form of expression.

We express no opinion as to the form of relief which should be granted, this being a matter for the lower courts to determine. We reverse and remand for further proceedings consistent with this opinion.

Reversed and remanded.

* * *

MR. JUSTICE BLACK, dissenting.

The Court's holding in this case ushers in what I deem to be an entirely new era in which the power to control pupils by the elected "officials of state supported public schools . . ." in the United States is in ultimate effect transferred to the Supreme Court. * * *

* * *

Assuming that the Court is correct in holding that the conduct of wearing armbands for the purpose of conveying political ideas is protected by the First Amendment * * * , the crucial remaining questions are whether students and teachers may use the schools at their whim as a platform for the exercise of free speech—"symbolic" or "pure"—and whether the courts will allocate to themselves the function of deciding how the pupils' school day will be spent. While I have always believed that under the First and Fourteenth Amendments neither the State nor the Federal Government has any authority to regulate or censor the content of speech, I have never believed that any person has a right to give speeches or engage in demonstrations where he pleases and when he pleases. * * *

While the record does not show that any of these armband students shouted, used profane language, or were violent in any manner, detailed testimony by some of them shows their armbands caused comments, warnings by other students, the poking of fun at them, and a warning by an older football player that other, nonprotesting students had better let them alone. There is also evidence that a teacher of mathematics had his lesson period practically "wrecked" chiefly by disputes with Mary Beth Tinker, who wore her armband for her "demonstration." Even a casual reading of the record shows that this armband did divert students' minds from their regular lessons, and that talk, comments, etc., made John Tinker "self-conscious" in attending school with his armband. While the absence of obscene remarks or boisterous and loud disorder perhaps justifies the Court's statement that the few armband students did not actually "disrupt" the classwork, I think the record overwhelmingly shows that the armbands did exactly what the elected school officials and principals foresaw they would, that is, took the students' minds off their classwork and diverted them to thoughts about the highly emotional subject of the Vietnam war. And I repeat that if the time has come when pupils of state-supported schools, kindergartens, grammar schools, or high schools, can defy and flout orders of school officials to keep their minds on their own schoolwork, it is the beginning of a new revolutionary era of permissiveness in this country fostered by the judiciary. The next logical step, it appears to me, would be to hold unconstitutional laws that bar pupils under 21 or 18 from voting, or from being elected members of the boards of education.

* * *

* * * But even if the record were silent as to protests against the Vietnam war distracting students from their assigned class work, members of this Court, like all other citizens, know, without being told, that the disputes over the wisdom of the Vietnam war have disrupted and divided this country as few other issues ever have. Of course students, like other people, cannot concentrate on lesser issues when black armbands are being ostentatiously displayed in their presence to call attention to the

wounded and dead of the war, some of the wounded and the dead being their friends and neighbors. It was, of course, to distract the attention of other students that some students insisted up to the very point of their own suspension from school that they were determined to sit in school with their symbolic armbands.

Change has been said to be truly the law of life but sometimes the old and the tried and true are worth holding. The schools of this Nation have undoubtedly contributed to giving us tranquility and to making us a more law-abiding people. Uncontrolled and uncontrollable liberty is an enemy to domestic peace. We cannot close our eyes to the fact that some of the country's greatest problems are crimes committed by the youth, too many of school age. School discipline, like parental discipline, is an integral and important part of training our children to be good citizens—to be better citizens. Here a very small number of students have crisply and summarily refused to obey a school order designed to give pupils who want to learn the opportunity to do so. One does not need to be a prophet or the son of a prophet to know that after the Court's holding today some students in Iowa schools and indeed in all schools will be ready, able, and willing to defy their teachers on practically all orders. This is the more unfortunate for the schools since groups of students all over the land are already running loose, conducting break-ins, sit-ins, lie-ins, and smash-ins. Many of these student groups, as is all too familiar to all who read the newspapers and watch the television news programs, have already engaged in rioting, property seizures, and destruction. They have picketed schools to force students not to cross their picket lines and have too often violently attacked earnest but frightened students who wanted an education that the pickets did not want them to get. Students engaged in such activities are apparently confident that they know far more about how to operate public school systems than do their parents, teachers, and elected school officials. It is not answer to say that the particular students here have not yet reached such high points in their demands to attend classes in order to exercise their political pressures. Turned loose with lawsuits for damages and injunctions against their teachers as they are here, it is nothing but wishful thinking to imagine that young, immature students will not soon believe it is their right to control the schools rather that the right of the States that collect the taxes to hire the teachers for the benefit of the pupils. This case, therefore, wholly without constitutional reasons in my judgment, subjects all the public schools in the country to the whims and caprices of their loudest-mouthed, but maybe not their brightest, students. I, for one, am not fully persuaded that school pupils are wise enough, even with this Court's expert help from Washington, to run the 23,390 public school systems in our 50 States. I wish, therefore, wholly to disclaim any purpose on my part to hold that the Federal Constitution compels the teachers, parents, and elected school officials to surrender control of the American public school system to public school students. I dissent.

Notes and Questions

It should be kept in mind that the freedom of expression protected in *Tinker* pertains to social, political, and economic issues. Insolence or disrespect on the part of students is not protected, nor is screaming or cursing at teachers in a classroom or at school administrators.

Tinker was filed as a legal action under §1983 of Title 42 of the United States Code. This section of the Civil Rights Act has been increasingly employed as a legal basis for bringing a suit involving students or teachers. See chapter 7, page 371 for a brief discussion of this act.

According to *Tinker*, "undifferentiated fear or apprehension of disturbance is not enough to overcome the right to freedom of expression," and school authorities must accept "mere disturbance" when students exercise their First Amendment rights. Only when students engage in conduct that would "*materially* and *substantially* interfere with the requirements of appropriate discipline in the operation of the school" (emphasis added) may authorities prohibit the conduct. Unfortunately, the Court did not provide a test that school authorities could employ to determine whether actual disruption or merely a forecast of "substantial disruption" was necessary before they could prohibit conduct where freedom of expression was at issue. Further complicating the picture for school administrators was the failure by the Court to provide sufficient guidance concerning the meaning of a forecast of "substantial disruption."

There is little doubt that school officials may enforce reasonable rules to ensure the orderly operation of the school. However, *Tinker* proclaimed that when freedom of expression is involved, school officials may not restrict this freedom because the viewpoint expressed displeases an official or has the potential to bring about a degree of disruption. Part of the desired political socialization of students is that they learn that a government official—a school authority in this instance—may not restrict freedom of expression merely because it may be annoying or somewhat disruptive. Although some school officials may feel uncomfortable with such a doctrine, its rationale is based on the notion that if students are to become full participants in a free and democratic society, they must thoroughly understand that they are free to express themselves on any social, political, or economic issue without undue restraint or reprisal from government. The Court's contention is that the school is the proper place for a student to come to this understanding through the observance of freedom of expression in the school environment rather than through lectures or through policies that imply that freedom of expression is conferred at a specific age or upon graduation from high school.

Those not agreeing with court decisions that seem to condone the use of vulgarity should understand the high status of freedom of expression in the panoply of individual rights. To date courts have been reluctant to curtail these rights unless obscenity, a clear and present danger, or—in the educational arena—material and substantial disruption are involved.

Shortly after the *Tinker* decision, the Sixth Circuit Court of Appeals addressed a factual situation similar to *Tinker*. In that case a group of students wore buttons and wished to distribute pamphlets soliciting participation in an antiwar demonstration. A federal appellate court upheld the suspension of these students and distinguished the case from *Tinker* on several grounds. Two primary factors were that the school had a long-standing, uniformly-applied no-button, no-symbol rule and that since the racial mix of the school was 70 percent black and 30 per cent white, the student's actions could provoke racial strife. See *Guzick* v. *Drebus,* 431 F.2d 594 (6th Cir. 1970), cert. denied, 401 U.S. 948 (1971).

Several classes of words are considered "unprotected" speech under the First Amendment. These include defamation, libel, obscenity, and "fighting words." Disciplinary action was upheld against a student who had directed the loud remark, "He's a prick!" at his teacher off campus on a Sunday evening. See *Fenton* v. *Stear,* 423 F. Supp. 767 (Pa. 1976). In another instance a court upheld the suspension of high school students who continued to wear "Fuck the Draft" buttons, although the principal had expressly ordered them not to wear such buttons. See *Hinze* v. *Superior Court of Marin County,* 119 Cal. App.3d 1005, 174 Cal. Rptr. 403 (1981).

A student was charged with violating a school code provision regarding the use of obscene or profane language or gestures resulting from a nominating speech filled with sexual innuendo. In upholding the student a federal court of appeals stated that punishment of the student was prohibited unless the speech brought about material and substantial disruption. See *Fraser* v. *Bethel School District,* 755 F.2d 1356 (9th Cir. 1985).

Students attending private schools do not have the First Amendment protections provided by the *Tinker* decision, nor do such students necessarily have civil rights guaranteed by other amendments through the Fourteenth Amendment. Such rights are available to public school students because the public school operates under the "color of the State"; however, private school activity is not considered "state action." A substantial linkage between a private school and the state or federal government would have to be present for a private school to be considered acting under the "color of the state." As a result, private school students do not have many of the rights afforded public school students discussed in the succeeding sections of this chapter. Disagreements over "student rights" in a private school setting are generally resolved by applying contract law to the agreement governing the student's attendance.

What are your school system's policies, if any, pertaining to students' freedom of expression?

B. Publications

Since *Tinker,* students have challenged school rules pertaining to prohibiting or restricting the distribution of literature on school grounds and have alleged censorship by school authorities of both the official newspaper and underground newspapers. Analysis of the multitude of decisions discussing these issues reveals that courts are extremely sensitive to restrictions inhibiting written freedom of expression among students. Although school authorities may restrict publication or distribution of literature when not doing so would result in material and substantial disruption, school authorities may not do so merely because the material is "offensive to good taste" or would incite some disturbance.

1. Distribution of "Indecent Speech"

Although the factual situation involved a college campus, the United States Supreme Court clearly expressed its view regarding the distribution of material that may be offensive to some in *Papish* v. *Board of Curators of the University of Missouri.* The *Papish* decision, along with *Tinker,* appears to solidify the position that students may express themselves on political, social, and economic issues, even if such expression causes substantial consternation for school authorities.

Papish v. Board of Curators of the University of Missouri

Supreme Court of the United States, 1973
410 U.S. 667

PER CURIAM.

Petitioner, a graduate student in the University of Missouri School of Journalism, was expelled for distributing on campus a newspaper "containing forms of indecent speech" in violation of a bylaw of the Board of Curators. The newspaper, the Free Press Underground, had been sold on this state university campus for more than four years pursuant to an authorization obtained from the University Business Office. The particular newspaper issue in question was found to be unacceptable for two reasons. First, on the front cover the publisher had reproduced a political cartoon previously printed in another newspaper depicting policemen raping the Statue of Liberty and the Goddess of Justice. The caption under the cartoon read: " . . . With Liberty and Justice for All." Secondly, the issue contained an article entitled "M-----f------ Acquitted," which discussed the trial and acquittal on an assault charge of a New York City youth who was a member of an organization known as "Up Against the Wall, M-----f------."

Following a hearing, the Student Conduct Committee found that petitioner had violated Par. B of Art. V of the General Standards of Student Conduct which requires students "to observe generally accepted standards of conduct" and specifically prohibits "indecent conduct or speech." Her expulsion, after affirmance first by the Chancellor of the University and then by its Board of Curators, was made effective in the middle of the spring semester. Although she was then permitted to remain on campus until the end of the semester, she was not given credit for the one course in which she made a passing grade.

After exhausting her administrative review alternatives within the University, petitioner brought an action for declaratory and injunctive relief pursuant to 42 U.S.C. § 1983 in the United States District Court for the Western District of Missouri. She claimed that her expulsion was improperly premised on activities protected by the First Amendment. The District court denied relief * * * , and the Court of Appeals affirmed, one judge dissenting. * * * Rehearing *en banc* was denied by an equally divided vote of all the judges in the Eighth Circuit.

The District Court's opinion rests, in part, on the conclusion that the banned issue of the newspaper was obscene. The Court of Appeals found it unnecessary to decide that question. Instead, assuming that the newspaper was not obscene and that its distribution in the community at large would be protected by the First Amendment, the court held that on a university campus "freedom of expression" could properly be "subordinated to other interests such as, for example, the conventions of decency in the use and display of language and pictures." * * * The court concluded that "[t]he Constitution does not compel the University . . . [to allow] such publications as the one in litigation to be publicly sold or distributed on its open campus." * * *

This case was decided several days before we handed down *Healy* v. *James,* 408 U.S. 169 (1972), in which, while recognizing a state university's undoubted prerogative to enforce reasonable rules governing student conduct, we reaffirmed that "state colleges and universities are not enclaves immune from the sweep of the First Amendment." * * * We think *Healy* makes it clear that the mere dissemination of ideas—no matter how offensive to good taste—on a state university campus may not be shut off in the name alone of "conventions of decency." Other recent precedents of this Court make it equally clear that neither the political cartoon nor the headline story involved in this case can be labeled as constitutionally obscene or otherwise unprotected * * * . There is language in the opinions below which suggests that the University's action here could be viewed as an exercise of its legitimate authority to enforce reasonable regulations as to the time, place, and manner of speech and its dissemination. While we have repeatedly approved such regulatory authority * * * , the facts set forth in the opinions below show clearly that petitioner was expelled because of the disapproved content of the newspaper rather than the time, place, or manner of its distribution.

Since the First Amendment leaves no room for the operation of a dual standard in the academic community with respect to the content of speech, and because the state University's action here cannot be justified as a nondiscriminatory application of reasonable rules governing conduct, the judgments of the courts below must be reversed. Accordingly the petition for a writ of certiorari is granted, the case is remanded to the District Court, and that court is instructed to order the University to restore to petitioner any course credits she earned for the semester in question and, unless she is barred from reinstatement for valid academic reasons, to reinstate her as a student in the graduate program.

Reversed and remanded.

MR. CHIEF JUSTICE BURGER, dissenting.

* * *

In theory, at least, a university is not merely an arena for the discussion of ideas by students and faculty; it is also an institution where individuals learn to express themselves in acceptable, civil terms. We provide that environment to the end that students may learn the self-restraint necessary to the functioning of a civilized society and understand the need for those external restraints to which we must all submit if group existence is to be tolerable.

* * * Students are, of course, free to criticize the university, its faculty, or the Government in vigorous, or even harsh, terms. But it is not unreasonable or violative of the Constitution to subject to disciplinary action those individuals who distribute publications which are at the same time obscene and infantile. To preclude a state university or college from regulating the distribution of such obscene materials does not protect the values inherent in the First Amendment; rather, it demeans those values. The anomaly of the Court's holding today is suggested by its use of the now familiar "code" abbreviation for the petitioner's foul language.

* * *

MR. JUSTICE REHNQUIST, with whom THE CHIEF JUSTICE and MR. JUSTICE BLACKMUN join, dissenting.

* * *

Petitioner Papish has for many years been a graduate student at the University of Missouri. Judge Stephenson, writing for the Court of Appeals in this case, summarized her record in these words:

> "Miss Papish's academic record reveals that she was in no rush to complete the requirements for her graduate degree in Journalism. She possesses a 1958 academic degree from the University of Connecticut; she was admitted to graduate school at the University of Missouri in September in 1963; and although she attended school through the fall, winter, and summer semesters, she was, after 6 years of work, making little, if any, significant progress toward the achievement of her stated academic objective. At the time of her dismissal, Miss Papish was enrolled in a one-hour course entitled 'Research Journalism' and in a three-hour course entitled 'Ceramics 4.' In the semester immediately preceding her dismissal, she was enrolled only in 'Ceramics 3.'" * * *

Whatever may have been her lack of ability or motivation in the academic area, petitioner had been active on other fronts. In the words of the Court of Appeals:

> "3. On November 1, 1967, the Faculty Committee on Student Conduct, after notice of charges and a hearing, placed Miss Papish on disciplinary probation for the remainder of her student status at the University. The basis for her probation was her violation of the general standard of student conduct. . . . This action arose out of events which took place on October 14, 1967 at a time when the University was hosting high school seniors and their parents for the purpose of acquainting them with its educational programs and other aspects of campus life. She specifically was charged, *inter alia,* with openly distributing, on University grounds, without the permission of appropriate University personnel, two non-University publications of the Students for Democratic Society (SDS). It was alleged in the notice of charges, and apparently established at the ensuing hearing, that one of these publications, the New Left Notes, contained 'pornographic, indecent and obscene words, "F---," "bulls---," and "sh--." The notice of charges also recites that the other publication, *The CIA at College: Into Twilight and Back,* contained 'a pornographic and indecent picture depicting two rats apparently fornicating on its cover. . . .'

> "4. Some two weeks prior to the incident causing her dismissal, Miss Papish was placed on academic probation because of prolonged submarginal academic progress. It was a condition of this probation that she pursue satisfactory work on her thesis, and that such work be evidenced by the completion and presentation of several completed chapters to her thesis advisor by the end of the semester. By letter dated January 31, 1969, Miss Papish was notified that her failure to comply with this special condition within the time specified would result in the termination of her candidacy for a graduate degree." * * *

It was in the light of this background that respondents finally expelled petitioner for the incident described in the Court's opinion. The Court fails to note, however, two findings made by the District Court with respect to the circumstances under which petitioner hawked her newspaper near the memorial tower of the University.

> "The Memorial Tower is the central unit of integrated structures dedicated to the memory of those students who died in the Armed Services in World Wars I and II. Other adjacent units include the Student Union and a Non-Sectarian chapel for prayer and meditation. Through the Memorial Arch pass parents of students, guests of the University, students, including many persons under 18 years of age and high school students." * * * "The plaintiff knowingly and intentionally participated in distributing the publication to provoke a confrontation with the authorities by pandering the publication with crude, puerile, vulgar obscenities." * * *

* * *

* * * It simply does not follow under any of our decisions or from the language of the First Amendment itself that because petitioner could not be criminally prosecuted by the Missouri state courts for the conduct in question, she may not therefore be expelled from the University of Missouri for the same conduct. A state university is an establishment for the purpose of educating the State's young people, supported by the tax revenues of the State's citizens. The notion that the officials lawfully charged with the governance of the university have so little control over the environment for which they are responsible that they may not prevent the public distribution of a newspaper on campus which contained the language described in the Court's opinion is quite unacceptable to me, and I would suspect would have been equally unacceptable to the Framers of the First Amendment. * * *

The Court cautions that "disenchantment with Miss Papish's performance, understandable as it may have been, is no justification for denial of constitutional rights." Quite so. But a wooden insistence on equating, for constitutional purposes, the authority of the State to criminally punish with its authority to exercise even a modicum of control over the university which it operates, serves neither the Constitution nor public education well. There is reason to think that the "disenchantment" of which the Court speaks may, after this decision, become widespread among taxpayers and legislators. The system of tax-supported public universities which has grown up in this country is one of its truly great accomplishments; if they are to continue to grow and thrive to serve an expanding population, they must have something more than the grudging support of taxpayers and legislators. But one can scarcely blame the latter if, told by the Court that their only function is to supply tax money for the operation of the university, the "disenchantment" may reach such a point that they doubt the game is worth the candle.

Notes and Questions

Chief Justice Burger and Justices Rehnquist and Blackmun dissented in this per curiam decision. Interjected in their dissent are several factors the justices believe should be taken into account when examining Ms. Papish's conduct. These factors include Ms. Papish's lack of progress in her academic program, her "light" load, and placement on academic probation; the possibility that "disenchantment" on the part of taxpayers and legislators may reduce support for the university; the obscene and infantile nature of the publications; the appropriateness of the place of distribution, which included an area dedicated to the memory of deceased veterans, the student union, and a chapel; and the possibility that persons under age eighteen and high school students would be exposed to these publications. Do you agree that freedom of expression should be conditioned on such factors?

Although a college decision, does the reasoning in **Papish** have applicability for public school administrators?

Defining obscenity, which is not constitutionally protected, is difficult. See *Miller* v. *California*, 413 U.S. 15 (1973), reh. den., 414 U. S. 881 (1973) in which the U.S. Supreme Court outlines the following test applicable to material for adults:

> (1) whether the average person, applying contemporary community standards, would find that the work taken as a whole appeals to the prurient interest; (2) whether the work depicts or describes, in a patently offensive way, sexual conduct specifically described by the applicable state law; and (3) whether the work, taken as a whole, lacks serious literary, artistic, political or scientific value.

Vulgarity, on the other hand, has usually received court sanction.

High school students have attempted to distribute literature that school officials considered to be indecent, if not obscene. The statement "High School is fucked" and other "earthy" expressions, references to bodily functions, and the statement "Oral sex may prevent tooth decay" have been upheld by courts. See *Sullivan* v. *Houston Independent School District*, 475 F.2d 1071 (5th Cir. 1973), cert. denied, 414 U.S. 1032 (1973); *Jacobs* v. *Board of School Commissioners*, 490 F.2d 601 (7th Cir. 1973); and *Scoville* v. *Board of Education of Joliet Township High School District 204*, 425 F.2d 10 (7th Cir. 1970), cert. denied, 400 U.S. 826 (1970). However, see *Frasca* v. *Andrews*, 463 F. Supp. 1043 (N.Y. 1979), in which a principal was upheld who prevented a school newspaper from being published containing the words "pissed off" and "ass."

How do school authorities explain their allowing material that some consider to be offensive to be distributed on school grounds when some students, parents, and members of the community vehemently object to its distribution and not only disagree with court opinions allowing such conduct but strongly believe that such court decisions are primarily responsible for a general lowering of morality among young people? Proponents of decisions allowing "offensive" material to be published argue that an understanding of the First Amendment right of freedom of expression, which is vital in a democratic society, can be taught only by its practice and not by such cursory treatment as a week's unit in a civics class.

2. Prior Approval for Controversial Literature

Students occasionally attempt to distribute on school grounds literature that authorities may consider to be not only obscene but also libelous or in poor taste and possibly distressing to some students, teachers, parents, and others in the community. In an attempt to regulate such distribution, some states have passed statutes and many local school systems have instituted rules prescribing procedures for the review of content and for the orderly distribution of literature within a school. These statues and local rules have taken several forms, including a prohibition against the distribution of certain categories of material; a requirement for prior submission of material for informational purposes; and regulations specifying reasonable time, place, and manner for distribution of materials. Courts have agreed that reasonable time, place, and manner regulations are permissible; however, courts have not agreed on the extent, if any, to which school authorities may examine and pass judgment on a publication prior to its distribution and whether or not school authorities may prohibit distribution in the absence of showing that distribution will create a material and substantial disruption. Courts have addressed these types of questions in cases dealing with the distribution of "underground" newspapers, official school publications, and commercial and religious literature.

a. Official Publications

Gambino v. Fairfax County School Board

United States District Court, Eastern District of Virginia, 1977
429 F. Supp. 731, aff'd, 564 F.2d 157 (4th Cir. 1977)*

ALBERT V. BRYAN, Jr., District Judge.

This action was brought pursuant to 42 U.S.C. § 1983 and 28 U.S.C. § 1343 to enjoin the defendant from prohibiting the publication of an article entitled "Sexually Active Students Fail to Use Contraception" in

*Although affirmed by the United States Court of Appeals, Fourth Circuit, an edited version of the district court decision is presented here because of its greater detail in discussing the issues.

"The Farm News," a newspaper published in the Hayfield Secondary School (Hayfield). * * *

Hayfield is governed by the Fairfax County School Board (the School Board), an agency of the Commonwealth of Virginia. On August 11, 1976, the School Board issued notice 6130 which prohibited the schools from offering sex education until a decision was reached on a proposed program. * * * The article in question here was submitted for publication on November 22, 1976, while the School Board's notice was in effect. Pursuant to a prior agreement regarding potentially controversial material, this article was submitted to the principal, Doris Torrice, for review. Perceiving that portions of the submission containing information on contraceptives, apparently viewed apart from those portions incorporating results obtained from a canvass of Hayfield student attitudes toward birth control, violated notice 6130, she ordered plaintiffs not to publish it as written. Although plaintiffs were given the option of publishing the article with the objectionable passages excised, they chose to insist on printing all or none of the piece.

Ms. Torrice's decision was reviewed and upheld by the Advisory Board on Student Expression * * * .

The action of the Advisory Board was sustained by the Division Superintendent of the Fairfax County Public Schools and by the School Board. A few days before hearing plaintiffs' appeal, the School Board adopted Regulation 6131 approving a sex education program but specifically proscribing birth control as a subject of that program * * * .

* * * The Farm News is a student activity. Some staff members are enrolled in Journalism and receive academic credit for their work on the paper. * * * Other staff members work on the paper as an extra-curricular activity. The paper is written and edited in the school during school hours and at the homes of the participants. Revenues are generated from advertising, allocations by the School Board, sales of individual issues, and student subscriptions. This latter source involves a tie-in with the school yearbook, i.e., no student may receive the yearbook unless he also subscribes to the newspaper. * * * Additionally, the faculty advisor provided to supervise the paper was paid a salary supplement of $1,225.00. Copies of the newspaper usually are distributed to student subscribers in homeroom.

As the Court views it, this case turns upon one issue—whether The Farm News is a publication protected by the First Amendment. The authority of the School Board to determine course content in the school curriculum is not questioned. Nor is there any contention that the content of the article would fall outside the limits of First Amendment freedom if the newspaper otherwise is protected. In fact, upon an actual reading of the article, the Court is surprised at its innocuousness and that it could spawn the controversy at hand. Nevertheless, the defendants have perceived sufficient danger in the publication to warrant judicial resolution of the problem. Defendants also recognize that if the newspaper is found to be a First Amendment forum the regulations pursuant to which this suppression was undertaken are open to serious question.   *   *   *

The defendants rely on the contention that The Farm News is not a public forum entitled to First Amendment protection. They argue that the newspaper is essentially an "in-house" organ of the school system, or alternatively that the students in Hayfield are a "captive audience," rendering the publication subject to reasonable regulation.

While the state may have a particular proprietary interest in a publication that legitimately precludes it from being a vehicle for First Amendment expression, it may not foreclose constitutional security by mere labelling.   *   *   *   Once a publication is determined to be in substance a free speech forum, constitutional protections attach and the state may restrict the content of that instrument only in accordance with First Amendment dictates.

The extent of state involvement in providing funding and facilities for The Farm News does not determine whether First Amendment rights are applicable.   *   *   *

*   *   *

Defendants' fears of irresponsible journalism are met first by the fact that no evidence of it has surfaced in the past or in the article here in question, nor has there been any demonstrated likelihood of it in the future. More significantly, defendants have failed to appreciate the very real distinction between what a private citizen and the state constitutionally may do with regard to limiting otherwise protected speech.   *   *   *   The First Amendment mandate is directed toward state action, not private. As no contention has been made that the student editorial board of The Farm News acts as an agent of the state, the argument that the newspaper is powerless to control the content of its own publication is without merit. Irresponsible journalism may occur at some point in the future, but speculation is not a proper consideration in the decision of the case presently before the Court.

Turning to the substantive question of whether The Farm News was established as a vehicle for expression, the Court finds   *   *   *   that this instrument was conceived, established, and operated as a conduit for student expression on a wide variety of topics. It falls clearly within the parameters of the First Amendment.

*   *   *

Finally defendants argue that to allow the students to publish this article would permit them to override the decision of the School Board not to include birth control in the sex education curriculum. As noted above, the Court does not question the authority of the School Board to prescribe course content. Further, while even under principles of liberal construction a considerable effort is required to find the questioned portions of the article instructional, the Court assumes that the article does contain information which, if it appeared in material used in a sex education course, would contravene the School Board's policy.

A corollary of the finding that The Farm News was established as a vehicle for First Amendment expression and not as an official publication is that the newspaper cannot be construed objectively as an integral part of the curriculum offered at Hayfield. * * * Rather, it occupies a position more akin to the school library where more extensive and explicit information on birth control philosophy and methodology is available. * * * In either place, the material is not suppressible by reason of its objectionability to the sensibilities of the School Board or its constituents. * * * Therefore, because the newspaper is not in reality a part of the curriculum of the school, and because it is entitled to First Amendment protection, the power of the School Board to regulate course content will not support its action in this case.

Having determined that The Farm News is entitled to the First Amendment protection afforded a public forum, that the circumstances at Hayfield do not justify application of the "captive audience" theory, and that publication of the proposed article cannot be suppressed solely because its subject matter does not accord with the School Board's notion of appropriate course content, the Court finds that the application of the regulations under which the defendants acted in this instance was constitutionally invalid. * * * The Court declines, however, to declare the regulations facially invalid and limits its holding solely to the application of those regulations to prohibit publication in The Farm News of any portion of the article "Sexually Active Students Fail to Use Contraception."

Accordingly the plaintiffs are entitled to an injunction prohibiting the defendants, or those acting in concert with them, from banning the publication in The Farm News of those portions of the article which were found objectionable.

* * *

It is so ordered.

Notes and Questions

Gambino was upheld in a two-to-one split decision of a panel of the United States Court of Appeals for the Fourth Circuit.

Does the court's opinion in *Gambino* suggest that "official" school newspapers such as the "The Farm News" have no different status under the First Amendment than do "underground" publications?

Dissatisfaction with the content and censorship associated with a school's official publication has prompted some students to publish underground newspapers. These publications, which are generally published off campus, contain a variety of articles that may include criticism of teachers, administrators, school board members, and local school policy; discussions of economic, political, social, and religious issues; explicit sexual material dealing with such topics as masturbation, premarital sex, contraceptives, abortion, and homosexuality; obscenities and "earthy" expressions; and discussions that imply approval of various illegal drugs. Since these publications are offensive to many students, teachers, parents, and school officials, demands are often made that school authorities prohibit their distribution on campus. In one case the distribution and sale of an independent high school newspaper was upheld. The California Supreme Court indicated that school authorities retained the power to prohibit specified categories of objectionable material and to stop distribution of offensive material but not to exercise restraint of the content before publication. See *Bright* v. *Los Angeles Unified School District*, 134 Cal. Rptr. 639, 556 P.2d 1090 (1976).

May students be punished by school officials for publishing an allegedly "morally offensive, indecent, and obscene" publication printed outside school and not sold on campus? A federal appellate court ruled that public school officials could not punish such off-campus expression even if they could reasonably foresee that the publication would be distributed on campus. See *Thomas* v. *Board of Education, Granville Central School District*, 607 F.2d 1043 (2nd Cir. 1979), cert. denied, 444 U.S. 1081 (1980).

A federal appeals court upheld the censorship of a high school sex questionaire. Although the responses were to have been published in an anonymous, tabulated form in the student newspaper, the questions confronted responding students with such topics as premarital sex, contraception, homosexuality, masturbation, and the extent of their sexual experiences. The court held that the school authorities had not acted unreasonably in trying to protect the responding students from psychological pressures and emotional harm. Moreover, the court maintained that "it is not the function of the courts to reevaluate the wisdom of the actions of state officials charged with protecting the health and welfare of public school students." See *Trachtman* v. *Anker*, 563 F.2d 512 (2nd Cir. 1977).

May a school refuse to publish a student's picture in the yearbook because the student was in violation of the grooming code? The Ohio Supreme Court held that a picture of a student whose hair style was in violation of the code could not be excluded from the school yearbook, which was to be distributed after the school year ended. However, the school could refrain from publishing a yearbook. See *McClung* v. *Board of Education of City of Washington C. H.*, 46 Ohio St. 2d 149, 346 N.E.2d 691, 75 Ohio Op. 2d 197 (1976). Also see *Stanton* v. *Brunswick School Department*, 577 F. Supp. 1560 (Me. 1984), which addressed the appropriateness in a yearbook of a student-selected quotation vividly describing execution by electrocution. The court stated that the school had created a public forum by permitting students to include a quote under their pictures and that matters of taste may not be censored by vague, subjective, or nondiscrete standards.

Student publications occasionally contain allegedly libelous information concerning board members, administrators, or teachers. Since school board members and administrators are generally held to be public officials, they must accept a higher degree of criticism than the average citizen. There is some doubt as to whether teachers are considered public officials for these purposes. See *Franklin* v. *Lodge 1108, B.P.O.E.*, 97 Cal. App.3d 915, 159 Cal. Rptr. 131 (1979), which held that teachers were not public officials.

May visitors to a school be barred from distributing literature? See *Peterson* v. *Board of Education of School Dist. No. 1*, 370 F. Supp. 1208 (Neb. 1973), where the court stated:

> . . . I find no fault with the present policy of requiring "all visitors to . . . report to the school at the beginning of their visit." However, the banning of distribution of the newspaper because it may involve visitors, without any showing that the mere having of visitors will disrupt the school or result in danger to other persons on school grounds, is not constitutionally permissible. (P. 1215)

May school authorities deny official recognition to a group that is odious to them? See *Healy* v. *James*, 408 U.S. 169 (1972), which upheld the right of college students to establish a local chapter for Students for a Democratic Society. This allegedly radical group was vehemently opposed to American participation in the Vietnam War.

Does your school system have policies pertaining to prior approval of material intended for inclusion in an official school publication?

b. Non-School-Sponsored Commercial or Religious Literature

Hernandez v. *Hanson* addresses the issue of whether or not school authorities may require the prior approval for distribution of literature of non-school-sponsored organizations and prohibit that which is commercial and sectarian.

Hernandez v. Hanson

United States District Court, District of Nebraska, 1977
430 F. Supp. 1154

DENNEY, District Judge.

This matter comes before the Court upon the cross-motions of the parties for summary judgment, declaring unconstitutional and in violation of the First and Fourteenth Amendments to the United States Constitution and enjoining the enforcement of policies and regulations of the School District of Omaha, Nebraska, which require students to obtain prior approval before distributing literature on behalf of non-school sponsored organizations with the Omaha public schools. The case was brought pursuant to 42 U.S.C. § 1983. * * *

* * *

Since the filing of this lawsuit, the School Board has, in good faith, promulgated new policies and regulations which are presently under challenge. This Court abhors the task of intervening in the conduct of matters within the province of local school authorities and will not interfere with the day to day operations of schools. However, when fundamental constitutional rights come into play, all creatures of the State, including the Boards of Education, must be subject to judicial scrutiny. * * *

* * *

At the outset, it is important to note what this litigation does not involve. The plaintiffs do not challenge the constitutionality of the School Board's power to reasonably regulate the time, place and manner of distribution. "Just as in the community at large, reasonable regulations with respect to the time, the place, and the manner in which student groups conduct their speech-related activities must be respected." * * * Nor do the regulations require prior approval of all written distributions by students. At issue is the constitutionality of regulations requiring prior approval of literature on behalf of non-school sponsored organizations intended to be distributed by students and a prohibition on commercial and secular literature. Plaintiffs vigorously contend that prior approval is unconstitutional per se as a prior restraint in violation of the First Amendment.

* * *

Plaintiffs' contention that a sanction of a prior approval system in this case will open the door for similar infringements on free speech is simply misplaced. As the courts have previously noted, the rights of students are not coextensive with adults. The Court therefore holds that, given the nature and purpose of the public school, there is nothing per se unreasonable in requiring prior approval of written distributions so long as precedural safeguards are afforded.

However, this Court's sanction of a prior submission rule does not end the Court's inquiry. "Any system of prior restraint of expression comes to this Court bearing a heavy presumption against its constitutional validity." * * * The defendants, therefore, carry a heavy burden of showing a justification for the imposition of such a restraint. * * * The practice at issue requires prior approval "to distribute to several students literature, fliers or announcements . . . concerning events, meetings or programs of non-school sponsored organizations . . ." A prior approval rule as a means to forecast disruption and to control the time, manner and place of a *substantial* distribution is valid. However, in this case, the Board has overextended its reach in requiring the prior approval of non-school literature intended to be distributed to several students in that the likelihood of disruption of school activities is insignificant in such minor distributions. * * *

* * *

Plaintiffs attack the outright prohibition of distribution of literature commercial in nature or sectarian. Dr. Hanna testified by affidavit as follows:

> This prohibition rests upon the judgment that permitting distribution of such advertising would substantially and materially contribute to the erosion of the educational process by distracting student attention and time away from the major purpose of the student's presence at school: to obtain an education. Moreover, most of the students in the schools of the School District of Omaha are present in the schools because of Nebraska's Compulsory Attendance Law. These students are a "captive audience." If sectarian or commercial fliers were permitted to be distributed to students, the schools would undoubtedly be flooded with handouts.

* * *

The Supreme Court has recently held that there is not a First Amendment exception for "commercial speech." * * * *Tinker* allows a prior restraint only when the school officials can reasonably "forecast substantial disruption of or material interference with school activities." * * * The question is therefore whether the School Board can reasonably forecast that the distribution of commercial literature or sectarian literature anywhere within a school at any time would substantially disrupt or materially interfere with school activities. Given the power of the school to reasonably regulate the time, manner and place of expressive activities and that regulations "must be narrowly tailored to further the

State's legitimate interest," * * * the Court concludes as a matter of law that the outright prohibition of commercial literature is inconsistent with the First Amendment.

It cannot be doubted that leaflets advertising religious activities are protected by the constitutional guaranty of free speech and press to the same extent as "ordinary" speech. * * * However, defendants attempt to justify their position of official "neutrality" as consistent with the well-established principle of the separation of Church and State.

* * *

The Supreme Court has developed a three-prong test for determining whether a state statute or regulation violates the Establishment Clause. The statute or regulation must have a secular legislative purpose; it must have a "primary effect" that neither advances nor inhibits religion; and its administration must avoid excessive entanglement with religion. * * * In the view of this Court, to permit distribution of religious literature in the public schools is more than merely to accommodate religion. If students were permitted to distribute religious literature, "[i]n the eyes of the pupils and their parents the board of education [would have] placed its stamp of approval upon [the] distribution, and, in fact, upon the [religious literature] itself." * * * As the Second Circuit appropriately noted * * * "After all the States have been told about keeping the 'wall between church and state . . . high and impregnable,' * * * it would be rather bitter irony to chastise [defendants] for having built the wall too tall and too strong."

* * *

The Court concludes that the policy and practice is overbroad because: (1) it establishes a prior restraint on distribution without a requirement that the distribution interfere in a material and substantial way with the administration of school activity and discipline; and (2) because it prohibits any distribution of literature concerning non-school events or organizations commercial in nature.

* * *

Notes and Questions

This decision upholds the school board's policy of not allowing the distribution of leaflets advertising religious activities. Does this decision conflict with the Fifth Circuit's ruling in *Meltzer* (p. 51), which upheld "the distribution of religious literature at designated locations on the school premises?"

Can parents force school authorities to have students distribute a circular prepared by a parent? A federal appellate court held that a school may refuse to distribute certain materials, since such distribution would create a public forum. See *Buckel* v. *Prentice*, 572 F.2d 141 (6th Cir. 1978).

C. Participation in Patriotic Exercises

Students have challenged local policies or state statutes requiring their participation in patriotic exercises. The most common challenge centers around participation in the pledge of allegiance. *Lipp* **v.** *Morris* upheld the student's position and follows the rationale of other courts that have addressed this issue.

Lipp v. Morris

United States Court of Appeals, Third Circuit, 1978
579 F.2d 834

PER CURIAM:
This case involves the constitutionality of a New Jersey statute requiring school students to stand at attention during the salute to the flag. The appeal brings before the court two questions: (1) Did the District Judge abuse his discretion in declining to abstain because the New Jersey statute involved here is clear and unambiguous, and (2) Is the statute unconstitutional because it compels an affirmation of belief or punishes protected activity in violation of the First and Fourteenth Amendments of the Constitution of the United States.

* * *

Plaintiff, Deborah Lipp, a 16-year-old, alleged that because the statute directed that she stand during the recitation of the pledge of allegiance to the flag, compelling her to make what she termed a "symbolic gesture," it violated her rights under the First and Fourteenth Amendments. The action was brought under 42 U.S.C. § 1983 (1970). Plaintiff was a student at Mountain Lakes High School, New Jersey. Defendants were Harry Morris, principal of the high school * * * . Plaintiff emphasized that in her belief, the words of the pledge were not true and she stood only because she had been threatened if she did not do so.

Defendant argues first that the district court should have abstained from ruling on the constitutionality of the New Jersey statute to permit a New Jersey court to construe the law and thereby avoid a decision on federal constitutional grounds. The clearest answer to this argument is the statement of the District Judge which we adopt: "I can only do that [abstain] where the statute is open to an alternative construction which would avoid the Constitutional issue. This statute permits no such construction. It's plain, simple, blunt English." * * * Here we hold that the statute is not of an uncertain nature and, therefore, the case does not qualify for application of the abstention doctrine.

Secondly, defendant asserts that being required to stand while others engage in the flag salute ceremony is in no way a violation of the First and Fourteenth Amendments. The attorney general of New Jersey argues that mere standing does not rise to the level of "symbolic speech." Defendant suggests that standing silently is the same as just remaining seated, and that by the simple act of standing, the plaintiff in no way engages in protected activity.

* * * Deborah Lipp urges that her right to remain silent and not to be forced to stand springs directly from the precise First Amendment right against compelled participation in the flag ceremony recognized in *Barnette.*

Banks and *Goetz* are precisely on point. They interdict the state from requiring a student to engage in what amounts to implicit expression by standing at respectful attention while the flag salute is being administered and being participated in by other students. * * *

In the words of Judge Meanor: "I find this statute to be severable, that is, the portion thereof attacked as unconstitutional may rationally be severed from the remainder of the statute. * * * This mandatory condition upon the student's right not to participate in the flag salute ceremony is an unconstitutional requirement that the student engage in a form of speech and may not be enforced. The unconstitutionality of this severable portion of the statute is declared at this time." We concur.

Accordingly, * * * the judgment of the district court will be affirmed.

Notes and Questions

In an earlier decision, a student's position was upheld in a refusal to stand during the pledge, because he believed "that there [isn't] liberty and justice for all in the United States." The court did not agree that the option of either leaving the room or standing quietly during the pledge ceremony was a viable option. See *Goetz* v. *Ansell,* 477 F.2d 636 (2nd Cir. 1973).

The United States Supreme Court upheld the rights of Jehovah's Witnesses not to participate in the pledging of the flag. See *West Virginia*

State Board of Education v. *Barnette,* 319 U.S. 624 (1943). This opinion was rendered while the United States was engaged in World War II, and many observers contend that the decision is a dramatic espousal of the individual's right of freedom of expression. In often quoted sections, the Court stated:

> ... One's right to life, liberty and property, to free speech, a free press, freedom of worship and assembly, and other fundamental rights may not be submitted to vote; they depend on the outcome of no elections. (P. 638)

* * *

> If there is any fixed star in our constellation, it is that no official, high or petty, can prescribe what shall be orthodox in politics, nationalism, religion, or other matters of opinion or force citizens to confess by word or act their faith therein. If there are any circumstances which permit an exception, they do not now occur to us. (P. 642)

Georgia has a statutory provision that states:

> Each student in the public schools of the State of Georgia shall be afforded the opportunity to recite the Pledge of Allegiance to the flag of the United States of America during each school day. It shall be the duty of each local board of education to establish a policy setting the time and manner for recitation of the Pledge of Allegiance. Said policy shall be established in writing and shall be distributed to each teacher within the school (Ga. Code § 20-2-286, 1976).

Does your state have a provision addressing student participation in patriotic exercises? What is your local school system's policy on this issue?

II. Suspension, Expulsion, Transfer

Students may be excluded from school for failure to conform to legitimate rules. A student may be suspended; exclusion from school for ten days or less is the usual practice for minor violations of school rules. Expulsion is an exclusion from school for the remainder of a quarter, for a semester, for an academic year, or permanently and occurs upon repeated or major infractions of school rules or criminal conviction. Court opinions have held that since students have a valuable property interest in school attendance, students must be provided due process prior to their being excluded from school. Careful reading of these opinions reveals that the degree of due process that must be afforded a student varies in direct proportion to the length of the exclusion.

Students may also be transferred, for disciplinary reasons, to another school from the one they are attending. Consequently, courts have had to determine the degree of due process required, if any, prior to such a transfer.

A. Suspension

Goss v. Lopez

Supreme Court of the United States, 1975
419 U.S. 565

MR. JUSTICE WHITE delivered the opinion of the Court.

This appeal by various administrators of the Columbus, Ohio, Public School System (CPSS) challenges the judgment of a three-judge federal court, declaring that appellees—various high school students in the CPSS—were denied due process of law contrary to the command of the Fourteenth Amendment in that they were temporarily suspended from their high schools without a hearing either prior to suspension or within a reasonable time thereafter, and enjoining the administrators to remove all references to such suspensions from the students' records.

Ohio law, Rev. Code Ann. § 3313.64 (1972), provides for free education to all children between the ages of six and 21. Section 3313.66 of the Code empowers the principal of an Ohio public school to suspend a pupil for misconduct for up to 10 days or to expel him. In either case, he must notify the student's parents within 24 hours and state the reasons for his action. A pupil who is expelled, or his parents, may appeal the decision to the Board of Education and in connection therewith shall be permitted to be heard at the board meeting. The Board may reinstate the pupil following the hearing. No similar procedure is provided in § 3313.66 or any other provision of state law for a suspended student. Aside from a regulation tracking the statute, at the time of the imposition of the suspensions in this case the CPSS itself had not issued any written procedure applicable to suspensions. Nor, so far as the record reflects, had any of the individual high schools involved in this case. Each, however, had formally or informally described the conduct for which suspension could be imposed.

The nine named appellees, each of whom alleged that he or she had been suspended from public high school in Columbus for up to 10 days without a hearing pursuant to § 3313.66, filed an action under 42 U.S.C. § 1983 against the Columbus Board of Education and various administrators of the CPSS. The complaint sought a declaration that § 3313.66 was unconstitutional in that it permitted public school administrators to deprive plaintiffs of their rights to an education without a hearing of any kind, in violation of the procedural due process component of the Fourteenth Amendment. It also sought to enjoin the public school officials from issuing future suspensions pursuant to § 3313.66 and to require them to remove references to the past suspensions from the records of the students in question.

The proof below established that the suspensions arose out of a period of widespread student unrest in the CPSS during February and March 1971. Six of the named plaintiffs, Rudolph Sutton, Tyrone Washington, Susan Cooper, Deborah Fox, Clarence Byars, and Bruce Harris, were students at the Marion-Franklin High School and were each suspended for 10 days on account of disruptive or disobedient conduct committed in the presence of the school administrator who ordered the suspension. One of these, Tyrone Washington, was among a group of students demonstrating in the school auditorium while a class was being conducted there. He was ordered by the school principal to leave, refused to do so, and was suspended. Rudolph Sutton, in the presence of the principal, physically attacked a police officer who was attempting to remove Tyrone Washington from the auditorium. He was immediately suspended. The other four Marion-Franklin students were suspended for similar conduct. None was given a hearing to determine the operative facts underlying the suspension, but each, together with his or her parents, was offered the opportunity to attend a conference, subsequent to the effective date of the suspension, to discuss the student's future.

Two named plaintiffs, Dwight Lopez and Betty Crome, were students at the Central High School and McGuffey Junior High School, respectively. The former was suspended in connection with a disturbance in the lunchroom which involved some physical damage to school property. Lopez testified that at least 75 other students were suspended from his school on the same day. He also testified below that he was not a party to the destructive conduct but was instead an innocent bystander. Because no one from the school testified with regard to this incident, there is no evidence in the record indicating the official basis for concluding otherwise. Lopez never had a hearing.

Betty Crome was present at a demonstration at a high school other than the one she was attending. There she was arrested together with others, taken to the police station, and released without being formally charged. Before she went to school on the following day, she was notified that she had been suspended for a 10-day period. Because no one from the school testified with respect to this incident, the record does not disclose how the McGuffey Junior High School principal went about making the decision to suspend Crome, nor does it disclose on what information the decision was based. It is clear from the record that no hearing was ever held.

There was no testimony with respect to the suspension of the ninth named plaintiff, Carl Smith. The school files were also silent as to his suspension, although as to some, but not all, of the other named plaintiffs the files contained either direct references to their suspensions or copies of letters sent to their parents advising them of the suspension.

On the basis of this evidence, the three-judge court declared that plaintiffs were denied due process of law because they were "suspended without hearing prior to suspension or within a reasonable time thereafter," and that Ohio Rev. Code Ann. § 3313.66 (1972) and regulations issued pursuant thereto were unconstitutional in permitting such suspensions. It was ordered that all references to plaintiffs' suspensions be removed from school files.

Although not imposing upon the Ohio school administrators any particular disciplinary procedures and leaving them "free to adopt regulations providing for fair suspension procedures which are consonant with the educational goals of their schools and reflective of the characteristics of their school and locality," the District Court declared that there were "minimum requirements of notice and a hearing prior to suspension, except in emergency situations." In explication, the court stated that relevant case authority would: (1) permit "[i]mmediate removal of a student whose conduct disrupts the academic atmosphere of the school, endangers fellow students, teachers or school officials, or damages property"; (2) require notice of suspension proceedings to be sent to the student's parents within 24 hours of the decision to conduct them; and (3) require a hearing to be held, with the student present, within 72 hours of his removal. Finally, the court stated that, with respect to the nature of the hearing, the relevant cases required that statements in support of the charge be produced, that the student and others be permitted to make statements in defense or mitigation, and that the school need not permit attendance by counsel.

The defendant school administrators have appealed the three-judge court's decision. Because the order below granted plaintiffs' request for an injunction—ordering defendants to expunge their records—this Court has jurisdiction of the appeal pursuant to 28 U.S.C. § 1253. We affirm.

At the outset, appellants contend that because there is no constitutional right to an education at public expense, the Due Process Clause does not protect against expulsions from the public school system. This position misconceives the nature of the issue and is refuted by prior decisions. The Fourteenth Amendment forbids the State to deprive any person of life, liberty, or property without due process of law. Protected interests in property are normally "not created by the Constitution. Rather, they are created and their dimensions are defined" by an independent source such as state statutes or rules entitling the citizen to certain benefits. *   *   *

*   *   *

Although Ohio may not be constitutionally obligated to establish and maintain a public school system, it has nevertheless done so and has required its children to attend. *   *   * The authority possessed by the State to prescribe and enforce standards of conduct in its schools although concededly very broad, must be exercised consistently with constitutional safeguards. Among other things, the State is constrained to recognize a student's legitimate entitlement to a public education as a property interest which is protected by the Due Process Clause and which may not be taken away for misconduct without adherence to the minimum procedures required by that Clause.

The Due Process Clause also forbids arbitrary deprivations of liberty. "Where a person's good name, reputation, honor, or integrity is at stake because of what the government is doing to him," the minimal requirements of the Clause must be satisfied. * * * School authorities here suspended appellees from school for periods of up to 10 days based on charges of misconduct. If sustained and recorded, those charges could seriously damage the students' standing with their fellow pupils and their teachers as well as interfere with later opportunities for higher education and employment. It is apparent that the claimed right of the State to determine unilaterally and without process whether that misconduct has occurred immediately collides with the requirements of the Constitution.

Appellants proceed to argue that even if there is a right to a public education protected by the Due Process Clause generally, the Clause comes into play only when the State subjects a student to a "severe detriment or grievous loss." The loss of 10 days, it is said, is neither severe nor grievous and the Due Process Clause is therefore of no relevance. Appellants' argument is again refuted by our prior decisions; for in determining "whether due process requirements apply in the first place, we must look not to the 'weight' but to the *nature* of the interest at stake." * * * Appellees were excluded from school only temporarily, it is true, but the length and consequent severity of a deprivation, while another factor to weigh in determining the appropriate form of hearing, "is not decisive of the basic right" to a hearing of some kind. * * * The Court's view has been that as long as a property deprivation is not *de minimis*, its gravity is irrelevant to the question whether account must be taken of the Due Process Clause. * * * A 10-day suspension from school is not *de minimis* in our view and may not be imposed in complete disregard of the Due Process Clause.

A short suspension is, of course, a far milder deprivation than expulsion. But "education is perhaps the most important function of state and local governments," * * * and the total exclusion from the educational process for more than a trivial period, and certainly if the suspension is for 10 days, is a serious event in the life of the suspended child. Neither the property interest in educational benefits temporarily denied nor the liberty interest in reputation, which is also implicated, is so insubstantial that suspensions may constitutionally be imposed by any procedure the school chooses, no matter how arbitrary.

"Once it is determined that due process applies, the question remains what process is due." * * * We turn to that question, fully realizing as our cases regularly do that the interpretation and application of the Due Process Clause are intensely practical matters and that "[t]he very nature of due process negates any concept of inflexible procedures universally applicable to every imaginable situation." * * *

* * * At the very minimum, therefore, students facing suspension and the consequent interference with a protected property interest must be given *some* kind of notice and afforded *some* kind of hearing. "Parties whose rights are to be affected are entitled to be heard; and in order that they may enjoy that right they must first be notified." * * *

It also appears from our cases that the timing and content of the notice and the nature of the hearing will depend on appropriate accommodation of the competing interests involved. * * * The student's interest is to avoid unfair or mistaken exclusion from the educational process, with all of its unfortunate consequences. The Due Process Clause will not shield him from suspensions properly imposed, but it disserves both his interest and the interest of the State if his suspension is in fact unwarranted. The concern would be mostly academic if the disciplinary process were a totally accurate, unerring process, never mistaken and never unfair. Unfortunately, that is not the case, and no one suggests that it is. Disciplinarians, although proceeding in utmost good faith, frequently act on the reports and advice of others; and the controlling facts and the nature of the conduct under challenge are often disputed. The risk of error is not all trivial, and it should be guarded against if that may be done without prohibitive cost or interference with the educational process.

The difficulty is that our schools are vast and complex. Some modicum of discipline and order is essential if the educational function is to be performed. Events calling for discipline are frequent occurrences and sometimes require immediate, effective action. Suspension is considered not only to be a necessary tool to maintain order but a valuable educational device. The prospect of imposing elaborate hearing requirements in every suspension case is viewed with great concern, and many school authorities may well prefer the untrammeled power to act unilaterally, unhampered by rules about notice and hearing. But it would be a strange disciplinary system in an educational institution if no communication was sought by the disciplinarian with the student in an effort to inform him of his dereliction and to let him tell his side of the story in order to make sure that an injustice is not done. "[F]airness can rarely be obtained by secret, one-sided determination of facts decisive of rights. . . ." "Secrecy is not congenial to truth-seeking and self-righteousness gives too slender an assurance of rightness. No better instrument has been devised for arriving at truth than to give a person in jeopardy of serious loss notice of the case against him and opportunity to meet it." * * *

We do not believe that school authorities must be totally free from notice and hearing requirements if their schools are to operate with acceptable efficiency. Students facing temporary suspension have interests qualifying for protection of the Due Process Clause, and due process requires, in connection with a suspension of 10 days or less, that the student be given oral or written notice of the charges against him and, if he denies them, an explanation of the evidence the authorities have and an opportunity to present his side of the story. The Clause requires at least these rudimentary precautions against unfair or mistaken findings of misconduct and arbitrary exclusion from school.

There need be no delay between the time "notice" is given and the time of the hearing. In the great majority of cases the disciplinarian may informally discuss the alleged misconduct with the student minutes after it has occurred. We hold only that, in being given an opportunity to explain his version of the facts at this discussion, the student first be told what he is accused of doing and what the basis of the accusation is. Lower courts which have addressed the question of the nature of the procedures required in short suspension cases have reached the same conclusion. * * * Since the hearing may occur almost immediately following the misconduct, it follows that as a general rule notice and hearing should precede removal of the student from school. We agree with the District Court, however, that there are recurring situations in which prior notice and hearing cannot be insisted upon. Students whose presence poses a continuing danger to persons or property or an ongoing threat of disrupting the academic process may be immediately removed from school. In such cases, the necessary notice and rudimentary hearing should follow as soon as practicable, as the District Court indicated.

In holding as we do, we do not believe that we have imposed procedures on school disciplinarians which are inappropriate in a classroom setting. Instead we have imposed requirements which are, if anything, less than a fair-minded school principal would impose upon himself in order to avoid unfair suspensions. Indeed, according to the testimony of the principal of Marion-Franklin High School, that school had an informal procedure, remarkably similar to that which we now require, applicable to suspension generally but which was not followed in this case. * * *

We stop short of construing the Due Process Clause to require, countrywide, that hearings in connection with short suspensions must afford the student the opportunity to secure counsel, to confront and cross-examine witnesses supporting the charge, or to call his own witnesses to verify his version of the incident. Brief disciplinary suspensions are almost countless. To impose in each such case even truncated trial-type procedures might well overwhelm administrative facilities in many places and, by diverting resources, cost more than it would save in educational effectiveness. Moreover, further formalizing the suspension process and escalating its formality and adversary nature may not only make it too costly as a regular disciplinary tool but also destroy its effectiveness as part of the teaching process.

On the other hand, requiring effective notice and informal hearing permitting the student to give his version of the events will provide a meaningful hedge against erroneous action. At least the disciplinarian will be alerted to the existence of disputes about facts and arguments about cause and effect. He may then determine himself to summon the accuser, permit cross-examination, and allow the student to present his own witnesses. In more difficult cases, he may permit counsel. In any event, his discretion will be more informed and we think the risk of error substantially reduced.

Requiring that there be at least an informal give-and-take between student and disciplinarian, preferably prior to the suspension, will add little to the fact-finding function where the disciplinarian himself has witnessed the conduct forming the basis for the charge. But things are not always as they seem to be, and the student will at least have the opportunity to characterize his conduct and put it in what he deems the proper context.

We should also make it clear that we have addressed ourselves solely to the short suspension, not exceeding 10 days. Longer suspensions or explusions for the remainder of the school term, or permanently, may require more formal procedures. Nor do we put aside the possibility that in unusual situations, although involving only a short suspension, something more than the rudimentary procedures will be required.

The District Court found each of the suspensions involved here to have occurred without a hearing, either before or after the suspension, and that each suspension was therefore invalid and the statute unconstitutional insofar as it permits such suspensions without notice or hearing. Accordingly, the judgement is

Affirmed.

MR. JUSTICE POWELL, with whom THE CHIEF JUSTICE, MR. JUSTICE BLACKMUN, and MR. JUSTICE REHNQUIST join, dissenting.

The Court today invalidates an Ohio statute that permits student suspensions from school without a hearing "for not more than ten days." The decision unnecessarily opens avenues for judicial intervention in the operation of our public schools that may affect adversely the quality of education. The Court holds for the first time that the federal courts, rather than educational officials and state legislatures, have the authority to determine the rules applicable to routine classroom discipline of children and teenagers in the public schools. It justifies this unprecedented intrusion into the process of elementary and secondary education by identifying a new constitutional right: the right of a student not to be suspended for as much as a single day without notice and a due process hearing either before or promptly following the suspension.

The Court's decision rests on the premise that, under Ohio law, education is a property interest protected by the Fourteenth Amendment's Due Process Clause and therefore that any suspension requires notice and a hearing. In my view, a student's interest in education is not infringed by a suspension within the limited period prescribed by Ohio law. Moreover, to the extent that there may be some arguable infringement, it is too speculative, transitory, and insubstantial to justify imposition of a *constitutional* rule.

* * *

* * * [T]he Court ignores the experience of mankind, as well as the long history of our law, recognizing that there *are* differences which must be accommodated in determining the rights and duties of children as compared with those of adults. Examples of this distinction abound in our law: in contracts, in torts, in criminal law and procedure, in criminal sanctions and rehabilitation, and in the right to vote and to hold office. Until today, and except in the special context of the First Amendment issue in *Tinker,* the educational rights of children and teenagers in the elementary and secondary schools have not been analogized to the rights of adults or to those accorded college students. Even with respect to the first Amendment, the rights of children have not been regarded as "co-extensive with those of adults." * * *

* * *

The State's generalized interest in maintaining an orderly school system is not incompatible with the individual interest of the student. Education in any meaningful sense includes the inculcation of an understanding in each pupil of the necessity of rules and obedience thereto. This understanding is no less important than learning to read and write. One who does not comprehend the meaning and necessity of discipline is handicapped not merely in his education but throughout his subsequent life. In an age when the home and church play a diminishing role in shaping the character and value judgments of the young, a heavier responsibility falls upon the schools. When an immature student merits censure for his conduct, he is rendered a disservice if appropriate sanctions are not applied or if procedures for their application are so formalized as to invite a challenge to the teacher's authority—an invitation which rebellious or even merely spirited teenagers are likely to accept.

The lesson of discipline is not merely a matter of the student's self-interest in the shaping of his own character and personality; it provides an early understanding of the relevance of the social compact of respect for the rights of others. The classroom is the laboratory in which this lesson of life is best learned. * * *

* * *

One of the more disturbing aspects of today's decision is its indiscriminate reliance upon the judiciary, and the adversary process, as the means of resolving many of the most routine problems arising in the classroom. In mandating due process procedures the Court misapprehends the reality of the normal teacher-pupil relationship. There is an ongoing relationship, one in which the teacher must occupy many roles—educator, adviser, friend, and, at times, parent-substitute. It is rarely adversary in nature except with respect to the chronically disruptive or insubordinate pupil whom the teacher must be free to discipline without frustrating formalities.

The Ohio statute, providing as it does for due notice both to parents and the Board, is compatible with the teacher-pupil relationship and the informal resolution of mistaken disciplinary action. We have relied for generations upon the experience, good faith and dedication of those who staff our public schools, and the nonadversary means of airing grievances that always have been available to pupils and their parents. One would have thought before today's opinion that this informal method of resolving differences was more compatible with the interests of all concerned than resort to any constitutionalized procedure, however blandly it may be defined by the Court.

* * *

No one can foresee the ultimate frontiers of the new "thicket" the Court now enters. Today's ruling appears to sweep within the protected interest in education a multitude of discretionary decisions in the educational process. Teachers and other school authorities are required to make many decisions that may have serious consequences for the pupil. They must decide, for example, how to grade the student's work, whether a student passes or fails a course, whether he is to be promoted, whether he is required to take certain subjects, whether he may be excluded from interscholastic athletics or other extracurricular activities, whether he may be removed from one school and sent to another, whether he may be bused long distances when available schools are nearby, and whether he should be placed in a "general," "vocational," or "college-preparatory" track.

* * *

It hardly need be said that if a student, as a result of a day's suspension, suffers "a blow" to his "self esteem," "feels powerless," views "teachers with resentment," or feels "stigmatized by his teachers," identical psychological harms will flow from many other routine and necessary school decisions. The student who is given a failing grade, who is not promoted, who is excluded from certain extracurricular activities, who is assigned to a school reserved for children of less than average ability, or who is placed in the "vocational" rather than the "college preparatory" track, is unlikely to suffer any less psychological injury than if he were suspended for a day for a relatively minor infraction.

If, as seems apparent, the Court will now require due process procedures whenever such routine school decisions are challenged, the impact upon public education will be serious indeed. The discretion and judgment of federal courts across the land often will be substituted for that of the 50 state legislatures, the 14,000 school boards, and the 2,000,000 teachers who heretofore have been responsible for the administration of the American public school system. If the Court perceives a rational and analytically sound distinction between the discretionary decision by school authorities to suspend a pupil for a brief period, and the types of discretionary school decisions described above, it would be prudent to articulate it in today's opinion. Otherwise, the federal courts should prepare themselves for a vast new role in society.

Not so long ago, state deprivations of the most significant forms of state largesse were not thought to require due process protection on the ground that the deprivation resulted only in the loss of a state-provided "benefit." * * * In recent years the Court, wisely in my view, has rejected the "wooden distinction between 'rights' and 'privileges,'" * * * and looked instead to the significance of the state-created or state-enforced right and to the substantiality of the alleged deprivation. Today's opinion appears to abandon this reasonable approach by holding in effect that government infringement of any interest to which a person is entitled, no matter what the interest or how inconsequential the infringement, requires *constitutional* protection. As it is difficult to think of any less consequential infringement than suspension of a junior high school student for a single day, it is equally difficult to perceive any principled limit to the new reach of procedural due process.

Notes and Questions

Goss, a five-to-four decision, reveals a sharp division among the Court's justices. Does such a division make *Goss* any less the supreme law of the land? Is the due process requirement established in *Goss* educationally sound? Would seriatim ten-day suspensions for the same offense violate the rationale established in *Goss?*

Justice Byron "Whizzer" White, who wrote the *Goss* opinion, brought a unique background to the Supreme Court. He was a Phi Beta Kappa, Rhodes scholar, all-American football star at the University of

Colorado, professional football player (leading ground gainer in the National Football League in 1938), member of the Football Hall of Fame, decorated naval officer, Supreme Court clerk, lawyer, and a deputy attorney general. He was the leader of the Citizens for Kennedy in Colorado, and he was appointed to the Court by President Kennedy in 1962.

Does your state have a statutory provision pertaining to suspension? What are your local school system's rules regarding suspension?

B. Expulsion

Gonzales v. McEuen

United States District Court, Central District of California, 1977
435 F. Supp. 460

TAKASUGI, District Judge.

Eleven high school students, by their next friends, have brought this action under the Civil Rights Act, 42 U.S.C. § 1983, and the Due Process Clause of the Fourteenth Amendment to the Constitution of the United States. The case stems from the suspension and expulsion of the named plaintiffs from Oxnard Union High School following a period of student unrest on campus during October 14–15, 1976. The plaintiffs were charged with having committed certain acts which, it was alleged, led to a riot at Oxnard High School.

* * *

Plaintiffs' strongest and most serious challenge is to the impartiality of the Board. They contend that they were denied their right to an impartial hearing before an independent fact-finder. The basis for this claim is, first, overfamiliarity of the Board with the case; second, the multiple role played by defendents' counsel; and third, the involvement of the Superintendent of the District, Mr. McEuen, with the Board of Trustees during the hearings.

No one doubts that a student charged with misconduct has a right to an impartial tribunal * * * . There is doubt, however, as to what this means. Various situations have been identified in which experience teaches that the probability of actual bias on the part of the judge or decisionmaker is too high to be constitutionally tolerable. Bias is presumed to exist, for example, in cases in which the adjudicator has a pecuniary interest in the outcome; * * * or in which he has been the target of personal attack or criticism from the person before him. * * * The decision maker may also have such prior involvement with the case as to acquire a disqualifying bias. * * * The question before the Court is not whether the Board was actually biased, but whether, under the circumstances, there existed probability that the decisionmaker would be tempted to decide the issues with partiality to one party or the other. It is with this view that the plaintiffs' claims must be considered.

Much has been made of "The Red Book" which, it is claimed, contained information about the academic and disciplinary records of plaintiffs. It is alleged that the Board had access to this material from twenty to thirty days before the expulsion hearings. Depositions submitted to the court show that the members of the Board met with school officials prior to the hearings. Plaintiffs contend that this prior involvement by the Board deprived plaintiffs of the opportunity for a fair hearing. The court rejects this contention. Exposure to evidence presented in a nonadversary investigative procedure is insufficient in itself to impugn the fairness of the Board members at a later adversary hearing. * * * Nor is a limited combination of investigatory and adjudicatory functions in an administrative body necessarily unfair, absent a showing of other circumstances such as malice or personal interest in the outcome. * * * A school board would be amiss in its duties if it did not make some inquiry to know what was going on in the district for which it is responsible. Some familiarity with the facts of the case gained by an agency in the performance of its statutory role does not disqualify a decisionmaker. * * *

Turning now to the issue of the multiple roles performed by defendents' counsel, the court notes that the board members are defendants in this pending related action and may thereby become subject to personal liability.

It is undisputed that attorneys for the District who prosecuted the charges against the plaintiffs in the expulsion proceedings, also represent the Board members in this action. Plaintiffs claim that the attorneys acted in dual roles at the expulsion hearing: as prosecutors for the Administration and as legal advisors to the Board. Counsel for defendants admit that they advised the Board prior to the hearings with respect to its obligations regarding these expulsions, but they deny that they advised the Board during the proceedings themselves.

A reading of the transcripts reveals how difficult it was to separate the two roles. Special mention should be made of the fact that the Board enjoys no legal expertise and must rely heavily upon its counsel. This places defendants' attorneys in a position of intolerable prominence and influence.

It is the opinion of this court that the confidential relationship between the attorneys for the District and the members of the Board, reinforced by the advisory role played by the attorneys for the Board, created an unacceptable risk of bias. Bearing in mind also that the Board members are subject to personal liability in this action, the court concludes that bias can be presumed to exist.

Superintendent McEuen sat with the Board members during the expulsion hearings; he acted as Secretary of the Board on at least one occasion. By statute, Mr. McEuen is the chief advisor to the Board. The fact remains, however, that he is also the chief of the "prosecution" team, to wit, the District.

It is clear from the record that at least on one occasion, at the joint hearing of plaintiffs, Flores, Chavez and Rodriguez, Superintendent McEuen was present with the Board for approximately forty-five minutes during its deliberations on the issue of expelling these plaintiffs. The plaintiffs contend that their due process rights were violated by the involvement of Mr. McEuen with the Board. This court agrees.

Defendants' counsel maintain that Mr. McEuen did not participate in the deliberations and did no more, perhaps, than serve cookies and coffee to the Board members. Whether he did or did not participate, his presence to some extent might operate as an inhibiting restraint upon the freedom of action and expression of the Board. Defendants argue that there is no evidence that Mr. McEuen influenced or biased the Board. Proof of subjective reasoning processes are incapable of corroboration or disproval. Plaintiffs should not be forced to rely upon the memory or sense of fairness of Superintendent McEuen or the Board as to what occurred there. Pehaps Mr. McEuen's physical presence in deliberation becomes more offensive because of the pre-hearing comments which showed something less than impartiality.

The court concludes that the process utilized by the Board was fundamentally unfair. This raises a presumption of bias. In view of the alternatives for the selection of an impartial hearing body under California Education Code Section 10608, it would have been more reasonable to provide procedures that insured not only that justice was done, but also that it appeared to have been done.

* * *

Plaintiffs Barrington and Munden were expelled at a meeting of the Board on November 10, 1976. Neither Barrington nor Munden was present; neither was represented by either parent or counsel.

On October 29, 1976, letters had been sent to the parents advising them that the principal was recommending expulsion of the students. The letters contained a specific statement of the charges: in the case of Barrington, that he was involved in a riot at school at which time he had threatened physical violence against a teacher; in the case of Munden, that he was involved in a fight with another student, Wayne Berry. The letters contained no notice to the student or parent of the student's right to be present at the hearing, to be represented by counsel, and to present evidence. This was a clear violation of § 10608 of the California Education Code. The letters to the parents stated, "If you feel that the school does not have just cause for this recommendation, you may want to attend this meeting to present your reasons why [the students] should not be expelled."

* * *

Goss clearly anticipates that where the student is faced with the severe penalty of expulsion he shall have the right to be represented by and through counsel, to present evidence on his own behalf, and to confront and cross-examine adverse witnesses.

* * *

Notice to be adequate must communicate to the recipient the nature of the proceeding. In an expulsion hearing, the notice given to the student must include a statement not only of the specific charge, but also the basic rights to be afforded the student: to be represented by counsel, to present evidence, and to confront and cross-examine adverse witnesses. Section 10608 of the California Education Code provides, *inter alia,* for notice to the student and the parent of the specific charge, of the right to be represented by counsel, and of the right to present evidence. Federal due process requires no less.

Defendants next argue that even if the notice was defective, the court must still determine whether the plaintiffs were given a fair and impartial hearing. Defendants misapprehend the meaning of notice. It is not "fair" if the student does not know, and is not told, that he has certain rights which he may exercise at the hearing.

* * *

The court holds that the notice given to plaintiffs Barrington and Munden was defective in that it did not adequately inform them of their constitutional rights. It follows that their expulsions were improper.

* * *

Notes and Questions

According to **Gonzales,** a notice of expulsion hearing, to be adequate, must communicate the nature of the proceedings to the recipient. Such a notice must also include a statement of the specific charges and basic rights available to the student, such as the right to be represented by counsel, to present evidence, and to confront and cross-examine adverse witnesses. Several decisions prior to **Gonzales** did nor require notice of the right to be represented by counsel.

May a school superintendent participate, merely by being present at the expulsion deliberations, according to **Gonzales?**

The question of whether the same attorney may advise the school board and present the superintendentent's case at a hearing is discussed in *Breitling* v. *Solenberger*, 585 F. Supp. 289 (Va. 1984). The federal district court in this instance held that this dual role did not violate due process requirements.

Does your state have a statutory provision pertaining to expulsion? What are your local school system's rules or policies regarding expulsion?

C. Transfer

Jordan v. School District of City of Erie

United States Court of Appeals, Third Circuit, 1978
583 F. 2d 91

ROSENN, Circuit Judge.

These appeals present questions concerning the due process rights of students in the public schools who are temporarily removed and transferred because of behavioral problems from their regularly assigned school to another school designed to meet the needs of such students. * * *

* * * In essence, plaintiffs alleged that the school district's disciplinary procedures, involving the transfer of students from their regularly assigned schools to the New Directions Center, a facility designed especially to meet the needs of disruptive students, deprived students of their due process rights under the fourteenth amendment. After considerable pre-trial maneuvers, the parties * * * succeeded in negotiating a consent decree, approved by the district court. * * * Briefly, the consent decree provided for notice of the proposed disciplinary action to the student and his parents, and for informal and formal hearings concerning the decision to transfer.

* * *

Under the original consent decree, transfers for disciplinary purposes may be accomplished only after prior notice and hearing, except in special situations when students are disruptive and, in the professional judgment of the teacher, normal corrective measures are ineffective. In the event a student is removed from a required class, the consent decree provides that, if there is no similar required class within the school building, the removal should be deemed a recommendation for transfer and thereupon the procedures provided in the consent decree shall apply, including notice, the right to an informal meeting, and formal hearings. * * *

The district court held that the failure of the consent decree to provide specifically for notice and an opportunity for explanation prior to removal from class for disciplinary reasons or for notice and a rudimentary hearing to follow as soon as practicable for students "whose continuing presence poses continuing danger to persons or property or threatens disruption of the school process" rendered the decree deficient under *Goss v. Lopez*. It therefore directed that paragraph 32 be added to the consent decree.

Paragraph 32 requires that before a teacher can remove a student from class, notice, an explanation of the basis for the removal and an opportunity for the student to offer his version at an informal meeting with the building principal must be given. Only if, in the judgment of both the classroom teacher and the principal, the student's presence proves a continuing danger to persons or property or an ongoing threat of disrupting the academic process, may he be immediately removed from the class or school with the hearing to follow within three days. Thus, the effect of paragraph 32 is to neutralize the ability of a teacher acting alone to remove a disruptive student or one who poses a continuing danger to persons or property unless he or she first gives notice and the opportunity for an informal hearing.

The maintenance of "order and reasonable decorum in school buildings and classrooms is a major educational problem, and one which has increased significantly in magnitude in recent years." * * * The educational training, character-shaping of students and the maintenance of discipline in the classroom depends largely upon the capabilities and talents of the teacher. And the preservation of order in the classroom may depend upon the teacher's ability to cope promptly with a student disciplinary problem. "Events calling for discipline are frequent occurrences and sometimes require immediate, effective action." * * * The Association vigorously contends that the modification effectively removes the teacher from any determination of classroom discipline and destroys any right of the teacher to control the classroom and that the original consent decree adequately complies with *Goss v. Lopez*. The plaintiffs and the Commonwealth, on the other hand, contend that *Goss* requires the modification (para. 32) of the decree to allow for an immediate rudimentary hearing and for the principal to play the primary role in the process. As a federal court, our concern is only with the constitutionally protected rights of the parties, not with the operational and educational problems besetting complex public school systems in modern times.

The consent decree meets or exceeds in most respects due process rules enunciated by *Goss*. When a student faces removal from his regularly assigned classroom, and the consequential recommendation for transfer, the consent decree requires the principal to give written notice to both the student and his parents—in person or by certified mail—

detailing the reasons for the proposed transfer. * * * Further-more, the provisions of the consent decree provide for an informal meeting between the student, his parents, and the principal before the transfer, as well as two formal hearings at which evidence may be presented and witnesses examined. * * * In fact, a number of the provisions of the consent decree go far beyond the rudimentary precautions required by *Goss*. * * * Although there is no provision in the consent decree for notice or a hearing before a disruptive or dangerous student is physically removed from class, *Goss* indicated none is required as long as such removal is followed by appropriate notice and hearings, as is the case here. * * *

Although the parties to this proceeding appear to be concerned only with removal of disruptive students from a required class, it is possible under the language of the consent decree for a school disciplinarian to remove for disciplinary reasons a non-disruptive student or one whose presence does not pose a continuing danger to persons or property. In such circumstances, remote as they may be, the consent decree does not provide for notice, explanation of the basis for removal, and an opportunity for the student to offer his version of the incident triggering the disciplinary action prior to removal. We therefore direct the district court to add the following language as paragraph 32 to the consent decree:

> 32. Notwithstanding anything to the contrary contained herein, a student whose presence poses no continuing danger to persons or property or an ongoing threat of disrupting the academic process shall not be removed from class for disciplinary reasons until after notice of proposed action and basis therefore and opportunity to explain his version of the occurrence or occurrences at the informal meeting with the building principal as provided in paragraphs 2 and 3.

We conclude that the consent decree as thus amended conforms to the due process requirements of *Goss*, and we are satisfied that the students subject to its disciplinary procedures will receive sufficient due process protection. * * *

We will modify the order of the district court directing the addition of paragraph 32 as stated by it to the consent decree. * * *

Notes and Questions

May a lawyer be present at a "guidance conference" at which a student's transfer will be discussed? See *Madera v. Board of Education of the City of New York*, 386 F.2d 778 (2d Cir. 1967), cert. denied, 390 U.S. 1028 (1968) in which the court held that school officials did not have to permit the presence of counsel at such a conference.

III. Corporal Punishment

Corporal punishment may be defined as the use of such physical contact as striking, paddling, or spanking of a student by an educator. Although widely used, it is a controversial practice that has received much debate. Proponents view it as a necessary and educationally sound disciplinary measure. Those opposed view the practice as archaic, cruel, and inhuman and an unjustifiable act on the part of the state.

The issue had been repeatedly litigated until the United States Supreme Court upheld the practice in *Ingraham v. Wright.* In its opinion the Court addressed two major issues: whether or not the administration of corporal punishment represented cruel and unusual punishment in violation of the Eighth Amendment; and whether or not prior notice and an opportunity to be heard were required.

Ingraham v. Wright

Supreme Court of the United States, 1977
430 U.S. 651

MR. JUSTICE POWELL delivered the opinion of the Court.

This case presents questions concerning the use of corporal punishment in public schools: First, whether the paddling of students as a means of maintaining school discipline constitutes cruel and unusual punishment in violation of the Eighth Amendment; and, second, to the extent that paddling is constitutionally permissible, whether the Due Process Clause of the Fourteenth Amendment requires prior notice and an opportunity to be heard.

*   *   *

Petitioners' evidence may be summarized briefly. In the 1970–1971 school year many of the 237 schools in Dade County used corporal punishment as a means of maintaining discipline pursuant to Florida legislation and a local school board regulation. The statute then in effect authorized limited corporal punishment by negative inference, proscribing punishment which was "degrading or unduly severe" or which was inflicted without prior consultation with the principal or the teacher in charge of the school. *   *   *   The regulation *   *   *   contained explicit directions and limitations. The authorized punishment consisted of paddling the recalcitrant student on the buttocks with a flat wooden paddle measuring less than two feet long, three to four inches wide, and about one-half inch thick.

The normal punishment was limited to one to five "licks" or blows with the paddle and resulted in no apparent physical injury to the student. School authorities viewed corporal punishment as a less drastic means of discipline than suspension or expulsion. Contrary to the procedural requirements of the statute and regulation, teachers often paddled students on their own authority without first consulting the principal.

* * * Because he was slow to respond to his teacher's instructions, Ingraham was subjected to more than 20 licks with a paddle while being held over a table in the principal's office. The paddling was so severe that he suffered a hematoma requiring medical attention and keeping him out of school for several days. Andrews was paddled several times for minor infractions. On two occasions he was struck on his arms, once depriving him of the full use of his arm for a week.

* * *

In addressing the scope of the Eighth Amendment's prohibition on cruel and unusual punishment, this Court has found it useful to refer to "[t]raditional common-law concepts," * * * and to the "attitude[s] which our society has traditionally taken." * * * So, too, in defining the requirements of procedural due process under the Fifth and Fourteenth Amendments, the Court has been attuned to what "has always been the law of the land," * * * and to "traditional ideas of fair procedure." * * * We therefore begin by examining the way in which our traditions and our laws have responded to the use of corporal punishment in public schools.

The use of corporal punishment in this country as a means of disciplining schoolchildren dates back to the colonial period. It has survived the transformation of primary and secondary education from the colonials' reliance on optional private arrangements to our present system of compulsory education and dependence on public schools. Despite the general abandonment of corporal punishment as a means of punishing criminal offenders, the practice continues to play a role in the public education of schoolchildren in most parts of the country. Professional and public opinion is sharply divided on the practice, and has been for more than a century. Yet we can discern no trend toward its elimination.

At common law a single principle has governed the use of corporal punishment since before the American Revolution: Teachers may impose reasonable but not excessive force to discipline a child. * * * The basic doctrine has not changed. The prevalent rule in this country today privileges such force as a teacher or administrator "reasonably believes to be necessary for [the child's] proper control, training, or education." * * * To the extent that the force is excessive or unreasonable, the educator in virtually all States is subject to possible civil and criminal liability.

Although the early cases viewed the authority of the teacher as deriving from the parents, the concept of parental delegation has been replaced by the view—more consonant with compulsory education laws—that the State itself may impose such corporal punishment as is reasonably necessary "for the proper education of the child and for the maintenance of group discipline." * * * All of the circumstances are to be taken into account in determining whether the punishment is reasonable in a particular case. Among the most important considerations are the seriousness of the offense, the attitude and past behavior of the child, the nature and severity of the punishment, the age and strength of the child, and the availability of less severe but equally effective means of discipline. * * *

Of the 23 States that have addressed the problem through legislation, 21 have authorized the moderate use of corporal punishment in public schools. Of these States only a few have elaborated on the common-law test of reasonableness, typically providing for approval or notification of the child's parents, or for infliction of punishment only by the principal or in the presence of an adult witness. Only two States, Massachusetts and New Jersey, have prohibited all corporal punishment in their public schools. Where the legislatures have not acted, the state courts have uniformly preserved the common-law rule permitting teachers to use reasonable force in disciplining children in their charge.

Against this background of historical and contemporary approval of reasonable corporal punishment, we turn to the constitutional questions before us.

The Eighth Amendment provides: Excessive bail shall not be required, nor excessive fines imposed, nor cruel and unusual punishments inflicted." Bail, fines, and punishment traditionally have been associated with the criminal process, and by subjecting the three to parallel limitations the text of the Amendment suggests an intention to limit the power of those entrusted with the criminal-law function of government. An examination of the history of the Amendment and the decisions of this Court construing the proscription against cruel and unusual punishment confirms that it was designed to protect those convicted of crimes. We adhere to this long-standing limitation and hold that the Eighth Amendment does not apply to the paddling of children as a means of maintaining discipline in public schools.

The history of the Eighth Amendment is well known. The text was taken, almost verbatim, from a provision of the Virginia Declaration of Rights of 1776, which in turn derived from the English Bill of Rights of 1689. The English version, adopted after the accession of William and Mary, was intended to curb the excesses of English judges under the reign of James II. * * *

* * *

In light of this history, it is not surprising to find that every decision of this Court considering whether a punishment is "cruel and unusual" within the meaning of the Eighth and Fourteenth Amendments has dealt with a criminal punishment. * * *

* * *

In the few cases where the Court has had occasion to confront claims that impositions outside the criminal process constituted cruel and unusual punishment, it has had no difficulty finding the Eighth Amendment inapplicable. * * *

Petitioners acknowledge that the original design of the Cruel and Unusual Punishments Clause was to limit criminal punishments, but urge nonetheless that the prohibition should be extended to ban the paddling of schoolchildren. Observing that the Framers of the Eighth Amendment could not have envisioned our present system of public and compulsory education, with its opportunities for noncriminal punishments, petitioners contend that extension of the prohibition against cruel punishments is necessary lest we afford greater protection to criminals than to schoolchildren. It would be anomalous, they say, if schoolchildren could be beaten without constitutional redress, while hardened criminals suffering the same beatings at the hands of their jailors might have a valid claim under the Eighth Amendment. * * * Whatever force this logic may have in other settings, we find it an inadequate basis for wrenching the Eighth Amendment from its historical context and extending it to traditional disciplinary practices in the public schools.

* * *

The schoolchild has little need for the protection of the Eighth Amendment. Though attendance may not always be voluntary, the public school remains an open institution. Except perhaps when very young, the child is not physically restrained from leaving school during school hours; and at the end of the school day, the child is invariably free to return home. Even while at school, the child brings with him the support of family and friends and is rarely apart from teachers and other pupils who may witness and protest any instances of mistreatment.

The openness of the public school and its supervision by the community afford significant safeguards against the kinds of abuses from which the Eighth Amendment protects the prisoner. In virtually every community where corporal punishment is permitted in the schools, these safeguards are reinforced by legal constraints of the common law. Public school teachers and administrators are privileged at common law to inflict only such corporal punishment as is reasonably necessary for the proper education and discipline of the child; any punishment going beyond the privilege may result in both civil and criminal liability. * * * As long as the schools are open to public scrutiny, there is no reason to believe that the common-law constraints will not effectively remedy and deter excesses such as those alleged in this case.

We conclude that when public school teachers or administrators impose disciplinary corporal punishment, the Eighth Amendment is inapplicable. The pertinent constitutional question is whether the imposition is consonant with the requirements of due process.

The Fourteenth Amendment prohibits any state deprivation of life, liberty, or property without due process of law. Application of this prohibition requires the familiar two-stage analysis: We must first ask whether the asserted individual interests are encompassed within the Fourteenth Amendment's protection of "life, liberty or property"; if protected interests are implicated, we then must decide what procedures constitute "due process of law." * * * Following that analysis here, we find that corporal punishment in public schools implicates a constitutionally protected liberty interest, but we hold that the traditional common-law remedies are fully adequate to afford due process.

* * *

While the contours of this historic liberty interest in the context of our federal system of government have not been defined precisely, they always have been thought to encompass freedom from bodily restraint and punishment. * * * It is fundamental that the state cannot hold and physically punish an individual except in accordance with due process of law.

This constitutionally protected liberty interest is at stake in this case. There is, of course a *de minimis* level of imposition with which the Constitution is not concerned. But at least where school authorities, acting under color of state law, deliberately decide to punish a child for misconduct by restraining the child and inflicting appreciable physical pain, we hold that Fourteenth Amendment liberty interests are implicated.

"[T]he question remains what process is due." * * * Were it not for the common-law privilege permitting teachers to inflict reasonable corporal punishment on children in their care, and the availability of the traditional remedies for abuse, the case for requiring advance procedural safeguards would be strong indeed. But here we deal with a punishment—paddling—within that tradition, and the question is whether the common-law remedies are adequate to afford due process. * * * Whether in this case the common-law remedies for excessive corporal punishment constitute due process of law must turn on an analysis of the competing interests at stake, viewed against the background of "history, reason, [and] the past course of decisions." The analysis requires consideration of three distinct factors: "First, the private interest that will be affected . . . ; second, the risk of an erroneous deprivation of such interest . . . and the probable value, if any, of additional or substitute procedural safeguards; and finally, the [state] interest, including the function involved and the fiscal and administrative burdens that the additional or substitute procedural requirement would entail." * * *

Because it is rooted in history, the child's liberty interest in avoiding corporal punishment while in the care of public school authorities is subject to historical limitations. Under the common law, an invasion of personal security gave rise to a right to recover damages in a subsequent judicial proceeding. * * * But the right of recovery was qualified by the concept of justification. Thus, there could be no recovery against a teacher who gave only "moderate correction" to a child. * * * To the extent that the force used was reasonable in light of its purpose, it was not wrongful, but rather "justifiable or lawful." * * *

The concept that reasonable corporal punishment in school is justifiable continues to be recognized in the laws of most States. * * * It represents "the balance struck by this country" * * * between the child's interest in personal security and the traditional view that some limited corporal punishment may be necessary in the course of a child's education. Under that longstanding accommodation of interests, there can be no deprivation of substantive rights as long as disciplinary corporal punishment is within the limits of the common-law privilege.

This is not to say that the child's interest in procedural safeguards is insubstantial. The school disciplinary process is not "a totally accurate, unerring process, never mistaken and never unfair . . ." * * * . In any deliberate infliction of corporal punishment on a child who is restrained for that purpose, there is some risk that the intrusion on the child's liberty will be unjustified and therefore unlawful. In these circumstances the child has a strong interest in procedural safeguards that minimize the risk of wrongful punishment and provide for the resolution of disputed questions of justification.

We turn not to a consideration of the safeguards that are available under applicable Florida law.

Florida has continued to recognize, and indeed has strengthened by statute, the common-law right of a child not to be subjected to excessive corporal punishment in school. Under Florida law the teacher and principal of the school decide in the first instance whether corporal punishment is reasonably necessary under the circumstances in order to discipline a child who has misbehaved. But they must exercise prudence and restraint. For Florida has preserved the traditional judicial proceedings for determining whether the punishment was justified. If the punishment inflicted is later found to have been excessive—not reasonably believed at the time to be necessary for the child's discipline or training—the school authorities inflicting it may be held liable in damages to the child and, if malice is shown, they may be subject to criminal penalties.

Although students have testified in this case to specific instances of abuse, there is every reason to believe that such mistreatment is an aberration. The uncontradicted evidence suggests that corporal punishment in the Dade County schools was, "[w]ith the exception of a few cases, . . . unremarkable in physical severity." * * * Moreover, because paddlings are usually inflicted in response to conduct directly observed by teachers in their presence, the risk that a child will be paddled without cause is typically insignificant. In the ordinary case, a disciplinary paddling neither threatens seriously to violate any substantive rights nor condemns the child "to suffer grievous loss of any kind." * * *

In those cases where severe punishment is contemplated, the available civil and criminal sanctions for abuse—considered in light of the openness of the school environment—afford significant protection against unjustified corporal punishment. * * * Teachers and school authorities are unlikely to inflict corporal punishment unnecessarily or excessively when a possible consequence of doing so is the institution of civil or criminal proceedings against them.

It still may be argued, of course, that the child's liberty interest would be better protected if the common-law remedies were supplemented by the administrative safeguards of prior notice and a hearing. We have found frequently that some kind of prior hearing is necessary to guard against arbitrary impositions on interests protected by the Fourteenth Amendment. * * * But where the State has preserved what "has always been the law of the land," * * * the case for administrative safeguards is significantly less compelling.

* * *

But even if the need for advance procedural safeguards were clear, the question would remain whether the incremental benefit could justify the cost. Acceptance of petitioners' claims would work a transformation in the law governing corporal punishment in Florida and most other States. Given the impracticability of formulating a rule of procedural due process that varies with the severity of the particular imposition, the prior hearing petitioners seek would have to precede *any* paddling, however moderate or trivial.

Such a universal constitutional requirement would significantly burden the use of corporal punishment as a disciplinary measure. Hearings—even informal hearings—require time, personnel, and a diversion of attention from normal school pursuits. School authorities may well choose to abandon corporal punishment rather than incur the burdens of complying with the procedural requirements. Teachers, properly concerned with maintaining authority in the classroom, may well prefer to rely on other disciplinary measures—which they may view as less effective—rather than confront the possible disruption that prior notice and a hearing may entail. Paradoxically, such an alteration of disciplinary policy is most likely to occur in the ordinary case where the contemplated punishment is well within the common-law privilege.

Elimination or curtailment of corporal punishment would be welcomed by many as a societal advance. But when such a policy choice may result from this Court's determination of an asserted right to due process, rather than from the normal processes of community debate and legislative action, the societal costs cannot be dismissed as insubstantial. We are reviewing here a legislative judgment, rooted in history and reaffirmed in the laws of many States, that corporal punishment serves important educational interests. This judgment must be viewed in light of the disciplinary problems commonplace in the schools.   *   *   *

*   *   *   In view of the low incidence of abuse, the openness of our schools, and the common-law safeguards that already exist, the risk of error that may result in violation of a schoolchild's substantive rights can only be regarded as minimal. Imposing additional administrative safeguards as a constitutional requirement might reduce that risk marginally, but would also entail a significant intrusion into an area of primary educational responsibility. We conclude that the Due Process Clause does not require notice and a hearing prior to the imposition of corporal punishment in the public schools, as that practice is authorized and limited by the common law.

Petitioners cannot prevail on either of the theories before us in this case. The Eighth Amendment's prohibition against cruel and unusual punishment is inapplicable to school paddlings, and the Fourteenth Amendment's requirement of procedural due process is satisfied by Florida's preservation of common-law constraints and remedies. We therefore agree with the Court of Appeals that petitioners' evidence affords no basis for injunctive relief, and that petitioners cannot recover damages on the basis of any Eighth Amendment or procedural due process violation.

Affirmed.

Notes and Questions

Ingraham was a five-to-four decision. Chief Justice Burger and Justices Powell, Stewart, Blackmun, and Rehnquist composed the majority.

Justice Powell, who wrote the *Ingraham* decision, brought a background of public school experience to the Court. He was chairman of the Richmond, Virginia, School Board during the time public schools were being desegregated in the 1950s, and he headed the Virginia State Board of Education. Although a Democrat, he was nominated to the Court by President Nixon and took office in 1972.

According to *Ingraham,* in the absence of legislation to the contrary, teachers may inflict corporal punishment. States having statutes that authorized corporal punishment at the time of *Ingraham* included California (conditioned on written parental approval), Delaware, Florida, Georgia, Hawaii, Illinois, Indiana, Maryland (in specified counties), Michigan, Montana, Nevada, North Carolina, Ohio, Oklahoma, Pennsylvania, South Carolina, South Dakota, Vermont, Virginia, West Virginia, and Wyoming. Massachusetts and New Jersey prohibited all corporal punishment.

Is it possible to reconcile the majority opinion in *Ingraham* with the majority opinion in *Goss?*

Does the *Ingraham* decision cite empirical data that establish the effectiveness of corporal punishment? Are such data necessary to support the Court's ruling?

A decision discussing the doctrine of *in loco parentis* concluded that the application of corporal punishment to public school children by means of a paddle, whip, stick, or other mechanical devices could not be permitted under this doctrine; however, the doctrine did not prohibit spanking by hand, physically seizing and removing unruly students from a classroom, or using physical force to restrain students from fighting or engaging in destructive or illegal acts. See *Smith* v. *West Virginia State Board of Education,* 295 S.E.2d 680 (W. Va. 1982)

Are you familiar with the statutory provisions, if any, in your state pertaining to corporal punishment? Are practices in your school system regarding the administration of corporal punishment in conformance with state and local provisions?

IV. Search of Students and Lockers

The desire to have the Fourth Amendment included in the Bill of Rights grew out of British practices prior to the Revolutionary War. Early Americans wanted assurance that their homes would not be invaded without just cause. Many held that without this protection, government authorities could intimidate the citizenry by pursuing "fishing expeditions" such as conducting searches of homes of politically nonconforming citizens until something incriminating was found. With this fear in mind, the Fourth Amendment was included in the Bill of Rights, to protect the individual from possible harassment by an unresponsive government. Originally, the protection of the Fourth Amendment applied only to the federal government, as was the case with the other first eight amendments of the Constitution; however, as a result of decisions involving the Fourteenth Amendment, this protection for the individual is now also available against the state.

School officials may be placed in the position of searching a student because they have a reasonable suspicion that the student has stolen an article or money or has something illegal in his or her possession, such as drugs. Courts faced with such questions have had to balance an individual student's right to the Fourth Amendment's protection from unreasonable search against the duty of school officials to provide all students with a safe and secure school environment. Several factors have complicated the courts' attempt to grapple with the issue of student searches. Foremost among these has been the contention that protection under the Fourth Amendment applies only when a government official acting under the color of the state conducts the search. Therefore, courts have had to determine whether or not a school official could be considered to be a state official whose actions were indeed state action. Another question is the degree of suspicion a school official must have before a search may be conducted. Police must have probable cause to search someone. This is a higher standard than reasonable cause, which has been required by those courts upholding searches by school officials. Also, courts have made a distinction when a search involves any indignities toward students such as a mass or strip search. Such searches, according to several courts, require a standard higher than reasonable cause and, depending on the severity of the intrusion on the student, may require probable cause.

The majority of state courts that have addressed the issue have held that school officials require only reasonable cause to search a student. The United States Supreme Court decision in *New Jersey* **v. *T.L.O.*** agreed with this notion. ***Bellnier* v. *Lund*,** a district court decision, discusses the issue of so-called strip searches.

A. Student Search

New Jersey v. T.L.O.

Supreme Court of the United States, 1985
469 U.S. ___, 105 S.Ct. 733

JUSTICE WHITE delivered the opinion of the Court.

We granted certiorari in this case to examine the appropriateness of the exclusionary rule as a remedy for searches carried out in violation of the Fourth Amendment by public school authorities. Our consideration of the proper application of the Fourth Amendment to the public schools, however, has led us to conclude that the search that gave rise to the case now before us did not violate the Fourth Amendment. Accordingly, we here address only the questions of the proper standard for assessing the legality of searches conducted by public school officials and the application of that standard to the facts of this case.

On March 7, 1980, a teacher at Piscataway High School in Middlesex

County, N.J., discovered two girls smoking in a lavatory. One of the two girls was the respondent T.L.O., who at that time was a 14-year-old high school freshman. Because smoking in the lavatory was a violation of a school rule, the teacher took the two girls to the Principal's office, where they met with Assistant Vice Principal Theodore Choplick. In response to questioning by Mr. Choplick, T.L.O.'s companion admitted that she had violated the rule. T.L.O., however, denied that she had been smoking in the lavatory and claimed that she did not smoke at all.

Mr. Choplick asked T.L.O. to come into his private office and demanded to see her purse. Opening the purse, he found a pack of cigarettes, which he removed from the purse and held before T.L.O. as he accused her of having lied to him. As he reached into the purse for the cigarettes, Mr. Choplick also noticed a package of cigarette rolling papers. In his experience, possession of rolling papers by high school students was closely associated with the use of marihuana. Suspecting that a closer examination of the purse might yield further evidence of drug use, Mr. Choplick proceeded to search the purse thoroughly. The search revealed a small amount of marihuana, a pipe, a number of empty plastic bags, a substantial quantity of money in one-dollar bills, an index card that appeared to be a list of students who owed T.L.O. money, and two letters that implicated T.L.O. in marihuana dealing.

Mr. Choplick notified T.L.O.'s mother and the police, and turned the evidence of drug dealing over to the police. At the request of the police, T.L.O.'s mother took her daughter to police headquarters, where T.L.O. confessed that she had been selling marihuana at the high school. On the basis of the confession and the evidence seized by Mr. Choplick, the State brought delinquency charges against T.L.O. in the Juvenile and Domestic Relations Court of Middlesex County. Contending that Mr. Choplick's search of her purse violated the Fourth Amendment, T.L.O. moved to suppress the evidence found in her purse as well her confession, which, she argued, was tainted by the allegedly unlawful search. The Juvenile Court denied the motion to suppress.

* * *

Although we originally granted certiorari to decide the issue of the appropriate remedy in juvenile court proceedings for unlawful school searches, our doubts regarding the wisdom of deciding that question in isolation from the broader question of what limits, if any, the Fourth Amendment places on the activities of school authorities prompted us to order reargument on that question. Having heard argument on the legality of the search of T.L.O.'s purse, we are satisfied that the search did not violate the Fourth Amendment.

In determining whether the search at issue in this case violated the Fourth Amendment, we are faced initially with the question whether that

Amendment's prohibition on unreasonable searches and seizures applies to searches conducted by public school officials. We hold that it does.

It is now beyond dispute that "the Federal Constitution, by virtue of the Fourteenth Amendment, prohibits unreasonable searches and seizures by state officers." * * * Equally indisputable is the proposition that the Fourteenth Amendment protects the rights of students against encroachment by public school officials:

> "The Fourteenth Amendment, as now applied to the States, protects the citizen against the State itself and all of its creatures—Boards of Education not excepted. These have, of course, delicate, and highly discretionary functions, but none that they may not perform within the limits of the Bill of Rights. That they are educating the young for citizenship is reason for scrupulous protection of Constitutional freedoms of the individual, if we are not to strangle the free mind at its source and teach youth to discount important principles of our government as mere platitudes." *West Virginia State Bd. of Ed.* v. *Barnette,* 319 U.S. 624, 637 (1943).

These two propositions—that the Fourth Amendment applies to the States through the Fourteenth Amendment, and that the actions of public school officials are subject to the limits placed on state action by the Fourteenth Amendment—might appear sufficient to answer the suggestion that the Fourth Amendment does not proscribe unreasonable searches by school officials. On reargument, however, the State of New Jersey has argued that the history of the Fourth Amendment indicates that the Amendment was intended to regulate only searches and seizures carried out by law enforcement officers; accordingly, although public school officials are concededly state agents for purposes of the Fourteenth Amendment, the Fourth Amendment creates no rights enforceable against them.

It may well be true that the evil toward which the Fourth Amendment was primarily directed was the resurrection of the pre-Revolutionary practice of using general warrants or "writs of assistance" to authorize searches for contraband by officers of the Crown. * * * But this Court has never limited the Amendment's prohibition on unreasonable searches and seizures to operations conducted by the police. Rather, the Court has long spoken of the Fourth Amendment's strictures as restraints imposed upon "governmental action"—that is, "upon the activities of sovereign authority." * * * Accordingly, we have held the Fourth Amendment applicable to the activities of civil as well as criminal authorities: building inspectors, * * * and even firemen entering privately owned premises to battle a fire, * * * are all subject to the restraints imposed by the Fourth Amendment. As we observed * * * [t]he basic purpose of this Amendment, as recognized in countless decisions of this Court, is to safeguard the privacy and security of individuals against arbitrary invasions by governmental officials."

* * * Because the individual's interest in privacy and personal security "suffers whether the government's motivation is to investigate violations of criminal laws or breaches of other statutory or regulatory standards," * * * it would be "anomalous to say that the individual and his private property are fully protected by the Fourth Amendment only when the individual is suspected of criminal behavior." * * *

Notwithstanding the general applicability of the Fourth Amendment to the activities of civil authorities, a few courts have concluded that school officials are exempt from the dictates of the Fourth Amendment by virtue of the special nature of their authority over schoolchildren. * * * Teachers and school administrators, it is said, act *in loco parentis* in their dealings with students: their authority is that of the parent, not the State, and is therefore not subject to the limits of the Fourth Amendment.

Such reasoning is in tension with contemporary reality and the teachings of this Court. We have held school officials subject to the commands of the First Amendment, see *Tinker* v. *Des Moines Independent Community School District* * * * and the Due Process Clause of the Fourteenth Amendment, see *Goss* v. *Lopez,* * * * . If school authorities are state actors for purposes of the constitutional guarantees of freedom of expression and due process, it is difficult to understand why they should be deemed to be exercising parental rather than public authority when conducting searches of their students. More generally, the Court has recognized that "the concept of parental delegation" as a source of school authority is not entirely "consonant with compulsory education laws." *Ingraham* v. *Wright,* 430 U.S. 651, 662 (1977). Today's public school officials do not merely exercise authority voluntarily conferred on them by individual parents; rather, they act in furtherance of publicly mandated educational and disciplinary policies. * * * In carrying out searches and other disciplinary functions pursuant to such policies, school officials act as representatives of the State, not merely as surrogates for the parents, and they cannot claim the parents' immunity from the strictures of the Fourth Amendment.

To hold that the Fourth Amendment applies to searches conducted by school authorities is only to begin the inquiry into the standards governing such searches. Although the underlying command of the Fourth Amendment is always that searches and seizures be reasonable, what is reasonable depends on the context within which a search takes place. The determination of the standard of reasonableness governing any specific class of searches requires "balancing the need to search against the invasion which the search entails." * * * On one side of the balance are arrayed the individual's legitimate expectations of privacy and personal security; on the other, the government's need for effective methods to deal with breaches of public order.

We have recognized that even a limited search of the person is a substantial invasion of privacy. * * * We have also recognized that searches of closed items of personal luggage are intrusions on protected privacy interests, for "the Fourth Amendment provides protection to the owner of every container that conceals its contents from plain view." * * * A search of a child's person or of a closed purse or other bag carried on her person, no less than a similar search carried out on an adult, is undoubtedly a severe violation of subjective expectations of privacy.

Of course, the Fourth Amendment does not protect subjective expectations of privacy that are unreasonable or otherwise "illegitimate." * * * To receive the protection of the Fourth Amendment, an expectation of privacy must be one that society is "prepared to recognize as legitimate." * * * The State of New Jersey has argued that because of the pervasive supervision to which children in the schools are necessarily subject, a child has virtually no legitimate expectation of privacy in articles of personal property "unnecessarily" carried into a school. This argument has two factual premises: (1) the fundamental incompatibility of expectations of privacy with the maintenance of a sound educational environment; and (2) the minimal interest of the child in bringing any items of personal property into the school. Both premises are severely flawed.

Although this Court may take notice of the difficulty of maintaining discipline in the public schools today, the situation is not so dire that students in the schools may claim no legitimate expectations of privacy. We have recently recognized that the need to maintain order in a prison is such that prisoners retain no legitimate expectations of privacy in their cells, but it goes almost without saying that "[t]he prisoner and the schoolchild stand in wholly different circumstances, separated by the harsh facts of criminal conviction and incarceration." * * * We are not yet ready to hold that the schools and the prisons need be equated for purposes of the Fourth Amendment.

Nor does the State's suggestion that children have no legitimate need to bring personal property into the schools seem well anchored in reality. Students at a minimum must bring to school not only the supplies needed for their studies, but also keys, money, and the necessaries of personal hygiene and grooming. In addition, students may carry on their persons or in purses or wallets such nondisruptive yet highly personal items as photographs, letters, and diaries. Finally, students may have perfectly legitimate reasons to carry with them articles of property needed in connection with extracurricular or recreational activities. In short, schoolchildren may find it necessary to carry with them a variety of legitimate, noncontraband items, and there is no reason to conclude that they have necessarily waived all rights to privacy in such items merely by bringing them onto school grounds.

Against the child's interest in privacy must be set the substantial interest of teachers and administrators in maintaining discipline in the classroom and on school grounds. Maintaining order in the classroom has never been easy, but in recent years, school disorder has often taken particularly ugly forms: drug use and violent crime in the schools have become major social problems. * * * Even in schools that have been spared the most severe disciplinary problems, the preservation of order and a proper educational environment requires close supervision of schoolchildren, as well as the enforcement of rules against conduct that would be perfectly permissible if undertaken by an adult. "Events calling for discipline are frequent occurrences and sometimes require immediate, effective action." * * * Accordingly, we have recognized that maintaining security and order in the schools requires a certain degree of flexibility in school disciplinary procedures, and we have respected the value of preserving the informality of the student-teacher relationship. * * *

How, then, should we strike the balance between the schoolchild's legitimate expectations of privacy and the school's equally legitimate need to maintain an environment in which learning can take place? It is evident that the school setting requires some easing of the restrictions to which searches by public authorities are ordinarily subject. The warrant requirement, in particular, is unsuited to the school environment: requiring a teacher to obtain a warrant before searching a child suspected of an infraction of school rules (or of the criminal law) would unduly interfere with the maintenance of the swift and informal disciplinary procedures needed in the schools. Just as we have in other cases dispensed with the warrant requirement when "the burden of obtaining a warrant is likely to frustrate the governmental purpose behind the search," * * * we hold today that school officials need not obtain a warrant before searching a student who is under their authority.

The school setting also requires some modification of the level of suspicion of illicit activity needed to justify a search. Ordinarily, a search—even one that may permissibly be carried out without a warrant—must be based upon "probable cause" to believe that a violation of the law has occurred. * * * However, "probable cause" is not an irreducible requirement of a valid search. The fundamental command of the Fourth Amendment is that searches and seizures be reasonable, and although "both the concept of probable cause and the requirement of a warrant bear on the reasonableness of a search, . . . in certain limited circumstances neither is required." * * * Thus, we have in a number of cases recognized the legality of searches and seizures based on suspicions that, although "reasonable," do not rise to the level of probable cause. * * * Where a careful balancing of governmental and private interests suggests that the public interest is best served by a Fourth Amendment standard of reasonableness that stops short of probable cause, we have not hesitated to adopt such a standard.

We join the majority of courts that have examined this issue in concluding that the accommodation of the privacy interests of schoolchildren with the substantial need of teachers and administrators for freedom to maintain order in the schools does not require strict adherence to the requirement that searches be based on probable cause to believe that the subject of the search has violated or is violating the law. Rather, the legality of a search of a student should depend simply on the reasonableness, under all the circumstances, of the search. Determining the reasonableness of any search involves a twofold inquiry: first, one must consider "whether the . . . action was justified at its inception"; * * * second, one must determine whether the search as actually conducted "was reasonably related in scope to the circumstances which justified the interference in the first place." Under ordinary circumstances, a search of a student by a teacher or other school official will be "justified at its inception" when there are reasonable grounds for suspecting that the search will turn up evidence that the student has violated or is violating either the law or the rules of the school. Such a search will be permissible in its scope when the measures adopted are reasonably related to the objectives of the search and not excessively intrusive in light of the age and sex of the student and the nature of the infraction.

This standard will, we trust, neither unduly burden the efforts of school authorities to maintain order in their schools nor authorize unrestrained intrusions upon the privacy of schoolchildren. By focusing attention on the question of reasonableness, the standard will spare teachers and school administrators the necessity of schooling themselves in the niceties of probable cause and permit them to regulate their conduct according to the dictates of reason and common sense. At the same time, the reasonableness standard should ensure that the interests of students will be invaded no more than is necessary to achieve the legitimate end of preserving order in the schools.

There remains the question of the legality of the search in this case. We recognize that the "reasonable grounds" standard applied by the New Jersey Supreme Court in its consideration of this question is not substantially different from the standard that we have adopted today. Nonetheless, we believe that the New Jersey court's application of that standard to strike down the search of T.L.O.'s purse reflects a somewhat crabbed notion of reasonableness. Our review of the facts surrounding the search leads us to conclude that the search was in no sense unreasonable for Fourth Amendment purposes.

The incident that gave rise to this case actually involved two separate searches, with the first—the search for cigarettes—providing the suspicion that gave rise to the second—the search for marihuana. Although it is the fruits of the second search that are at issue here, the validity of the search for marihuana must depend on the reasonableness of the initial search for cigarettes, as there would have been no reason to suspect that T.L.O.

possessed marihuana had the first search not taken place. Accordingly, it is to the search for cigarettes that we first turn our attention.

The New Jersey Supreme Court pointed to two grounds for its holding that the search for cigarettes was unreasonable. First, the court observed that possession of cigarettes was not in itself illegal or a violation of school rules. Because the contents of T.L.O.'s purse would therefore have "no direct bearing on the infraction" of which she was accused (smoking in a lavatory where smoking was prohibited), there was no reason to search her purse. Second, even assuming that a search of T.L.O.'s purse might under some circumstances be reasonable in light of the accusation made against T.L.O., the New Jersey court concluded that Mr. Choplick in this particular case had no reasonable grounds to suspect that T.L.O. had cigarettes in her purse. At best, according to the court, Mr. Choplick had "a good hunch." * * *

Both these conclusions are implausible. T.L.O. had been accused of smoking, and had denied the accusation in the strongest possible terms when she stated that she did not smoke at all. Surely it cannot be said that under these circumstances, T.L.O.'s possession of cigarettes would be irrelevant to the charges against her or to her response to those charges. T.L.O.'s possession of cigarettes, once it was discovered, would both corroborate the report that she had been smoking and undermine the credibility of her defense to the charge of smoking. To be sure, the discovery of the cigarettes would not prove that T.L.O. had been smoking in the lavatory; nor would it, strictly speaking, necessarily be inconsistent with her claim that she did not smoke at all. But it is universally recognized that evidence, to be relevant to an inquiry, need not conclusively prove the ultimate fact in issue, but only have "any tendency to make the existence of any fact that is of consequence to the determination of the action more probable or less probable than it would be without the evidence." * * * The relevance of T.L.O.'s possession of cigarettes to the question whether she had been smoking and to the credibility of her denial that she smoked supplied the necessary "nexus" between the item searched for and the infraction under investigation. * * * Thus, if Mr. Choplick in fact had a reasonable suspicion that T.L.O. had cigarettes in her purse, the search was justified despite the fact that the cigarettes, if found, would constitute "mere evidence" of a violation.

Of course, the New Jersey Supreme Court also held that Mr. Choplick had no reasonable suspicion that the purse would contain cigarettes. This conclusion is puzzling. A teacher had reported that T.L.O. was smoking in the lavatory. Certainly this report gave Mr. Choplick reason to suspect that T.L.O. was carrying cigarettes with her; and if she did have cigarettes, her purse was the obvious place in which to find them. Mr. Choplick's suspicion that there were cigarettes in the purse was not an "inchoate and unparticularized suspicion or 'hunch,'" * * * rather, it was the sort of "common-sense conclusio[n] about human behavior" upon which "practical people"—including government officials—are entitled to rely. * * * Of course, even if the teacher's report were true, T.L.O. *might* not have had a pack of cigarettes with her; she might have borrowed a cigarette from someone else or have been sharing a cigarette with another student. But the requirement of reasonable suspicion is not a requirement of absolute certainty: "sufficient probability, not certainty, is the touchstone of reasonableness under the Fourth Amendment. . . ." * * * Because the hypothesis that T.L.O. was carrying cigarettes in her purse was itself not unreasonable, it is irrelevant that other hypotheses were also consistent with the teacher's accusation. Accordingly, it cannot be said that Mr. Choplick acted unreasonably when he examined T.L.O.'s purse to see if it contained cigarettes.

Our conclusion that Mr. Choplick's decision to open T.L.O.'s purse was reasonable brings us to the question of the further search for marihuana once the pack of cigarettes was located. The suspicion upon which the search for marihuana was founded was provided when Mr. Choplick observed a package of rolling papers in the purse as he removed the pack of cigarettes. Although T.L.O. does not dispute the reasonableness of Mr. Choplick's belief that the rolling papers indicated the presence of marihuana, she does contend that the scope of the search Mr. Choplick conducted exceeded permissible bounds when he seized and read certain letters that implicated T.L.O. in drug dealing. This argument, too, is unpersuasive. The discovery of the rolling papers concededly gave rise to a reasonable suspicion that T.L.O. was carrying marihuana as well as cigarettes in her purse. This suspicion justified further exploration of T.L.O.'s purse, which turned up more evidence of drug-related activities: a pipe, a number of plastic bags of the type commonly used to store marihuana, a small quantity of marihuana, and a fairly substantial amount of money. Under these circumstances, it was not unreasonable to extend the search to a separate zippered compartment of the purse; and when a search of that compartment revealed an index card containing a list of "people who owe me money" as well as two letters, the inference that T.L.O. was involved in marihuana trafficking was substantial enough to justify Mr. Choplick in examining the letters to determine whether they contained any further evidence. In short, we cannot conclude that the search for marihuana was unreasonable in any respect.

Because the search resulting in the discovery of the evidence of marihuana dealing by T.L.O. was reasonable, the New Jersey Supreme Court's decision to exclude that evidence from T.L.O.'s juvenile delinquency proceedings on Fourth Amendment grounds was erroneous. Accordingly, the judgment of the Supreme Court of New Jersey is

Reversed.

B. Strip Search

Bellnier v. Lund

United States District Court, Northern District of New York, 1977
438 F. Supp. 47

MUNSON, District Judge.

This is an action whereby the plaintiff children, through their parents *comme* next friends, seek redress for an allegedly unlawful strip search claimed to have been conducted or condoned by defendants, all of whom are employed by the Auburn Enlarged City School District in one capacity or another. Plaintiffs seek legal, injunctive, and declaratory relief in their action, which is maintained under 42 U.S.C. §§ 1983 and 1985, as well as the Fourth, Ninth and Fourteenth Amendments of the United States Constitution. * * *

On the morning of December 6, 1974, plaintiffs and their classmates, members of the fifth grade class at Auburn's Lincoln Elementary School, arrived at the classroom in their usual fashion. Each of the students entered the classroom and placed his outer garment in a coatroom located wholly within, and accessible only from, the classroom itself. The teacher of the class, defendant Reardon, stood at or near the classroom door during this time while the student teacher, defendant Olson, remained inside the classroom. Once inside the room, no student left prior to the alleged search now the subject of this action.

Sometime that morning, and prior to the commencement of class, plaintiff Leonti complained to defendant Olson that he was missing $3.00 from his coat pocket. Plaintiff Leonti stated that he was sure that he had $4.00 when he arrived at school, showing defendant Reardon the four raffle ticket stubs indicating sales proceeds in the amount of $4.00, only $1.00 of which remained in Leonti's pocket.

An appeal by defendant Reardon to the class regarding knowledge of the missing money proved fruitless. Being aware of prior complaints from class members of missing money, lunches, and other items, and knowing that no one had left the classroom that morning, defendant Reardon commenced a search of the class, with the aid of fellow teachers and school officials, all of whom are named as defendants herein.

The outer garments hanging in the coatroom were searched initially. The students were then asked to empty their pockets and remove their shoes. A search of those items failed to reveal the missing money. The class members were then taken to their respective restrooms, the girls to the girls' room by defendants Olson and Butcher, and the boys to the boys' room by defendants Reardon, Parker, and Lund. The students were there ordered to strip down to their undergarments, and their clothes were searched. When the strip searches proved futile, the students were returned to the classroom. There, a search was conducted of their desks, books, and once again of their coats.

The entire search lasted approximately two hours, with the strip searches taking about fifteen minutes. The missing money was never located.

* * *

In finding that the Fourth Amendment does apply in this case, this Court does not mean to imply that a showing of probable cause is necessary in order to uphold the search as reasonable. In analyzing the search to determine reasonableness, the Court must weigh the danger of the conduct, evidence of which is sought, against the students' right of privacy and the need to protect them from the humiliation and psychological harms associated with such a search. * * * In doing so the Court must take into account the special duties and responsibilities imposed upon school officials to provide a safe atmosphere for a student to develop, the attendant limited powers which the school officials possess *in loco parentis* to effectuate the maintenance of proper discipline. * * *

This Court holds that, while there need not be a showing of probable cause in a case such as this, there must be demonstrated the existence of some articulable facts which together provided reasonable grounds to search the students, and that the search must have been in furtherance of a legitimate purpose with respect to which school officials are empowered to act, such as the maintenance of discipline or the detection and punishment of misconduct. * * * In making such an analysis, some factors which warrant consideration are: 1) the child's age; 2) the child's history and record in school; 3) the seriousness and prevalence of the problem to which the search is directed; and 4) the exigency requiring an immediate warrantless search. * * *

On balance, the facts of this case mitigate against the validity of the search in issue. It is entirely possible that there was reasonable suspicion, and even probable cause, based upon the facts, to believe that *someone* in the classroom has possession of the stolen money. There were no facts, however, which allowed the officials to particularize with respect to which students might possess the money, something which has time and again, with exceptions not relevant to this case, been found to be necessary to a reasonable search under the Fourth Amendment. * * * For this reason, the search must be held to have been invalid under the Fourth Amendment, there being no reasonable suspicion to believe that each student searched possessed contraband or evidence of a crime.

The Court is not unmindful of the dilemma which confronts school officials in a situation such as this. However, in view of the relatively slight danger of the conduct involved (as opposed to drug possession, for example), the extent of the search, and the age of the students involved, this Court cannot in good conscience say that the search undertaken was reasonable.   *   *   *

*   *   *

Notes and Questions

In another decision dealing with a strip search, a federal appellate court, *M.M.* v. *Anker*, 607 F.2d 588 (2nd Cir. 1979), contended that

> . . . teachers have a unique relationship to their students, both in administering discipline as part of their educational function, and in protecting the well-being of all children in their care and custody. Accordingly, these interests justify greater flexibility when applying the Fourth Amendment in a school setting. . . .
>
> We are also of the view that as the intrusiveness of the search intensifies, the standard of Fourth Amendment "reasonableness" approaches probable cause, even in the school context. . . . Thus, when a teacher conducts a highly intrusive invasion such as the strip search in this case, it is reasonable to require that probable cause be present . . . (P. 589).

Prior to the Court's decision in *T.L.O.* virtually all state and federal courts had held that school officials only required reasonable cause to search a student. *Louisiana v. Mora,* 330 So. 2d 900 (La. 1976), cert. denied, 429 U.S. 1004 (1976), represents a minority viewpoint. In that decision, the Louisiana Supreme Court held that school officials are government agents, that a warrantless search is in violation of the Fourth Amendment, and that evidence obtained in such a manner was not admissible in the subsequent criminal proceeding.

How do you account for the fact that students have essentially the same First Amendment rights of freedom of expression as adults, but apparently do not have the same Fourth Amendment rights?

May a school official search a car in the school parking lot when there is a reasonable suspicion that the car contains drugs? firearms or other weapons? liquor?

May school officials conduct a schoolwide search for drugs by using drug-detecting dogs and then engage in a strip search of suspected students? A federal appellate court has held that sniffing by a dog was not a search and therefore not protected by the Fourth Amendment; requesting students to empty their pockets and purses did not violate the Fourth Amendment; but conducting a nude search of a student as a result of the dog's alert was unreasonable. In entitling the student to damages, the court contended that a nude search was not only unconstitutional, but also contrary to common decency. See *Doe v. Renfrow,* 635 F.2d 582 (7th Cir. 1980), cert. denied, 451 U.S. 1022 (1981).

The Fifth Circuit Court of Appeals rejected the *Doe* rationale concerning the use of trained "sniffer" dogs and held that it was a search within the purview of the Fourth Amendment. This court contended that the intrusion in dignity that accompanies canine sniffing of students "cannot be justified by the need to prevent abuse of drugs and alcohol when there is not individualized suspicion." Canine sniffing of lockers and cars was not considered a search since they are unattended and in public view. See *Horton* v. *Goose Creek Independent School District,* 690 F.2d 470 (5th Cir. 1982), cert. denied, 463 U.S. 1207 (1983).

Some school systems have considered testing students for drug use as a condition of their attending school. Would such testing be a violation of a student's Fourth Amendment rights?

Courts have tended to allow school officials to search a student's locker without a warrant and without the student's permission. The court's reasoning is often that schools retain ultimate control over lockers and act *in loco parentis.* This issue was addressed in *Kansas* v. *Stein,* 203 Kan. 638, 456 P.2d 1, cert. denied, 397 U.S. 947 (1970), which discussed the public nature of student lockers. The court held that school authorities must protect both the school's educational functions and the students' welfare and may, therefore, inspect lockers to prevent their illicit use.

What is the policy in your school system regarding searches of students or their lockers?

V. Dress and Grooming

Challenges against dress codes and grooming regulations over the last decade clearly demonstrate that some parents will not idly accept school rules they believe to be unfair or anachronistic. There have not been as many challenges to dress codes, nor the emotion and fervor, as there have been to grooming regulations. In both cases parents usually maintain that they are responsible for their child's dress and grooming, and if questions of health or safety are not involved, school authorities should be able to demonstrate a relationship between their dress or grooming policy and an educationally sound program. School authorities, on the other hand, generally contend that they have the necessary experience and expertise to determine proper policies that will aid in maintaining order and discipline.

A. Dress

Courts, to date, have not been consistent in their decisions pertaining to dress. Generally, dress codes have been upheld that prohibited immodest or suggestive clothing, dress that would create a disturbance or distraction, and clothing that was unsanitary or created a health hazard.

Since there was no showing that the wearing of blue jeans inhibited or tended to inhibit the educational process, a New Hampshire federal court, in **Bannister v. Paradis,** invalidated the prohibition against wearing jeans.

Bannister v. Paradis

United States District Court, District of New Hampshire, 1970
316 F. Supp. 185

BOWNES, District Judge.

* * *

Prior to hearing, the parties entered into a stipulation of facts as follows. Kevin Bannister is twelve years old and is a student in the sixth grade of the Pittsfield High School which runs from the fifth through the twelfth grades, and is a public school. The present version of the dress code was adopted unanimously by the School Board on April 27, 1970, and the only section of the dress code in issue is the section * * * referring to dungarees. The plaintiff, however, does not agree that the dress code is constitutional as to its other provisions. Kevin was sent home for violation of the dress code because he was wearing blue jeans. At no time was force used to require Kevin to leave school.

At the outset, the Court has had some difficulty defining the word "dungarees." The principal of the school defined "dungarees" as working clothes made of a coarse cotton blue fabric. The Chairman of the School Board defined "dungarees" as a denim fabric pant used for work with color of no significance. Webster's Third International Dictionary defines "dungarees" as heavy cotton work clothes usually made of blue dungaree. For purposes of this case, the Court finds that blue jeans and dungarees are synonymous and that Kevin Bannister deliberately violated the school dress code on at least two occasions by wearing blue jeans to school. These violations were with the full knowledge and consent, if not the actual urging, of Kevin's parents. At the time the violations occurred, the blue jeans were neat and clean, as was all of Kevin's ensemble.

There was no evidence that the wearing of dungarees of any color had ever caused any disturbance at the school or given rise to any disciplinary problems. Kevin's wearing of blue jeans did not cause any disturbance and there was no disciplinary problem involved except the one involving Kevin himself. It can be fairly concluded that wearing clean blue jeans does not constitute a danger to the health or safety of other pupils and that wearing them does not disrupt the other pupils.

The principal of the school, Mr. Paradis, who has had a total of seven years' experience in teaching and school administration, testified that discipline is essential to the educational process, and that proper dress is part of a good educational climate. It was his opinion that if students wear working or play clothes to school, it leads to a relaxed attitude and such an attitude detracts from discipline and a proper educational climate. Mr. Paradis stated further that students with patches on their clothes and students with dirty clothes, regardless of the type of clothing, should be sent home. The Court notes there that there is nothing in the dress code specifically stating that clothes should be neat and clean. The dress code, as to the boys, is directed primarily to specific prohibitions and does not promulgate any positive standards to follow. On cross-examination, the principal stated: "I apply the dress code as I see it. We don't define the term dungarees as to what it is."

The Chairman of the School Board, E. Windsor Burbank, testified that it was his opinion, and the opinion of the School Board, that the relaxed atmosphere induced by wearing work or play clothes to school does not fit into the atmosphere of discipline and learning. This opinion was based on the Chairman's assertion that California students had poor academic records and that this was due to the sloppy and casual attire worn by them to school. The Chairman is a full time pilot for TWA Airlines and his knowledge of the type of school dress worn by students in California was based on his observations at the times that his airplane schedule took him to various sections of California. The Chairman did not explain the basis for his assertion that California high school students have poor academic records.

Prior to the adoption of a revised dress code in 1970, the Student Council had recommended that the prohibition against dungarees be eliminated. The School Board did not accede to this request, but no reasons were given for its refusal.

*   *   *

There was no suggestion that the wearing of blue jeans, clean or otherwise, in any way constitutes a right of expression. The First Amendment, therefore, does not apply and is not an issue.

Certainly, the prohibition against the wearing of blue jeans or dungarees cannot by any stretch of the imagination touch the right of privacy *   *   * .

If it were not for the case of Richards v. Thurston, 424 F.2d 1281 (1st Cir. 1970), the Court might be tempted to dispose of this matter on the ground that there was no deprivation of any constitutional rights. The language and reasoning of that case, however, convinces us that a person's right to wear clothes of his own choosing provided that, in the case of a schoolboy, they are neat and clean, is a constitutional right protected and guaranteed by the Fourteenth Amendment. Judge Coffin, in writing the opinion, * * * stated:

> No right is held more sacred, or is more carefully guarded, by the common law, than the right of every individual to the possession and control of his own person, free from all restraint or interference of others, unless by clear and unquestionable authority of law.

Surely, the commodious concept of liberty invoked by Judge Coffin, embracing freedoms great and small, is large enough to include within its embrace the right to wear clean blue jeans to school unless there is an outweighing state interest justifying their exclusion. * * *

Since we have determined that a personal liberty is involved, and that the plaintiff has stated a claim under 42 U.S.C. § 1983, we now consider the second question, and that is whether or not the regulations against the wearing of dungarees is justified under these circumstances. Going again to Richards v. Thurston, *supra,* for our guidelines, we take into account the nature of the liberty asserted, the context in which it is asserted, and the extent to which the intrusion on the liberty is confined to the legitimate public interest to be served.

On the scale of values of constitutional liberties, the right to wear clean blue jeans to school is not very high. There was no suggestion by the plaintiff that he could not afford pants other than blue jeans, although there was testimony by another parent that she had sent her son to school at the end of the year in blue jeans because she could not afford to buy him a pair of dress pants.

On the other hand, there was no showing that the wearing of dungarees in any way inhibited or tended to inhibit the education process. The Court is, of course, mindful of the testimony of the principal and the Chairman of the School Board that wearing work clothes or play clothes is subversive of the educational process because students tend to become lax and indifferent. The Court confesses, however, that it has considerable difficulty accepting this proposition. There was no expert testimony to this effect with the exception of that of Mr. Paradis. While the Court realizes that Mr. Burbank's experience on the School Board of eight years' standing does give him certain credentials, it does not qualify him as an expert in the field of education and teaching. There was no evidence as to how many other school boards in the state followed a similar dress code nor, with the exception of Mr. Burbank's rather casual observations of the California school system, was there any testimony as to the type of dress worn by other pupils in any other schools.

* * *

We realize that a school can, and must, for its own preservation exclude persons who are unsanitary, obscenely or scantily clad. Good hygiene and the health of the other pupils require that dirty clothes of any nature, whether they be dress clothes or dungarees, should be prohibited. Nor does the Court see anything unconstitutional in a school board prohibiting scantily clad students because it is obvious that the lack of proper covering, particularly with female students, might tend to distract other pupils and be disruptive of the educational process and school discipline.

While the Court recognizes that school boards do have power to adopt reasonable restrictions on dress as part of its educational policy and as an educational device, the school board's power must be limited to that required by its function of administering public education. The observation in Westley v. Rossi, *supra,* is pertinent.

> The standards of appearance and dress of last year are not those of today nor will they be those of tomorrow. Regulation of conduct by school authorities must bear a reasonable basis to the ordinary conduct of the school curriculum or to carrying out the responsibility of the school. (305 F. Supp. 714)

The Court rules that the defendants have not justified the intrusion on the personal liberty of Kevin Bannister, small as that intrusion may be, and that the prohibition against wearing dungarees is unconstitutional and invalid. The School Board and the principal of the Pittsfield High School are permanently enjoined from enforcing that portion of the dress code which prohibits boys from wearing dungarees. * * *

So ordered.

Notes and Questions

A federal district court examined specific portions of a school's dress code by employing a test that determined whether or not dress regulations had the effect of promoting legitimate objectives, such as safety, health, decency, and classroom decorum. The court ruling upheld portions of the dress code prohibiting the wearing of skirts more than six inches above the knee and excessively tight skirts or pants. However, the court invalidated dress regulations pertaining to "knicker suits," "jump suits," skirts more than six inches below the knee, frayed trousers or jeans, shirttails outside pants, tie-dyed clothing, "shirts or clothing having slogans, pictures, or emblems," and the mandatory wearing of socks by boys at all times. The major reason offered by the court for invalidating these specific regulations was an insufficiency in establishing a relationship between the specific regulation and a legitimate school objective. See *Wallace v. Ford,* 346 F. Supp. 156 (Ark. 1972).

A dress regulation requiring proper attire to participate in a graduation ceremony was upheld. The court maintained that receiving a diploma at a commencement program was not a property right under state law, and the student was entitled to receive his diploma separately after the program. See *Fowler* v. *Williamson,* 39 N.C. App. 715, 251 S.E.2d 889 (1979).

Some observers suggest that at one time in our history, schools, especially when serving a homogeneous community, were accepted as a socializing agency that was the arbiter of "proper" dress. If this is an accurate assessment, what factors have contributed to the demise of such a role for the school?

Does your school system have dress regulations?

B. Grooming

Court decisions dealing with grooming issues have not been consistent. Judicial views range from upholding the right of males to wear "long" hair, on the basis that this right is protected by the federal Constitution, to declaring the question an unworthy one for federal court attention. Since the constitutional right of male students to wear "long" hair is apparently determined geographically, depending upon the state or the federal circuit involved, it would be prudent, in the absence of a definitive statement by the United States Supreme Court, for educators to apprise themselves of appropriate federal decisions and state appellate opinions.

Davenport v. Randolph County Board of Education

United States Court of Appeals, Eleventh Circuit, 1984
730 F.2d 1395

KRAVITCH. Circuit Judge:

The plaintiffs. Jonathan Davenport and Micky Lazar O'Neal, are high school students who brought suit to challenge the "clean shaven" policy of defendant Ronald Watters, coach of the football and basketball teams at Randolph County High School (RCHS). Defendant Watters suspended Davenport from the RCHS basketball team in December 1981 for refusing to shave and barred both plaintiffs from participating on the football team for the 1982 season because of their refusal to abide by his grooming policy.

Defendant Watters' grooming policy prohibited team members from having beards, wearing mustaches extending beyond the corners of their mouths, or growing sideburns below the ear lobes. The plaintiffs' fathers approved of their sons' decisions not to abide by the coach's policy because they had suffered skin problems when shaving as youths and thus did not want their sons to shave. Defendant Randolph County School Board first considered the issue in March 1982 and recommended that coaches not require a minor to shave if the parents objected. At a later meeting, however, the Board reversed its position and endorsed Coach Watters' "clean shaven" policy. Plaintiffs proceeded to institute this suit pursuant to 42 U.S.C. § 1983 and the fourteenth amendment, requesting declaratory judgment and issuance of an injunction to prevent the defendants from refusing to allow the plaintiffs to participate in athletics at RCHS.

The plaintiffs contend that the "clean shaven" policy is unconstitutional because it is arbitrary and unreasonable to require fourteen and fifteen year-old adolescents to shave in order to participate in high school athletics. This court has previously ruled that in the high school environment there is "a per se rule that [grooming regulations] are constitutionally valid." *Karr v. Schmidt*, 460 F.2d 609, 617 (5th Cir. 1972) (en banc);* see also, *Stevenson v. Board of Education of Wheeler County, Georgia*, 426 F.2d 1154 (5th Cir.), cert. denied, 400 U.S. 957. * * * (1970) ("clean shaven" policy not irrational). The rule announced in *Karr* is founded on the premise that grooming regulations are a "reasonable means of furthering the school board's undeniable interest in teaching hygiene, instilling discipline, asserting authority, and compelling uniformity." * * *

This case falls squarely within the holdings of *Karr* and *Stevenson*. The district court found that the policy was "adopted to accomplish the legitimate objective of presenting the school in the light deemed most favorable to the school by the students and coaches at the school." The court further found, and the plaintiffs do not disagree, that there was no evidence that the policy was racially motivated.

The plaintiffs attempt to distinguish the above cases primarily on the ground that their objections to the grooming code are based on a concern that shaving will cause them skin problems. The plaintiffs' fathers testified that they had suffered such problems as youths, and the district court recognized that blacks are prone to such medical problems. No evidence, however, was presented to the court or the school board that the plaintiffs themselves would be likely to suffer from such problems, and defendant Watters testified that he would not enforce the policy if it would have injurious results. Without such medical evidence, we find it unnecessary

*The Eleventh Circuit, in the en banc decision *Bonner v. City of Prichard*, 661 F.2d 1206, 1209 (11th Cir. 1981), adopted as precedent decisions of the former Fifth Circuit rendered prior to October 1, 1981.

to decide whether enforcement of the "clean shaven" policy in such a context would amount to a constitutional violation outside the holding of *Karr's* per se rule. * * * (per se rule does not apply if grooming policy has arbitrary effect or is discriminatorily enforced).

* * *

Having found that the disputed policy is within the school board's power to regulate grooming and that the plaintiffs have not proven unique circumstances that would render the policy arbitrary or unreasonable, the district court's denial of relief is

Affirmed.

Notes and Questions

Although grooming regulations were a much-litigated issue in the late 1960s and early 1970s, there was a lack of unanimity among federal appellate courts deciding such cases. Federal appellate courts in the Fifth, Sixth, Ninth, and Tenth Circuits either upheld grooming regulations or contended that grooming regulations were unworthy of their attention. See *Ferrell* v. *Dallas Independent School District,* 392 F.2d 697 (5th Cir. 1968), cert. denied, 393 U.S. 856 (1968); *Jackson* v. *Dorrier,* 424 F.2d 213 (6th Cir. 1970), cert. denied, 400 U.S. 850 (1970); *King* v. *Saddleback Junior College District,* 445 F.2d 932 (9th Cir. 1971); *Freeman* v. *Flake,* 448 F.2d 258 (10th Cir. 1971). In contrast the First, Fourth, Seventh, and Eighth Circuits found regulations limiting the length of hair invalid. See *Richards* v. *Thurston,* 424 F.2d 1281 (1st Cir. 1970); *Massie* v. *Henry,* 455 F.2d 779 (4th Cir. 1972); *Breen* v. *Kahl,* 419 F.2d 1034 (7th Cir. 1969), cert. denied, 398 U.S. 937 (1970); *Bishop* v. *Colaw,* 450 F.2d 1069 (8th Cir. 1971). To date the United States Supreme Court has not rendered a substantive decision in school grooming cases, denying certiorari in cases that concerned male students' hair length.

State courts in Oklahoma, Oregon, and Alaska have held that schools do not have the authority to regulate hair styles. See *Independent School District No. 8 of Seiling* v. *Swanson,* 553 P.2d 496 (Okla. 1976); *Neuhaus* v. *Federico,* 12 Or. App. 314, 505 P.2d 939 (1973); and *Breese* v. *Smith,* 501 P.2d 159 (Alaska, 1972). However, Supreme Courts in Missouri and Kansas have not held similarly. See *Kraus* v. *Board of Education of the City of Jennings,* 492 S.W.2d 783 (Mo. 1973) and *Blaine* v. *Board of Education, Haysville Unified School District No. 261,* 210 Kan. 560, 502 P.2d 693 (1972).

Several courts have addressed the issue of hair regulations that apply only to males. See *Mercer* v. *Board of Trustees, North Forest Independent School District,* 538 S.W. 2d 201 (Tex. Civ. App. 1976) and *Trent* v. *Perritt,*

391 F. Supp. 171 (Miss. 1975), which upheld the schools' regulations. Are grooming regulations that apply only to males a form of sex discrimination in education?

Federal actions concerning this issue have not been consistent. Rules and regulations for Title IX of the Education Amendments of 1972, which made such grooming regulations a violation of Title IX, were deleted in 1978 by Secretary Califano of the Department of Health, Education and Welfare and later reinstated by Secretary Harris.* In 1981 Secretary Bell of the Department of Education† revoked these federal dress and grooming regulations.

VI. Pregnancy, Parenthood, Marriage

Not too long ago public school policies often excluded students who were married or pregnant or who were parents. The rationale for such policies was that exclusion would serve as a deterrent and thereby discourage students from becoming pregnant or getting married. Such policies, which in practice applied disproportionately to females, were successfully attacked in the courts in recent years. Enactment of Title IX of the Education Amendments of 1972 addressed the issue on the basis of prohibiting sexual discrimination in any educational programs receiving federal funds. Section 86.40, Marital or Parental Status, of the implementing regulations for Title IX states:

Marital or parental status.

(a) Status generally. A recipient shall not apply any rule concerning a student's actual or potential parental, family, or marital status which treats students differently on the basis of sex.

(b) Pregnancy and related conditions. (1) A recipient shall not discriminate against any student, or exclude any student from its education program or activity, including any class or extracurricular activity, on the basis of such student's pregnancy, childbirth, false pregnancy, termination of pregnancy or recovery therefrom, unless the student requests voluntarily to participate in a separate portion of the program or activity of the recipient.

(2) A recipient may require such a student to obtain the certification of a physician that the student is physically and emotionally able to continue participation in the normal education program or activity so long as such a certification is required of all students for other physical or emotional conditions requiring the attention of a physician.

(3) A recipient which operates a portion of its education program or activity separately for pregnant students, admittance to which is completely volun-

---

*See appendix D for edited implementing regulations for Title IX of the Education Amendments of 1972.
†The Office of Education, formerly within the Department of Health, Education and Welfare, was given separate department status in 1980.

tary on the part of the student as provided in paragraph (b) (1) of this section shall ensure that the instructional program in the separate program is comparable to that offered to non-pregnant students.

(4) A recipient shall treat pregnancy, childbirth, false pregnancy, termination of pregnancy and recovery therefrom in the same manner and under the same policies as any other temporary disability with respect to any medical or hospital benefit, service, plan or policy which such recipient administers, operates, offers, or participates in with respect to students admitted to the recipient's educational program or activity.

(5) In the case of a recipient which does not maintain a leave policy for its students, or in the case of a student who does not otherwise qualify for leave under such a policy, a recipient shall treat pregnancy, childbirth, false pregnancy, termination of pregnancy and recovery therefrom as a justification for a leave of absence for so long a period of time as is deemed medically necessary by the student's physician, at the conclusion of which the student shall be reinstated to the status which she held when the leave began. 45 C.F.R. § 86.40.*

Does your local school system or state have a policy regarding students who are married or pregnant or who are parents?

VII. Education of Handicapped Students

Prior to the 1970s the state of affairs regarding the education of handicapped students may be characterized by the following: a philosophy that placed the burden of educating handicapped children primarily on the family, a notion that the severely handicapped or those not toilet trained were not the responsibility of the public schools, and the resulting exemption of many handicapped children from compulsory-education laws. Nationwide, adequate and uniform services for handicapped public school children were not available. Support among states for such services was uneven and not extensive. A handful of local school systems provided services; however, the offerings rarely included the entire spectrum of services advocated by those working for reform.

A series of court decisions, the passage of state and federal laws and other governmental involvement beginning in the 1970s dramatically altered the relationship between handicapped students and public schools. Some of the earliest federal legislation included the Elementary and Secondary Education Act of 1965 and Title VI, which was a 1966 amendment to that act. In 1970 Title VI was repealed and replaced by the Education of the Handicapped Act of 1970. The passage of this legislation brought increased national attention to policy issues regarding handicapped students. A Bureau of Education for the Handicapped was created, and,

*See appendix D for edited implementing regulations for Title IX of the Education Amendments of 1972.

although early legislation did not provide for "mainstreaming" or a free and appropriate education, it established the groundwork for future legislation dealing with those issues.

Several successful court challenges to existing practices also altered the historic relationship between handicapped students and the public schools. Two of these decisions are particularly noteworthy. A federal district court in *Pennsylvania Association for Retarded Children* v. *Pennsylvania*, 343 F. Supp. 279 (Pa. 1972), held that mentally retarded students between the ages of six and twenty-one should be provided with access to a free public education and that handicapped students should be placed in regular classrooms when possible or in special classes when necessary. In *Mills* v. *Board of Education of the District of Columbia*, 348 F. Supp. 866 (D.C. 1972) another federal district court extended this doctrine to all school-age handicapped children, holding that they must be provided with a free and adequate public education.

Subsequent federal law embodied many of the principles enunciated in these court decisions. Section 504 of the Rehabilitation Act of 1973 represented a national commitment to end discrimination in any program receiving federal funds. The Education for All Handicapped Children Act of 1975 (P.L. 94-142) heralded a national policy under which federal funds would subsidize special education in those states meeting qualification requirements. The cornerstone of this act required states to adopt policies that assure all handicapped children a "free appropriate public education."

Owing to its complexity, the act and its implementing regulations have been extensively litigated. **Board of Education of the Hendrick Hudson Central School District** v. **Rowley,** a six-to-three United States Supreme Court decision, addressed the issue of whether an eight-year-old deaf child would be provided a sign-language interpreter in the classroom. The decision represented the first time that the Court had an opportunity to define the phrase "free appropriate public education."

Board of Education of the Hendrick Hudson Central School District v. Rowley

Supreme Court of the United States, 1982
458 U.S. 176

JUSTICE REHNQUIST delivered the opinion of the Court.

This case presents a question of statutory interpretation. Petitioners contend that the Court of Appeals and the District Court misconstrued the requirements imposed by Congress upon States which receive federal funds under the Education of the Handicapped Act. We agree and reverse the judgment of the Court of Appeals.

The Education of the Handicapped Act (Act), 84 Stat. 175, as amended, 20 U.S.C. §1401 *et seq.* (1976 ed. and Supp. IV), provides federal money to assist state and local agencies in educating handicapped children, and conditions such funding upon a State's compliance with extensive goals and procedures. The Act represents an ambitious federal effort to promote the education of handicapped children, and was passed in response to Congress' perception that a majority of handicapped children in the United States "were either totally excluded from schools or [were] sitting idly in regular classrooms awaiting the time when they were old enough to 'drop out.' " *   *   *

*   *   *

In order to qualify for federal assistance under the Act, a State must demonstrate that it "has in effect a policy that assures all handicapped children the right to a free appropriate public education." *   *   * That policy must be reflected in a state plan submitted to and approved by the Secretary of Education *   *   * which describes in detail the goals, programs, and timetables under which the State intends to educate handicapped children within its borders. *   *   * States receiving money under the Act must provide education to the handicapped by priority, first "to handicapped children who are not receiving an education" and second "to handicapped children . . . with the most severe handicaps who are receiving an inadequate education," *   *   * and "to the maximum extent appropriate" must educate handicapped children "with children who are not handicapped." *   *   * The Act broadly defines "handicapped children" to include "mentally retarded, hard of hearing, deaf, speech impaired, visually handicapped, seriously emotionally disturbed, orthopedically impaired, [and] other health impaired children. [and] children with specific learning disabilities." *   *   *

The "free appropriate public education" required by the Act is tailored to the unique needs of the handicapped child by means of an "individualized educational program" (IEP). *   *   * The IEP, which is prepared at a meeting between a qualified representative of the local educational agency, the child's teacher, the child's parents or guardian, and, where appropriate, the child, consists of a written document containing

"(A) a statement of the present levels of educational performance of such child, (B) a statement of annual goals, including short-term instructional objectives, (C) a statement of the specific educational services to be provided to such child, and the extent to which such child will be able to participate in regular educational programs, (D) the projected date for initiation and anticipated duration of such services, and (E) appropriate objective criteria and evaluation procedures and schedules for determining, on at least an annual basis, whether instructional objectives are being achieved." *   *   *

Local or regional educational agencies must review, and where appropriate revise, each child's IEP at least annually. * * *

In addition to the state plan and the IEP already described, the Act imposes extensive procedural requirements upon States receiving federal funds under its provisions. Parents or guardians of handicapped children must be notified of any proposed change in "the identification, evaluation, or educational placement of the child or the provision of a free appropriate public education to such child," and must be permitted to bring a complaint about "any matter relating to" such evaluation and education. * * * Complaints brought by parents or guardians must be resolved at "an impartial due process hearing," and appeal to the State educational agency must be provided if the initial hearing is held at the local or regional level. * * * Thereafter, "[a]ny party aggrieved by the findings and decision" of the state administrative hearing has "the right to bring a civil action with respect to the complaint . . . in any State court of competent jurisdiction or in a district court of the United States without regard to the amount in controversy." * * *

Thus, although the Act leaves to the States the primary responsibility for developing and executing educational programs for handicapped children, it imposes significant requirements to be followed in the discharge of that responsibility. Compliance is assured by provisions permitting the withholding of federal funds upon determination that a participating state or local agency has failed to satisfy the requirements of the Act, * * * and by the provision for judicial review. At present, all States except New Mexico receive federal funds under the portions of the Act at issue today. * * *

This case arose in connection with the education of Amy Rowley, a deaf student at the Furnace Woods School in the Hendrick Hudson Central School District, Peekskill, N.Y. Amy has minimal residual hearing and is an excellent lip-reader. During the year before she began attending Furnace Woods, a meeting between her parents and school administrators resulted in a decision to place her in a regular kindergarten class in order to determine what supplemental services would be necessary to her education. Several members of the school administration prepared for Amy's arrival by attending a course in sign-language interpretation, and a teletype machine was installed in the principal's office to facilitate communication with her parents who are also deaf. At the end of the trial period it was determined that Amy should remain in the kindergarten class, but that she should be provided with an FM hearing aid which would amplify words spoken into a wireless receiver by the teacher or fellow students during certain classroom activities. Amy successfully completed her kindergarten year.

As required by the Act, an IEP was prepared for Amy during the fall of her first-grade year. The IEP provided that Amy should be educated in a regular classroom at Furnace Woods, should continue to use the FM hearing aid, and should receive instruction from a tutor for the deaf for one hour each day and from a speech therapist for three hours each week. The Rowleys agreed with parts of the IEP but insisted that Amy also be provided a qualified sign-language interpreter in all her academic classes in lieu of the assistance proposed in other parts of the IEP. Such an interpreter had been placed in Amy's kindergarten class for a 2-week experimental period, but the interpreter had reported that Amy did not need his services at that time. The school administrators likewise concluded that Amy did not need such an interpreter in her first-grade classroom. They reached this conclusion after consulting the school district's Committee on the Handicapped, which had received expert evidence from Amy's parents on the importance of a sign-language interpreter, received testimony from Amy's teacher and other persons familiar with her academic and social progress, and visited a class for the deaf.

When their request for an interpreter was denied, the Rowleys demanded and received a hearing before an independent examiner. After receiving evidence from both sides, the examiner agreed with the administrators' determination that an interpreter was not necessary because "Amy was achieving educationally, academically, and socially" without such assistance. * * *

The examiner's decision was affirmed on appeal by the New York Commissioner of Education on the basis of substantial evidence in the record. * * * Pursuant to the Act's provision for judicial review, the Rowleys then brought an action in the United States District Court for the Southern District of New York, claiming that the administrators' denial of the sign-language interpreter constituted a denial of the "free appropriate public education" guaranteed by the Act.

The District Court found that Amy "is a remarkably well-adjusted child" who interacts and communicates well with her classmates and has "developed an extraordinary rapport" with her teachers. * * * It also found that "she performs better than the average child in her class and is advancing easily from grade to grade," * * * but "that she understands considerably less of what goes on in class than she could if she were not deaf" and thus "is not learning as much, or performing as well academically, as she would without her handicap," * * * This disparity between Amy's achievement and her potential led the court to decide that she was not receiving a "free appropriate public education," which the court defined as "an opportunity to achieve [her] full potential commensurate with the opportunity provided to other children." * * * According to the District Court, such a standard requires that the potential of the handicapped child be measured and compared to his or her performance, and that the resulting differential or 'shortfall' be compared to the shortfall experienced by non-handicapped children." * * * District Court's definition arose from its assumption that the responsibility for "giv[ing] content to the requirement of an 'appropriate education' " had "been left entirely to the [federal] courts and the hearing officers." * * *

* * *

This is the first case in which this Court has been called upon to interpret any provision of the Act. * * *

* * *

According to the definitions contained in the Act, a "free appropriate public education" consists of educational instruction specially designed to meet the unique needs of the handicapped child, supported by such services as are necessary to permit the child "to benefit" from the instruction. Almost as a checklist for adequacy under the Act, the definition also requires that such instruction and services be provided at public expense and under public supervision, meet the State's educational standards, approximate the grade levels used in the State's regular education, and comport with the child's IEP. Thus, if personalized instruction is being provided with sufficient supportive services to permit the child to benefit from the instruction, and the other items on the definitional checklist are satisfied, the child is receiving a "free appropriate public education" as defined by the Act.

Other portions of the statute also shed light upon congressional intent. Congress found that of the roughly eight million handicapped children in the United States at the time of enactment, one million were "excluded entirely from the public school system" and more than half were receiving an inappropriate education. * * * In addition, as mentioned in Part I, the Act requires States to extend educational services first to those children who are receiving no education and second to those children who are receiving an "inadequate education." * * * When these express statutory findings and priorities are read together with the Act's extensive procedural requirements and its definition of "free appropriate public education," the face of the statute evinces a congressional intent to bring previously excluded handicapped children into the public education systems of the States and to require the States to adopt *procedures* which would result in individualized consideration of and instruction for each child.

Noticeably absent from the language of the statute is any substantive standard prescribing the level of education to be accorded handicapped children. Certainly the language of the statute contains no requirement like the one imposed by the lower courts—that States maximize the potential of handicapped children "commensurate with the opportunity provided to other children." * * * That standard was expounded by the District Court without reference to the statutory definitions or even to the legislative history of the Act. Although we find the statutory definition of "free appropriate public education" to be helpful in our interpretation of the Act, there remains the question of whether the legislative history indicates a congressional intent that such education meet some additional substantive standard. * * *

As suggested in Part I, federal support for education of the handicapped is a fairly recent development. Before passage of the Act some States had passed laws to improve the educational services afforded handicapped children, but many of these children were excluded completely from any form of public education or were left to fend for themselves in classrooms designed for education of their nonhandicapped peers. The House Report begins by emphasizing this exclusion and misplacement, noting that millions of handicapped children "were either totally excluded from schools or [were] sitting idly in regular classrooms awaiting the time when they were old enough to 'drop out.' " * * *

* * *

This concern, stressed repeatedly throughout the legislative history, confirms the impression conveyed by the language of the statute: By passing the Act, Congress sought primarily to make public education available to handicapped children. But in seeking to provide such access to public education, Congress did not impose upon the States any greater substantive educational standard than would be necessary to make such access meaningful. Indeed, Congress expressly "recognize[d] that in many instances the process of providing special education and related services to handicapped children is not guaranteed to produce any particular outcome." * * * Thus, the intent of the Act was more to open the door of public education to handicapped children on appropriate terms than to guarantee any particular level of education once inside.

* * *

Respondents contend that "the goal of the Act is to provide each handicapped child with an equal educational opportunity." * * * We think, however, that the requirement that a State provide specialized educational services to handicapped children generates no additional requirements that the services so provided be sufficient to maximize each child's potential "commensurate with the opportunity provided other children." Respondents and the United States correctly note that Congress sought "to provide assistance to the States in carrying out their responsibilities under * * * the Constitution of the United States to provide equal protection of the laws." * * * But we do not think that such statements imply a congressional intent to achieve strict equality of opportunity or services.

The educational opportunities provided by our public school systems undoubtedly differ from student to student, depending upon a myriad of factors that might affect a particular student's ability to assimilate information presented in the classroom. The requirement that States provide "equal" educational opportunities would thus seem to present an entirely unworkable standard requiring impossible measurements and comparisons. Similarly, furnishing handicapped children with only such services as are available to nonhandicapped children would in all probability fall short of the statutory requirement of "free appropriate public education"; to require, on the other hand, the furnishing of every special service necessary to maximize each handicapped child's potential is, we think, further than Congress intended to go. Thus to speak in terms of "equal" services in one instance gives less than what is required by the Act and in another instance more. The theme of the Act is "free appropriate public education," a phrase which is too complex to be captured by the word "equal" whether one is speaking of opportunities or services.

* * *

The District Court and the Court of Appeals thus erred when they held that the Act requires New York to maximize the potential of each handicapped child commensurate with the opportunity provided nonhandicapped children. Desirable though that goal may be, it is not the standard that Congress imposed upon States which receive funding under the Act. Rather, Congress sought primarily to identify and evaluate handicapped children, and to provide them with access to a free public education.

* * *

The determination of when handicapped children are receiving sufficient educational benefits to satisfy the requirements of the Act presents a more difficult problem. The Act requires participating States to educate a wide spectrum of handicapped children, from the marginally hearing-impaired to the profoundly retarded and palsied. It is clear that the benefits obtainable by children at one end of the spectrum will differ dramatically from those obtainable by children at the other end, with infinite variations in between. One child may have little difficulty competing successfully in an academic setting with nonhandicapped children while another child may encounter great difficulty in acquiring even the most basic of self-maintenance skills. We do not attempt today to establish any one test for determining the adequacy of educational benefits conferred upon all children covered by the Act. Because in this case we are presented with a handicapped child who is receiving substantial specialized instruction and related services and who is performing above average in the regular classrooms of a public school system, we confine our analysis to that situation.

The Act requires participating States to educate handicapped children with nonhandicapped children whenever possible. When that "mainstreaming" preference of the Act has been met and a child is being educated in the regular classrooms of a public school system, the system itself monitors the educational progress of the child. Regular examinations are administered, grades are awarded, and yearly advancement to higher grade levels is permitted for those children who attain an adequate knowledge of the course material. The grading and advancement system thus constitutes an important factor in determining educational benefit. Children who graduate from our public school systems are considered by our society to have been "educated" at least to the grade level they have completed, and access to an "education" for handicapped children is precisely what Congress sought to provide in the Act.

When the language of the Act and its legislative history are considered together, the requirements imposed by Congress become tolerably clear. Insofar as a State is required to provide a handicapped child with a "free appropriate public education," we hold that it satisfies this requirement by providing personalized instruction with sufficient support services to permit the child to benefit educationally from that instruction. Such instruction and services must be provided at public expense, must meet the State's educational standards, must approximate the grade levels used in the State's regular education, and must comport with the child's IEP. In addition, the IEP, and therefore the personalized instruction, should be formulated in accordance with the requirements of the Act and, if the child is being educated in the regular classrooms of the public education system, should be reasonably calculated to enable the child to achieve passing marks and advance from grade to grade.

* * *

Applying these principles to the facts of this case, we conclude that the Court of Appeals erred in affirming the decision of the District Court. Neither the District Court nor the Court of Appeals found that petitioners had failed to comply with the procedures of the Act, and the findings of neither court would support a conclusion that Amy's educational program failed to comply with the substantive requirements of the Act. On the contrary, the District Court found that the "evidence firmly establishes that Amy is receiving an 'adequate' education, since she performs better than the average child in her class and is advancing easily from grade to grade." * * * In light of this finding, and of the fact that Amy was receiving personalized instruction and related services calculated by the Furnace Woods school administrators to meet her educational needs, the lower courts should not have concluded that the Act requires the provision of a sign-language interpreter. Accordingly, the decision of the Court of Appeals is reversed, and the case is remanded for further proceedings consistent with this opinion.

So ordered.

Notes

Another decision by the United States Supreme Court raised the issue of whether or not clean intermittent catheterization (CIC) was a "related service" under the Education of the Handicapped Act, (P.L. 91-230, as amended by the Education of All Handicapped Children Act of 1975, P.L. 94-142). In this case the parents of an eight-year-old daughter born with spina bifida requested that CIC be performed during school hours. The Court held that such services should be provided and should not be subject to exclusion as medical services. The Court reasoned that the child could not benefit from special education without such services and that such services were "no less related to the effort to educate than are services that enable a child to reach, enter, or exit a school." See *Irving Independent School District* v. *Tatro*, 468 U.S. ___, 104 S.Ct. 3371 (1984).

In examining another issue related to the education of handicapped students, the Eleventh Circuit Court of Appeals held that the Georgia policy of refusing to provide more than 180 days of schooling to handicapped children violated P.L. 94-142 and Section 504 of the Rehabilitation Act. The court contended that the law requires an "appropriate education" suited to the individual needs of the students; for some students the 180-day limit may conflict with the requirement. See *Georgia Association of Retarded Citizens* v. *McDaniel*, 716 F.2d 1565, (11th Cir. 1983), cert. denied, 469 U.S. ___, 105 S.Ct. 1228 (1985).

Two federal courts of appeals have addressed the issue of long-term expulsion of handicapped students. Both courts held that expulsion of a handicapped child constitutes a change in educational placement within the meaning of P.L. 94-142; therefore, change of placement procedures defined in the law must be followed. The courts also reasoned that a student may be expelled if the current special-education placement is determined to be appropriate and the behavior is not related to the handicapping condition. However, the courts contended that under no circumstances may educational services to the handicapped child be completely terminated even during a period of suspension. See *S-1* v. *Turlington*, 635 F.2d 342 (5th Cir. 1981), and *Kaelin* v. *Grubbs*, 682 F.2d 595 (6th Cir. 1982).

Parents may be reimbursed for expenditures for private special education if a school system cannot provide the educational needs for a handicapped child. Often occurring, however, is the question of parents' entitlement to reimbursement when they place their child in a private setting during the review process of a contested individualized educational program (I.E.P.). In addressing this issue the United States Supreme Court ruled that "parents who unilaterally change their child's placement during the pendency of review proceedings, without the consent of state or local school officials, do so at their own financial risk." Consequently parents will be reimbursed only if they ultimately prevail in the proceedings. See *Burlington School Committee* v. *Department of Education of Massachusetts*, 471 U.S. ___, 105 S. Ct. 1996 (1985).

VIII. Participation in Extracurricular Activities

Extracurricular activities are usually thought of as those that are normally conducted outside the classroom before or after regular school hours, usually noncredit, generally supervised by school officials, academically nonremedial and of a voluntary nature on the part of the students. They may include activities such as athletics, drama, clubs, band, cheerleading, and debate.

Two basic legal issues have surfaced when policies excluding a student from extracurricular activities are attacked. One of the issues raises the question of the status of extracurricular activities as a protected property interest and the requisite process due, if any. The other issue deals with the equal protection claim that an excluded student is the victim of a school's arbitrary classification scheme.

A. Legal Status of Extracurricular Activities

In following *Goss,* courts have generally held that students have a property interest in the entire educational process. However, courts have not agreed whether or not participation in one aspect of the process, such as extracurricular activities, is a constitutionally protected property interest. If it is held that such a property interest does exist, courts must then decide the extent of due process which must be provided. These issues were examined by the Supreme Court of Nebraska in *Braesch v. DePasquale.*

Braesch v. DePasquale

Supreme Court of Nebraska, 1978
200 Neb. 726, 265 N.W.2d 842
cert. denied, 439 U.S. 1068 (1979)

MCCOWN, J.

The plaintiffs brought this proceeding in the District Court for Washington County, Nebraska, to enjoin the defendant school officials from enforcing any rules of conduct that would prevent full participation by the plaintiffs in the interscholastic basketball program of the Arlington Public Schools. The District Court granted a permanent injunction enjoining defendants from preventing plaintiffs from full participation in the interscholastic basketball teams of Arlington, Nebraska. The defendants have appealed.

The plaintiffs in this action were all minors under the age of 19 and represented by their respective parents. All five plaintiffs were senior members of either the boys or the girls interscholastic basketball teams of Arlington High School. Rules of conduct for boys and girls basketball teams were distributed at the beginning of the 1976–77 basketball season. Participants in the basketball program were required to sign them and obtain one parent's signature on a copy of the rules. The rule involved here was: "DRINKING, SMOKING OR DRUGS: Do not come out for basketball if you plan on using any of the above. Any use of them will result in the immediate expulsion from the squad." Each of the plaintiffs and one or more of the parents had signed the rule.

On Saturday evening, January 8, 1977, a party was held at the home of one of the plaintiffs. The other plaintiffs, along with other seniors who were not members of the interscholastic basketball teams, attended the party. A few days later, Robert Krempke, the coach of the boys basketball team, overheard conversations at school about the party and learned that a senior boy not on the basketball team had been arrested on the evening of the party on a charge of minor in possession. On January 12, 1977, the coach approached the plaintiff who had been the host for the party and questioned him about the party. The plaintiff host admitted that there had been beer at the party and that he and other members of the basketball team were "involved." After consulting with the school principal, the basketball coach talked with each of the plaintiff members of the boys basketball team. Each admitted being at the party and drinking. The coach told them to leave basketball practice, and told them that he would arrange a meeting with them and their parents, and the principal, the following morning. The following morning, January 13, 1977, Daniel DePasquale, the principal of the high school, and Mr. Krempke, the coach, met with two of the boys involved, and on the next morning with the third. Each boy was accompanied by a parent or adult member of his family. At these brief meetings the coach told the persons present that the rules required expulsion from the basketball team, and the principal supported the coach. The principal testified that at the conclusion of these meetings he considered the boys suspended from the team and told them the decision would be confirmed by mail.

On January 13, 1977, Eloise Hiemke, the girls basketball coach learned about the drinking party from one of the girls involved and from an assistant coach. On the morning of January 14, 1977, the girls coach met with the two girls involved, asked each of them if they had been at the party, and if they had had any alcoholic beverages to drink. Each of the girls admitted she had. The principal and the girls basketball coach met with the girls and their parents on the afternoon of January 14, 1977.

The principal and the girls coach advised the girls and their parents that they felt the girls should be expelled from the team, and that an official letter would be mailed to them advising them of the decision and telling them what could be done to appeal the decision. The principal opinion expressed by the parents at the various meetings was that the penalty was too severe.

By letter dated January 18, 1977, the principal notified all the plaintiffs and their parents that each of the plaintiffs had been suspended from the basketball team until January 31, 1977, and then expelled from the team for the remainder of the season. The letter also informed them that they had 5 days in which to give written notice of their desire to appeal to the board of education, and that at the hearing they would each have the right to present their side of the issue, present any documents or statements, and cross-examine witnesses and be represented by counsel. By letters dated January 20, 1977, each of the plaintiffs requested a hearing.

* * *

On January 28, 1977, following a hearing, the District Court granted a temporary injunction enjoining the defendants from preventing the plaintiffs from full participation on the interscholastic basketball teams. Trial on the permanent injunction was later set for and held on February 18, 1977. Following the hearing, the court specifically found that the right to participate in interscholastic basketball activities was "a constitutional right protected by the due process clause of the state and federal constitutions" and that plaintiffs had been deprived of that right without due process. The District Court entered a permanent injunction enjoining defendants from preventing plaintiffs' full participation in the interscholastic basketball teams of Arlington High School. The defendants have appealed.

* * *

There is some disagreement between the parties as to whether participation in high school athletics is a constitutional right or is a privilege not protected by any constitutional principle. * * * [T]he Supreme Court of the United States has abandoned much of the former dichotomy between rights and privileges in constitutional classifications. The Fourteenth Amendment's protection of property extends to benefits which, under state law or practice, a person has a claim or entitlement. * * * The Supreme Court of the United States has also held that temporary suspension from public school infringes upon property or liberty interests protected by the due process clause of the Fourteenth Amendment. * * *

The State of Nebraska, as a part of its program for public education, has provided athletic opportunities to all public school students. Participation in interscholastic athletics ordinarily has significantly less important constitutional dimensions than does participation in traditional academic education. A student's interest in participation in high school athletics is nevertheless a significant one. * * * In the light of these constitutional principles, the question is whether the due process clause limits the power of the defendants to exclude the plaintiffs from participation in the interscholastic athletic program of Arlington High School.

Assuming that the application of the rule of conduct involved here implicates a property or liberty interest which is protected by the Fourteenth Amendment, the question becomes one of what process was due the plaintiffs under the circumstances of this case. Due process is not a technical fixed concept to be applied in all conditions, but must be flexible. It calls for such procedural protection as may be appropriate to meet the particular situation. In Goss v. Lopez, * * * the Supreme Court held that due process requires that a student facing a temporary *academic* suspension for disciplinary reasons be given oral or written notice of the charges against him, and, if he denies them, an explanation of the evidence the authorities have and an opportunity to explain his side of the story. The Supreme Court required those rudimental precautions against unfair or mistaken findings and arbitrary exclusion from school. Certainly no greater requirements should be imposed for expulsion from interscholastic athletics.

There can be no doubt that each of the plaintiffs here had specific advance notice of the rule of conduct involved, and notice of the date, time, and place of the violation charged. Each of the plaintiffs admitted his or her violation of the rule. Courts that have considered the issue have generally concluded that when the acts which are the basis for disciplinary action are admitted, the requirements of due process are far less stringent, and that due process requirements with respect to the "guilt" finding process have been met by the admissions. * * *

In the case before us the plaintiffs do not dispute that there was a specific rule of conduct for interscholastic basketball participants; that each of them and their parents had actual notice of the rule in advance; and that each of the plaintiffs violated the rule. The plaintiffs' position is simply that the rule was arbitrary and unreasonable or that the penalty was too great.

Rules prohibiting use of alcoholic liquor or drugs by participants in interscholastic athletics are clearly appropriate. * * * [T]his court upheld the right of public schools to make reasonable rules for student conduct, and held that in order to overturn such rules on the ground that they were unreasonable or arbitrary, or that they invade private rights, the evidence of such facts must be clear and satisfactory. This court said: "The wisdom or expediency of a rule adopted by a school board and the motive prompting it are not open to judicial inquiry, where it is within the administrative power of that body." Rules governing the conduct of participants in interscholastic athletics duly and regularly adopted by school authorities ought to be valid and enforceable unless they are clearly arbitrary and unreasonable and serve no legitimate end of educational athletic policy.

The rule involved in this case, even though the penalty of expulsion for the season might be deemed severe by some persons, clearly serves a legitimate rational interest and directly affects the discipline of student athletes. It cannot be said that the prescribed penalty was an arbitrary and unreasonable means to attain the legitimate end of deterrence of the use of alcoholic liquor by student athletes. * * *

Although due process may also contemplate an opportunity to be heard on the question of the penalty to be imposed where the penalty is discretionary rather than prescribed, the opportunity was also provided here. In addition to the informal procedures and meetings, which met all rudimentary requirements of due process, the plaintiffs here were also given the right to appear at a formal hearing with a right to present evidence, cross-examine witnesses, and be represented by counsel. A hearing examiner was appointed and a date set for hearing but the plaintiffs declined to participate in any of the appeals procedures established by the school board. Instead, they commenced this injunction action 1 day after they had requested the appeals procedures offered by defendants, and the temporary injunction was obtained in the District Court 2 days after the date set for the school hearing which plaintiffs had already refused. Under such circumstances courts should be reluctant to interfere prior to completion of prompt and reasonable procedures for obtaining a final order of the school board. A few days suspension from interscholastic athletic competition can hardly be said to constitute such irreparable harm as to justify judicial interference with orderly and prompt school board procedures.

* * *

It is clear in this case that the school board had the power to change or reduce the penalty if it were determined to be arbitrary and unreasonable. The plaintiffs refused to exhaust that remedy or to pursue it to the point of finality at which it might be ripe for judicial review. Where a board of education has provided effective, reasonable, and prompt procedures for notice, hearing, and review of an order of expulsion from participation in interscholastic athletics, and the athlete neglects or refuses to follow or comply with such procedures and exhaust such remedies, such neglect or refusal ordinarily constitutes a waiver of any right to subsequent injunctive relief.

The action of the District Court in granting the injunction here was erroneous and is therefore reversed.

Reversed.

Notes and Questions

Several federal courts have addressed this issue. In *Dallam* v. *Cumberland Valley School District*, 391 F. Supp. 358 (Pa. 1975) the court stated:

> ... [T]he property interest in education created by the state is participation in the entire process. The myriad activities which combine to form that educational process cannot be dissected to create hundreds of separate property rights, each cognizable under the Constitution. Otherwise, removal from an athletic team, a club or any extracurricular activity, would each require ultimate satisfaction of procedural due process. (P. 361)

In *Pegram* v. *Nelson*, 469 F. Supp. 1134 (N.C. 1979) the court declared:

> Since there is not a property interest in each separate component of the "educational process," denial of the opportunity to participate in merely one of several extracurricular activities would not give rise to a right to due process. However, *total exclusion* from participation in that part of the educational process designated as extracurricular activities for a *lengthy period of time* could, depending upon the particular circumstances, be a sufficient deprivation to implicate due process. (P. 1140)

And in *Albach* v. *Olde*, 531 F.2d 983 (10th Cir. 1976) the court maintained that

> ... The educational process is a broad and comprehensive concept with a variable and indefinite meaning. It is not limited to classroom attendance but includes innumerable separate components, such as participation in athletic activity and membership in school clubs and social groups, which combine to provide an atmosphere of intellectual and moral advancement. We do not read *Goss* to establish a property interest subject to constitutional protection in each of these separate components. (P. 985)

Potential for litigation exists in such individual sports as swimming, track, and possibly tennis. Consider the situation where an athlete refuses to participate in an event designated by the coach. In such a situation the coach's decision is often based on the notion that athletes should be deployed in a manner to gain as many points as possible for the team. The athlete's refusal, however, is based on the concern that following the coach's decision may reduce the athlete's opportunity to excel in his or her specialty, thereby reducing or eliminating the opportunity for an athletic scholarship. Assuming the issue was justiciable, how would a court rule? Does a partial answer to this dilemma lie in determining whether a sport is an "individual" or a "team" sport?

Courts have addressed the issue of academic requirements for participation in extracurricular activities. The West Virginia Supreme Court upheld a state requirement that students maintain a *C* average in order to participate in nonacademic extracurricular activities. Additionally, the court sustained a county board of education rule requiring students to receive passing grades in all classes in order to participate in nonacademic activities. See *Bailey* v. *Truby*, 321 S.E.2d 302 (W.Va. 1984).

What is your school system's policy regarding the restriction of students from participating in extracurricular activities?

B. Athletics

Exclusion or suspension from participation in athletics makes up the vast majority of court cases dealing with extracurricular activities. Rules barring married students, females, and handicapped students from participation in athletics are frequently challenged. Those barred generally allege that they have not received equal protection guaranteed under the Fourteenth Amendment or that the school conduct violates a federal statute.

1. Married Students

Cases dealing with married students barred from participating in athletics have often involved "star" athletes who claim they will be deprived of an opportunity to be considered for athletic scholarships. Those barred have also alleged that such rules infringe upon the fundamental right of marriage. Historically, courts had upheld rules barring married students from participating in athletics. However, beginning in the early 1970s courts have uniformly and consistently invalidated such rules.

Beeson v. Kiowa County School District RE-1

Colorado Court of Appeals, 1977
567 P.2d 801

RULAND, Judge

* * *

Plaintiff was a senior in high school, married, and the mother of a child at the time she initiated this action seeking to enjoin the school board from enforcing its policy so that she could participate on the girl's varsity basketball team. * * *

* * *

The facts pertinent to this review are not disputed. Plaintiff was a "star player" on the girls' varsity basketball team during her freshman year in high school. However, she married the following summer and a child was born to the married couple during her sophomore year. Plaintiff was aware of the policy at the time she married.

Plaintiff did not seek to participate on the varsity team during either her sophomore or junior years. Plaintiff sought, however, to rejoin the team for her senior year, but was precluded by the school policy from doing so. While she was allowed to practice with the team, she was not allowed to participate in interscholastic competition.

Plaintiff testified that by reason of her inability to compete on the varsity team during her senior year, she lost any opportunity for a college athletic scholarship. She expressed the belief that she would have been offered an athletic scholarship based on her previously demonstrated ability and on the fact that her sister had been offered such a scholarship at sometime in the past.

Various reasons were offered by the members of the school board as the basis for its policy. First and foremost, the board members felt that the policy discouraged teenagers from marrying until after their high school education was completed. On the other hand, some members felt that if a student did marry, that student must be encouraged to devote the time necessary to fulfill the resultant family responsibilities. In the view of these members, prohibiting participation in extracurricular activities was a means to that end. By the same reasoning, they felt that the additional family responsibility left time only for the pursuit of a basic education. As to this particular plaintiff, some members have expressed the opinion that it was necessary for her to spend as much time as possible with her minor child.

Some board members believed that the policy discouraged unwanted pregnancies. They were also concerned about the influence that a married student could have on other students in promoting a lack of discipline among the students participating in the extracurricular activity. Finally, various members were concerned about the liability the school district might incur if a married woman student participated in athletics and suffered injury while in the process of an undetected pregnancy.

During the course of the trial, there was no challenge to the good faith and concern of the school board in initially adopting this policy some 20 years ago and in maintaining it in effect at the time of plaintiff's request to play varsity basketball. Rather, plaintiff challenged the policy on the basis that it, in effect, punished her for exercising a fundamental right to marry, as well as on the basis that it infringed upon her fundamental right to obtain an education. She also complained that the policy deprived her of the potential opportunity to obtain a college education through the assistance of an athletic scholarship. In response to these contentions, the trial court determined that plaintiff had no fundamental right to marry because the consent of her parents was required at the time of her marriage, that plaintiff had no fundamental right to participate in extracurricular activities, as distinguished from the right to obtain a basic education, and that whether plaintiff could qualify for a college scholarship or whether she even intended to attend college was purely a matter of speculation. The court therefore concluded that the school board's policy was a reasonable regulation as requiring students to choose between the rights and responsibilities of students "subject to parental guidance and discipline." The court reasoned that "if such a regulation can be successfully challenged, then it is likely the authority of the school board would be almost totally destroyed because almost every regulation which is a condition on a student's right to participate would be a denial of equal protection."

We first emphasize that the issue on appeal is whether the school board's policy is valid in the context of plaintiff being a married student. Therefore, we do not consider the validity of a policy which would preclude plaintiff from participating in extracurricular activities because she was the mother of a young child, or whether a policy would be valid if it required married women to meet certain requirements in order to assure the board that no injuries would result from an undetected pregnancy. The additional considerations inherent in such policies are irrelevant here because the policy at issue excluded plaintiff from participating in extracurricular activities based solely on the fact that she was married.

According to § 14–12–101, C.R.S. 1973, "[i]t is the declared public policy of this state . . . to promote and foster the marriage relationship. . . ." We are therefore compelled to hold that the creation of a "marriage relationship" is a fundamental right in this jurisdiction. * * *

Nor is this fundamental right vitiated by the fact that plaintiff needed parental consent to enter her marriage. Plaintiff's marriage was entered into in compliance with § 14–2–106, C.R.S. 1973, of the Uniform Marriage Act. That Act has as one of its purposes "to strengthen and preserve the integrity of marriage and to safeguard meaningful family relationships." * * * [T]he General Assembly has obviously determined that this purpose is fulfilled, if as here, parental consent for plaintiff's marriage is first obtained. Hence, it is clear that a board policy which discriminates against those who exercise that right violates the equal protection clause of the Fourteenth Amendment, unless there exists a compelling interest which justifies that discrimination. * * *

The State, acting through the General Assembly, is obligated to provide a "thorough and uniform system of free public school throughout the state, wherein all residents of the state, between the ages of six and twenty-one years may be educated gratuitously." * * * The school district acts as a political subdivision of the State for that purpose. * * * As such it is authorized to adopt policies "not inconsistent with law, which may relate to the study, discipline, conduct, safety and welfare of all pupils." * * * However, we find only one instance wherein the General Assembly has felt compelled to address the issue of marriage in the context of the public schools, and that comes in the form of a prohibition against employment based upon marital status. * * * Hence, we find no specific legislative support for a policy which discriminates against married students.

Looking then to the reasons offered by the school board, we conclude that the acknowledged intent to discourage eligible persons from marrying obviously contravenes the declared public policy of this State "to promote and foster the marriage relationship." * * * Illustrative of the inhibiting effect of the policy is evidence in the record indicating that another star basketball player in the same school district who had fathered a child during his senior year remained eligible for interscholastic competition because he did not marry the mother until after his graduation.

This impact of the policy upon the marriage relationship requires us to consider whether the discrimination created by the board's policy is justified by the need to require married students to focus on their basic education and their family responsibilities by excluding them from extracurricular activities. We find no support for the discrimination here. The focus on basic education can be supplied by a board policy which establishes academic requirements for both married and unmarried students to be eligible for extracurricular activities. On the other hand, the fulfillment of family responsibilities may, in many cases, depend upon further education at the college level, and depriving students of the opportunity to earn a college athletic scholarship, or to participate in extracurricular activities to broaden their general background, could close the door to any opportunity to obtain that education. * * *

Finally, we must evaluate the board's contention that married students who participate in extracurricular activities may tend to promote a lack of discipline among the other students and may not be dependable because of their family responsibility. Since the policy has been in effect for approximately 20 years, we understand why no incidents were cited by the board where these problems have arisen. On the other hand, we are unable to perceive why the same policies which govern the discipline and dependability of unmarried students who participate in extracurricular activities would not serve to resolve any such problems. At least we cannot characterize this potential problem, standing alone, as sufficient justification for discrimination against the fundamental right to marry.
* * *

Accordingly, the judgment of the district court is reversed and the cause remanded with directions to enter judgment declaring the board's policy invalid as a denial of equal protection under the Fourteenth Amendment.

Notes and Questions

May a divorced student be barred from engaging in extracurricular activities? See *Romans* v. *Crenshaw*, 354 F. Supp. 868 (Tex. 1972), which upheld a divorced student's right to engage in such activities.

Does your state have a statutory provision pertaining to married students participating in extracurricular activities? What are your local school system's rules or policies regarding married students engaging in such activities?

2. Female Participation

Historically, there has been both de facto and de jure segregation of male and female public school students. In some school systems entire schools have been segregated on the basis of sex. More common, however, has been the separation of the sexes in certain classes and in interscholastic athletic participation. A flagrant example has been the routine assignment of girls to home economics classes and boys to "shop" courses. Opportunities for females in athletic competition were limited, and the stereotypic role for a female was often that of cheerleader, flag girl, or pom-pom girl.

Many female students and their parents considered such treatment, especially in the limited opportunity for athletic competition, to be in violation of the equal protection provision of the Fourteenth Amendment and a form of sex discrimination. Many courts have agreed with this contention, and although Title IX addresses this issue, litigation pertaining to female participation in athletic programs has not abated. *Leffel* **v.** *Wisconsin Interscholastic Athletic Association* represents an example of the post-Title IX cases brought before the courts.

Leffel v. Wisconsin Interscholastic Athletic Association

United States District Court, Eastern District of Wisconsin, 1978
444 F. Supp. 1117

MYRON L. GORDON, District Judge.

*   *   *

In these actions, the plaintiffs seek a declaration that a provision of the constitution of the Wisconsin Interscholastic Athletic Association (WIAA) which limits coeducational interscholastic activities violates the equal protection clause of the fourteenth amendment to the United States Constitution. They also seek a permanent injunction enjoining its enforcement.   *   *   *

The following facts are undisputed. In case no. 75–C–174, the named plaintiffs, female students at De Pere High School, were denied permission to qualify for competition with male students on the high school interscholastic varsity baseball team. The high school offered no separate female team for interscholastic competition. In case no. 73–C–269, the named plaintiffs, female students at Washington High School, were denied permission to qualify for competition with male students on the high school's interscholastic varsity swim team and tennis team. The school sponsored a girls' swim team but no girls' tennis team.

In both cases, the school officials excluded the plaintiffs from trying out for the teams based on the following provision of the WIAA constitution:

> "The Board of Control shall prohibit all types of interscholastic activity involving boys and girls competing with or against each other."

The WIAA is a voluntary, unincorporated, nonprofit organization whose purpose is to organize, develop, direct, and control interscholastic athletic programs for students in the public high schools of Wisconsin. Under the organization's constitution, member schools agree to conduct their athletic program according to the constitution, by-laws and rules of eligibility of the organization. Since most of the state's public high schools and junior high schools were members of the organization at the time these actions were commenced, interscholastic competition with most Wisconsin public high schools depended upon compliance with the prohibition on coeducational competition.

During the pendency of these actions, Title IX of the Education Amendments of 1972 * * * (Title IX) was enacted. Title IX prohibits sex discrimination in any educational program receiving federal funds. The regulations promulgated by the Department of Health, Education and Welfare pursuant to 20 U.S.C. § 1682 include specific provisions relating to sex discrimination in athletics. 45 C.F.R. § 86.41(a) generally prohibits separate athletic programs based on sex, but § 86.41(b) permits separate teams for members of each sex where selection for such teams is based on competitive skills or the activity involved is a contact sport. The same section also provides that "where a recipient [educational institution] operates or sponsors a team in a particular sport for members of one sex but operates or sponsors no such team for members of the other sex, and athletic opportunities for members of that sex have previously been limited, members of the excluded sex must be allowed to try out for the team offered unless the sport involved is a contact sport."

After these actions were commenced, and in response to Title IX and the corresponding regulations, the WIAA amended the challenged provision of its constitution to read as follows:

"The Board of Control shall prohibit all types of interscholastic activity involving boys and girls competing with or against each other *except (a) as prescribed by state and federal law and (b) as determined by Board of Control interpretations of such law.*"(emphasis added)

The defendants argue that their rule is in full compliance with Title IX and its corresponding regulations. Their position is that Title IX encompasses all that is required by federal law, including the equal protection clause of the fourteenth amendment, thereby insulating their rule from constitutional challenge. The defendants urge that a constitutional attack cannot be waged against the WIAA rule until Title IX itself is determined to be unconstitutional.

In my opinion, the defendants' argument is meritless. The enactment of Title IX did not remove the problem of sex discrimination from constitutional concern; congressional enactments cannot preempt provisions of the Constitution. Moreover, Title IX merely created an administrative remedy, subject to judicial review, to enforce the prohibition of sex discrimination in educational programs receiving federal financial assistance. It does not displace the plaintiffs' right to enforce the commands of the fourteenth amendment through an action under 42 U.S.C. § 1983. * * *

Originally, the plaintiffs argued that the WIAA rule was unconstitutional on its face and as applied. The amended rule, however, permits coeducational athletic activity to the extent required by federal law. The claim of facial unconstitutionality is therefore no longer tenable, but the claim of unconstitutional application remains.

In the complaints filed in these cases, the plaintiffs sought a declaration that the WIAA rule "deprives the plaintiffs and the class they represent of their constitutional rights to be free from state establishment and enforcement of sex-based exclusions unrelated to merit" and an injunction enjoining any such rule or practice. The requested declaration was considerably broader than the declaration sought in the present motion.

The plaintiffs now seek summary judgment declaring that the challenged rule, as applied, deprives the plaintiffs and their class of equal protection under any of the following circumstances:

(1) where their school does not provide a girls' team in a particular sport;

(2) where the girls' team in a particular sport at their school does not provide a program comparable to that maintained for boys;

(3) where the level of competition for the boys' team in a particular sport is higher than the level of competition for the corresponding girls' team.

The plaintiffs also seek a permanent injunction enjoining the defendants from enforcing the rule under such circumstances.

From the manner in which the plaintiffs have narrowed their demand for relief, it is apparent that they do not question whether separate teams for boys and girls, with comparable support and funding, are permissible under the fourteenth amendment. Several other courts have dealt with this problem and have approved of the concept of "separate but equal" teams for male and female high school students. * * *

With respect to "noncontact" sports, the defendants do not dispute that the plaintiffs would be denied equal protection of the laws under the first two circumstances listed above. They argue, however, that Title IX permits different treatment of male and female students insofar as "contact" sports are concerned. The defendants disagree that the plaintiffs have a valid constitutional grievance under the third circumstance.

The defendants' argument that Title IX permits different treatment of boys and girls insofar as "contact" sports are concerned must be rejected in view of my determination that in this case the defendants' rule and policies must be measured against the fourteenth amendment, rather than Title IX.

In its present posture, the case is therefore reduced to the following two issues: First, have the defendants violated the equal protection clause by denying female high school students the opportunity to qualify for a position on a boys' varsity interscholastic team engaging in a contact sport where no separate team is provided for girls, or where the separate team provided does not have a comparable program? Secondly, as to both contact and noncontact sports, does the equal protection clause of the fourteenth amendment require that female high school students be permitted to attempt to qualify for a position on a boys' varsity interscholastic team where the boys' team has a higher level of competition than the corresponding girls' team? The second issue will be addressed first.

There is no dispute that the WIAA rule in question and the defendants' application of the rule is an intentional discrimination, i.e., for what they deem to be legitimate purposes, the defendants intentionally treat boy and girl athletes differently. Since an intentional discrimination is involved, the fourteenth amendment's equal protection clause is implicated. * * *

However, there are no allegations in the instant complaints that the the defendants have intentionally imposed different levels of competition on boys and girls. Any such differences arise from the abilities of the team members themselves. Thus, the plaintiffs' claim for declaratory and injunctive relief cannot encompass the concept of equal levels of competition.

The governmental objective posited to the defendants is the prevention of injury to female athletes. The defendants argue that "anatomical and physiological differences between boys and girls" and "differences in athletic abilities" justify the prohibition of coeducational teams in contact sports. The defendants offer affidavits to support the proposition that anatomical and physiological differences between boys and girls will leave girls exposed to unreasonable risk of injury if they were to compete with or against boys.

The plaintiffs do not dispute that the defendants' stated objectives are legitimate, but they argue that the correlation between gender and athletic ability is too weak to withstand equal protection scrutiny. Even if the defendants' generalizations are assumed to be true, I nevertheless find that the exclusion of girls from all contact sports in order to protect female high school athletes from an unreasonable risk of injury is not fairly or substantially related to a justifiable governmental objective in the context of the fourteenth amendment.

The defendant advances no governmental objective whatsoever to justify providing boys with the opportunity to participate in varsity inter-scholastic competition in contact sports while *absolutely* denying the same opportunity to girls. It is doubtful that any such legitimate governmental objective exists. * * * The defendants do not argue that girls will be exposed to an unreasonable risk of injury in a separate girls' athletic pro-gram for contact sports; they argue that girls will be exposed to an un-reasonable risk of injury if allowed to compete on boys teams. However, coeducational teams are only one possible remedy for the defendants' con-stitutional violation. The defendants have the other two alternatives of (1) dropping all varsity interscholastic competition, and (2) establishing sepa-rate girls' teams for contact sports. * * * As noted previously, the demand for relief of the plaintiffs at bar would be met by the establishment of separate girls' teams with a comparable program; thus, I need not decide whether the concept of separate girls' teams presents a problem of equal protection.

The state public schools are under no constitutional compulsion to provide interscholastic competition in any sport, but once they choose to do so, this educational opportunity must be provided to all on equal terms. * * * Although the plaintiffs do not have a constitutional right to compete on boys' teams in contact or noncontact sports, the defendants may not afford an educational opportunity to boys that is denied to girls.

It should be noted, however, that a denial of equal protection ex-ists only where members of the plaintiff class request and are denied the opportunity to participate in a particular varsity interscholastic sport. * * *

* * *

It is declared that the defendants' exclusion of the plaintiffs and the class they represent from participation in a varsity interscholastic athletic program in a particular sport where such a program is provided for male students violates the equal protection clause of the fourteenth amendment.

The defendants are hereby permanently enjoined from excluding the plaintiffs and the class they represent from participation in a varsity interscholastic athletic program in a particular sport where such a program is provided for male students.

* * *

Notes

Section 86.41, Athletics, of the implementing regulations for Title IX stipulates as follows:

Athletics.

(a) General. No person shall, on the basis of sex, be excluded from participation in, be denied the benefits of, be treated differently from one another or otherwise be discriminated against in any interscholastic, intercollegiate, club or intramural athletics offered by a recipient, and no recipient shall provide any such athletics separately on such basis.

(b) Separate teams. Notwithstanding the requirements of paragraph (a) of this section, a recipient may operate or sponsor separate teams for members of each sex where selection for such teams is based upon competitive skill or the activity involved is a contact sport. However, where a recipient operates or sponsors a team in a particular sport for members of one sex but operates or sponsors no such team for members of the other sex, and athletic opportunities for members of that sex have previously been limited, members of the excluded sex must be allowed to try out for the team offered unless the sport involved is a contact sport. For the purposes of this part, contact sports include boxing, wrestling, rugby, ice hockey, football, basketball, and other sports the purpose of major activity of which involves bodily contact.

(c) Equal opportunity. A recipient which operates or sponsors interscholastic, intercollegiate, club or intramural athletics shall provide equal athletic opportunity for members of both sexes. In determining whether equal opportunities are available the Director will consider, among other factors:

    (1) Whether the selection of sports and levels of competition effectively accommodate the interests and abilities of members of both sexes;
    (2) The provision of equipment and supplies;
    (3) Scheduling of games and practice time;
    (4) Travel and per diem allowance;
    (5) Opportunity to receive coaching and academic tutoring;
    (6) Assignment and compensation of coaches and tutors;
    (7) Provision of locker rooms, practice and competitive facilities;
    (8) Provision of medical and training facilities and services;
    (9) Provision of housing and dining facilities and services;
  (10) Publicity.

Unequal aggregate expenditures for members of each sex or unequal expenditures for male and female teams if a recipient operates or sponsors separate teams will not constitute non-compliance with this section, but the Director may consider the failure to provide necessary funds for teams for one sex in assessing equality of opportunity for members of each sex.

(d) Adjustment period. A recipient which operates or sponsors interscholastic, intercollegiate, club or intramural athletics at the elementary school level shall comply fully with this section as expeditiously as possible but in no event later than one year from the effective date of this regulation. A recipient which operates or sponsors interscholastic, intercollegiate, club or intramural athletics at the secondary or post-secondary school level shall comply fully with this section as expeditiously as possible but in no event later than three years from the effective date of this regulation. 45 C.F.R. § 86.41.*

Rules for girls' basketball, which require split court play, six rather than five players, and permit only forwards to shoot, are not unconstitutional according to *Cape* v. *Tennessee Secondary School Athletic Association*, 563 F.2d 793 (6th Cir. 1977).

3. Participation of Handicapped Students

A handicapped student's desire to participate in athletics requires the balancing of the student's and the school system's interest. The student may wish to have the most well-rounded school experience possible; yet, the school has the responsibility of protecting the physical well-being of the student. Most significant in these cases is the determination of possible injury to the handicapped student if he or she is allowed to participate in interscholastic athletics.

Kampmeier v. Nyquist

United States Court of Appeals, Second Circuit, 1977
553 F.2d 296

LUMBARD, Circuit Judge:

Two junior high school students, each with vision in only one eye, and their parents, appeal from an order by Judge Burke in the Western District of New York denying their motion for a preliminary injunction against public school authorities in Pittsford and Canandaigua, New York, who have refused to allow the students to participate in contact sports at school. Plaintiffs contend that the school system's prohibition on participation by one-eyed students in contact sports violates section 504 of the Rehabilitation Act of 1973, 29 U.S.C. § 794, and also deprives them of their fourteenth amendment right to equal protection of the law. Having considered the possible irreparable consequences that may flow from

*See appendix D for edited implementing regulations for Title IX of the Education Amendments of 1972.

whichever decision the court should choose to make, we conclude that the appellants have not made a sufficient factual showing of likely success of the merits to warrant preliminary relief. Accordingly, we affirm the order of the district court.

In their complaint filed on April 14, 1976, plaintiffs alleged the following: Margaret Kampmeier has a congenital cataract in one eye. As of the beginning of her seventh-grade year in 1975, she was one of the best athletes in her class. Her parents have provided her with protective glasses which have industrial quality safety lenses, wire mesh side shields, and extended ear pieces. The Kampmeiers have also announced their willingness to release the school and its employees from liability for any athletics injury to Margaret's good eye. Steven Genecco is a grade ahead of Margaret. He has been virtually blind in one eye since an injury at age six. Prior to the 1975–76 school year, he had been allowed to participate in all school sports. During 1975 he participated in interscholastic basketball and a community association football league as well as the regular school physical education program. On recommendation by a school physician, each child has now been prohibited from participating in any contact sports at school, solely because of lack of vision in one eye.

In response to plaintiffs' motion for a preliminary injunction, the defendants submitted affidavits explaining that under regulations promulgated by the New York State Commissioner of Education, * * * approval from the school medical officer is required before any student may be allowed to participate in interscholastic athletics. Pamphlets distributed to school officials by the Commissioner list blindness in one eye as a disqualifying condition for participation in contact sports, but not noncontact sports. The lists of disqualifications are advisory only: "[t]hese guidelines . . . are only guidelines and are not absolute mandates for the school physician." "Some of the disqualifying conditions listed are subject to evaluation by the responsible physician with respect to anticipated risks, the otherwise athletic fitness of the candidate, special protective preventive measures that might be utilized, and the nature of the supervisory control." * * *

Letters from physicians who had examined the children were submitted. Their opinions were divided.

* * *

As we read § 504, however, exclusion of handicapped children from a school activity is not improper if there exists a substantial justification for the school's policy. Section 504 prohibits only the exclusion of handicapped persons who are "otherwise qualified." Here, the defendants have relief on medical opinion that children with sight in only one eye are not qualified to play in contact sports because of the high risk of eye injury. The plaintiffs have presented little evidence—medical, statistical, or otherwise—which would cast doubt on the substantiality of this rationale. On the record before us, they have not made a clear showing of probable success on the merits.

Both sides have demonstrated the possibility of irreparable injury. On the one hand, athletics play an important part in the life and growth of teenage children, * * * and the plaintiffs are being deprived of the freedom to participate in sports of their choice. On the other hand, public school officials have a parens patriae interest in protecting the well-being of their students; the defendants, relying on medical opinion, are concerned about the risk of injury to a child's one good eye. In view of the host of noncontact sports which remain open to the plaintiffs, we conclude that the balance of hardships does not tip decidedly in their favor.

The motion for a preliminary injunction was properly denied.

Judgment affirmed.

Notes and Questions

Two federal laws often serve as the basis for a lawsuit involving handicapped students. Section 504 of the Rehabilitation Act of 1973 is mentioned in **Kampmeier.** The other is the Education for All Handicapped Children Act of 1975—Public Law 94-142.

Title IX has been responsible for increased participation of females in interscholastic athletics. Do you think Section 504 of the Rehabilitation Act of 1973 and Public Law 94-142 will provide an impetus for the increased participation of handicapped students, perhaps by requiring separate teams, in interscholastic athletics?

What is your local school system's policy regarding the participation of handicapped students in athletics?

IX. School Punishment for Out-of-School Offenses

Out-of-school conduct of students may have an impact on the overall well-being of the school. When there is a problem with out-of-school conduct, school authorities must reconcile their control of student conduct necessary for the orderly operation of the school with their obligation to comply with the standards of constitutionality and reasonableness required by the judiciary to ensure that students receive just treatment.

Several court decisions have addressed issues dealing with noncriminal student off-campus activity. In one case it was alleged that two students were assaulted by a group of others while they were all walking home after school. Although the court agreed that school authorities may punish students for out-of-school physical abuse directed at other students, punishment such as expulsion may not be based on unsigned and unidentified statements by student witnesses. See *Tibbs* v. *Board of Education of the Township of Franklin*, 114 N.J. Super. 287, 276 A.2d 165 (1971).

Parking an automobile off campus contrary to school rules was an issue in *McLean Independent School District* v. *Andrews*, 333 S.W.2d 886 (Tex. Civ. App. 1960). A student's suspension for breaking the school rules was upheld, primarily on the basis of promoting the safety of student pedestrians on the streets adjacent to the school during noon recess. The court noted, however, that the rule in question might provide future complications as students parked at more remote distances from the campus.

An Ohio appellate court, in *McNaughton* v. *Circleville Board of Education*, 46 Ohio Misc. 12, 345 N.E.2d 649, 75 Ohio Op.2d 47 (Ohio C.P. 1974), upheld the suspension from school and from participation in athletic activities of students who held an out-of-school initiation and hazing of new members of an officially recognized high school club. The club's advisor had not been notified nor was he present at the initiation, which occurred at the home of one of the offending students. Initiates were struck with belts, forced to eat onions, and required to rub tabasco sauce on the faces of fellow initiates.

Cases have addressed the dismissal of students from school chapters of the National Honor Society owing to their violation of a rule against the use of alcohol. In two such cases, *Warren* v. *National Association of Secondary School Principals*, 375 F. Supp. 1043 (Tex. 1974) and *Ector County Independent School District* v. *Hopkins*, 518 S.W.2d 576 (Tex. Civ. App. 1975), the violative drinking took place off campus. These courts stressed that students facing dismissal from an honor society as a result of their drinking had to be afforded appropriate due process.

Courts have held that public school students' out-of-school criminal conduct may be subject to school disciplinary hearings, although as a practical matter the particular kind of school response will be influenced by the nature and seriousness of the criminal charges. A non-school-related speeding charge, for instance, might be ignored by authorities, while a murder or rape charge would not be.

R.R. v. *Board of Education of the Shore Regional High School District*, 109 N.J. Super. 337, 263 A.2d 180 (1970) addressed the question of whether public school officials can deprive a student of his or her right to attend school because of criminal acts committed off school grounds. In this instance, a fifteen-year-old boy stabbed a girl during an altercation in a neighbor's house after the boy had returned home at the end of a school day. This court concluded that officials do have the right to expel or suspend students for out-of-school activities when it is reasonably necessary either for the transgressing student's physical or emotional safety and well-being or for the safety and well-being of other students, teachers, or public school property. Despite this conclusion, the court ordered the school to readmit the student because of due process violations.

A California court upheld the suspension of students involved in such offenses as kidnapping, rape, assault with a bumper jack, assault resulting in the death of a boy whose head struck a sidewalk curb, carrying a concealed weapon, and disturbing the peace. The California court made no attempt to distinguish between offenses that occurred on campus and those that occurred off campus. See *S. v. Board of Education, San Francisco Unified School District*, 20 Cal. App. 3d 83, 97 Cal. Rptr. 422 (1971).

A federal district court in *Caldwell* v. *Cannady*, 340 F. Supp. 835 (Tex. 1972) upheld the reasonableness of a local school board policy mandating the expulsion of any student possessing, using, or selling dangerous or narcotic drugs. In this instance students were disciplined after they were arrested when marijuana was found in their automobile in a series of incidents at night and away from school.

Authority of school officials to discipline a student acquitted of out-of-school reckless driving charges was addressed by the Supreme Court of Wyoming in *Clements* v. *Board of Trustees of the Sheridan County School District No. 2*, 585 P.2d 197 (Wyo. 1978). The student had been charged with reckless driving for purposely impeding the progress of a school bus. The court held that school authorities may discipline pupils for out-of-school conduct having a direct and immediate effect on the discipline or general welfare of the school.

Constitutional questions regarding double jeopardy and self-incrimination have been raised in the cases ruling on the legality of actions taken by public school officials in response to charges of out-of-school criminal violations against students. Courts have consistently held that both school sanctions and judicial sanctions are permitted without violating the Fifth Amendment prohibition against double jeopardy. They maintain that school hearings and criminal proceedings have different purposes, with school responses being civil or remedial while judicial responses are punitive. Although acknowledging that school discipline has punitive effects, the courts contend that its underlying purpose is the protection of the school environment.

Courts have also held that public school students' out-of-school criminal conduct properly may be the subject of school disciplinary hearings without violating Fifth Amendment rights against compulsory self-incrimination. Students may not be required to testify in these proceedings, and if students' rights are infringed upon in the hearings, courts reason, the students may then ask for a judicial review of the proceedings.

Analysis reveals that the judiciary supports the rationale that students may be subject to school discipline, including suspension or expulsion, if their out-of-school conduct threatens the efficient operation of the school. Generally the courts recognize that the authority to make and enforce policies designed to protect the safety and welfare of students is a reasonable and necessary exercise of the power invested in local school boards. Nevertheless, courts will support the use of that authority over out-of-school criminal conduct only when they perceive the conduct as having a direct and substantial impact on the school and its programs.

When the out-of-school conduct has involved physical violence or otherwise threatened the safety or well-being of students, the judiciary has not been concerned with whether the conduct occurred out of school or in school. Decisions indicate that the test of the public school's authority to control student conduct is not the time or place of the conduct, but rather its effect on the morale and efficiency of the school. It may be concluded that the nature and seriousness of the conduct and its potential impact on the public school and its programs are more important than where the conduct occurred.

teachers
and the law

INTRODUCTION

In recent years teachers have increasingly employed the courts to remedy treatment by school authorities with which they disagreed. In many instances personnel practices that had become institutionalized through custom have been challenged as being discriminatory, violative of statutory or constitutional provisions, or unfair. Although teachers have not always been successful in actions brought before the judiciary, their willingness to employ the courts for a redress of grievances has produced a climate in which public school administrators have become more sensitive to the necessity of treating teachers in a legally defensible manner.

This chapter will focus on issues dealing with nonrenewal and dismissal; freedom of expression; academic freedom; dress and grooming; the teacher as an exemplar; discrimination based on sex, race, or age; reduction in force; teacher bargaining; and the political rights of teachers.

I. Nonrenewal and Dismissal

Over the years the development of state statutory provisions and the existence of a sizable body of case law have provided teachers with safeguards against arbitrary dismissal. Although school administrators have the primary task of evaluating teachers and determining their fitness, this task must be done in accordance with state statutory provisions and in the light of constitutional protections.

According to a United States Supreme Court decision, **Board of Regents of State Colleges v. Roth,** a nontenured teacher need not be given reasons for nonrenewal unless the nonrenewal deprived the teacher of a "liberty" interest or if there was a "property" interest in continued employment. Any statement regarding the reason for the nonrenewal could result in the teacher's requesting a due process hearing.

Depending on a state's statutory provisions, dismissal of a tenured teacher or one under a continuing contract must be in conformance with the state law. State provisions usually contain grounds for dismissal such as nonperformance of duty, incompetency, insubordination, conviction of crimes involving moral turpitude, failure to comply with reasonable orders, violation of contract provisions or local rules or regulations, persistent failure or refusal to maintain orderly discipline of students, and revocation of the teaching certificate. Additionally, all of the procedural aspects of the hearing process provided by state statute must be afforded the teacher. These often include the following requirements: proper notice, containing charges and the names and nature of the testimony of witnesses and stating the time and place of the hearing; compulsory process or subpoena requiring the attendance of witnesses and the production of relevant papers and documents; a fair hearing; and an opportunity for appeal.

A. Nonrenewal of Untenured Teacher

Board of Regents of State Colleges v. Roth

Supreme Court of the United States, 1972
408 U.S. 564

MR. JUSTICE STEWART delivered the opinion of the Court.

In 1968 the respondent, David Roth, was hired for his first teaching job as assistant professor of political science at Wisconsin State University-

Oshkosh. He was hired for a fixed term of one academic year. The notice of his faculty appointment specified that his employment would begin on September 1, 1968, and would end on June 30, 1969. The respondent completed that term. But he was informed that he would not be rehired for the next academic year.

The respondent had no tenure rights to continued employment. Under Wisconsin statutory law a state university teacher can acquire tenure as a "permanent" employee only after four years of year-to-year employment. Having acquired tenure, a teacher is entitled to continued employment "during efficiency and good behavior." A relatively new teacher without tenure, however, is under Wisconsin law entitled to nothing beyond his one-year appointment. There are no statutory or administrative standards defining eligibility for re-employment. State law thus clearly leaves the decision whether to rehire a nontenured teacher for another year to the unfettered discretion of university officials.

The procedural protection afforded a Wisconsin State University teacher before he is separated from the University corresponds to his job security. As a matter of statutory law, a tenured teacher cannot be "discharged except for cause upon written charges" and pursuant to certain procedures. A nontenured teacher, similarly, is protected to some extent *during* his one-year term. Rules promulgated by the Board of Regents provide that a nontenured teacher "dismissed" before the end of the year may have some opportunity for review of the "dismissal." But the Rules provide no real protection for a nontenured teacher who simply is not re-employed for the next year. He must be informed by February 1 "concerning retention or non-retention for the ensuing year." But "no reason for non-retention need be given. No review or appeal is provided in such case."

In conformance with these Rules, the President of Wisconsin State University-Oshkosh informed the respondent before February 1, 1969, that he would not be rehired for the 1969–1970 academic year. He gave the respondent no reason for the decision and no opportunity to challenge it at any sort of hearing.

The respondent then brought this action in Federal District Court alleging that the decision not to rehire him for the next year infringed his Fourteenth Amendment rights. He attacked the decision both in substance and procedure. First, he alleged that the true reason for the decision was to punish him for certain statements critical of the University administration, and that it therefore violated his right to freedom of speech. Second, he alleged that the failure of University officials to give him notice of any reason for nonretention and an opportunity for a hearing violated his right to procedural due process of law.

The District Court granted summary judgment for the respondent on the procedural issue, ordering the University officials to provide him with reasons and a hearing.   * * *   The Court of Appeals, with one judge dissenting, affirmed this partial summary judgment.   * * *   We granted certiorari.   * * *   The only question presented to us at this stage in the case is whether the respondent had a constitutional right to a statement of reasons and a hearing on the University's decision not to rehire him for another year. We hold that he did not.

The requirements of procedural due process apply only to the deprivation of interests encompassed by the Fourteenth Amendment's protection of liberty and property. When protected interests are implicated, the right to some kind of prior hearing is paramount. But the range of interests protected by procedural due process is not infinite.

The District Court decided that procedural due process guarantees apply in this case by assessing and balancing the weights of the particular interests involved. It concluded that the respondent's interest in re-employment at Wisconsin State University-Oshkosh outweighed the University's interest in denying him re-employment summarily.   * * *   Undeniably, the respondent's re-employment prospects were of major concern to him—concern that we surely cannot say was insignificant. And a weighing process has long been a part of any determination of the *form* of hearing required in particular situations by procedural due process. But, to determine whether due process requirements apply in the first place, we must look not to the "weight" but to the *nature* of the interest at stake.   * * *   We must look to see if the interest is within the Fourteenth Amendment's protection of liberty and property.

"Liberty" and "property" are broad and majestic terms. They are among the "[g]reat [constitutional] concepts . . . purposely left to gather meaning from experience . . . [T]hey relate to the whole domain of social and economic fact, and the statesmen who founded this Nation knew too well that only a stagnant society remains unchanged."   * * *   For that reason, the Court has fully and finally rejected the wooden distinction between "rights" and "privileges" that once seemed to govern the applicability of procedural due process rights. The Court has also made clear that the property interests protected by procedural due process extend well beyond actual ownership of real estate, chattels, or money. By the same token, the Court has required due process protection for deprivations of liberty beyond the sort of formal constraints imposed by the criminal process.

Yet, while the Court has eschewed rigid or formalistic limitations on the protection of procedural due process, it has at the same time observed certain boundaries. For the words "liberty" and "property" in the Due Process Clause of the Fourteenth Amendment must be given some meaning.

"While this Court has not attempted to define with exactness the liberty . . . guaranteed [by the Fourteenth Amendment], the term has received much consideration and some of the included things have been definitely stated. Without doubt, it denotes not merely freedom from bodily restraint but also the right of the individual to contract, to engage in any of the common occupations of life, to acquire useful knowledge, to marry, establish a home and bring up children, to worship God according to the dictates of his own conscience, and generally to enjoy those privileges long recognized . . . as essential to the orderly pursuit of happiness by free men." * * * In a Constitution for a free people, there can be no doubt that the meaning of "liberty" must be broad indeed. * * *

There might be cases in which a State refused to reemploy a person under such circumstances that interests in liberty would be implicated. But this is not such a case.

The State, in declining to rehire the respondent, did not make any charge against him that might seriously damage his standing and associations in his community. It did not base the nonrenewal of his contract on a charge, for example, that he had been guilty of dishonesty, or immorality. Had it done so, this would be a different case. For "[w]here a person's good name, reputation, honor, or integrity is at stake because of what the government is doing to him, notice and an opportunity to be heard are essential." * * * In such a case, due process would accord an opportunity to refute the charge before University officials. In the present case, however, there is no suggestion whatever that the respondent's "good name, reputation, honor, or integrity" is at stake.

Similarly, there is no suggestion that the State, in declining to reemploy the respondent, imposed on him a stigma or other disability that foreclosed his freedom to take advantage of other employment opportunities. The State, for example, did not invoke any regulations to bar the respondent from all other public employment in state universities. Had it done so, this, again, would be a different case. * * *

To be sure, the respondent has alleged that the nonrenewal of his contract was based on his exercise of his right to freedom of speech. But this allegation is not now before us. The District Court stayed proceedings on this issue, and the respondent has yet to prove that the decision not to rehire him was, in fact, based on his free speech activities.

Hence, on the record before us, all that clearly appears is that the respondent was not rehired for one year at one university. It stretches the concept too far to suggest that a person is deprived of "liberty" when he simply is not rehired in one job but remains as free as before to seek another. * * *

The Fourteenth Amendment's procedural protection of property is a safeguard of the security of interests that a person has already acquired in specific benefits. These interests—property interests—may take many forms.

Thus, the Court has held that a person receiving welfare benefits under statutory and administrative standards defining eligibility for them has an interest in continued receipt of those benefits that is safeguarded by procedural due process. * * * Similarly, in the area of public employment, the Court has held that a public college professor dismissed from an office held under tenure provisions * * * and college professors and staff members dismissed during the terms of their contracts * * * have interests in continued employment that are safeguarded by due process. Only last year, the Court held that this principle "proscribing summary dismissal from public employment without hearing or inquiry required by due process" also applied to a teacher recently hired without tenure or a formal contract, but nonetheless with a clearly implied promise of continued employment. * * *

Certain attributes of "property" interests protected by procedural due process emerge from these decisions. To have a property interest in a benefit, a person clearly must have more than an abstract need or desire for it. He must have more than a unilateral expectation of it. He must, instead, have a legitimate claim of entitlement to it. It is a purpose of the ancient institution of property to protect those claims upon which people rely in their daily lives, reliance that must not be arbitrarily undermined. It is a purpose of the constitutional right to a hearing to provide an opportunity for a person to vindicate those claims.

Property interests, of course, are not created by the Constitution. Rather, they are created and their dimensions are defined by existing rules or understandings that stem from an independent source such as state law—rules or understandings that secure certain benefits and that support claims of entitlement to those benefits. Thus, the welfare recipients * * * had a claim of entitlement to welfare payments that was grounded in the statute defining eligibility for them. The recipients had not yet shown that they were, in fact, within the statutory terms of eligibility. But we held that they had a right to a hearing at which they might attempt to do so.

Just as the welfare recipients' "property" interest in welfare payments was created and defined by statutory terms, so the respondent's "property" interest in employment at Wisconsin State University-Oshkosh was created and defined by the terms of his appointment. Those terms secured his interest in employment up to June 30, 1969. But the important fact in this case is that they specifically provided that the respondent's employment was to terminate on June 30. They did not provide for contract renewal absent "sufficient cause." Indeed, they made no provision for renewal whatsoever.

Thus, the terms of the respondent's appointment secured absolutely no interest in re-employment for the next year. They supported absolutely no possible claim of entitlement to re-employment. Nor, significantly, was there any state statute or University rule or policy that secured his interest in re-employment or that created any legitimate claim to it. In these circumstances, the respondent surely had an abstract concern in being rehired, but he did not have a *property* interest sufficient to require the University authorities to give him a hearing when they declined to renew his contract of employment.

Our analysis of the respondent's constitutional rights in this case in no way indicates a view that an opportunity for a hearing or a statement of reasons for nonretention would, or would not, be appropriate or wise in public colleges and universities. For it is a written Constitution that we apply. Our role is confined to interpretation of that Constitution.

We must conclude that the summary judgment for the respondent should not have been granted, since the respondent has not shown that he was deprived of liberty or property protected by the Fourteenth Amendment. The judgment of the Court of Appeals, accordingly, is reversed and the case is remanded for further proceedings consistent with this opinion.

It is so ordered.

Notes and Questions

Roth was a five-to-three decision. In his dissent, Justice Douglas argued that:

> . . . Nonrenewal of a teacher's contract is tantamount in effect to a dismissal and the consequences may be enormous. Nonrenewal can be a blemish that turns into a permanent scar and effectively limits any chance the teacher has of being rehired as a teacher, at least in his State.

Do you agree with his assessment?

Another United States Supreme Court decision dealt with an issue that may have significance in states without tenure statutes. In that decision the Court held that if a teacher had de facto tenure—an expectation of continued employment after many years of satisfactory service although a formal tenure system did not exist—a hearing could be requested to challenge grounds for nonretention. See *Perry v. Sindermann,* 408 U.S. 593 (1972).

The United States Supreme Court upheld the dismissal of a tenured teacher who refused to comply with a continuing education policy requiring teachers who held only a bachelor's degree to earn at least five semester hours of college credit every three years. See *Harrah Independent School District v. Martin,* 440 U.S. 194 (1979).

A nontenured teacher's nonrenewal was not upheld in *Stoddard v. School District No. 1.,* 590 F.2d 829 (10th Cir. 1979). The teacher in this case was advised in a letter from her principal that her contract would not be renewed because of failure to maintain order in the classroom and lack of dynamics in motivating students. The teacher alleged that in a private conversation the principal informed her that the "real" reasons for non-renewal were (1) rumors regarding an affair with another resident of her trailer park, (2) her propensity for playing cards and not attending church regularly, and (3) her obesity, which was the "lack of dynamics" referred to in the letter.

A school district's refusal to renew a teacher's contract for violating a policy against outside employment was not upheld because the policy was not uniformly applied. See *Gosney* v. *Sonora Independent School District*, 603 F.2d 522 (5th Cir. 1979). The court declared that the district's no-outside-employment policy was not itself unconstitutional.

The United States Supreme Court has upheld a New York statute forbidding permanent certification as a public school teacher of any person who is not a United States citizen unless that person has manifested an intention to apply for citizenship. See *Ambach* v. *Norwick*, 441 U.S.68 (1979).

State statutes often contain a catchall phrase such as "for other due and sufficient cause" as a ground for dismissal. The question of over-breadth and vagueness of such a phrase was discussed in *diLeo* v. *Greenfield*, 541 F.2d 949 (2d Cir. 1976), and the court agreed that the phrase was not general.

In the private sector federal statutes protect union members, women, minority-group members, and the handicapped from arbitrary dismissal; however, nonunion employees in the private sector generally fall under the common-law "employment at will" legal doctrine, which allows for dismissal without cause. The doctrine is followed in most states; yet recent court actions appear to be eroding the doctrine. There have been successful court challenges when private sector dismissal involved: an employee's refusal to break a law; failure to discharge a long-service worker "fairly" or "in good faith"; improper notice of dissatisfaction; a broken promise of job security; the false advertisement of a "permanent position"; and jury service. A new phrase, "corporate due process," has been coined by those examining this area of law.

Does your state have statutory provisions dealing with nonrenewal and dismissal of teachers? What are your local school system's policies regarding nonrenewal and dismissal?

II. Freedom of Expression

Public school teachers' status regarding their rights of freedom of expression has received considerable court attention in recent years. Prior to this, several historic forces had contributed to the commonly held view that public employees, which included teachers, had a limited right of freedom of expression. The strongest force contributing to this view was that public employment was considered a privilege rather than a right. Although this distinction has been modified, the belief that public employment was a privilege had received considerable credibility, especially since 1892, as the result of Justice Holmes' often-quoted statement, "The petitioner may have a constitutional right to talk politics, but he has no constitutional right to be a policeman." This judicial view, coupled with the notion that the quid pro quo for government employees' increased job security (a result of the ravages of the spoils system), had the effect of allowing the forfeiture of certain constitutional rights. Formal restrictions of government employees' political activities were embodied in the Hatch Act at the federal level. Several states have enacted "little Hatch Acts," and other states have statutory provisions restricting certain activities of state employees and/or teachers. Such legislation, combined with a judicial view that public employment was a privilege and not a right, tended to solidify the long-held contention that government employees, which included teachers, had a limited right of freedom of expression.

A heightened concern with individual rights during the 1960s, combined with a seemingly receptive federal judiciary, resulted in some teachers challenging the position that teachers had a limited right of freedom of expression. Several Supreme Court and lower court decisions have upheld the teachers' contention.

Pickering v. *Board of Education of Township High School District 205,* a Supreme Court decision, established the principle that public school teachers have the First Amendment right of freedom of expression. Pickering was dismissed from his teaching position for writing a letter, published in a newspaper, critical of several of the school board's actions. These included allocation of school funds between educational and athletic programs and the board's and superintendent's methods of informing, or neglecting to inform, the school district's taxpayers of the real reasons why additional tax revenues were being sought for the schools. In attempting to balance the teacher's interest as a citizen in making public comments, against the state's interest in promoting the efficiency of its employees' public services, the court struck the balance on the side of the teacher.

Another Supreme Court decision, *Mt. Healthy City School District Board of Education* v. *Doyle,* involved an untenured teacher who had been in an altercation with a colleague, argued with school cafeteria employees, swore at students, and made obscene gestures to female pupils. He also called a radio station and provided them with a memorandum from the principal relating to teacher dress and appearance. Doyle alleged that his not being rehired was due to his exercising his First Amendment rights in calling the radio station. The Court, in vacating the lower court's decision, reasoned that the proper test in such a case is whether or not the school board would have rehired the teacher even in "the absence of the protected conduct."

A provision in a collective bargaining agreement granting exclusive access to teacher mailboxes and the interschool mail system to the association that represented the majority of teachers was upheld by a five-to-four decision of the United States Supreme Court in *Perry Education Association* v. *Perry Local Educators' Association.* The Court found that the mail system was not a public forum and that ample alternative channels for communication existed, such as bulletin boards, meeting facilities, and the United States mail.

A. Tenured Teacher's Public Expression

Pickering v. Board of Education

Supreme Court of the United States, 1968
391 U.S. 563

MR. JUSTICE MARSHALL delivered the opinion of the Court.

Appellant Marvin L. Pickering, a teacher in Township High School District 205, Will County, Illinois, was dismissed from his position by the appellee Board of Education for sending a letter to a local newspaper in connection with a recently proposed tax increase that was critical of the way in which the Board and the district superintendent of schools had handled past proposals to raise new revenue for the schools. Appellant's dismissal resulted from a determination by the Board, after a full hearing, that the publication of the letter was "detrimental to the efficient operation and administration of the schools of the district" and hence, under the relevant Illinois statute,   * * *   that "interests of the school require[d] [his dismissal]."

* * *

In February of 1961 the appellee Board of Education asked the voters of the school district to approve a bond issue to raise $4,875,000 to erect two new schools. The proposal was defeated. Then, in December of 1961, the Board submitted another bond proposal to the voters which called for the raising of $5,500,000 to build two new schools. This second proposal passed and the schools were built with the money raised by the bond sales. In May of 1964 a proposed increase in the tax rate to be used for educational purposes was submitted to the voters by the Board and was defeated. Finally, on September 19, 1964, a second proposal to increase the tax rate was submitted by the Board and was likewise defeated.

It was in connection with this last proposal of the School Board that appellant wrote the letter to the editor * * * that resulted in his dismissal.

Prior to the vote on the second tax increase proposal a variety of articles attributed to the District 205 Teachers' Organization appeared in the local paper. These articles urged passage of the tax increase and stated that failure to pass the increase would result in a decline in the quality of education afforded children in the district's schools. A letter from the superintendent of schools making the same point was published in the paper two days before the election and submitted to the voters in mimeographed form the following day. It was in response to the foregoing material, together with the failure of the tax increase to pass, that appellant submitted the letter in question to the editor of the local paper.

The letter constituted, basically, an attack on the School Board's handling of the 1961 bond issue proposals and its subsequent allocation of financial resources between the schools' educational and athletic programs. It also charged the superintendent of schools with attempting to prevent teachers in the district from opposing or criticizing the proposed bond issue.

The Board dismissed Pickering for writing and publishing the letter. Pursuant to Illinois law, the Board was then required to hold a hearing on the dismissal. At the hearing the Board charged that numerous statements in the letter were false and that the publication of the statements unjustifiably impugned the "motives, honesty, integrity, truthfulness, responsibility and competence" of both the Board and the school administration. The Board also charged that the false statements damaged the professional reputations of its members and of the school administrators, would be disruptive of faculty discipline, and would tend to foment "controversy, conflict and dissension" among teachers, administrators, the Board of Education, and the residents of the district. * * *

* * *

To the extent that the Illinois Supreme Court's opinion may be read to suggest that teachers may constitutionally be compelled to relinquish the First Amendment rights they would otherwise enjoy as citizens to comment on matters of public interest in connection with the operation of the public schools in which they work, it proceeds on a premise that has been unequivocally rejected in numerous prior decisons of this Court. * * * At the same time it cannot be gainsaid that the State has interests as an employer in regulating the speech of its employees that differ significantly from those it possesses in connection with regulation of the speech of the citizenry in general. The problem in any case is to arrive at a balance between the interests of the teacher, as a citizen, in commenting upon matters of public concern and the interest of the state, as an employer, in promoting the efficiency of the public services it performs through its employees.

* * * Because of the enormous variety of fact situations in which critical statements by teachers and other public employees may be thought by their superiors, against whom the statements are directed, to furnish grounds for dismissal, we do not deem it either appropriate or feasible to attempt to lay down a general standard against which all such statements may be judged. However, in the course of evaluating the conflicting claims of First Amendment protection and the need for orderly school administration in the context of this case, we shall indicate some of the general lines along which an analysis of the controlling interests should run.

An examination of the statements in appellant's letter objected to by the Board reveals that they, like the letter as a whole, consist essentially of criticism of the Board's allocation of school funds between educational and athletic programs, and of both the Board's and the superintendent's methods of informing, or preventing the informing of, the district's taxpayers of the real reasons why additional tax revenues were being sought for the schools. The statements are in no way directed towards any person with whom appellant would normally be in contact in the course of his daily work as a teacher. Thus no question of maintaining either discipline by immediate superiors or harmony among coworkers is presented here. Appellant's employment relationships with the Board and, to a somewhat lesser extent, with the superintendent are not the kind of close working relationships for which it can persuasively be claimed that personal loyalty and confidence are necessary to their proper functioning. * * *

We next consider the statements in appellant's letter which we agree to be false. The Board's original charges included allegations that the publication of the letter damaged the professional reputations of the Board and the superintendent and would foment controversy and conflict among the Board, teachers, administrators, and the residents of the district. However, no evidence to support these allegations was introduced at the hearing. So far as the record reveals, Pickering's letter was greeted by everyone but its main target, the Board, with massive apathy and total disbelief. The Board must, therefore, have decided, perhaps by analogy with the law of libel, that the statements were *per se* harmful to the operation of the schools.

However, the only way in which the Board could conclude, absent any evidence of the actual effect of the letter, that the statements contained therein were *per se* detrimental to the interest of the schools was to equate the Board members' own interests with that of the schools. Certainly an accusation that too much money is being spent on athletics by the administrators of the school system * * * cannot reasonably be regarded as *per se* detrimental to the district's schools. Such an accusation reflects rather a difference of opinion between Pickering and the Board as to the preferable manner of operating the school system, a difference of opinion that clearly concerns an issue of general public interest.

In addition, the fact that particular illustrations of the Board's claimed undesirable emphasis on athletic programs are false would not normally have any necessary impact on the actual operation of the schools, beyond its tendency to anger the Board. For example, Pickering's letter was written after the defeat at the polls of the second proposed tax increase. It could, therefore, have had no effect on the ability of the school district to raise necessary revenue, since there was no showing that there was any proposal to increase taxes pending when the letter was written.

More importantly, the question whether a school system requires additional funds is a matter of legitimate public concern on which the judgment of the school administration, including the School Board, cannot, in a society that leaves such questions to popular vote, be taken as conclusive. On such a question free and open debate is vital to informed decision-making by the electorate. Teachers are, as a class, the members of a community most likely to have informed and definite opinions as to how funds allotted to the operation of the schools should be spent. Accordingly, it is essential that they be able to speak out freely on such questions without fear of retaliatory dismissal.

In addition, the amounts expended on athletics which Pickering reported erroneously were matters of public record on which his position as a teacher in the district did not qualify him to speak with any greater authority than any other taxpayer. The Board could easily have rebutted appellant's errors by publishing the accurate figures itself, either via a letter to the same newspaper or otherwise. We are thus not presented with a situation in which a teacher has carelessly made false statements about matters so closely related to the day-to-day operations of the schools that any harmful impact on the public would be difficult to counter because of the teacher's presumed greater access to the real facts. Accordingly, we have no occasion to consider at this time whether under such circumstances a school board could reasonably require that a teacher make substantial efforts to verify the accuracy of his charges before publishing them.

What we do have before us is a case in which a teacher has made erroneous public statements upon issues then currently the subject of public attention, which are critical of his ultimate employer but which are neither shown nor can be presumed to have in any way either impeded the teacher's proper performance of his daily duties in the classroom or to have interfered with the regular operation of the schools generally. In

these circumstances we conclude that the interest of the school administration in limiting teachers' opportunities to contribute to public debate is
not significantly greater than its interest in limiting a similar contribution
by any member of the general public.

* * *

In sum, we hold that, in a case such as this, absent proof of false
statements knowingly or recklessly made by him, a teacher's exercise of
his right to speak on issues of public importance may not furnish the basis
for his dismissal from public employment. * * *

Notes

Justice Thurgood Marshall, who wrote the **Pickering** opinion, became the
first black to be named to the Supreme Court. He was appointed by
President Johnson in 1967. He had been counsel for the National Association for the Advancement of Colored People and the NAACP Legal Defense and Educational Fund for twenty-five years. During that time he
argued many civil rights cases, including the 1954 landmark public school
desegregation case, and he "won" twenty-nine out of the thirty-two cases
in which he appeared before the Court.

Reminiscent of **Tinker,** a teacher's dismissal for refusing to remove a
black armband worn in class to protest against the Vietnam War was
invalidated. See *James* v. *Board of Education of Central School District No. 1,*
461 F.2d 566 (2d Cir. 1972), cert. denied, 409 U.S. 1042 (1972).

Although the case did not involve educators, the United States Supreme Court, in a 5–4 decision, did not extend the **Pickering** rationale to
a questionnaire circulated within a district attorney's office. In this case an
assistant district attorney was transferred to different job responsibilities.
In protest she circulated among her co-workers a questionnaire related
primarily to the transfer policy. In approving her termination, the Court
contended that protecting the circulation of the questionnaire would "require a public office to be run as a roundtable for employee complaints
over internal office affairs" and that normal office functioning would be
endangered. Additionally, the Court asserted: "When employee expression cannot be fairly considered as relating to any matter of political,
social, or other concern to the community, government officials should
enjoy wide latitude in managing their offices, without intrusive oversight
by the judiciary in the name of the First Amendment." However, the
majority reiterated the following caveat from **Pickering:** "Because of the
enormous variety of fact situations in which critical statements by . . . public employees may be thought by their superiors . . . to furnish grounds
for dismissal, we do not deem it either appropriate or feasible to lay down

a general standard against which all such statements may be judged." See *Connick* v. *Myers*, 461 U.S. 138 (1983).

A school counselor, who had received a master's degree with special training in counseling children of Mexican-American ancestry, was transferred from one school to another for advising parents to seek legal aid concerning a particular school policy. Under the disputed policy, students were being placed in classes for the mentally retarded because they were tested in English rather than their native tongue. See *Bernasconi* v. *Tempe Elementary School District No. 3*, 548 F.2d 857 (9th Cir. 1977), cert. denied, 434 U.S. 825 (1977) in which the court reversed a lower-court decision that had denied relief to the counselor. In its decision the federal appellate court concluded that the counselor's transfer was based partially upon retaliation for the exercise of First Amendment rights.

A track coach alleged that his nonrenewal was based on a protest letter to a newspaper. In this case a proposed discontinuance of a junior high track program by the school board sparked a public controversy. A letter was published in the local newspaper, in which the coach denied recommending that the track program be discontinued and in which he stated his reasons for supporting it. A federal appellate court found that the school district had violated the coach's First Amendment rights in firing him for writing a protest letter to the newspaper. The court held that there was ample evidence for the jury to find that the letter was the motivating factor in the board's decision not to renew plaintiff's contract. In reaching this conclusion, the court contended that it is not enough for a teacher to show that he was fired after engaging in constitutionally protected conduct. He also bears the initial burden of showing that such conduct was a motivating factor in the board's decision not to rehire. The burden then shifts to the board, which must show, by a preponderance of evidence, that it would have reached the same decision in the absence of the protected conduct. See *McGee* v. *South Pemiscot School District R-V*, 712 F.2d 339 (8th Cir. 1983).

A teacher's dismissal based on her privately expressed complaints and opinions to her principal was addressed in *Givhan* v. *Western Line Consolidated School District*, 439 U.S. 410 (1979). Here the Court announced that teachers do not forfeit their protection against governmental abridgement of freedom of speech if they decide to express their views privately rather than publicly.

Pickering would not apply to private school teachers because a private school does not operate under the "color of the state." Nor would private school teachers necessarily have civil rights protections available to public school teachers. Rights of private school teachers would be governed by their individual contracts with their school and the degree to which a linkage existed betweeen a private school and the state or federal government.

B. Nontenured Teacher's Freedom of Expression

Mr. Healthy City School District Board of Education v. Doyle

Supreme Court of the United States, 1977
429 U.S. 274

MR. JUSTICE REHNQUIST delivered the opinion of the Court.

Respondent Doyle sued petitioner Mt. Healthy Board of Education in the United States District Court for the Southern District of Ohio. Doyle claimed that the Board's refusal to renew his contract in 1971 violated his rights under the First and Fourteenth Amendments to the United States Constitution. After a bench trial the District Court held that Doyle was entitled to reinstatement with backpay. The Court of Appeals for the Sixth Circuit affirmed the judgment.   *   *   *

*   *   *

Doyle was first employed by the Board in 1966. He worked under one-year contracts for the first three years, and under a two-year contract from 1969 to 1971. In 1969 he was elected president of the Teachers' Association, in which position he worked to expand the subjects of direct negotiation between the Association and the Board of Education. During Doyle's one-year term as president of the Association, and during the succeeding year when he served on its executive committee there was apparently some tension in relations between the Board and the Association.

Beginning early in 1970, Doyle was involved in several incidents not directly connected with his role in the Teachers' Association. In one instance, he engaged in an argument with another teacher which culminated in the other teacher's slapping him. Doyle subsequently refused to accept an apology and insisted upon some punishment for the other teacher. His persistence in the matter resulted in the suspension of both teachers for one day, which was followed by a walk-out by a number of other teachers, which in turn resulted in the lifting of the suspensions.

On other occasions, Doyle got into an argument with employees of the school cafeteria over the amount of spaghetti which had been served him; referred to students in connection with a disciplinary complaint, as "sons of bitches"; and made an obscene gesture to two girls in connection with their failure to obey commands made in his capacity as cafeteria supervisor. Chronologically the last in the series of incidents which respondent was involved in during his employment by the Board was a telephone call by him to a local radio station. It was the Board's consideration of this incident which the court below found to be a violation of the First and Fourteenth Amendments.

In February 1971, the principal circulated to various teachers a memorandum relating to teacher dress and appearance, which was apparently prompted by the view of some in the administration that there was a relationship between teacher appearance and public support for bond issues. Doyle's response to the receipt of the memorandum—on a subject which he apparently understood was to be settled by joint teacher-administration action—was to convey the substance of the memorandum to a disc jockey at WSAI, a Cincinnati radio station, who promptly announced the adoption of the dress code as a news item. Doyle subsequently apologized to the principal, conceding that he should have made some prior communication of his criticism to the school administration.

Approximately one month later the superintendent made his customary annual recommendations to the Board as to the rehiring of nontenured teachers. He recommended that Doyle not be rehired. The same recommendation was made with respect to nine other teachers in the district, and in all instances, including Doyle's, the recommendation was adopted by the Board. Shortly after being notified of this decision, respondent requested a statement of reasons for the Board's actions. He received a statement citing "a notable lack of tact in handling professional matters which leaves much doubt as to your sincerity in establishing good school relationships." That general statement was followed by references to the radio station incident and to the obscene-gesture incident.

The District Court found that all of these incidents had in fact occurred. It concluded that respondent Doyle's telephone call to the radio station was "clearly protected by the First Amendment," and that because it had played a "substantial part" in the decision of the Board not to renew Doyle's employment, he was entitled to reinstatement with backpay. * * * The District Court did not expressly state what test it was applying in determining that the incident in question involved conduct protected by the First Amendment, but simply held that the communication to the radio station was such conduct. The Court of Appeals affirmed in a brief *per curiam* opinion. * * *

Doyle's claims under the First and Fourteenth Amendments are not defeated by the fact that he did not have tenure. Even though he could have been discharged for no reason whatever, and had no constitutional right to a hearing prior to the decision not to rehire him, * * * he may nonetheless establish a claim to reinstatement if the decision not to rehire him was made by reason of his exercise of constitutionally protected First Amendment freedoms. * * *

That question of whether speech of a government employee is constitutionally protected expression necessarily entails striking "a balance between the interests of the teacher, as a citizen, in commenting upon matters of public concern and the interest of the State, as an employer, in promoting the efficiency of the public services it performs through its employees." *Pickering v. Board of Education*, 391 U.S. 563, 568 (1968). There is no suggestion by the Board that Doyle violated any established policy, or that its reaction to his communication to the radio station was anything more than an ad hoc response to Doyle's action in making the memorandum public. We therefore accept the District Court's finding that the communication was protected by the First and Fourteenth Amendments. We are not, however, entirely in agreement with that court's manner of reasoning from this finding to the conclusion that Doyle is entitled to reinstatement with backpay.

The District Court made the following "conclusions" on this aspect of the case:

> "1) If a non-permissible reason, e.g., exercise of First Amendment rights, played a substantial part in the decision not to renew—even in the face of other permissible grounds—the decision may not stand (citations omitted).

> "2) A non-permissible reason did play a substantial part. That is clear from the letter of the Superintendent immediately following the Board's decision, which stated two reasons—the one, the conversation with the radio station clearly protected by the First Amendment. A court may not engage in any limitation of First Amendment rights based on 'tact'—that is not to say that the "tactfulness" is irrelevant to other issues in this case." * * *

At the same time, though, it stated that

> "[i]n fact, as this Court sees it and finds, both the Board and the Superintendent were faced with a situation in which there did exist in fact reason . . . independent of any First Amendment rights or exercise thereof, to not extend tenure." * * *

Since respondent Doyle had no tenure, and there was therefore not even a state-law requirement of "cause" or "reason" before a decision could be made not to renew his employment, it is not clear what the District Court meant by this latter statement. Clearly the Board legally *could* have dismissed respondent had the radio station incident never come to its attention. One plausible meaning of the court's statement is that the Board and the Superintendent not only could, but in fact *would* have reached that decision had not the constitutionally protected incident of the telephone call to the radio station occurred. We are thus brought to the issue whether, even if that were the case, the fact that the protected conduct played a "substantial part" in the actual decision not to renew would necessarily amount to a constitutional violation justifying remedial action. We think that it would not.

A rule of causation which focuses solely on whether protected conduct played a part, "substantial" or otherwise, in a decision not to rehire, could place an employee in a better position as a result of the exercise of constitutionally protected conduct than he would have occupied had he done nothing. The difficulty with the rule enunciated by the District Court is that it would require reinstatement in cases where a dramatic and perhaps abrasive incident is inevitably on the minds of those responsible for the decision to rehire, and does indeed play a part in that decision—even if the same decision would have been reached had the incident not occurred. The constitutional principle at stake is sufficiently vindicated if such an employee is placed in no worse a position than if he had not engaged in the conduct. A borderline or marginal candidate should not have the employment question resolved against him because of constitutionally protected conduct. But that same candidate ought not to be able, by engaging in such conduct, to prevent his employer from assessing his performance record and reaching a decision not to rehire on the basis of that record, simply because the protected conduct makes the employer more certain of the correctness of its decision.

This is especially true where, as the District Court observed was the case here, the current decision to rehire will accord "tenure." The long-term consequences of an award of tenure are of great moment both to the employee and to the employer. They are too significant for us to hold that the Board in this case would be precluded, because it considered constitutionally protected conduct in deciding not to rehire Doyle, from attempting to prove to a trier of fact that quite apart from such conduct Doyle's record was such that he would not have been rehired in any event.

* * *

Initially, in this case, the burden was properly placed upon respondent to show that his conduct was constitutionally protected, and that this conduct was a "substantial factor"—or, to put it in other words, that it was a "motivating factor" in the Board's decision not to rehire him. Respondent having carried that burden, however, the District Court should have gone on to determine whether the Board had shown by a preponderance of the evidence that it would have reached the same decision as to respondent's reemployment even in the absence of the protected conduct.

We cannot tell from the District Court opinion and conclusions, nor from the opinion of the Court of Appeals affirming the judgment of the District Court, what conclusions those courts would have reached had they applied this test. The judgment of the Court of Appeals is therefore vacated, and the case remanded for further proceedings consistent with this opinion.

So ordered.

Notes

The Court's opinion in **Doyle** reaffirms the doctrine that nontenured teachers have First Amendment rights, and they may establish a claim to reinstatement if the reason for not being rehired was in violation of these rights. However, as the Court stresses, engaging in constitutionally protected conduct may not prevent an employer from dismissing a teacher on the basis of his or her total performance record.

A probationary teacher may not be terminated solely for refusing to participate in a flag-salute ceremony. The teacher stood silently at attention during daily classroom recitation of the pledge of allegiance, in which school regulations required her to participate. See *Russo* v. *Central School District No. 1,* 469 F.2d 623 (2nd Cir. 1972), cert. denied, 411 U.S. 932 (1973). However, see *Palmer* v. *Board of Education of the City of Chicago,* 603 F.2d 1271 (7th Cir. 1979), cert. denied, 444 U.S. 1026 (1980), which upheld the discharge of a teacher who, based on her Jehovah's Witness faith, refused to lead her kindergarten students in patriotic exercises and failed to comply with certain aspects of the curriculum. In upholding the discharge, the court distinguished between the freedom to believe in certain religious tenets and following an appropriate curriculum.

See *Norbeck* v. *Davenport Community School District,* 545 F.2d 63 (8th Cir. 1976), cert. denied, 431 U.S. 917 (1977), which upheld the nonrenewal of a principal who acted as the chief negotiator for the Davenport Education Association. The principal had claimed that the board had infringed upon his constitutional right of association.

C. Use of School-System Mail

Perry Education Association v. Perry Local Educators' Association

Supreme Court of the United States, 1983
460 U.S. 37

JUSTICE WHITE delivered the opinion of the Court.

Perry Education Association is the duly elected exclusive bargaining representative for the teachers of the Metropolitan School District of Perry Township, Ind. A collective-bargaining agreement with the Board of Education provided that Perry Education Association, but no other union, would have access to the interschool mail system and teacher mailboxes in the Perry Township schools. The issue in this case is whether the denial of similar access to the Perry Local Educators' Association, a rival teacher group, violates the First and Fourteenth Amendments.

The Metropolitan School District of Perry Township, Ind., operates a public school system of 13 separate schools. Each school building contains a set of mailboxes for the teachers. Interschool delivery by school employees permits messages to be delivered rapidly to teachers in the District. The primary function of this internal mail system is to transmit official messages among the teachers and between the teachers and the school administration. In addition, teachers use the system to send personal messages and individual school building principals have allowed delivery of messages from various private organizations.

Prior to 1977, both the Perry Education Association (PEA) and the Perry Local Educators' Association (PLEA) represented teachers in the School District and apparently had equal access to the interschool mail system. In 1977, PLEA challenged PEA's status as *de facto* bargaining representative for the Perry Township teachers by filing an election petition with the Indiana Education Employment Relations Board (Board). PEA won the election and was certified as the exclusive representative, as provided by Indiana law. * * *

The Board permits a school district to provide access to communication facilities to the union selected for the discharge of the exclusive representative duties of representing the bargaining unit and its individual members without having to provide equal access to rival unions. Following the election, PEA and the School District negotiated a labor contract in which the School Board gave PEA "access to teachers' mailboxes in which to insert material" and the right to use the interschool mail delivery system to the extent that the School District incurred no extra expense by such use. The labor agreement noted that these access rights were being accorded to PEA "acting as the representative of the teachers" and went on to stipulate that these access rights shall not be granted to any other "school employee organization"—a term of art defined by Indiana law to mean "any organization which has school employees as members and one of whose primary purposes is representing school employees in dealing with their school employer." The PEA contract with these provisions was renewed in 1980 and is presently in force.

The exclusive-access policy applies only to use of the mailboxes and school mail system. PLEA is not prevented from using other school facilities to communicate with teachers. PLEA may post notices on school bulletin boards; may hold meetings on school property after school hours; and may, with approval of the building principals, make announcements on the public address system. Of course, PLEA also may communicate with teachers by word of mouth, telephone, or the United States mail. Moreover, under Indiana law, the preferential access of the bargaining agent may continue only while its status as exclusive representative is insulated from challenge. * * * While a representation contest is in progress, unions must be afforded equal access to such communication facilities.

PLEA and two of its members filed this action under 42 U. S. C. § 1983 against PEA and individual members of the Perry Township School Board. Plaintiffs contended that PEA's preferential access to the internal mail system violates the First Amendment and the Equal Protection

Clause of the Fourteenth Amendment. They sought injunctive and declaratory relief and damages. Upon cross-motions for summary judgment, the District Court entered judgment for the defendants. * * *

The Court of Appeals for the Seventh Circuit reversed. * * * The court held that once the School District "opens its internal mail system to PEA but denies it to PLEA, it violates both the Equal Protection Clause and the First Amendment." It acknowledged that PEA had "legal duties to the teachers that PLEA does not have" but reasoned that "[w]ithout an independent reason why equal access for other labor groups and individual teachers is undesirable, the special duties of the incumbent do not justify opening the system to the incumbent alone." * * *

* * *

The primary question presented is whether the First Amendment, applicable to the States by virtue of the Fourteenth Amendment, is violated when a union that has been elected by public school teachers as their exclusive bargaining representative is granted access to certain means of communication, while such access is denied to a rival union. There is no question that constitutional interests are implicated by denying PLEA use of the interschool mail system. "It can hardly be argued that either students or teachers shed their constitutional rights to freedom of speech or expression at the schoolhouse gate." *Tinker* v. *Des Moines School District* * * * The First Amendment's guarantee of free speech applies to teacher's mailboxes as surely as it does elsewhere within the school, *Tinker* v. *Des Moines School District, supra,* and on sidewalks outside * * * . But this is not to say that the First Amendment requires equivalent access to all parts of a school building in which some form of communicative activity occurs. "[N]owhere else [have we] suggested that students, teachers, or anyone else has an absolute constitutional right to use all parts of a school building or its immediate environs for . . . unlimited expressive purposes." * * * The existence of a right of access to public property and the standard by which limitations upon such a right must be evaluated differ depending on the character of the property at issue.

In places which by long tradition or by government fiat have been devoted to assembly and debate, the rights of the State to limit expressive activity are sharply circumscribed. At one end of the spectrum are streets and parks which "have immemorially been held in trust for the use of the public and, time out of mind, have been used for purposes of assembly, communicating thoughts between citizens, and discussing public questions." * * * In these quintessential public forums, the government may not prohibit all communicative activity. For the State to enforce a content-based exclusion it must show that its regulation is necessary to serve a compelling state interest and that it is narrowly drawn to achieve that end. * * * The State may also enforce regulations of the time, place, and manner of expression which are content-neutral, are narrowly tailored to serve a significant government interest, and leave open ample alternative channels of communication. * * *

A second category consists of public property which the State has opened for use by the public as a place for expressive activity. The Constitution forbids a State to enforce certain exclusions from a forum generally open to the public even if it was not required to create the forum in the first place. * * * Although a State is not required to indefinitely retain the open character of the facility, as long as it does so it is bound by the same standards as apply in a traditional public forum. Reasonable time, place, and manner regulations are permissible, and a content-based prohibition must be narrowly drawn to effectuate a compelling state interest. * * *

Public property which is not by tradition or designation a forum for public communication is governed by different standards. We have recognized that the "First Amendment does not guarantee access to property simply because it is owned or controlled by the government." * * * In addition to time, place, and manner regulations, the State may reserve the forum for its intended purposes, communicative or otherwise, as long as the regulation on speech is reasonable and not an effort to suppress expression merely because public officials oppose the speaker's view. * * * As we have stated on several occasions, "[t]he State, no less than a private owner of property, has power to preserve the property under its control for the use to which it is lawfully dedicated." * * *

The school mail facilities at issue here fall within this third category. The Court of Appeals recognized that Perry School District's interschool mail system is not a traditional public forum: "We do not hold that a school's internal mail system is a public forum in the sense that a school board may not close it to all but official business if it chooses." * * * The internal mail system, at least by policy, is not held open to the general public. It is instead PLEA's position that the school mail facilities have become a "limited public forum" from which it may not be excluded because of the periodic use of the system by private non-school-connected groups, and PLEA's own unrestricted access to the system prior to PEA's certification as exclusive representative.

Neither of these arguments is persuasive. The use of the internal school mail by groups not affiliated with the schools is no doubt a relevant consideration. If by policy or by practice the Perry School District has opened its mail system for indiscriminate use by the general public, then PLEA could justifiably argue a public forum has been created. This, however, is not the case. As the case comes before us, there is no indication in the record that the school mailboxes and interschool delivery system are open for use by the general public. Permission to use the system to communicate with teachers must be secured from the individual building principal. There is no court finding or evidence in the record which demonstrates that this permission has been granted as a matter of course to all who seek to distribute material. We can only conclude that the schools do allow some outside organizations such as the YMCA, Cub Scouts, and other civic and church organizations to use the facilities. This type of selective access does not transform government property into a public forum. In *Greer* v. *Spock* * * * the fact that other civilian speakers and entertainers had sometimes been invited to appear at Fort Dix did not convert the military base into a public forum. And in *Lehman* v. *Shaker Heights*, * * * a plurality of the Court concluded that a city transit system's rental of space in its vehicles for commercial advertising did not require it to accept partisan political advertising.

Moreover, even if we assume that by granting access to the Cub Scouts, YMCA's, and parochial schools, the School District has created a "limited" public forum, the constitutional right of access would in any event extend only to other entities of similar character. While the school mail facilities thus might be a forum generally open for use by the Girl Scouts, the local boys' club, and other organizations that engage in activities of interest and educational relevance to students, they would not as a consequence be open to an organization such as PLEA, which is concerned with the terms and conditions of teacher employment.

* * *

We believe it is more accurate to characterize the access policy as based on the *status* of the respective unions rather than their views. Implicit in the concept of the nonpublic forum is the right to make distinctions in access on the basis of subject matter and speaker identity. These distinctions may be impermissible in a public forum but are inherent and inescapable in the process of limiting a nonpublic forum to activities compatible with the intended purpose of the property. The touchstone for evaluating these distinctions is whether they are reasonable in light of the purpose which the forum at issue serves.

* * *

We observe that providing exclusive access to recognized bargaining representatives is a permissible labor practice in the public sector. We have previously noted that the "designation of a union as exclusive representative carries with it great responsibilities. The tasks of negotiating and administering a collective-bargaining agreement and representing the interests of employees in settling disputes and processing grievances are continuing and difficult ones." * * * Moreover, exclusion of the rival union may reasonably be considered a means of insuring labor peace within the schools. The policy "serves to prevent the District's schools from becoming a battlefield for inter-union squabbles."

* * *

* * * The judgment of the Court of Appeals is *Reversed.*

Notes

Prior to *Perry,* courts had allowed the granting of exclusive rights to use bulletin boards, school mailboxes, and meeting rooms to teacher organizations to which a majority of teachers belong. See *Connecticut State Federation of Teachers* v. *Board of Education Members,* 538 F.2d 471 (2nd Cir. 1976) and *Memphis American Federation of Teachers* v. *Board of Education of Memphis City Schools,* 534 F.2d 699 (6th Cir. 1976).

A controversy grew out of attempts by a teacher association to disseminate documents to teachers, to send speakers to school meetings, and to arrange meetings at the schools. A federal appellate court held the policy concerning literature distribution to be unconstitutional both facially and as applied; however, the policy regulating visitors on school campuses was held not to be facially unconstitutional. See *Hall* v. *Board of School Commissioners of Mobile County,* 681 F.2d 965 (5th Cir. 1982).

III. Academic Freedom

Academic freedom is difficult to conceptualize definitively, since its extent is influenced by such factors as grade level and the nature of certain courses. Litigation often occurs when a school system's views regarding academic freedom are not in congruence with a teacher's perception of autonomy in determining specific subject matter for a particular class, appropriate teaching methods, and the selection of appropriate materials. In this type of litigation, teachers generally allege that they have a constitutional right to present material to which students, parents, or school officials may object. Although courts have recognized that teachers have the right to academic freedom, as with other constitutional rights, it is not absolute and must be balanced against the competing interests of the larger society.

A. Appropriate Materials

Brubaker v. Board of Education, School District 149

United States Court of Appeals, Seventh Circuit, 1974
502 F.2d 973, aff'd. by an equally divided en banc court,
502 F.2d 1000 (1974), cert. denied, 421 U.S. 965 (1975)

O'SULLIVAN, Senior Circuit Judge.

This appeal concerns the discharge by defendant Board of Education of three public school teachers—plaintiff-appellants—for distributing or causing to be distributed to their eighth grade pupils allegedly obscene and improper reading materials. * * * The litigation was concluded in the District Court by an order granting defendant-appellees' motion for summary judgment. From such order, plaintiffs appeal.

We affirm.

Clara S. Brubaker, John W. Brubaker and Ronald K. Sievert were teachers of eighth grade students in public schools operated by the Board of Education of District 149, Cook County, Illinois. They were all non-tenured, and their respective one-year contracts were to expire on June 12, 1970. Prior to the events here involved, the Brubakers had been advised that they would not be rehired, while Sievert had been notified that he would be retained for the 1970–71 school year.

In April, 1970, Clara Brubaker and another teacher, not involved here, attended the movie "Woodstock" which documented the 1969 rock festival by the name. A number of relevant brochures were acquired at the theatre. These contained various articles, poems and pictures. One article—or poem—entitled "Getting Together" contained material which brought about the discharge of the plaintiffs. Its total content is set out in the brochure "Woodstock." * * * Those parts relating to drugs, sexual behavior and what might be called vulgarities are as follows:

"Woodstock felt like home. *A place to take acid. A place to make love.* Felt like a place we'd been before, but hard to remember, like yesterday's vision, like last night's dream. But now it's all now *and it feels like we're never turning back.*

*   *   *   *   *   *

Woodstock felt like a swell of energy, wave of elation that fills the heart *and flows on over the lover beside you.*

Woodstock was freedom. Don't ever forget that. Don't ever settle for less.

*   *   *   *   *   *

Oh joy overflowing, *oh lover caressing,* I am what I have to share, oh take me completely!

*   *   *   *   *   *

Grass smoked together.

Stink of our shit; Music of Laughter.

Gathering together.

Bodies naked into the water, touching each other, opening hearts into greater awareness of being together
of living on the planet
of being part of something—a movement, a motion, like a drop of water in the crest of the tide, moving together *we're a big fucking wave . . . !*

*   *   *   *   *   *

It's only the beginning.

*   *   *   *   *   *

Old world crumbling, new world being born."

(Emphasis supplied.)

As a message to the minds of eighth graders, the brochure's poetry can and probably must be fairly read as an alluring invitation and a beckoning for them to throw off the dull discipline imposed on them by the moral environment of their home life, and in exchange to enter into a new world of love and freedom—freedom to use acid and grass, freedom to take their clothes off and to get an early start in the use of such vulgarities as "shit," "fucking," and their companions.

It is probably a fair inference that by second or third year high school most American males have become familiar with, and at times employ, these and like words. Is it only a forlorn hope, however, that most of our young ladies will never employ that kind of speech?

Clara Brubaker, who taught French at various primary grade schools, placed some of these brochures in the teachers' lounges and also gave copies to her husband, John Brubaker, and to Ronald Sievert, alleged for use in their classes. She did not herself distribute any brochures to students, but did display one of the brochure's posters in her classroom.

Copies of the brochure were then made available to the eighth grade students in John Brubaker's and Ronald Sievert's classes. In due time, these brochures found their way into the homes of some of the students. * * *

* * *

The complaint set out that Clara Brubaker had placed a number of the brochures in the teachers' lounges at four or five schools where she taught French, gave a number of copies to plaintiffs John Brubaker and Ronald K. Sievert, and "display[ed] the poster contained therein [in the brochure] in her classroom." She made no allegation that the brochure or its contents were in any way relevant to what she was teaching. It was further alleged that plaintiffs John Brubaker and Ronald K. Sievert had placed the brochures on their desks to be available to their students.

Appellants claim that the brochure had relevancy to what was being taught to the eighth grade students. Appellant Sievert said it had relevancy to his teaching assignment—Language Arts—because under his guidance his class was studying the history of rock music. * * *

* * *

Appellant John Brubaker's teaching assignment was solely "Industrial Arts." As to the relevancy of the Woodstock brochure to that subject, he said: "I think that this whole thing contributed to the interest of my class in musical instruments." He added that such would be true of the poetry also, saying that as to the words of the poem, "there was nothing wrong with them   *   *   *   they were part of the regular vocabulary of youngsters of this age." Neither Brubaker nor Sievert explained to their students any claimed relevancy of the Woodstock brochure.

*   *   *

At the relevant public hearings, testimony was presented by plaintiffs and by the Board. Plaintiffs produced two eminently educated men who expressed the view that the poem "Getting Together" was proper material to be given to eighth grade students. Both had received Ph.D's from important American universities, and had studied and were currently active in the field of education.

*   *   *

*   *   *   When asked whether the distribution of the brochure *Woodstock* would fit the "preponderant" opinion of the teaching profession, he answered, "it is the kind of material that is in public circulation and is, therefore, part of the material of the classroom." He thought also that providing such material to the students would help to develop a "rapport with these students   *   *   *   as this all increases the general fluidity and realism of the classrooms."

*   *   *

*   *   *   The other referred to his research for the National Institute of Child Health and Human Development. Thus the above quoted excerpts portray the attitudes and beliefs of some of the *teachers of the teachers* of today's children. It was their opinion that teachers should not be required to get approval from school authorities before distributing such material as the Woodstock brochure to their students. Such a requirement, it was said, "demeans the teacher"   *   *   *   .

*   *   *

One of the plaintiffs' experts found hypocrisy in the contrast between contemporary society's professed notions of morality and the total conduct of that society. He said,

> "but as a social scientist it is my considered opinion that society in the form and conduct of that society is indeed a *sick society*."

We ponder, then whether a vaccine or therapy to be given to our eighth grades for this sickness—the hypocrisy of their seniors—may be found in exposure to Woodstock and its invitations.

*   *   *

A member of the staff of the Superintendent of Public Instruction for the State of Illinois testified in support of the action of the defendant Board. He was director of the state program for gifted children. By education and experience he was qualified to express his view that the Woodstock brochure and its poetry had no educational value and was inappropriate for distribution to grammar school children. He found invalid the offered excuse that appellants had not read the brochure's poem "Getting Together" before distributing it. We share this view. Parents of children who had brought the Woodstock brochure home also testified in support of the Board's action.

We think it right also to observe that upon learning of the Board's reaction to what had happened, none of the plaintiffs expressed any regret over the matter; neither did any of them seek reinstatement by assurance that corrective measures would be taken. They made no effort to come to a friendly solution with the Board. Their first step was employment of a lawyer who demanded a plenary hearing. This lawsuit followed almost a year thereafter. Whatever their ambivalence as to whether what they did was at most an innocent mistake or done after deliberation, their lawsuit insists and relies solely upon a position that what they did—providing, with their apparent approval, the Woodstock poetry—was but an exercise of the academic freedom guaranteed them by the United States Constitution.

* * *

We have set out the factual background of this case at the above length because we believe that such recitation exposes the correctness of our affirmance of the District Court's holding that the School Board's action was not arbitrary or capricious, and was not an invasion of the appellants' constitutional rights. Appellants assert that making available to their eighth grade students the Woodstock brochure's poem "Getting Together" was an exercise of their Civil Rights, protection of which is vouchsafed to them by 42 U.S.C. § 1983. They said that their dismissal invaded their Right of Academic Freedom, and they suggest that what was done would have a "chilling effect" on the exercise of academic freedom by other teachers.

We do not believe that however much the reach of the First Amendment has been extended and however eager today's courts have been to protect the many varieties of claims to civil rights, the appellee school board had to put up with the described conduct of appellants.

* * *

Appellants further argue that they were denied due process,

"because there existed a lack of ascertainable standards by which they could measure their conduct."

They do not attempt definition of the relevant and ascertainable standards which they say the School Board should have promulgated. We will not fault a school board for not anticipating that eighth grade teachers might distribute to their students, without explanation or assigned reason therefor, poetry of the caliber of "Getting Together." Appellants say that the Board was wrong because it reached a conclusion as to the poetry's impropriety,

> "[w]ithout the benefit of any supporting expert testimony in the fields of literature, obscenity or drugs."

Experts should not be needed to support a conclusion that is obvious. Moreover, the Supreme Court, in Paris Adult Theatre I v. Slaton, 413 U.S. 49, 56 (1973), rejected the contention that " 'expert' affirmative evidence that the materials were obscene," was necessary when the alleged obscene material was itself placed in evidence. Similarly in this case no "expert" testimony was required.

Relative to the brochure's admitted invitation to the use of drugs, the evidence disclosed that Ill.Rev.Stat. ch.122, § 27–10 required that the "Nature and effect of alcoholic drinks and narcotics and their effects on the human system" be taught to pupils below the second year of high school and above the third year of elementary school work. Appellants argue that they were not aware of such statute, and that, therefore, it "did not constitute the kind of constitutionally permissible ascertainable standard which should have placed plaintiffs on notice that their conduct in distributing the Woodstock brochure [with its glorification of grass and acid] would subject them to dismissal." Whether they knew of the statute or not, we consider that these teachers should have known better than to hand to their young students something that invited the use of the described drugs. Additionally, appellants had been aware of and had participated in previously presented teaching programs expounding upon the baleful consequences of the use of drugs and alcohol.

* * *

The validity of our conclusion that the District Court properly found no violation of appellants' First Amendment or Civil Rights emerges so clearly that we decline to add, by our own extended dissertation, to the already abundant literature on the subject we deal with.

* * *

FAIRCHILD, Circuit Judge (dissenting).

I do not believe that the Woodstock brochure was either so irrelevant to educational goals or patently offensive that the plaintiffs were precluded from exercising their judgment as teachers and electing to employ it in their classes. Accordingly, I respectfully dissent from the majority's conclusion that the district court correctly held these discharges did not violate first amendment rights.

Freedom to discuss controversial or unpopular ideas in the schools is "a special concern of the First Amendment, which does not tolerate laws that cast a pall of orthodoxy over the classroom." * * * Academic freedom "does not grant teachers a license to say or write in class whatever they may feel like." * * * However, particularly where the school board has not formulated standards to guide him, academic freedom affords a teacher a certain latitude in judging whether material is suitable and relevant to his instruction. "First Amendment freedoms need breathing space to survive. . . ." * * *

These instructors did not exceed the bounds which germaneness places on protected classroom speech. The discussion and distribution of the Woodstock brochure consumed no significant amount of school time. * * * Further, it was arguably relevant to the course of instruction. Sievert's class had just completed study of the history of rock music; Brubaker's was considering the construction of musical instruments. The 1969 rock music festival at Woodstock, New York had at least some significance to these subjects, significance which was perhaps more evident in April, 1970 than it is today. More importantly, however, the appropriateness of a particular classroom discussion topic cannot be gauged solely by its logical nexus to the subject matter of instruction. A teacher may be more successful with his students if he is able to relate to them in philosophy of life, and, conversely, students may profit by learning something of a teacher's views on general subjects. Academic freedom entails the exchange of ideas which promote education in its broadest sense.

The Woodstock brochure was not so offensive that its classroom use was obviously improper. The school board had not promulgated any standards against which plaintiffs could measure this type of literature to determine whether board policy forbade its use. The board points out that certain conduct patently exceeds "the bounds of the recognized standards of propriety" and a particular rule giving advance notice that it is forbidden is unnecessary. * * * However, the material in question does not fall into this category.

First, plaintiff's experts in the field of education characterized the Woodstock pamphlet as suitable, even admirable, teaching material for eighth grade students. Whether or not this opinion be accepted, the classroom use of this work can hardly be considered "conduct, generally condemned by responsible men." * * * Second, the brochure is not obscene in the legal sense. The use of profanity does not transform the controversial into the obscene. * * * Miller v. California, 413 U.S. 1524 (1973) described obscenity as limited to "works which, taken as a whole, appeal to the prurient interest in sex, which portray sexual conduct in a patently offensive way, and which, taken as a whole, do not have serious literary, artistic, political, or scientific value." The bulk of the pamphlet consists of inoffensive factual accounts of the Woodstock festival. Even assuming the continuing validity of the variable obscenity doctrine, and making the widest allowances for the age of plaintiffs' students, neither the brochure as a whole nor the poem "Getting Together" begin to satisfy the *Miller* criteria.   *   *   *

Whether the board could constitutionally have promulgated specific rules which would have prohibited the classroom use of this literature by eighth grade students is not the issue presented. I cannot conclude that these materials are so clearly improper as to justify the mid-term discharge of an instructor who elected to use them in his teaching.

I would reverse the district court's summary judgment for defendants and remand for determination of the amount of back pay due plaintiffs as a result of their unlawful discharge.

*   *   *

Notes

A badly divided Supreme Court, as evidenced by seven separate opinions, addressed the issue of a school board's authority to remove books from a school library. Although there was no majority opinion, the plurality opinion does offer some guidance. School authorities may not exercise their discretion in the removal of books for narrow partisan or political purposes or to deny students access to ideas with which school authorities disagree. Additionally, the justices suggested several constitutionally legitimate standards that could be applied in determining a book's candidacy for removal, such as the book's educational suitability. Specific suitability criteria could include relevance to the curriculum and appropriateness for an age level. A book considered obscene for minors, pervasively vulgar, or offensive in its language could also be legitimately excluded. See *Board of Education, Island Trees Union Free School District No. 26* v. *Pico*, 457 U.S. 853 (1982).

B. Political Speakers

Wilson v. Chancellor

United States District Court, District of Oregon, 1976
418 F. Supp. 1358

BURNS, District Judge.

Plaintiffs Wilson and Logue seek declaratory and injunctive relief from a school board order banning "all political speakers" from Molalla

Union High School (MHS). They contend that the order violates the First Amendment and the equal protection clause of the Fourteenth Amendment, and is unconstitutionally vague and overbroad. * * *

Wilson teaches the political science class at MHS in which Logue was a student. This dispute arose when Wilson invited a Communist, Anton Kchmareck, to speak to that class. Wilson already and without objection had presented a Democrat, a Republican, and a member of the John Birch Society. The Communist was to be the last of this quadrumvirate through which Wilson hoped to present, in the words of the adherent, each of four points of view.

Wilson followed customary procedure and reported this invitation to the principal. The principal approved. Defendant school board discussed the invitation at its November 1975 meeting and also approved. This procedure was neither unprecedented nor customary.

The board's approval inspired mixed reviews. Two severe critics called a community meeting on December 4 where they circulated a petition asking the board to reverse the decision; approximately 800 persons eventually signed it. Several townsfolk, in letters to the local newspaper, mentioned the possibility of voting down all school budgets and voting out the members of the board.

Faced with this petition and many outraged residents, the board on December 11 reversed its decision and issued orally an order banning "all political speakers" from the high school.

The case came on for hearing on plaintiffs' motion for preliminary injunction. The parties submitted written statements and offered testimony and exhibits. The parties then agreed that the court could regard the hearing as a full trial on the merits because all necessary evidence was in.

Miss Logue contends the order violates her First Amendment right to hear the speech of others.

The right to hear customarily is invoked by prisoners denied access to periodicals, * * * members of a potential audience for a speaker prohibited from speaking, * * * or persons asserting either the public's "right to know," * * * or the emerging right of privacy * * * .

Of these cases, only the potential audience cases are applicable here. * * * These cases and my recognition that the First Amendment exists to protect a broad range of interests persuade me that Logue suffered an infringement of her First Amendment rights. * * *

Few courts have considered whether and to what extent the First Amendment protects academic freedom. Honored in Germanic tradition and prominent in academic debates, the theory rarely surfaces in legal opinions. Moreover, even its most enthusiastic advocates usually distinguish between the freedom to be accorded university professors and that to be accorded elementary and secondary school teachers. It seems to be assumed that the former engage in the search for knowledge and therefore should have far greater freedom than the latter who merely disseminate knowledge.

The Supreme Court of the United States has discussed academic freedom in "eloquent and isolated statements." * * * Lower courts have spoken more frequently, but none has clearly defined the theory's legal contours. Nor will I. This case can be decided by using purely conventional freedom of expression analysis.

A teacher's teaching is expression to which the First Amendment applies. The right to freedom of expression is not absolute; it may be restricted, and restrictions on a teacher's expression should be judged in light of the "special characteristics of the school environment." * * *

In imposing restrictions and making other decisions, school boards should be allowed great discretion. No court should intervene merely because a board's decision seems unwise. But if school boards, in exercising their discretion, act so as to interfere impermissibly with the constitutional rights of students or teachers, or both, courts must and will intervene if their jurisdiction is properly invoked.

These considerations in mind, I address two pivotal questions: First, is a teaching method or vehicle a form of expression protected by the First Amendment? Second, if so, is the restriction at issue here reasonable?

Three cases have treated teaching methods as protected forms of expression: *Keefe v. Geanakos*, 418 F.2d 359 (1st Cir. 1969), *Parducci v. Rutland*, 316 F. Supp. 352 (M.D. Ala. 1970), and *Sterzing v. Fort Bend Independent School Dist.*, 376 F. Supp. 657 (S.D.Tex. 1972).

The teacher in *Keefe* assigned his class an Atlantic Monthly article containing a word which "admittedly highly offensive, is a vulgar term for an incestuous son."

A school committee summoned Keefe to defend his conduct. When he was asked to agree not to use the word again, he declined. He subsequently was suspended, and sought a temporary injunction against the committee's dismissal hearing.

The district court denied an interlocutory injunction pending a decision on the merits. The court of appeals reversed, holding that plaintiff had demonstrated he probably would succeed on his lack of notice and academic freedom claims.

In *Parducci*, the teacher assigned her eleventh grade English class a Kurt Vonnegut, Jr. short story, "Welcome to the Monkey House." Several parents complained. School officials admonished the teacher not to use the story in any of her classes, and threatened to dismiss her if she refused. The teacher resigned. In her suit for injunctive relief she contended that the school's action violated her First Amendment rights.

The court recognized such a right, but concluded that it must be balanced against competing societal interests, most prominently the "state's vital interest in protecting its young people from any form of extreme propagandism in the classroom." * * * The court also recognized that *Tinker* * * * requires the state to demonstrate that

"[T]he forbidden conduct would 'materially and substantially interfere with the requirements of appropriate discipline in the operation of the school.' " * * *

The court then held that because the assignment was appropriate and presented no threat of disruption, the teacher's dismissal for assigning the short story violated her First Amendment rights.

In *Sterzing* a teacher disclosed to his civics class his lack of opposition to interracial marriage. After several parents complained, school officials urged Sterzing to confine his teaching to the assigned textbook. He ignored this request and several times departed from the text during the ensuing five months. Shortly after Sterzing administered an allegedly propagandistic test on race relations, the school board voted to discharge him for insubordination.

The district court ordered that Sterzing be reinstated. It held that a teacher has a substantive right to choose teaching methods which serve a demonstrated educational purpose. "A responsible teacher," wrote the court, "must have freedom to use the tools of his profession as he sees fit." * * *

Although these three cases involved actual or threatened dismissal, a teacher's freedom of expression can be impermissibly restricted even if dismissal is not threatened; prohibitions against certain teaching practices impliedly carry a threat of sanction and thereby restrict a teacher's freedom of expression.

These cases also recognize the validity of a popular maxim, "the medium is the message." The expresser's medium can affect the persuasiveness of his message, the duration of its influence, and the size and type of audience which it reaches. The act of teaching is a form of expression, and the methods used in teaching are media. Wilson's use of political speakers was his medium for teaching; similarly, the short story was Parducci's medium, the pamphlets were Sterzing's media, and the article containing the controversial words was Keefe's medium. The various school boards which restricted the media employed by Wilson here, and by Keefe, Parducci, and Sterzing in the cases cited, suppressed expression which the First Amendment protects.

But the school boards may restrict teachers' expression if the restrictions are reasonable in light of the special circumstances of the school environment. Thus, question two: was this order reasonable?

I conclude that the order was not reasonable and therefore violated the First Amendment.

The order barred political speakers absolutely, yet no disruptions had occurred in Wilson's classes, or at other school gatherings where political subjects were discussed. Further, none were expected in the future.

The defendants have not shown that outside speakers impair high school education. If they did, the board still would lack justification for banning only outside *political* speakers. Moreover, the evidence demonstrated that the use of outside speakers is widely recommended, widely practiced, and professionally accepted.

The boards cannot justify the ban by contending that political subjects are inappropriate in a high school curriculum. Political subjects frequently are discussed at Molalla High School and other schools throughout the country, as required by law. Nor does the board have a valid interest in suppressing, as it did, political expression occurring in the course of recognized extracurricular activities.

The board cannot contend it was acting within its discretionary power to exclude incompetent speakers. It acted under pressure from those who feared, rather than doubted, the speaker's competence by banning all speakers without regard to competence.

The board's only apparent reason for issuing the order which suppressed protected speech was to placate angry residents and taxpayers. The First Amendment forbids this; neither fear of voter reaction nor personal disagreement with views to be expressed justifies a suppression of free expression, at least in the absence of any reasonable fear of material and substantial interference with the educational process.

The order, by granting school officials discretion to bar political speakers before those persons speak, creates a system of prior restraint.

Prior restraints are not unconstitutional per se, but their invalidity is heavily presumed. * * * They are valid only if they include criteria to be followed by school authorities in determining whether to allow or forbid the expression and procedural safeguards in the form of an expeditious review procedure. * * *

The Molalla board order was completely bare; it failed to include either criteria by which to define "political speakers" or procedural safeguards in any form.

The order therefore constitutes an invalid prior restraint. Although our language contains many words and phrases which require no further definition, the phrase "political speakers" is not among them. * * *

* * *

The challenged order discriminates against political speakers by banning only them from the high school. It also discriminates against teachers of politically-oriented subjects by prohibiting only them from using outside speakers in the classroom.

Legislation invariably classifies and discriminates; whenever it grants benefits to some classes it denies them to others. These classifications are inherent in the legislative act, and are unconstitutional only under prescribed circumstances.

Classifications which restrain conduct protected by the First Amendment are unconstitutional unless they suitably further an appropriate governmental interest. * * * Appropriate governmental interests include the desire to promote effective education by preventing material disruptions of classroom work, substantial disorders, or invasions of the rights of others, * * * or by averting a clear and present danger * * * .

Because I already have concluded that the order did not further any appropriate governmental interests, and therefore violated the First Amendment, I must also conclude that it violated the equal protection clause. The order exists to silence absolutely the expression of an unpopular political view, solely out of fear that some will listen. This the government, acting through the school board, cannot do.

The board discriminated in a third way. It allowed Wilson to invite a Republican, a Democrat, and a member of the John Birch Society to speak to his class, but it forbade him from inviting a Communist.

The effect was discriminatory. Persons with palatable views could speak; those with less readily digestible views could not.

An order prohibiting Wilson from inviting a Republican to class after a Democrat had spoken there clearly would be discriminatory. That Wilson invited a Communist rather than a champion of the current political orthodoxy has no constitutional significance.

* * *

I do not imply that members of a community now may sue to compel schools to open their doors to particular outside speakers. Such compulsion would restrict a teacher's freedom rather than protect it, contrary to the important policies that I have outlined.

Nor do I suggest that Federal courts stand ready to regulate the regimen and to control the curricula of our public schools. A teacher is not required to have outside speakers contribute to class. I hold only that this regulation, as it applied in this particular set of facts, does not withstand constitutional scrutiny.

And I do not malign the defendant board members. Their position is sensitive, at once both a challenge and an opportunity. They serve a community in which many persons equate Communism with violence, deception, and imperialism. Yet violence, deception, and imperialism have occurred under many flags and in the name of many creeds. School boards could eliminate much of the high schools' curricula by restricting them to theories, philosophies, and practices of resolutely pacifistic, honest, nonexpansionist societies.

It seems these same residents fear that young Molallans will become young Marxists and Maoists, virtually overnight. Because Oregon law * * * requires the schools to specially emphasize our form of government, respect for the flag, and obedience to our laws, this fear seems ill-founded. Moreover, today's high school students are surprisingly sophisticated, intelligent, and discerning. They are far from easy prey to even the most forcefully expressed, cogent, and persuasive words.

Finally, I am firmly convinced that a course designed to teach students that a free and democratic society is superior to those in which freedoms are sharply curtailed will fail entirely if it fails to teach one important lesson: that the power of the state is never so great that it can silence a man or woman simply because there are those who disagree. Perhaps that carries with it a second lesson: that those who enjoy the blessings of a free society must occasionally bear the burden of listening to others with whom they disagree, even to the point of outrage.

* * *

Notes and Questions

Who has the *ultimate* authority to decide what will or will not take place in a classroom? a teacher? building-level administrators? central office administrators? the local school board? state department of education? state legislature? the Department of Education? courts? What factors would influence your decision? Does grade level and/or nature of the subject matter being taught affect the decision?

Apparently, academic freedom may be bargained away. A teacher's association negotiated an agreement with a provision that the board shall have the right to "determine the processes, techniques, methods and means of teaching any and all subjects." Several English teachers challenged the school board's action in directing that certain books not be purchased or assigned. The court held for the school board but contended it would have held for the teachers if the negotiated agreement had not existed. See *Cary v. Board of Education of Adams-Arapahoe School Dist. 28-J,* 598 F.2d 535 (10th Cir. 1979).

IV. Dress and Grooming

Personal appearance of teachers in respect to dress and grooming has received considerable attention in the courts. School authorities generally contend that proper dress and grooming establish a professional image for teachers, promote good grooming among students, and aid in the maintenance of respect and decorum in the classroom. Teachers, on the other hand, generally allege that local regulations governing their personal appearance invade their rights of privacy and liberty. Issues raised in these conflicts include the wearing of "long" hair or sideburns for males, wearing of a beard, wearing of a tie and/or jacket for a male, and improper skirt length for a female.

East Hartford Education Association v. Board of Education of Town of East Hartford

United States Court of Appeals, Second Circuit, 1977
562 F.2d 838

* * *

Before KAUFMAN, Chief Judge, and SMITH, FEINBERG, MANS-
FIELD, MULLIGAN, OAKES, TIMBERS, GURFEIN, VAN GRAAFEI-
LAND and MESKILL, Circuit Judges.

On petition for Rehearing En Banc

MESKILL, Circuit Judge:

Although this case may at first appear too trivial to command the
attention of a busy court, it raises important issues concerning the proper
scope of judicial oversight of local affairs. The appellant here, Richard
Brimley, is a public school teacher reprimanded for failing to wear a
necktie while teaching his English class. Joined by the teachers union, he
sued the East Hartford Board of Education, claiming that the reprimand
for violating the dress code deprived him of his rights of free speech and
privacy. Chief Judge Clarie granted summary judgment for the defendants. * * * A divided panel of this Court reversed and remanded
for trial. 562 F.2d at 838-856 (1977). At the request of a member of the
Court, a poll of the judges in regular active service was taken to determine if the case should be reheard *en banc*. A majority voted for rehearing. We now vacate the judgment of the panel majority and affirm the
judgment of the district court.

The facts are not in dispute. In February, 1972, the East Hartford
Board of Education adopted "Regulations For Teacher Dress." At that
time, Mr. Brimley, a teacher of high school English and filmmaking,
customarily wore a jacket and sport-shirt, without a tie. His failure to wear
a tie constituted a violation of the regulation and he was reprimanded for
his delict. Mr. Brimley appealed to the school principal and was told that
he was to wear a tie while teaching English, but that his informal attire
was proper during filmmaking classes. He then appealed to the superintendent and the board without success, after which he began formal arbi-
tration proceedings, which ended in a decision that the dispute was not
arbitrable. This lawsuit followed. Although Mr. Brimley initially complied
with the code while pursuing his remedies, he has apparently returned to
his former mode of dress. * * *

In the vast majority of communities, the control of public schools is
vested in locally-elected bodies. This commitment to local political bodies
requires significant public control over what is said and done in school.
* * * It is not the federal courts, but local democratic processes, that
are primarily responsible for the many routine decisions that are made in
public school systems. Accordingly, it is settled that "[c]ourts do not and

cannot intervene in the resolution of conflicts which arise in the daily operation of school systems and which do not directly and sharply implicate basic constitutional values." * * *

* * *

Because the appellant's clash with his employer has failed to "directly and sharply implicate basic constitutional values," we refuse to upset the policies established by the school board.

Mr. Brimley claims that by refusing to wear a necktie he makes a statement on current affairs which assists him in his teaching. In his brief, he argues that the following benefits flow from his tielessness:

> (a) He wishes to present himself to his students as a person who is not tied to "establishment conformity."
>
> (b) He wishes to symbolically indicate to his students his association with the ideas of the generation to which those students belong, including the rejection of many of the customs and values, and of the social outlook, of the older generation.
>
> (c) He feels that dress of this type enables him to achieve closer rapport with his students, and thus enhances his ability to teach.

Appellant's claim, therefore, is that his refusal to wear a tie is "symbolic speech," and, as such, "is protected against governmental interference by the First Amendment."

We are required here to balance the alleged interest in free expression against the goals of the school board in requiring its teachers to dress somewhat more formally than they might like. * * * When this test is applied, the school board's position must prevail.

Obviously, a great range of conduct has the symbolic, "speech-like" aspect claimed by Mr. Brimley. To state that activity is "symbolic" is only the beginning, and not the end, of constitutional inquiry. * * * Even though intended as expression, symbolic speech remains conduct, subject to regulation by the state. * * *

As conduct becomes less and less like "pure speech" the showing of governmental interest required for its regulation is progressively lessened. * * * In those cases where governmental regulation of expressive conduct has been struck down, the communicative intent of the actor was clear and "closely akin to 'pure speech.' " * * * Thus, the First Amendment has been held to protect wearing a black armband to protest the Vietnam War, * * * burning an American Flag to highlight a speech denouncing the government's failure to protect a civil rights leader, * * * or quietly refusing to recite the Pledge of Allegiance. * * *

In contrast, the claims of symbolic speech made here are vague and unfocused. Through the simple refusal to wear a tie, Mr. Brimley claims that he communicates a comprehensive view of life and society. It may well be, in an age increasingly conscious of fashion, that a significant portion of the population seeks to make a statement of some kind through its clothes. * * * However, Mr. Brimley's message is sufficiently vague to place it close to the "conduct" end of the "speech-conduct" continuum described above. * * * While the regulation of the school board must still pass constitutional muster, the showing required to uphold it is significantly less than if Mr. Brimley had been punished, for example, for publicly speaking out on an issue concerning school administration. * * *

At the outset, Mr. Brimley had other, more effective means of communicating his social views to his students. He could, for example, simply have told them his views on contemporary America; if he had done this in a temperate way, without interfering with his teaching duties, we would be confronted with a very different First Amendment case. * * * The existence of alternative, effective means of communication, while not conclusive, is a factor to be considered in assessing the validity of a regulation of expressive conduct. * * *

Balanced against appellant's claim of free expression is the school board's interest in promoting respect for authority and traditional values, as well as discipline in the classroom, by requiring teachers to dress in a professional manner. A dress code is a rational means of promoting these goals. * * *

This balancing test is primarily a matter for the school board. Were we local officials, and not appellate judges, we might find Mr. Brimley's arguments persuasive. However, our role is not to choose the better educational policy. We may intervene in the decisions of school authorities only when it has been shown that they have strayed outside the area committed to their discretion. If Mr. Brimley's argument were to prevail, this policy would be completely eroded. Because teaching is by definition an expressive activity, virtually every decision made by school authorities would raise First Amendment issues calling for federal court intervention.

The very notion of public education implies substantial public control. Educational decisions must be made by someone; there is no reason to create a constitutional preference for the views of individual teachers over those of their employers. * * * [T]he First Amendment claim made here is so insubstantial as to border on the frivolous. We are unwilling to expand First Amendment protection to include a teacher's sartorial choice.

Mr. Brimley also claims that the "liberty" interest grounded in the due process clause of the Fourteenth Amendment protects his choice of attire. * * * This claim will not withstand analysis.

* * *

* * * If Mr. Brimley has any protected interest in his neckwear, it does not weigh very heavily on the constitutional scales. As with most legislative choices, the board's dress code is presumptively constitutional. It is justified by the same constitutional concerns for respect, discipline

and traditional values described in our discussion of the First Amendment claim.

The rights of privacy and liberty in which appellant seeks refuge are important and evolving constitutional doctrines. To date, however, the Supreme Court has extended their protection only to the most basic personal decisions. * * * Nor has the Supreme Court been quick to expand these rights to new fields. * * * As with any other constitutional provision, we are not given a "roving commission" to right wrongs and impose our notions of sound policy upon society. There is substantial danger in expanding the reach of due process to cover cases such as this. By bringing trivial activities under the constitutional umbrella, we trivialize the constitutional provision itself. If we are to maintain the vitality of this new doctrine, we must be careful not to "cry wolf" at every minor restraint on a citizen's liberty. * * *

The two other Courts of Appeals which have considered this issue have reached similar conclusions. In *Miller* v. *School District*, 495 F.2d 658 (7th Cir. 1974), the Seventh Circuit upheld a grooming regulation for teachers. * * * The First Circuit reached the same result in *Tardif* v. *Quinn*, 545 F.2d 761 (1st Cir. 1976), where a school teacher was dismissed for wearing short skirts. * * *

Both *Miller* and *Tardif* are stronger cases for the plaintiff's position than the instant case. Both involved dismissals rather than, as here, a reprimand. Moreover, *Miller* involved a regulation of hair and beards, as well as dress. Thus, Miller was forced to appear as his employers wished both on and off the job. In contrast, Mr. Brimley can remove his tie as soon as the school day ends. If the plaintiffs in *Miller* and *Tardif* could not prevail, neither can Mr. Brimley.

Each claim of substantive liberty must be judged in the light of that case's special circumstances. In view of the uniquely influential role of the public school teacher in the classroom, the board is justified in imposing this regulation. As public servants in a special position of trust, teachers may properly be subjected to many restrictions in their professional lives which would be invalid if generally applied. * * * We join the sound views of the First and Seventh Circuits, and follow *Kelley* [425 U.S. 238 (1976), a challenge to a police department's hair grooming regulations], by holding that a school board may, if it wishes, impose reasonable regulations governing the appearance of the teachers it employs. There being no material factual issue to be decided, the grant of summary judgment is affirmed.

Notes

Other federal courts of appeals have held similarly to the **East Hartford** decision. The wearing of beards by untenured teachers at the high school and junior high school levels was addressed in *Ball* v. *Board of Trustees of* *the Kerrville Independent School District,* 584 F.2d 684 (5th Cir. 1978), cert. denied, 440 U.S. 972 (1979) and *Miller* v. *School District No. 167,* 495 F.2d 658 (7th Cir. 1974). However, a midcontract dismissal of a junior college instructor who refused to shave his beard was held to be unconstitutional. See *Hander* v. *San Jacinto Junior College,* 519 F.2d 273 (5th Cir. 1975).

V. Teacher as Exemplar

Not too many years ago a teacher's lifestyle was determined to a large extent by a school system's formal or informal, often rigid rules. An example is Rules of Conduct for Teachers, which was published by a local West Virginia Board of Education in 1915.

Rules of Conduct for Teachers

1. You will not marry during the term of your contract.

2. You are not to keep company with men.

3. You must be home between the hours of 8:00 P.M. and 6:00 A.M. unless attending a school function.

4. You may not loiter downtown in ice cream stores.

5. You may not travel beyond the city limits unless you have the permission of the chairman of the board.

6. You may not ride in a carriage or automobile with any man unless he is your father or brother.

7. You may not smoke cigarettes.

8. You may not dress in bright colors.

9. You may under no circumstances dye your hair.

10. You must wear at least two petticoats.

11. Your dresses must not be any shorter than two inches above the ankle.

12. To keep the schoolroom neat and clean, you must sweep the floor at least once daily; scrub the floor at least once a week with hot, soapy water; clean the blackboards at least once a day, and start the fire at 7:00 A.M. so the room will be warm by 8:00 A.M.

All school teachers did not work under such restrictive rules. However, a belief had developed over the years that teachers should act as examples to their charges and that they should be exemplars to their students in such areas as dress, grooming, the social amenities, and morals.

Although it may at times have been difficult for a teacher to uphold the community's view of exemplary conduct, this expectation was generally well known to the teacher. In those days a teacher knew that improper dress or grooming, being seen drunk in public, and, for females, divorce would result not only in school authorities' disapproval but possibly in dismissal. The same rules applied to extramarital affairs, "improper" or "immoral" conduct on the part of single teachers, and homosexuality.

Changing lifestyles and frequent lack of agreement regarding not necessarily exemplary but merely "proper" conduct may make it difficult for a teacher to know when a norm is transgressed or exceeds school authorities' or a community's zone of acceptance. This problem is further heightened by the fact that teacher conduct which may be tolerated in a metropolitan area may not be in a small town with a homogeneous population that considers itself conservative.

Since state statutes may cite "immorality" as a ground for teacher dismissal, courts have been called upon repeatedly to adjudicate issues dealing with controversial lifestyles. Some of these issues have included homosexuality, adultery, unmarried members of the opposite sex living together, unwed pregnant teachers, sex-change operations, and sexual advances by teachers toward students. Although court decisions have not been consistent, they have determined that in certain areas of personal conduct, teachers do not necessarily have to be exemplars. An overriding factor in most of the cases is whether or not a questionable lifestyle or persuasion hampers a teacher's effectiveness. Courts have demonstrated a reluctance to enforce or bar conduct solely on the basis of conformity, historical precedent, or "expert" opinion. Rather, they have required that there be a connection between the conduct in question and actual teaching performance.

To date courts have been inconsistent in their treatment of adulterous teachers or unmarried couples living together. However, they have generally not upheld dismissals of teachers for being unmarried and pregnant but have consistently upheld dismissals based on homosexuality or sexual advances toward students. In one instance, *In re Grossman*, 127 N.J. Super. 13, 316 A.2d 39 (1974), a court upheld the dismissal of a male tenured teacher who underwent sex-reassignment surgery to change his external anatomy to that of a female.

A. Homosexual Teacher

Gaylord v. Tacoma School District No. 10

Supreme Court of Washington, 1977
88 Wash.2d 286, 559 P.2d 1340, cert. denied,
434 U.S. 879 (1977)

HOROWITZ, Associate Justice.

Plaintiff-appellant, James Gaylord, appeals a judgment of the trial court upholding Gaylord's discharge from employment as a high school teacher by defendant school district. A prior appeal resulted in a remand to the trial court to enter new findings based upon application of the proper statutory burden of proof of the district.   *   *   *   The case now before us is an appeal from the judgment entered on new findings and conclusions entered by the trial court on remand.

*   *   *

We need consider only the assignments of error which raise two basic issues: (1) whether substantial evidence supports the trial court's conclusion plaintiff-appellant Gaylord was guilty of immorality; (2) whether substantial evidence supports the findings, that as a known homosexual, Gaylord's fitness as a teacher was impaired to the injury of the Wilson High School, justifying his discharge by the defendant school district's board of directors. The relevant findings of the trial court may be summarized as follows.

Gaylord knew of his homosexuality for 20 years prior to his trial, actively sought homosexual company for the past several years, and participated in homosexual acts. He knew his status as a homosexual, if known, would jeopardize his employment, damage his reputation and hurt his parents.

Gaylord's school superior first became aware of his sexual status on October 24, 1972, when a former Wilson High student told the school's vice-principal he thought Gaylord was a homosexual. The vice-principal confronted Gaylord at his home that same day with a written copy of the student's statement. Gaylord admitted he was a homosexual and attempted unsuccessfully to have the vice-principal drop the matter.

On November 21, 1972, Gaylord was notified the board of directors of the Tacoma School Board had found probable cause for his discharge due to his status as a publicly known homosexual. This status was contrary to school district policy No. 4119(5), which provides for discharge of school employees for "immorality." After hearing, the defendant board of directors discharged Gaylord effective December 21, 1972.

The court found an admission of homosexuality connotes illegal as well as immoral acts, because "sexual gratification with a member of one's own sex is implicit in the term 'homosexual.'" These acts were proscribed by RCW 9.79.120 (lewdness) and RCW 9.79.100 (sodomy).

After Gaylord's homosexual status became publicly known, it would and did impair his teaching efficiency. A teacher's efficiency is determined by his relationship with his students, their parents, the school administration and fellow teachers. If Gaylord had not been discharged after he became known as a homosexual, the result would be fear, confusion, suspicion, parental concern and pressure on the administration by students, parents and other teachers.

The court concluded "appellant was properly discharged by respondent upon a charge of immorality upon his admission and disclosure that he was a homosexual" and that relief sought should be denied.

Was Gaylord guilty of immorality?

Our concern here is with the meaning of immorality in the sense intended by school board policy No. 4119(5). School boards have broad management powers. * * * Under RCW 28A.58.100(1) the school board may discharge teachers for "sufficient cause." Policy No. 4119(5) adopted by the school board and in effect during the term of Gaylord's teaching contract with defendant school district permits the Tacoma School Board of Directors to treat "immorality" as sufficient cause for discharge.

"Immorality" as used in policy No. 4119(5) does not stand alone. RCW 28A.67.110 makes it the duty of all teachers to "endeavor to impress on the minds of their pupils the principles of morality, truth, justice, temperance, humanity, and patriotism . . . " RCW 28A.70.140 requires an applicant for a teacher's certificate be "a person of good moral character." RCW 28A.70.160 makes "immorality" a ground for revoking a teacher's certificate. Other grounds include the commission of "crimes against the laws of the state." The moral conduct of a teacher is relevant to a consideration of that person's fitness or ability to function adequately as a teacher of the students he is expected to teach—in this case high school students. * * *

"Immorality" as a ground of teacher discharge would be unconstitutionally vague if not coupled with resulting actual or prospective adverse performance as a teacher. * * * The basic statute permitting discharge for "sufficient cause" (RCW 38A.58.100(1)) has been construed to require the cause must adversely affect the teacher's performance before it can be invoked as a ground for discharge. * * *

It follows the term "immorality" is not to be construed in its abstract sense apart from its effect upon teaching efficiency or fitness to teach. In its abstract sense the term is not and perhaps cannot be comprehensively defined although it can be illustrated.

When, as in the case here, the term "immorality" has not been defined in policy No. 4119(5), it would seem reasonable to give the term its ordinary, common, everyday meaning as we would when construing an undefined term in a statute. * * *

* * *

The medical and psychological and psychiatric literature on the subject of homosexuality distinguishes between the overt homosexual and the passive or latent homosexual. An overt homosexual has homosexual inclinations consciously experienced and expressed in actual homosexual behavior as opposed to latent. A latent homosexual is one who has "an erotic inclination toward members of the same sex, not consciously experienced or expressed in overt action; opposite of overt." * * * However, it has been pointed out that "actually individual homosexuals do not necessarily maintain an active or passive attitude exclusively in a given relationship, inasmuch as they alternate in the male and female roles." * * *

Moreover, homosexual experience of an overt nature varies among homosexuals, from males who are more or less exclusively homosexual to males that are only occasionally so. * * *

In the instant case Gaylord "admitted his status as a homosexual" * * * [a]nd "from appellant's own testimony it is unquestioned that homosexual acts were participated in by him, although there was no evidence of any overt act having been committed." * * *

* * *

This rule of construction concerning his admission of homosexuality is supported by evidence that Gaylord was and had been a homosexual for 20 years. He also testified that in the 2-year period before his discharge, he actively sought out the company of other male homosexuals and participated actively as a member of the Dorian Society (a society of homosexuals). He responded to a blind advertisement in the society's paper for homosexual company. He concealed his homosexuality from his parents until compelled to reveal it by the present dispute.

If Gaylord meant something other than homosexual in the usual sense, he failed to explain what he meant by his admission of homosexuality or being a homosexual so as to avoid any adverse inference, although he had adequate opportunity at trial to do so. He clearly had a right to explain that he was not an overt homosexual and did not engage in the conduct the court ascribed to him which the court found immoral and illegal. Evidence that explains the admission or qualifies it is clearly admissible. * * * There was uncontroverted evidence plaintiff was a competent and intelligent teacher so the court could reasonably assume Gaylord knew what homosexuality could mean. It was not a word to be thoughtlessly or lightly used. Gaylord's precaution for 20 years to keep his status of being a homosexual secret from his parents is eloquent evidence of his knowledge of the serious consequences attendant upon an undefined admission of homosexuality.

He testified that in June 1970 he realized that if he was "ever going to have [homosexual] friends . . . that I needed, that I was going to have to make more efforts of my own to find these people because I wasn't going to stumble across them by accident as I expected." It was about that time he joined the Dorian Society. He testified he "felt very comfortable with the people there." Eventually he began to attend a good many of their functions. On one occasion a high school boy conferred with the plaintiff about homosexuality and learned that plaintiff was "deeply involved" for a period of a month with a person whose advertisement he had answered. It would have been a simple matter for Gaylord to have explained the physical side, if any, of his relationship but he did not do so.

Our next inquiry is whether homosexuality as commonly understood is considered immoral. Homosexuality is widely condemned as immoral and was so condemned as immoral during biblical times. * * *

A sociologist testified in the instant case: "A majority of people and adults in this country react negatively to homosexuality." A psychiatrist testified "I would say in our present culture and certainly, in the last few hundred years in Western Europe and in America this [homosexuality] has been a frightening idea . . ."

The court found "sexual gratification with a member of one's own sex is implicit in the term 'homosexual.' " * * * This finding would not necessarily apply to latent homosexuals, however, the court in effect found from the evidence and reasonable inferences therefrom, it applied to Gaylord. These acts—sodomy and lewdness—were crimes during the period of Gaylord's employment and at the time of his discharge. * * *

Volitional choice is an essential element of morality. One who has a disease, for example, cannot be held morally responsible for his condition. Homosexuality is not a disease, however. Gaylord's witness, a psychiatrist, testified on cross-examination that homosexuality except in a case of hormonal or congenital defect (not shown to be present here) is not inborn. Most homosexuals have a "psychological or acquired orientation." Only recently the Board of the American Psychiatric Association has stated: "homosexuality . . . by itself does not necessarily constitute a psychiatric disorder." * * *

Nevertheless it is a disorder for those who wish to change their homosexuality which is acquired after birth. In the instant case plaintiff desired no change and has sought no psychiatric help because he feels comfortable with his homosexuality. He has made a voluntary choice for which he must be held morally responsible. * * *

The remaining question on this point is whether the repeal of the sodomy statute (RCW 9.79.100), while this case was pending, deprives sodomy of its immoral character. In the first place the repeal did not go into effect until July 1, 1976, sometime after Gaylord's discharge. Sodomy between consenting adults is no longer a crime. * * * Generally the fact that sodomy is not a crime no more relieves the conduct of its immoral status than would consent to the crime of incest.

The next question is whether the plaintiff's performance as a teacher was sufficiently impaired by his known homosexuality to be the basis for discharge. The court found that Gaylord, prior to his discharge on December 21, 1972, had been a teacher at the Wilson High School in the Tacoma School District No. 10 for over 12 years, and had received favorable evaluations of his teaching throughout this time. * * *

First, he argues his homosexuality became known at the school only after the school made it known and that he should not be responsible therefore so as to justify his discharge as a homosexual. The difficulty with this argument is twofold. First, by seeking out homosexual company he took the risk his homosexuality would be discovered. It was he who granted an interview to the boy who talked to him about his homosexual problems. The boy had been referred to Gaylord for that purpose by the homosexual friend to whom Gaylord had responded favorably in answering his advertisement in the paper of the Dorian Society. As a result of that interview the boy came away with the impression plaintiff was a homosexual and later told the assistant high school principal about the matter. The latter in turn conferred with plaintiff for the purpose of verifying the charge that had been made. It was the vice-principal's duty to report the information to his superiors because it involved the performance capabilities of Gaylord. The school cannot be charged with making plaintiff's condition known so as to defeat the school board's duty to protect the school and the students against the impairment of the learning process in all aspects involved.

Second, there is evidence that at least one student expressly objected to Gaylord teaching at the high school because of his homosexuality. Three fellow teachers testified against Gaylord remaining on the teaching staff, testifying it was objectionable to them both as teachers and parents. The vice-principal and the principal, as well as the retired superintendent of instruction, testified his presence on the faculty would create problems. There is conflicting evidence on the issue of impairment but the court had the power to accept the testimony it did on which to base complained of findings. * * * The testimony of the school teachers and administrative personnel constituted substantial evidence sufficient to support the findings as to the impairment of the teacher's efficiency.

It is important to remember that Gaylord's homosexual conduct must be considered in the context of his position of teaching high school students. Such students could treat the retention of the high school teacher by the school board as indicating adult approval of his homosexuality. It would be unreasonable to assume as a matter of law a teacher's ability to perform as a teacher required to teach principles of morality * * * is not impaired and creates no danger of encouraging expression of approval and of imitation. Likewise to say that school directors must wait for prior specific overt expression of homosexual conduct before they act to prevent harm from one who chooses to remain "erotically attracted to a notable degree towards persons of his own sex and is psychologically, if not actually disposed to engage in sexual activity prompted by this attraction" is to ask the school directors to take an unacceptable risk in discharging their fiduciary responsibility of managing the affairs of the school district.

We do not deal here with homosexuality which does not impair or cannot reasonably be said to impair his ability to perform the duties of an occupation in which the homosexual engages and which does not impair the effectiveness of the institution which employs him. However, even the federal civil service regulations on which Gaylord relies to show a change in attitude towards homosexuals provides:

> [W]hile a person may not be found unsuitable based on substantiated conclusions concerning possible embarrassment to the Federal service, a person may be dismissed or found unsuitable for Federal employment where the evidence establishes that such person's sexual conduct affects job fitness.

* * * It must be shown that "the conduct of the individual may reasonably be expected to interfere with the ability of the person's fitness in the job or against the ability to discharge its responsibility." * * * These principles are similar to those applicable here. The challenged findings and conclusions are supported by substantial evidence.

Affirmed.

DOLLIVER, Associate Justice (dissenting).

The appellant, Mr. Gaylord, had been a teacher at Wilson High School for over 12 years at the time of his discharge. In college, he had been an outstanding scholar: he graduated Phi Beta Kappa from the University of Washington and was selected "Outstanding Senior" in the political science department. He later received a masters degree in librarianship. As a teacher, the evaluations made of Mr. Gaylord were consistently favorable. The most recent evaluation of this teaching performance stated that "Mr. Gaylord continues his high standards and thorough teaching performance. He is both a teacher and student in his field."

Despite this outstanding record, the trial court found that Mr. Gaylord should be discharged for "immorality." To uphold this dismissal, we must find substantial evidence supporting the finding that Mr. Gaylord was discharged for "sufficient cause."

* * *

There is not a shred of evidence in the record that Mr. Gaylord participated in any of the acts stated above. While we have held in the past that "sufficient cause" requires certain *conduct* * * * , we are presented here with a record showing no illegal or immoral conduct; we have only an admission of a homosexual status and Gaylord's testimony that he sought male companionship. * * *

Undoubtedly there are individuals with a homosexual identity as there are individuals with a heterosexual identity, who are not sexually active. Mr. Gaylord, for all we know, may be one of these individuals.

Certainly in this country we should be beyond drawing severe and far-reaching inferences from the admission of a status—a status which may be no more than a state of mind. Furthermore, there are homosexual activities involving a physical relationship which are not prohibited by statute. * * *

The trial court made a most puzzling finding that, "From appellant's own testimony it is unquestioned that homosexual acts were participated in by him, although there was no evidence of any overt acts having been committed." The trial court essentially found that, as an admitted homosexual, unless Mr. Gaylord denied doing a particular immoral or illegal act, he can be assumed to have done the act. The court has placed upon the appellant the burden to negate what it asserts are the implications that may be drawn from his testimony although he never was accused of participating in acts of sodomy or lewdness.

We must require here, as we have in the past, proof of conduct to justify a dismissal. The only conceivable testimony on conduct was the comment of the student that Gaylord and another male were "deeply involved" for about a month. This hardly qualifies as testimony either as to "immorality," sodomy or lewdness. Finding no conduct, I am unwilling to take the leap in logic accepted by the majority that admission of a status or identity implies the commission of certain illegal or immoral acts.

* * *

Surely the majority has adopted a novel approach. Mr. Gaylord was never at any time accused of performing any "homosexual acts." Yet because of his declared status, he must assume the burden of proving he did not commit certain illegal or immoral acts which have at no time been referred to or mentioned, much less described, by the school board. Presumably under this reasoning, an unmarried male who declares himself to be heterosexual will be held to have engaged in "illegal or immoral acts." The opportunities for industrious school districts seem unlimited.

The majority goes to great lengths to differentiate between an overt and a latent homosexual. Authority is cited that overt homosexuality is "consciously experienced and expressed in actual homosexual behavior." Yet there is no evidence in the record of any actual behavior of acts, and the findings of the trial court specifically state "there was no evidence of any overt act having been committed." The real problem faced by the majority is that the term "homosexual" is not mentioned once in the Revised Code of Washington. There is no law in this state against being a homosexual. All that is banned (prior to July 1, 1976) are certain acts, none of which Mr. Gaylord was alleged to have committed and none of which can it be either assumed or inferred he committed simply because of his status as a homosexual.

The second glaring error in this proceeding is the respondent's failure to establish that Mr. Gaylord's performance as a teacher was impaired by his homosexuality. As pointed out by the trial court in its findings, the evidence is quite clear that, having been a homosexual for the entire time he taught at Wilson High School, the fact of Mr. Gaylord's homosexuality did not impair his performance as a teacher. In other words, homosexuality per se does not preclude competence.   *   *   *

The evidence before the court is uncontroverted—Mr. Gaylord carefully kept his private life quite separate from the school.   *   *   *   He made no sexual advances toward his professional contemporaries or his students. There is absolutely no evidence that Mr. Gaylord failed in any way to perform the duties listed in RCW 28A.67.110. In over 12 years of teaching at the same school, his best friends on the teaching staff were unaware of his homosexuality until the time of his discharge. Gaylord did not use his classroom as a forum for discussing homosexuality. Given the discretion with which Gaylord conducted his private life, it appears that public knowledge of Gaylord's homosexuality occurred, as the trial court found, at the time of his dismissal.   *   *   *

At the trial, a variety of witnesses speculated on the effect that Gaylord's homosexuality might have on his effectiveness in the classroom. The speculation varied considerably. Certainly there were witnesses who testified that Gaylord's effectiveness would be damaged. There were also those who testified to the contrary. As a result, the trial court found that "the continued employment of appellant after he became known as a homosexual would result, had he not been discharged, in confusion, suspicion, fear, expressed parental concern and pressure upon the administration." The question this court must ask is whether a finding of detrimental effect can be made on the basis of conjecture alone.

*   *   *

Historically, the private lives of teachers have been controlled by the school districts in many ways. There was a time when a teacher could be fired for a marriage, a divorce, or for the use of liquor or tobacco.   *   *   * Although the practice of firing teachers for these reasons has ceased, there are undoubtedly those who could speculate that any of these practices would have a detrimental effect on a teacher's classroom efficiency as well as cause adverse community reaction. I find such speculation to be an unacceptable method for justifying the dismissal of a teacher who has a flawless record of excellence in his classroom performance.   *   *   *

What if Mr. Gaylord's status was as a black, a Roman Catholic, or a young heterosexual single person, instead of a male homosexual? Would his dismissal be handled in such a manner? Mere speculation coupled with status alone is not enough.   *   *   *   In this finding, substitute the words "black" or "female" for "homosexual" and the defect of the majority approach is brought into sharp focus.

*   *   *

Notes and Questions

Tangential to the issue of dismissal of a homosexual teacher for unfitness or immorality is a freedom-of-expression issue; namely, may teachers express their sexual preferences or advocate homosexuality? Courts have addressed these issues in several decisions.

A nontenured vocational guidance counselor informed several colleagues that she was bisexual and had a female lover. In upholding her nonrenewal a federal appellate court held that her First Amendment rights had not been violated. In citing *Connick* v. *Myers*, 461 U.S. 138 (1983) the court stated, "If a public employee's statement cannot be fairly characterized as constituting speech on a matter of public concern, it is unnecessary to scrutinize the reasons for the discharge." The court opined that the teacher was speaking in her personal interest and that there was no evidence of any public concern in the high school or community with the issue of bisexuality among school personnel. See *Rowland* v. *Mad River School District,* 730 F.2d 444 (6th Cir. 1984), cert. denied, 470 U.S. ___, 105 S.Ct. 1373 (1985). Justice Brennan, joined by Justice Marshall in a lengthy dissent, chastised the Court's majority for not accepting the case for review.

The Tenth Circuit Court of Appeals upheld a portion of an Oklahoma statute proscribing homosexual activity, but it declared unconstitutional the portion prohibiting the advocacy of such activity. Specifically, the court found fault with a section that barred "advocating, soliciting, imposing, encouraging or promoting public or private homosexual activity in a manner that creates a substantial risk that such conduct will come to the attention of school children or school employees .... ." The court stated that this provision purported to regulate "pure speech" and that the first amendment protects advocacy of legal as well as illegal conduct as long as such advocacy does not incite imminent lawlessness. See *National Gay Task Force* v. *Board of Education of Oklahoma City,* 729 F.2d 1270 (10th Cir. 1984), aff'd. by an equally divided Court, 470 U.S. ___, 105 S.Ct. 1858 (1985).

A number of other decisions have addressed the issue of dismissing or revoking certificates of homosexual teachers. See *Ross* v. *Springfield School District No. 19,* 71 Or. App. 57, 691 P.2d 509 (1984); *Gish* v. *Board of Education of the Borough of Paramus,* 145 N.J. Super. 96, 366 A.2d 1337 (1977), cert. denied, 434 U.S. 879 (1977); *Board of Education of Long Beach Unified School District* v. *Jack M.,* 19 Cal.3d 691, 566 P.2d 602, 139 Cal. Rptr. 700 (1977); *Burton* v. *Cascade School District Union High School No. 5,* 512 F.2d 850 (9th Cir. 1975), cert. denied, 423 U.S. 839 (1975); *Acanfora* v. *Board of Education of Montgomery County,* 491 F.2d 498 (4th Cir. 1974), cert. denied, 419 U.S. 836 (1974); *McConnell* v. *Anderson,* 451 F.2d 193 (8th Cir. 1971), cert. denied, 405 U.S. 1046 (1972); and *Morri-*

son v. *State Board of Education,* 1 Cal.3d 214, 461 P.2d 375, 82 Cal. Rptr. 175 (1969).

Do school authorities have a duty to ferret out homosexual teachers? A reading of several decisions suggests that teaching effectiveness is impaired if homosexual teachers bring undue attention to themselves. Does this suggest that homosexuality among teachers is acceptable if it is not admitted or overt?

B. Adulterous Teacher

Erb v. Iowa State Board of Public Instruction

Supreme Court of Iowa, 1974
216 N.W.2d 339

McCORMICK, Justice.

In this appeal plaintiff Richard Arlan Erb challenges the revocation of his teaching certificate. The certificate was revoked by defendant Board of Educational Examiners after a hearing on July 16, 1971. Erb brought an action in certiorari alleging the board's action was illegal. After the trial the writ of certiorari was annulled. Erb appealed. We reverse.

* * *

Erb, a native Iowan, military veteran, and holder of a master's degree in fine arts, received his Iowa teaching certificate in 1963. Since then he has taught art in the Nishna Valley Community School which serves an area including the towns of Strahn, Emerson, Hastings, and Stanton. He resides in Emerson, is married and has two young sons. In addition to teaching he has coached wrestling, assisted with football, and acted as senior class sponsor.

The complaint against Erb was made by Robert M. Johnson, a farmer whose wife Margaret taught home economics in the Nishna Valley School. Johnson told the board his goal was removal of Erb from the school and not revocation of his teaching certificate. He read an extensive statement in which he detailed his observations relating to an adulterous liaison between Erb and Johnson's wife which began and ended in spring 1970.

Margaret planned to quit teaching and open a boutique in Red Oak. Her association with Erb began in early spring when he agreed to assist her with design of the store. They saw each other often. By May, Johnson became suspicious of Margaret's frequent late-night absences from home.

He suspected Margaret and Erb were meeting secretly and engaging in illicit activity in the Johnson automobile. One night in May he hid in the trunk of the car. Margaret drove the car to school, worked there for some time, and later drove to a secluded area in the country where she met Erb. Margaret and Erb had sexual intercourse in the back seat of the car while Johnson remained hidden in the trunk. Johnson did not disclose his presence or his knowledge of the incident.

Instead he consulted a lawyer with a view toward divorcing Margaret. He told the board he was advised his interests in a divorce action would be better served if he had other witnesses to his wife's misconduct. After several days of fruitless effort to catch Margaret and Erb in a compromising situation, he and his "raiding party" eventually located them one night in June parked in a remote area. Johnson and the others surrounded the car and took photographs of Margaret and Erb who were partially disrobed in the back seat. Johnson told Margaret not to come home and that further communication would be through lawyers. He told Erb to disclose the affair to his wife.

Erb did so. He and Margaret terminated their affair. Erb offered to resign his teaching position, but the local school board unanimously decided not to accept his resignation. The board president testified Erb's teaching was highly rated by his principal and superintendent, he had been forgiven by his wife and the student body, and he had maintained the respect of the community. Erb was retained for the ensuing school year and continued to teach in the Nishna Valley school.

Witnesses before the board included Erb's past and present high school principals, his minister, a parent of children in the school, and a substitute teacher. All vouched for his character and fitness to teach. His superintendent gave essentially the same testimony in district court. The board refused to allow Erb's attorney to cross-examine Johnson or two witnesses in support of Erb's character and fitness to teach. Trial court ruled in its pretrial order that under the admitted record Erb's teacher-student relationship had not been impaired by his conduct.

The board voted five to four to revoke Erb's teaching certificate and, without making any findings of fact or conclusions of law, ordered it revoked. Revocation was stayed by trial court and then by this court pending outcome of the certiorari action and appeal. Trial court held Erb's admitted adulterous conduct was sufficient basis for revocation of his certificate and annulled the writ.

* * * In this appeal Erb contends the board acted illegally (1) in denying his right to cross-examine witnesses against him and limiting the number of his witnesses, (2) in failing to make findings, and (3) in revoking his teaching certificate without substantial evidence that he is not morally fit to teach.

Limitations at the hearing. Erb did not object before the board to the board's denial of his right of cross-examination and limitation on the number of his witnesses. These questions cannot be presented for the first time here. Erb was obliged to raise them before the board and the trial court. * * * Since he did not do so he failed to preserve error in these respects for review here.

Failure of the board to make findings. A different situation exists concerning the board's failure to make findings of fact. Erb's first opportunity to complain of the absence of board findings was in his certiorari action, and he did raise the issue there. We hold the board acted illegally in failing to make findings of fact.

Although Iowa does not have an administrative procedure act to guide administrative boards, we have held such boards are required, even without statutory mandate, to make findings of fact on issues presented in any adjudicatory proceeding. Such findings must be sufficiently certain to enable a reviewing court to ascertain with reasonable certainty the factual basis and legal principle upon which the administrative body acted. * * *

The board violated this precept in the present case. No findings were made. This would be sufficient basis to hold trial court should have sustained the writ of certiorari. However, reversing the case on that basis would return the case to the board which could make its findings on the present record and would not answer the remaining issue whether there is substantial evidence in the record which would permit the board to find Erb is not morally fit to teach. If that issue is resolved favorably to Erb, the case will be ended now in his favor rather than sent back to the board for findings.

Sufficiency of the evidence. Since the board made no findings there is no intelligible way to determine what interpretation the board gave to its statutory authorization to revoke the certificate of one not "morally fit to teach." But nothing prevents us from determining whether there is substantial evidence in the record which would have supported revocation if the proper standard had been applied. Erb contends there is not. We agree. We will first examine the standard and then the sufficiency of the evidence.

This court has not previously been called upon to decide what constitutes moral unfitness to teach. The legislature provided no definition in code chapter 260.

* * *

The board contends the fact Erb admitted adultery is sufficient in itself to establish his unfitness to teach. This assumes such conduct automatically and invariably makes a person unfit to teach. We are unwilling to make that assumption. It would vest the board with unfettered power to revoke the certificate of any teacher whose personal, private conduct incurred its disapproval regardless of its likely or actual effect upon his teaching. The legislature did not give the board that kind of power in Code § 260.23. The label applied to the teacher's conduct is only a lingual abstraction until given content by its likely or actual effect on his fitness to teach. Morrison v. State Board of Education, 1 Cal.3d 214, 82 Cal.Rptr. 175, 194, 461 P.2d 375, 394 (1969); * * * 68 Am Jur. 2d Schools § 134 at 465 ("Where the courts have been presented with the question whether or not specific conduct of a teacher constitutes moral unfitness which would justify revocation, they have apparently required that the conduct must adversely affect the teacher-student relationship before revocation will be approved.").

As observed by the Morrison court, "Surely incidents of extramarital heterosexual conduct against a background of years of satisfactory teaching would not constitute 'immoral conduct' sufficient to justify revocation of a life diploma without any showing of an adverse effect on fitness to teach." * * *

We emphasize the board's power to revoke teaching certificates is neither punitive nor intended to permit exercise of personal moral judgment by members of the board. Punishment is left to the criminal law, and the personal moral views of board members cannot be relevant. A subjective standard is impermissible and contrary to obvious legislative intent. The sole purpose of the board's power under § 260.23 is to provide a means of protecting the school community from harm. Its exercise is unlawful to the extent it is exercised for any other purpose.

In Morrison the California court discussed factors relevant to application of the standard:

> "In determining whether the teacher's conduct thus indicates unfitness to teach the board may consider such matters as the likelihood that the conduct may have adversely affected students or fellow teachers, the degree of such adversity anticipated, the proximity or remoteness in time of the conduct, the type of teaching certificate held by the party involved, the extenuating or aggravating circumstances, if any, surrounding the conduct, the praiseworthiness or blameworthiness of the motives resulting in the conduct, the likelihood of the recurrence of the questioned conduct, and the extent to which disciplinary action may inflict an adverse impact or chilling effect upon the constitutional rights of the teacher involved or other teachers." * * *

These factors have relevance in deciding whether a teacher is morally fit to teach under Code § 260.2. Since the same standard is applicable in determining whether a certificate should be revoked under Code § 260.23, a certificate can be revoked only upon a showing before the board of a reasonable likelihood that the teacher's retention in the profession will adversely affect the school community.

There was no evidence of such adverse effect in the present case. No one even asserted such an effect. The complainant himself acknowledged his purpose was to remove Erb from the school rather than from teaching. The evidence showed Erb to be a teacher of exceptional merit. He is dedicated, hardworking and effective. There was no evidence to show his affair with Margaret Johnson had or is likely to have an adverse effect upon his relationship with the school administration, fellow teachers, the student body, or the community. Overwhelming and uncontroverted evidence of local regard and support for Erb is a remarkable testament to the ability of a community to understand, forgive and reconcile.

There was no evidence other than that Erb's misconduct was an isolated occurrence in an otherwise unblemished past and is not likely to recur. The conduct itself was not an open or public affront to community mores; it became public only because it was discovered with considerable effort and made public by others. * * * Erb made no effort to justify it; instead he sought to show he regretted it, it did not reflect his true character, and it would not be repeated.

* * * [W]e are persuaded the evidence adduced before the board would not support a finding that Erb is morally unfit to teach in Iowa.

The board acted illegally in revoking his certificate. Trial court erred in annulling the writ of certiorari.

Reversed.

Notes and Questions

Would a state supreme court have ruled the same way in the **Erb** case twenty years ago? fifty years ago?

A school board's dismissal, in midterm, of a single female elementary school teacher who was openly living with a man was upheld. The court in *Sullivan* v. *Meade Independent School District No. 101*, 530 F.2d 799 (8th Cir. 1976) contended that

> . . . Ms. Sullivan's conduct violated local mores, that her students were aware of this, and that, because of the size of the town, this awareness would continue. . . . Ms. Sullivan was shown to have generated deep affection from her students, increasing the probability of emulation. . . . (P. 804)

> * * *

> . . .[however,] the parameters of the newly evolving constitutional right to privacy are not yet clear. While the right of a couple to live together without benefit of matrimony eventually may be held to fall within the penumbra of the constitutional right to privacy, it had not been so held at the time the Board dismissed the appellant. . . . (P. 806)

Would the dismissal by the school board of a male in similar circumstances have been upheld by this court?

See *Fisher* v. *Snyder*, 476 F.2d 375 (8th Cir. 1973), in which the court did not uphold the dismissal of a high school teacher accused of having men not related to her staying in her apartment. This court concluded that:

> ... while a school board may legitimately inquire into the character and integrity of its teachers, ... it must be certain that it does not arbitrarily or capriciously dismiss a teacher based on unsupported conclusions drawn from such inquiries.
>
> *   *   *
>
> But here, there is no proof of improper conduct. The only whit of evidence offered as support for the board's conclusion that Mrs. Fisher was guilty of unbecoming conduct was the fact that she had overnight guests. But the presence of these guests in her home provides no inkling beyond subtle implication and innuendo which would impugn Mrs. Fisher's morality. Idle speculation certainly does not provide a basis in fact for the board's conclusory inference that "there was strong potential of sexual misconduct" and that, therefore Mrs. Fisher's activity was "social misbehavior that is not conducive to the maintenance of the integrity of the public school system." We agree with the district court that "At most, the evidence may be said to raise a question of Mrs. Fisher's good judgment in her personal affairs, when measured against an undefined standard which someone could suppose exists in a small town in Nebraska." (Pp. 377–378)

What appears to be the reason for the seemingly opposite holdings in *Sullivan* and *Fisher*?

C. Unwed Pregnant Teacher

Avery v. Homewood City Board of Education

United States Court of Appeals, Fifth Circuit, 1982
674 F.2d 337

TJOFLAT, Circuit Judge:

Jean Avery brought this action in the district court, alleging that the termination of her teaching contract by the Homewood City Board of Education was unlawful. Following a bench trial, the court concluded that although one of the grounds of Avery's discharge was arguably impermissible, the presence of another, permissible, ground rendered the termination lawful. Accordingly, the court entered judgment for the defendants. The district court erred by holding that the mere presence of a permissible ground for Avery's discharge rendered the discharge lawful. On the record before it, the court was required to enter judgment for Avery. We therefore vacate the judgment of the district court and direct the entry of judgment for the plaintiff.

Jean Avery, a black woman, taught remedial reading at Shades Cahaba Elementary School in Homewood City, Alabama, from 1972 until her discharge on February 8, 1977. A written policy of the Homewood City Board of Education (the Board) required teachers who became pregnant so to inform the Superintendent of Education (the Superintendent) no later than the fourth month of pregnancy (the notice rule). In mid-November, 1976, Avery, who was not married, informed her principal that she was expecting to give birth in late December. The principal commented that Avery was in violation of the notice rule and instructed her to inform the Superintendent of her pregnancy, which Avery did.

Avery and the Superintendent, Dr. French, discussed Avery's situation in early December, 1976. According to Dr. French's testimony, he emphasized Avery's violation of the notice rule. According to Avery, Dr. French urged her to resign because of the "moral issue" of conception out of wedlock.

In any event, Dr. French notified Avery by letter of December 15, 1976, that the Board would meet to determine whether to cancel her contract for three reasons: insubordination, neglect of duty, and immorality. As Superintendent, Dr. French was authorized to recommend Avery's dismissal, and the three grounds stated in the December 15 letter were charges he would be bringing before the Board. As Dr. French testified, both "insubordination" and "neglect of duty" referred to Avery's violation of the notice rule, and "immorality" referred to her pregnancy out of wedlock.

On February 8, 1977, the Board voted to terminate Avery's employment immediately, and instructed Dr. French so to inform Avery. Dr. French did so by letter of February 11, 1977, specifying no reasons for the discharge.   *   *   *

Avery sued the Board, Dr. French, and the Board members (collectively appellees), alleging that her discharge violated Title VII of the Civil Rights Act of 1964, 42 U.S.C. § 2000e *et seq.* (1976); Title IX of the Education Amendments Act of 1972, 20 U.S.C. § 1681 et seq. (1976); 42 U.S.C. §1981 (1976); and, because it deprived her of rights guaranteed by the equal protection and due process clauses of the fourteenth amendment, 42 U.S.C. § 1983 (1976). She sought reinstatement with back pay, tenure status, lost benefits, declaratory and injunctive relief, and attorney's fees. Underlying each legal theory in the complaint was the premise that the Board unlawfully based its decision to dismiss Avery on her immoral conception of a child out of wedlock. Avery has at no time claimed that the notice rule is unlawful either facially or as applied.

The district court found that Avery's employment had been terminated in part for immorality and acknowledged that a discharge for that reason might be unconstitutional. However, the court found that it was not necessary to reach the issue:

> Immorality was only one of the grounds for termination. Defendants contend that the plaintiff's employment was also terminated on the grounds of insubordination or neglect of duty in not reporting her pregnancy. Clearly she did not comply with the school rules with respect to reporting. . . . The notice rule . . . is reasonable, and the School Board was justified in terminating her for this refusal. That being the case, the court finds it unnecessary to reach the constitutional issue and the other issues raised by plaintiff.

The district court held in effect that, without regard to the immorality charge, Avery's dismissal was lawful because it was based in part on a permissible ground. This holding contravened the standards of proof and causation mandated by the Supreme Court for mixed-motive discharge cases such as this one. See *Mt. Healthy City School Dist. Bd. of Educ. v. Doyle*, 429 U.S. 274. * * *

The Court concluded that the fact that constitutionally protected conduct played a substantial part in the termination decision did not necessarily indicate a constitutional violation justifying remedial action.

* * * Rather, the proper test would protect against the invasion of constitutional rights without commanding consequences not necessary to the assurance of those rights:

> Initially, . . . the burden was properly placed upon [the plaintiff] to show that his conduct was constitutionally protected, and that this conduct was a "substantial factor"—or to put it in other words, that it was a "motivating factor" in the Board's decision not to rehire him. [Plaintiff] having carried that burden, however, the District Court should have gone on to determine whether the Board had shown by a preponderance of the evidence that it would have reached the same decision as to [plaintiff's] reemployment even in the absence of the protected conduct. * * *

The framework of proof established in *Mt. Healthy* applies to Avery's constitutional claims. The burden was initially on Avery to show that her conduct was constitutionally protected and was a substantial or a motivating factor in the Board's decision to discharge her. We assume, *arguendo*, that Avery's out of wedlock pregnancy was constitutionally protected. The district court found that the pregnancy was one of the reasons for Avery's discharge; the appellees did not dispute at trial that a motivating factor in Avery's discharge was immorality, and do not challenge the district court's finding to that effect on appeal.

Having found that Avery had carried her initial burden, the district court should have gone on to determine whether the appellees had proven by a preponderance of the evidence that they would have discharged Avery even in the absence of her out of wedlock pregnancy. Since the court instead held that the other, unchallenged, ground for

Avery's dismissal rendered the Board's decision lawful, the district court's judgment must be vacated.

Having concluded that the district court's application of the wrong framework of proof caused it to neglect an essential factual inquiry, our usual course would be to remand the case to the district court for that inquiry. Having thoroughly reviewed the record, however, we are convinced that the district court could not permissibly find that the appellees proved by a preponderance of the evidence that the Board would have discharged Avery even absent her out of wedlock pregnancy.

The appellees insist that the record shows that Avery's violation of the notice rule was a substantial factor in the Board's decision to discharge her. This is correct, but irrelevant; the appellees' burden was to prove not that their decision was substantially motivated by that violation, but rather that Avery would have been dismissed even in the absence of her out of wedlock pregnancy. The record includes no evidence whatever to permit that inference. Dr. French charged Avery with immorality when he recommended her discharge and, according to Dr. French's testimony, the reasons for her discharge were the three grounds specified in his December 15 letter. Neither Dr. French nor the one Board member who testified offered any evidence, direct or circumstantial, to suggest what they would have done about Avery's violation of the notice rule if she had been married. The appellees offered no evidence of the Board's treatment of married teachers who had violated the notice rule. Since no evidence in the record supports the proposition that Avery would have been dismissed absent consideration of her out of wedlock pregnancy, we would set aside as clearly erroneous a finding by the district court that the appellees proved that proposition by a preponderance of the evidence. Fed.R.Civ.P. 52(a). Therefore, we find that the appellees did not carry their burden to show that they would have discharged Avery even absent her asserted immorality.

The only remaining question is whether a discharge on account of pregnancy out of wedlock is, as Avery maintains, unlawful. As we have noted, Avery challenges her dismissal on both statutory and constitutional grounds. Ordinarily, we would address the statutory claims first. However, the presence in this case of controlling authority that Avery's discharge on account of unwed pregnancy was unconstitutional counsels that we address Avery's constitutional claims first.

In *Andrews* v. *Drew Municipal Separate School Dist.*, 507 F.2d 611 (5th Cr. 1975). *cert. dismissed as improvidently granted*, 425 U.S. 559, * * * (1976), the defendant school district automatically disqualified from employment any parent of an illegitimate child. In a suit brought by an affected teacher aide and an affected applicant for a position as a teacher aide, we held that the prohibition against the employment of unwed parents violated the equal protection clause of the fourteenth amendment. Inquiring whether the classification established by the school district's policy was rationally related to a legitimate government interest, we rejected all three rationales offered in support of the contention that the rule furthered the creation of a properly moral scholastic environment: (1) that unwed parenthood is prima facie proof of immorality; (2) that unwed parents are unfit role models; (3) that employment of an unwed parent in a scholastic environment materially contributes to the problem of school-girl pregnancies. * * *

The appellees argue, as did the school district in *Andrews*, that unwed parenthood is *per se* proof of immorality and that a parent of an illegitimate child is an unfit role model. The appellees offer no support for either assertion that was not before us in *Andrews*, nor do the appellees offer any meaningful distinction between *Andrews* and this case. Therefore, we hold that Avery's discharge was in violation of her rights under the equal protection clause of the fourteenth amendment. So holding, we need not reach her other claims.

The judgment of the district court is vacated. The case is remanded to the district court, which is instructed to determine the relief to which Avery is entitled and to enter judgment accordingly.

VACATED and REMANDED, with instructions.

Notes and Questions

Several other courts have ruled similarly to **Avery.** See *Cochran* v. *Chidester School District*, 456 F.Supp. 390 (Ark. 1978); *Brown* v. *Bathke*, 566 F.2d 588 (8th Cir. 1977); *New Mexico State Board of Education* v. *Stoudt*, 91 N.M. 183, 571 P.2d 1186 (1977); *Andrews* v. *Drew Municipal Separate School District*, 507 F.2d 611 (5th Cir. 1975); and *Drake* v. *Covington County Board of Education*, 371 F. Supp. 974 (Ala. 1974).

What would be the status of a single female teacher who had been artificially inseminated or who became a surrogate mother?

D. Criminal Activities

Gillett v. Unified School District No. 276

Supreme Court of Kansas, 1980
605 P.2d 105

PRAGER, Justice:
This case involves a controversy between a school teacher and school board over the nonrenewal of her teaching contract. Unified school dis-

trict No. 276 appeals from a judgment of the district court reversing the school board's decision not to renew the teacher's employment contract. The trial court ordered the teacher to be reinstated with back pay.

The facts in the case are not greatly in dispute and essentially are as follows: Unified school district No. 276 is located in Jewell County. Jessie Mae Gillett is a tenured teacher who had been continuously employed by the school district for a period of seven years. Her last term of employment covered the 1976–77 school year. On March 11, 1977, the school board delivered to Mrs. Gillett a notice of nonrenewal of her teaching contract for the following year pursuant to K.S.A. 1977 Supp. 72–5437. The notice, which was contained in a letter from the president and clerk of the school board, was in the form required by statute. The reason given for nonrenewal was the existence of criminal charges of shoplifting pending against Mrs. Gillett in Hastings, Nebraska. Mrs. Gillett promptly filed a request for a due process hearing on the matter. On May 5, 1977, the board served on the teacher a notice which contained a supplemental list of reasons for nonrenewal including the following:

1. Inability to properly handle school funds;
2. Excessive absences from teaching school duties for allegedly being ill;
3. Improper use of sick leave;
4. Physical and mental instability; and
5. Loss of community, student, and school board respect for this teacher.

Mrs. Gillett, through her counsel, objected to the consideration of the supplemental reasons contending they were not timely served. The hearing committee overruled the objection, stating that it would consider the supplementary reasons.

* * *

The recommendation of the hearing committee was delivered to the school board, which considered all of the evidence presented in the case together with arguments and briefs of counsel. The board unanimously decided to follow its previous decision of nonrenewal of Mrs. Gillett's contract. The board made no findings of fact and gave no specific reason in writing for rejecting the committee's recommendation. Mrs. Gillett then appealed the school board's decision to the district court, using K.S.A. 60–2101(d) as required by K.S.A. 1977 Supp. 72–5443. The district court reviewed the transcript of the evidence presented at the due process hearing and heard arguments of counsel. The district court entered judgment in favor of Mrs. Gillett, ordering her reinstated with back pay. * * *

* * *

The primary issue raised on this appeal is whether the district court erred in holding that the school board had failed to present substantial evidence to support its reason for nonrenewal. From the evidentiary record in the case, we have concluded that there was substantial competent evidence showing good cause which justified the school board in its decision not to renew the teaching contract of Mrs. Gillett. In the original notice of nonrenewal served on the teacher on March 11, 1977, the reason given for nonrenewal was the criminal charges pending against Mrs. Gillett in Hastings, Nebraska. The evidence of the pendency of these two criminal cases was undisputed. Although Mrs. Gillett did not take the stand herself, the evidence presented on her behalf showed without question that she had taken articles at two stores in Hastings, Nebraska, on October 16, and November 17, 1976. The teacher did not deny that she took the articles of property. Her defense to the accusation was that, because of her mental condition at the time, she was not criminally responsible for her actions. Dr. Dale W. Peters, a practicing psychiatrist, testified that he was a consultant to the Sunflower Guidance Center in Concordia. Mrs. Gillett was referred to that center for psychiatric evaluation in March of 1977. Dr. Peters examined her to determine her mental capacity and state of health, primarily for determining her mental state in relationship to the shoplifting incidents in Hastings, Nebraska. From these examinations, he concluded that, although she was not mentally ill, she was subject to altered states of consciousness resulting from sensitive reactions to a wide variety of foods. Various tests showed her sensitive to numerous foods which at times interfered with the functioning of her brain cells. During these attacks, she would become mentally disturbed and her judgment adversely affected.

At the time of her arrests in Hastings, Nebraska, it appeared that Mrs. Gillett was acting strangely and out of touch with reality. The thrust of Dr. Peters testimony was that, at the time of the shoplifting incidents in Hastings, Nebraska, Mrs. Gillett, being in an altered state of consciousness, was not responsible for her actions. The evidence showed that she had been involved in another shoplifting incident in 1973. Apparently on a number of occasions, she had become confused and lost while driving her motor vehicle. Each of these situations involved an altered state of consciousness which came on gradually. Dr. Peters testified that acute episodes can be dramatic. Such episodes could last up to one hour and could occur at any time, including during classroom hours. Dr. Peters conceded that Mrs. Gillett could again be involved in shoplifting incidents in the future and that she was still under treatment at the time of the hearing. Although Dr. Peters was of the opinion that there was no danger to the students in the classroom, he indicated an attack during class could be disruptive. Similar attacks could occur either from the consumption of certain foods or from a withdrawal from such foods. At the time of the hearing Mrs. Gillett was in the course of an elimination diet which, hopefully, might eliminate her problem. If it did not work, then additional testing and treatment would be required. Dr. Peters mentioned over 80 foods which could cause Mrs. Gillett to go into an altered state of consciousness. He further stated that this list was inconclusive and that there might be other foods which could affect her in the same way.

A teacher testified that at one time she had observed Mrs. Gillett in an altered state of consciousness while seated in her automobile. After the arrests at Hastings, she heard a student discussing the fact that Mrs. Gillett had been arrested. Another teacher testified that she had also heard students mention the fact that Mrs. Gillett had been arrested. This was the first time the teacher had known about it. There was no evidence presented at the hearing as to the ultimate outcome of the criminal actions. There was testimony tending to show that Mrs. Gillett had been careless in keeping candy sale proceeds in her desk drawer and in failing to make daily deposits at the bank as directed by the school superintendent. However, there was no proof of any misappropriation or loss of any money as the result of Mrs. Gillett's handling of the school funds. In regard to excessive absences from teaching duties for allegedly being ill, the record is devoid of any misconduct on the part of the teacher in this regard. In regard to loss of community, student, and school respect for the teacher, the president of the school board testified that in his opinion the school board had community support in the nonrenewal of Mrs. Gillett's contract. A substitute teacher testified about a classroom incident where students were caught copying. When she told them copying wasn't allowed, the students responded: "The teacher can get away with it."

Mr. Ralph Hooten, who was president of the school board at the time the letter of nonrenewal was delivered to Mrs. Gillett, testified that the school board had unanimously decided that Mrs. Gillett's teaching contract should not be renewed because of the criminal charges of shoplifting pending in Nebraska. This conclusion was reached only after substantial discussion by the board over a period of hours. The board had concluded that these shoplifting charges reduced her efficiency as a teacher. It appeared to him that, with the charges pending, the learning atmosphere would be improved if her contract was not renewed. Mr. Hooten stated that the board was aware of a similar charge of shoplifting in the year 1973 which was subsequently dismissed. At the time the board decided not to pursue the matter further. When the charges came up again in 1976, the board felt that they could not ignore those charges, having knowledge of the prior incident in 1973. It is fair to conclude, from Mr. Hooten's testimony, that the school board was very much concerned about the criminal charges against Mrs. Gillett, that the board spent hours discussing the situation, and that they decided to nonrenew her contract rather than to terminate her in midyear.

The issue to be determined here is whether there is substantial evidence in the record sufficient to establish good cause, justifying the school board's decision of nonrenewal of the teaching contract. The district court found that there was not. We have concluded there was. The problem presented in this case was obviously one of great difficulty for the school board. The trial court specifically found that the school board had not arbitrarily and fraudulently refused to accept the findings of the hearing committee. The district court was correct in that finding. It is difficult to reconcile that finding with the additional finding that there was no substantial evidence to support the board's reason for nonrenewal. Here the evidence was undisputed that, for a period of at least three years, the teacher had been subject to altered states of consciousness, during which she did not know what she was doing and her judgment and her conduct were adversely affected. At the time of the hearing, a testing and treatment program for Mrs. Gillett had been undertaken but not completed. She was attempting to get to the cause of her problem and was taking appropriate action to do something about it. However, we do not believe that, at that time, the school board acted unreasonably in concluding that it would be for the best interests of the school system to nonrenew Mrs. Gillett's teaching contract for the following school year.

We think it significant that in this case the teacher did not personally take the witness stand to give her own explanation as to her physical and mental condition or to deny that she, knowingly with larcenous intent, took property from the stores in Hastings, Nebraska. She did not testify that the treatment then being administered was effective or was beginning to solve her problem. She did not testify as to her relationship with the students, or with other teachers, or with the school administrators. Not a single witness testified as to any contributions she was making to the educational program of the school district.

We cannot in good conscience find from the evidence that the board's action was not taken in good faith, or that it was arbitrary, irrational, unreasonable, or irrelevant to the school board's objective of maintaining an efficient school system for the students in the school district. It follows that the judgment of the district court must be reversed and the case remanded to the district court with directions to enter judgment in favor of the school board.

It is so ordered.

Note

In a similar case a permanent teacher's indefinite contract was terminated because of three instances of alleged immoral conduct: stealing a teapot that was a prop in a school play, twenty dollars from a basketball game's receipts, and a set of the school's books. See *Kimble* v. *Worth County R-III Board of Education*, 669 S.W.2d 949 (Mo. App. 1984).

E. Sexual Advances toward Students

Moore v. Knowles

United States Court of Appeals, Fifth Circuit, 1973
482 F.2d 1069

ON PETITION FOR REHEARING
PER CURIAM:

*　*　*

Moore, the plaintiff below, was a male teacher in the eighth grade of a Texas school system, teaching both male and female students. In early 1970, female pupils made assertions to law enforcement officers that Moore had engaged in or attempted misconduct with them of a sexual nature. Immediately school officials excluded Moore from classroom teaching. Subsequently the school board, without a proper hearing, suspended him from teaching duties, with pay, for the remainder of the 1969–70 school year. Later the board, without hearing, refused to consider renewal of Moore's contract for the 1970–71 school year.

*　*　*

The exclusion of Moore from continuing to perform his teaching duties occurred on January 7, 1970, immediately after the girl students made their assertions to law enforcement officers. In a conference on January 7, attended by law enforcement officers, Moore was informed of the pupils' charges. He was not then formally suspended but was barred from continuing his classroom teaching duties. His pay continued. We agree with the analysis of the District Court that, upon balancing all the considerations involved, the board did not violate due process by forthwith, and pending further developments, directing that Moore must not continue teaching his classes. School officials, responsible for the safety of teenage students, had a range of discretion in acting to meet what reasonably could be considered as an emergency situation and to keep school going. *　*　*

On January 28 the county grand jury indicted Moore on four charges: two separate charges of aggravated assault and battery and one of contributing to delinquency of a minor, all allegedly relating to one child; one charge of assault with intent to rape and indecent exposure, allegedly concerning another child. Beginning around January 13 Moore had begun to seek a hearing before the board. On February 11, without a proper hearing, the school board notified Moore that he was relieved from his teaching duties for the remainder of the school year, with pay, pending further investigation by the board and further consideration of the matter. For the same considerations spelled out above, plus the intervening indictments by the grand jury, we consider that the board did not err in changing Moore's status, without a hearing, from that of teacher without portfolio to suspension from teaching duties for the remainder of the year, with pay. In reaching this conclusion we consider the grand jury's actions to have special significance, which we discuss below.

We turn now to the refusal to consider renewal of Moore's contract. On February 27 the superintendent informed Moore that the renewal of his contract for 1970–71 would not be acted upon pending resolution of the "problems with which you are acquainted." In the subsequent litigation in District Court board members acknowledged that their actions concerning Moore were taken as a consequence of the outstanding indictments and that in other respects he was a qualified teacher. The court found that Moore had an expectancy of employment and that the school board's failure to give him a hearing on its refusal to renew his contract for 1970–71 was a violation of due process, and the court awarded him back pay for 1970–71 plus attorney fees. We reversed as to the failure to renew the contract for 1970–71, based on Perry v. Sindermann, 408 U.S. 593 (1972), in which the Supreme Court held that the mere expectancy of employment did not necessitate a hearing.

* * *

But this case involves considerations not present in the Supreme Court's hypothetical "different case." The law enforcement machinery of the State of Texas had intervened. Undoubtedly the board's acts in first suspending Moore from teaching duties for the remainder of the year and then declining to consider his contract for renewal added to the damage to Moore's reputation, but the real "badge of infamy" flowed from the indictments and not from what the board did in reacting to them, and no action by the board could clear Moore's name. * * *

We conclude that the action of the board in declining, without hearing, to consider renewal of Moore's contract, was not a violation of due process under *Roth*. The fact of indictments was not in dispute. Moore had knowledge of the indictments and had notice of the board's reasons for refusing to act on his contract. Implicitly, if not explicitly, the board concluded, as had the superintendent initially, that a male eighth grade teacher charged with sexual misconduct with his teenage female pupils should not be in contact with them in the teaching process. A public employing body, having knowledge of the existence of charges such as were here made, as part of its ultimate conclusion must consider the extent to which the charges reflect the possibility of culpability. Had the board itself leveled the misconduct charges against Moore, or had it relied upon only the charges by the girl students, Moore would have been entitled to a hearing. ＊ ＊ ＊ But once the underlying charges were presented to and acted upon by the grand jury—the state body whose function is to consider evidence of crime and to determine whether there exist sufficient grounds to hold an accused for trial—the board was entitled to accept that body's probable cause determination. After the grand jury had acted, the issue for the board was not whether Moore had committed the acts charged by the girls or whether he was guilty or innocent under the indictments but whether the existence and pendency of the indictments justified his suspension and the refusal to act upon the matter of his contract renewal.

＊ ＊ ＊ A hearing before the board on the issue of Moore's guilt, or the issue of probable cause of guilt, would have placed the board in an unseemly position vis-a-vis the law enforcement structure of the state. The board was not the proper body to try guilt or innocence or to retry probable cause. Board findings in one direction would have injured the interests of the state, and in another direction would have damaged those of Moore.

＊ ＊ ＊

Our prior opinion is withdrawn. The judgment of the District Court is affirmed in part, vacated in part, and the cause is remanded to the District Court for further proceedings not inconsistent with this opinion.

VI. Discrimination

Certain personnel practices pertaining to women, minorities, older persons, and handicapped persons have been challenged as being discriminatory. Although it has been argued that some of these practices may have reflected custom and did not have an overt discriminatory intent when instituted, those directly affected by them have alleged that they were in fact discriminatory. Challenged practices that have received court and/or statutory attention include discriminatory treatment of pregnant teachers, discriminatory employment practices toward females, racial discrimination, and age discrimination.

A. Sex Discrimination

Section 703 of the Civil Rights Act of 1964, Title VII, provides in part that:

> (a) It shall be an unlawful employment practice for an employer—
> 1. to fail or refuse to hire or to discharge any individual, or otherwise to discriminate against any individual with respect to his compensation, terms, conditions, or privileges of employment, because of such individual's race, color, religion, sex, or national origin: or

2. to limit, segregate, or classify his employees in any way which would deprive or tend to deprive any individual of employment opportunities or otherwise adversely affect his status as an employee, because of such individual's race, color, religion, sex, or national origin.

(b) It shall be an unlawful employment practice for an employment agency to fail or refuse to refer for employment, or otherwise to discriminate against, any individual because of his race, color, religion, sex, or national origin, or to classify or refer for employment any individual on the basis of his race, color, religion, sex, or national origin. 12 C.F.R. § 528

Although not challenged on the basis of Title VII, *Marshall* v. *Kirkland* addresses the issue of sex-based discrimination in not hiring females for administrative and specialty positions.

Marshall v. Kirkland

United States Court of Appeals, Eighth Circuit, 1979
602 F.2d 1282

HANSON, Senior District Judge.

*   *   *

Appellants' complaint . . . alleges gender-based discrimination. Women have predominated as teachers in Barton-Lexa School District by a ratio of between three and four to one. Evidence was presented to the district court which indicated that the assignment to "specialty" positions (a position with extra duties for which an increment in compensation was provided), and promotion to one of the three administrative positions in the district (principal of the elementary school, principal of the high school, and superintendent of the district) was influenced by the sex of the employee and statistically favored males with a concomitant differential in pay as between men and women.

The district court concluded:

the plaintiffs have failed in their burden of presenting any testimony to the effect that discrimination due to sex existed within a period of 3 years from the commencement of this litigation.

*   *   *   Plaintiffs appeal from this determination that they failed to prove a prima facie case of sex discrimination.

*   *   *

* * * The district court held that a prima facie case of unconstitutional sex discrimination had not been made and that no rebuttable presumption arose. We conclude that the district court's finding in this regard is clearly erroneous and contrary to recently articulated constitutional principles with respect to the assignment of specialty personnel and promotion of teachers to administrative positions.

Appellants do not distinguish the elements involved in a constitutional as opposed to a Title VII statutory claim of sex discrimination. The two actions are different, however, as the Supreme Court has recently made clear. The evidence raises the question of whether defendants violated the right of female teachers, administrators, and applicants to equal protection of the law, a claim cognizable under 42 U.S.C. § 1983. Title VII is not involved.

As a general proposition, the equal protection clause of the Fourteenth Amendment, substantively inherent in the Fifth Amendment, grants to public employees "a federal constitutional right to be free from gender discrimination" unless a gender classification serves important governmental objectives and is substantially related to the achievement of those objectives. * * *

In *Feeney* the Supreme Court elaborated on what constitutes "discriminatory purpose": "It implies that the decisionmaker . . . selected or reaffirmed a particular course of action at least in part 'because of,' not merely 'in spite of,' its adverse effects upon an identifiable group." -- U.S. at --, 99 S.Ct. at 2296. If employment decisions or policies in the public employment area are made in part "because it would accomplish the collateral goal of keeping women in a stereotypic and predefined place," the Constitution is violated. * * *

* * *

The record indicates that during the relevant years there were ten or eleven administrative and specialty positions. As noted, the administrative positions were the superintendent and the elementary and high school principals. The seven or eight specialty positions, which carried an increment in pay because of extra duties involved, consisted of various jobs—coaching, physical education, counselor, agriculture and home economics teachers. The practice of the school district was that the three administrators usually came from the ranks of teachers, and the specialists were of course teachers compensated for extra duties.

With regard to the specialty positions, the home economics and girls' physical education teacher positions were occupied by women during the relevant years, while the other specialty positions were filled by men. Women teachers outnumbered men by a ratio of three or four to one with the net result that all or nearly all male teachers in the district had specialty positions while the great majority of women did not. With regard to pay, the women specialty teachers received less than the males, though this evidence was poorly developed. School board president W. F. Burney testified that "[i]t has . . . been the policy of the school to hire men" for coaching positions, * * * and he agreed "that the men always get specialty jobs and the women almost never get specialty jobs." * * * School superintendent Kirkland, prior to 1973 the principal at the high school and like Burney, a decisionmaker, agreed that the football, basketball, and track coaches had traditionally been men and that, with the exception of the girls' basketball coach (a special pay job established relatively recently), should continue to be men. * * * Kirkland candidly testified;

> [T]here is no evidence, to indicate that only men could perform those jobs, but again, this is something that has been traditionally done in this Country and I concur with it.

* * * He also testified that men had previously taught girls' physical education and that men would be capable of coaching girls' basketball. In contrast, women were not qualified to coach male athletic teams because "I just feel that a man could do [a] better job of handling a group of young men like that, than a woman." * * *

With respect to administrators, the evidence suggests that at the time of trial women were virtually disqualified from holding the position of high school principal and, as a consequence, superintendent. Mrs. Todd, the elementary principal during the relevant years, was the lowest paid of the three administrators. In 1973 David Bagley, a high school teacher, was promoted to high school principal to replace Mr. Kirkland who assumed the duties of superintendent. Mrs. Todd was concededly better qualified than Bagley, * * * but was not considered for the job. Mrs. Todd testified and did not indicate any interest in the high school principal or superintendent positions. However, Superintendent Kirkland did not indicate in his testimony that Todd's lack of interest was a factor in failing to consider her for the position. Instead, he testified that Todd was not considered "[b]ecause with the situation we had, and the students we had, I felt that we needed a man for the job." * * * Thereupon occurred the following colloquy between appellants' counsel and Mr. Kirkland:

> Q Now, fully explain that please. The situation you had and the students you had . . .
> A Because with high school students I feel that men are stronger disciplinarians than women are, and this particular instance I felt we needed a man in this position because part of the job was to be at athletic events, this sort of thing . . . to see that things . . . everything goes off as it should and I felt that a man could do a better job than a woman.

Q Well, what is the objective evidence that you have for arriving at the conclusion that a woman can't do those things?

A I don't have any, Mr. Walker.

Q Is that just a natural bias?

A I suppose it is.   *   *   *

Coupled with objective evidence showing a clear pattern of disproportionate gender representation in administrative and specialty positions, the testimony of school board president Burney and former principal and superintendent Kirkland strongly indicates that the sex of a teacher was an important part of assignment and promotion decisions in this area of the school district's employment. At the very least, appellants made a prima facie showing that decisionmakers in the school district sought to maintain women teachers in a "stereotypic and predefined place" in the school district and the district court clearly erred in finding otherwise.   *   *   * Indeed, the testimony of Burney and Kirkland would support a factual finding that the school district had a discernible policy or practice of hiring only men (or women) for certain specific administrative or specialty jobs. Such a finding would raise the question of whether the non-neutral gender classification could be justified as bearing a close and substantial relationship to important governmental objectives.   *   *   *

*   *   *

The district court observed that the school district "presented substantial testimony that no sex discrimination existed in the operation of the school system," but the court did not elaborate in view of its finding on the prima facie issue. Accordingly, on remand the district court should, on the basis of the present record, determine (1) by appropriate order whether the named plaintiffs may sue as representative parties on behalf of the class of all female teachers and applicants; (2) if the cause may be maintained as a class action, whether the evidence of no sex discrimination referred to by the district court rebuts the presumption in favor of class-wide equitable relief   *   *   *   ; and (3) whether the presumption in favor of individual relief has been rebutted with respect to those women who testified. Judgment may then be entered on the district court's supplemental findings and conclusions.

*   *   *

*   *   *   We reverse the district court's dismissal of the class and individual claims for relief predicated on alleged unconstitutional sex discrimination to the extent it relates to the assignment of female teachers to specialty positions and promotion to administrative positions. We remand the cause to the district court for further proceedings consistent with this opinion.

Though the results here is mixed, because on this appeal appellants' counsel has successfully established a prima facie case of sex discrimination, we award costs on appeal to appellants including $500 in attorney fees. 42 U.S.C. § 1988.

* * *

Notes

See *Jepsen* v. *Florida Board of Regents*, 610 F.2d 1379 (5th Cir. 1980) for an action brought under the Civil Rights Act of 1964, Title VII rather than under 42 U.S.C. § 1983.

Title IX regulations were vague on the question of whether the amendment covered employment practices of schools and colleges. A six-to-three decision by the United States Supreme Court reasoned that Congress had intended Title IX to cover employment. See *North Haven Board of Education* v. *Bell*, 456 U.S. 512 (1982). However, in *Grove City College* v. *Bell*, 465 U.S. 555 (1984), the Supreme Court, referring to private institutions, declared that Title IX did not apply to schools and colleges as a whole but only to those parts of an institution that received federal aid directly.

A religiously-oriented private school did not renew a pregnant teacher's contract because the school's tenets included "the importance of the mother in the home during the early years of child growth." Although such action would be considered discriminatory in a public school setting, a federal appellate court upheld the private school's action. This decision reveals that a private school with a religious affiliation may be immune from governmental anti-discriminatory regulations when its policies are grounded in religious beliefs. See *Dayton Christian Schools* v. *Ohio Civil Rights Commission*, 766 F.2d 932 (6th Cir. 1985).

A Fifth Circuit Court of Appeals recognized that a teacher's decision to breastfeed her baby had some constitutional dimensions. In its decision the court contended that the teacher's right to breastfeed her baby could be limited if this practice interfered with important educational interests that were furthered by the rules that prohibited teachers from bringing their children to work with them for any reason. See *Dike* v. *School Board of Orange County*, 650 F.2d 783 (5th Cir. 1981).

B. Pregnancy

A challenge to local school board policies that provided for mandatory leave at a particular time in a pregnancy and rules pertaining to reemployment after delivery has been heard by the United States Supreme Court. In its decision in *Cleveland Board of Education* v. *La Fleur*, 414 U.S. 632 (1974), the Court held that mandatory maternity termination provisions stating the number of months before anticipated childbirth violated the due process clause of the Fourteenth Amendment. The court reasoned that arbitrary cutoff dates have no valid relationship to the state's interest in preserving continuity of instruction, as long as the teacher is required to give substantial advance notice that she is pregnant. And the Court stated that the challenged provisions created a conclusive presumption that every teacher is physically incapable of continuing her duties at a specified time in her pregnancy. Additionally, the Court struck down the provision that a mother could not return to work until the next regular semester after her child was three months old.

Shortly after this decision many court challenges were brought against policies pertaining to disability benefits, sick leave, and health insurance involving pregnancy. The issue was addressed by the United States Supreme Court in a non-educator-related case, *General Electric Company* v. *Gilbert*, 429 U.S. 125 (1976). Largely as a result of the *Gilbert* decision, which upheld the exclusion of pregnancy-related disabilities from General Electric's comprehensive disability plan, Congress passed the Pregnancy Discrimination Act, which went into effect in 1979.*

This act is an amendment to Title VII of the Civil Rights Act of 1964, which prohibits, among other things, discrimination in employment on the basis of sex. The Pregnancy Discrimination Act makes it clear that "because of sex" or "on the basis of sex" as used in Title VII, includes "because of or on the basis of pregnancy, childbirth or related medical conditions." Therefore, Title VII prohibits discrimination in employment against women affected by pregnancy or related conditions.

The basic principle of the Act is that women so affected must be treated the same as other applicants and employees, on the basis of their ability or inability to work. A woman is therefore protected against such practices as being fired, or refused a job or promotion, because she is pregnant or has had an abortion. She usually cannot be forced to go on leave as long as she can still work. If other employees who take disability leave are entitled to resume their jobs when they are able to work again, so are women who have been unable to work because of pregnancy. Generally, there is no guarantee of returning to one's former position or school.

In the area of fringe benefits, such as disability benefits, sick leave, and health insurance, the same principle applies. A woman unable to work for pregnancy-related reasons is entitled to disability benefits or sick leave on the same basis as employees unable to work for other temporary medical reasons. Also, any health insurance provided must cover expenses for pregnancy-related conditions on the same basis as coverage given for other medical conditions. However, health insurance for expenses resulting from abortion is not required, except where the life of

*See appendix D for the text of this act.

the mother would be endangered if the fetus were carried to term or where medical complications have arisen from such an abortion.

In a seven-to-two decision the Court established that an insurance plan violated the 1964 Civil Rights Act and the Pregnancy Discrimination Act because it offered full hospitalization benefits to husbands of female workers but excluded pregnancy from the full coverage offered to the wives of male workers. The decision stated that under the plan "husbands of female employees receive a specified level of hospitalization coverage for all conditions; the wives of male employees receive such coverage except for pregnancy-related conditions. . . . The 1978 act makes clear that it is discriminatory to treat pregnancy-related conditions less favorably than other medical conditions." Therefore, the plan "unlawfully gives married male employees a benefit package for their dependents that is less inclusive than the dependency coverage provided to married female employees." See *Newport News Shipbuilding and Dry Dock Company* v. *Equal Employment Opportunity Commission, 462 U.S. 669 (1983).*

C. Racial Discrimination

Court action and statutory provisions such as those included in Title VII of the Civil Rights Act of 1964 and elsewhere have clearly stated that teachers should not suffer racial discrimination. Involuntary termination of black teachers in school systems that have been under court order to desegregate has resulted in severe action against the offending school system. In one such case in which black teachers had been involuntarily terminated, in the period between 1969 and 1976, a consent decree in a federal district court required the following from the school system: back pay for the terminated teachers; damages of $3,000 to individual teachers in several instances; attorneys' fees; court costs; expenses incurred by the teachers in bringing the action; reinstatement at the beginning of the next school year to their former teaching positions or if that was not possible, to positions with at least the same responsibilities, salaries, fringe benefits, privileges, and other requisites at least equal to those afforded other professionals holding similar positions and possessing similar employment; no hiring of white teachers, counselors, or administrators until all of the involuntarily terminated teachers had been reinstated; a list sent to the court for the next three years of the names and races of all staff members who were not rehired for the next school year, explaining the reasons for dismissal; a list sent to the court for the next three years of the names and races of all persons who applied for an employment position, the action taken, and the reasons for such action; and maintenance of a file for three years of the applications of all black persons who applied for a position, reconsideration each school year of the application of each black person who had not been hired the previous year, and a report to the court on the action taken. See *Hilson* v. *Ouzts*, No. 78-2449 (M.D. Ga. 1978).

Title VII was employed by a black assistant principal who had been denied the position of director of vocational education in favor of a white applicant. In upholding the white's selection, a court recognized that superior qualifications were a valid, nondiscriminatory reason. See *Clark* v. *Huntsville City Board of Education*, 717 F.2d 525 (11th Cir. 1983).

Although not a decision dealing with educators, a six-to-three Supreme Court decision upheld the "last-hired–first-fired" principle as applied to Memphis firefighters. The Court asserted that seniority systems, as long as they are unbiased, may not be disrupted to save the jobs of newly hired minority workers. The decision states: "It is inappropriate to deny an innocent employee the benefits of his seniority in order to provide a remedy in a pattern or practice suit such as this." *Firefighters Local Union No. 1784* v. *Stotts*, 467 U.S. 561 (1984).

D. Age Discrimination

For many years state statutes and local school board policies establishing mandatory retirement for teachers varied greatly across the country, although in many instances the mandatory retirement age was sixty-five. Passage of the federal Age Discrimination in Employment Act of 1967 established a uniform mandatory retirement age.

Under that act it became unlawful for an employer to discriminate against any employee or potential employee on the basis of age except "where age is a bona fide occupational qualification reasonably necessary to the normal operation of the particular business, or where the differentiation is based on reasonable factors other than age." Originally the protection of the act was limited to workers between the ages of forty and sixty-five. However, the Age Discrimination in Employment Act amendments of 1978 raised the upper limit to age seventy and removed the cap entirely for federal workers. As originally passed in 1967, the act did not apply to the federal government, to the states or their political subdivisions, or to employers with fewer than twenty-five employees. In 1974 Congress extended the substantive prohibitions of the act to employers having at least twenty workers and to the federal and state governments.

The issue of involuntary retirement at ages below the act's upper limit has been addressed by the Supreme Court. In *Massachusetts Board of Retirement* v. *Murgia*, 427 U.S. 307 (1976), the court upheld a state law requiring the mandatory retirement of uniformed police at age fifty. And in *Equal Employment Opportunity Commission* v. *Wyoming*, 460 U.S. 226 (1983), the court upheld the involuntary retirement, pursuant to a Wyoming statute, of a supervisor for the Wyoming Game and Fish Department. This five-to-four decision also upheld the extension of the Age

Discrimination in Employment Act to cover state and local governments as a valid exercise of Congress' power under the Commerce Clause.

However, the Court upheld an airline captain's contention that he should be allowed to serve as a flight engineer after he reached the mandatory retirement age of sixty. In a unanimous decision the Court maintained that Federal Aviation Administration regulations that provided for the mandatory retirement of pilots at age sixty did not apply to flight engineers—a flight-crew position that does not call for the operation of the flight controls unless the captain and first officer become incapacitated. See *Western Airlines Inc.* v. *Criswell*, 472 U.S. ___, 105 S.Ct. 2743 (1985).

Whether or not a school board's policy favoring the hiring of less experienced teachers violated the Age Discrimination in Employment Act was addressed in *Geller v. Markham.*

Geller v. Markham

United States Court of Appeals, Second Circuit, 1980
635 F.2d 1027, cert. denied, 451 U.S. 945 (1981)

MANSFIELD, Circuit Judge:

Miriam Geller, a 55-year-old teacher, brought a class action in the District Court for the District of Connecticut under the Age Discrimination in Employment Act of 1967 (ADEA), * * * claiming that defendants-appellants violated her rights by denying her employment as a teacher because of her age. She sought damages, equitable relief (including reinstatement, pension rights, benefits and seniority) and attorney's fees. A jury trial before Judge M. Joseph Blumenfeld resulted in an award of $15,190 damages. Following the trial, Judge Blumenfeld denied her application for equitable relief but awarded attorney's fees. From this denial she appeals. * * *

We affirm the finding of defendants' liability, since the record reveals that defendants subjected Ms. Geller to a hiring practice with both discriminatory impact, * * * and illegally disparate treatment, * * * the principles of which may be applied in ADEA cases. * * * We also affirm the district court's refusal to award reinstatement, but reverse its decision not to award pension benefits.

Ms. Geller applied for a position as a teacher at Bugbee School in West Hartford in late August, 1976. She was then 55 years old. She had gained considerable experience as a tenured teacher in New Jersey, where she had lived until shortly before applying for the Bugbee job, and she had done some work as a substitute teacher in the Connecticut schools. She was interviewed for a permanent position to fill a "sudden opening" in the Bugbee School on September 3, 1976, and was told to be ready to begin teaching art on September 7. Meanwhile, school officials continued to interview other candidates for the job.

Ms. Geller prepared the art room over Labor Day weekend, and taught school until September 17, when she was replaced by a 25-year-old woman who had not applied for the job until September 10. Shortly thereafter, Ms. Geller brought the present suit, alleging violations of ADEA, and pointing in particular to the "Sixth Step Policy" adopted by the West Hartford Board of Education ("Board"). This cost-cutting policy, which was derived from a statement included by the previous Bugbee School Superintendent in his budget report to the Board, read:

> "Except in special situations and to the extent possible, teachers needed in West Hartford next year will be recruited at levels below the sixth step of the salary schedule."

The sixth step is the salary grade reached by teachers with more than five years' experience.

At trial plaintiff introduced expert statistical testimony establishing that 92.6% of Connecticut teachers between 40 and 65 years old (the protected age group under ADEA) have more than 5 years experience, while only 62% of teachers under 40 have taught more than five years. She also presented considerable evidence in the form of witnesses' testimony that individual defendants had discussed the "sixth step" policy with her, and had taken the policy into account when deciding to replace her. Defendants countered that the ratio of hirees over 40 years of age to under-40 hirees had not changed substantially since the announcement of the "sixth step" policy. From these latter statistics, which were offered not by an expert statistician but by Mr. Hedrick, a named defendant, defendants argued that the "sixth step" policy had never been applied to discriminate on the basis of age. They claimed that Ms. Geller had been replaced by a younger woman because hiring officials considered the younger woman more qualified, not because the school board was unwilling to pay a woman with her experience. Defendants also argue that even if the "sixth step" was applied, they were justified in applying it because an "experience-cost criterion" for hiring was necessary in view of declining enrollments and rising school costs.

Largely on the strength of plaintiff's expert statistical evidence, Judge Blumenfeld found that defendants' "sixth step" policy was discriminatory as a matter of law. * * * He declined to accept defendants' contention that proof of a violation of ADEA required establishment of discriminatory motive. With respect to plaintiff's claim of disparate treatment, * * * however, he took the view that to sustain this claim plaintiff must ultimately prove a discriminatory motive on the defendants' part and that proof that they discharged her because of the application of the "sixth step" policy was insufficient * * * .

After instructing the jury that the "sixth step" policy was discriminatory on the basis of age as a matter of law, Judge Blumenfeld submitted to it the question of whether this policy had been applied to Ms. Geller. First, in his oral instructions to the jury, he asked it to determine "if the decision about Mrs. Geller was made in whole or in part, because she was above the fifth step," and if the "sixth step" policy "made a difference" in the decision to replace her with the younger woman, stating:

> There could have been more than one reason for defendants' decision about [Mrs. Geller's] employment but she is nevertheless entitled to recover if one factor was her [age] and if it made a difference in determining whether she would be employed. If it did not make any difference, if it was not a reason that entered into the decision, then of course she has not proved her case. But if it did, then she has.

> "If defendants' decision about Mrs. Geller was made in whole or in part because she was above the fifth step on the salary scale, . . . Mrs. Geller is entitled to recover. . . ."

* * *

As the Supreme Court pointed out, * * * discriminatory or disparate treatment in violation of Title VII occurs where "[t]he employer simply treats some people less favorably than others because of their race, color, religion, sex or national origin. Proof of discriminatory motive is critical, although it can in some situations be inferred from the mere fact of differences in treatment." "Disparate impact," on the other hand, results from the use of "employment practices that are facially neutral in their treatment of different groups but that in fact fall more harshly on one group than another and cannot be justified by business necessity." * * * Proof of motive is not required to sustain a claim of disparate impact.

* * *

A prima facie case of discriminatory impact may be established by showing that an employer's facially neutral practice has a disparate impact upon members of plaintiff's class, in this case teachers over 40 years of age. * * * Such a discriminatory impact is frequently evidenced by statistics from which it may be inferred that an employer's selection methods or employment criteria result in employment of a larger share of one group (here, teachers under 40 years of age) than of another (teachers over 40). * * * The employer may defend by showing that the employment practice is justified by business necessity or need and is related to successful performance of the job for which the practice is used. * * * In that event the plaintiff must be given an opportunity to show that other selection methods having less discriminatory effects would serve the employer's legitimate interest in competent performance of the job. * * *

A prima facie case of discriminatory treatment may be made out by the plaintiff's showing:

"(i) that he belongs to a racial minority; (ii) that he applied and was qualified for a job for which the employer was seeking applicants; (iii) that, despite his qualifications, he was rejected; and (iv) that, after his rejection, the position remained open and the employer continued to seek applicants from persons of complainant's qualifications." * * * The burden then shifts to the employer to go forward with evidence of "some legitimate, nondiscriminatory reason for the employee's rejection," * * * in which event the plaintiff, who has the ultimate burden, must be afforded the opportunity to demonstrate by competent evidence that the employer's presumptively valid reasons are a cover-up or pretext. * * * If the plaintiff succeeds in this showing the employer's articulated reason will not stand. * * *

Turning to the present case, the plaintiff showed through an accredited expert (Dr. Alan Hunt), based on his statistical analysis of the relationship between age and years of experience for teachers in Connecticut, that 92.6% of all teachers over 40 years of age have five or more years of teaching experience, which he characterized as "very significant" statistically or about "600 times the level generally required for statistical significance." Although the significance of the 92.6% figure is somewhat weakened by evidence that over 60% of teachers under 40 also have had more than five years' experience, we agree with Judge Blumenfeld's finding that the high correlation between experience and membership in the protected age group (40 to 65 years of age) would render application of the "sixth step" policy discriminatory as a matter of law, * * * since, absent countervailing statistics, the likelihood of a person over 40 being selected under the policy would be substantially less than that of a person under 40. The purpose of the "sixth step" policy was to economize by employing less experienced teachers, which would inevitably open more teaching opportunities to younger less experienced applicants than to the older, who were more experienced.

Defendants have offered two lines of defense, both of which are unpersuasive. First they contend that, although the "sixth step" policy appears to be correlated strongly to membership in the group over 40, the policy did not in fact result in discrimination against this group since the percentage of over-40 teachers hired to fill job openings before and after the application of the policy was about the same. The uncorroborated statistics offered in support of this contention, however, were so defective as to justify the district court's refusal to give them any weight. They were prepared by a named defendant in the case, a former Personnel Director for the West Hartford schools who had no expertise as a statistician and had a direct interest in the outcome of the case. He not only failed to produce any competent evidence of the applicant pool for the periods, which is essential to a statistical determination of hiring patterns, but he employed such dubious analytical techniques as obtaining an overall percentage figure by averaging annual percentages for several different years, thus contravening the basic, well-recognized principle that such averaging by percentages produces meaningless and often misleading results. Moreover it appears that there were dramatic changes in the size of the applicant pool and in the number of teachers hired in the West Hartford School District during the mid-1970's, which cast serious doubt upon the statistical significance of the defendants' evidence of allegedly unchanging hiring patterns. In 1968 and 1969, according to defendants' own figures, West Hartford hired 129 and 136 teachers, of whom 28 and 33, respectively, were above the fifth step, and 17 (13%) and 15 (8%), respectively, were over 40. In 1975 and 1976, by contrast, the District hired only 35 and 53 teachers, a substantially smaller group, of whom 7 and 10 were above the fifth step and 2 (6%) and 4 (8%), respectively, were over 40.

* * *

Here Judge Blumenfeld rightly found that the "sixth step" policy was discriminatory on its face. From there, he apparently declined to rely on statistics either to establish as a matter of law plaintiff's position that the policy was applied or to support defendants' position that it was not applied. Absent statistics regarding any changes in the applicant pool for teaching jobs as over-all hiring decreased, comparative evidence of overall hiring percentages carries little weight, since these percentages may have remained constant despite an increase or fall-off in over-40 applicants. In the face of these deficiencies in the statistical proof and the existence of testimony that the "sixth step" policy was applied in Ms. Geller's individual case, which was disputed, Judge Blumenfeld properly submitted the issue of whether it was applied to the jury, which resolved the question in her favor by finding that the "sixth step" policy was one reason for the hiring of a younger replacement.

Defendants' second line of defense, somewhat inconsistent with their contention that the "sixth step" policy was never followed, is that the policy, if applied, was supportable as a necessary cost-cutting gesture in the face of tight budgetary constraints. This cost justification must fail, however, because of the clear rule that "a general assertion that the average cost of employing older workers as a group is higher than the average cost of employing younger workers as a group will not be recognized as a differentiation under the terms and provisions of the Act, unless one of the other statutory exceptions applies. To classify or group employees solely on the basis of age for the purpose of comparing costs, or for any other purpose, necessarily rests on the assumption that the age factor alone may be used to justify a differentiation—an assumption plainly contrary to the terms of the Act and the purpose of Congress in enacting it. Differentials so based would serve only to perpetuate and promote the very discrimination at which the Act is directed." * * *

* * *

The record also reveals that, in addition to making out a case of disparate impact, Ms. Geller established a prima facie case of discriminatory treatment * * * satisfying the oft-repeated four conditions prescribed by the Court. * * * At age 55 she was clearly within the protected group under ADEA. She applied for the teaching job, was concededly qualified for it, and was even hired temporarily to perform it. She was then released, and saw a younger person placed in the job for which she was concededly qualified. These undisputed facts are sufficient to place upon the defendants the burden of rebutting her prima facie case. For reasons already stated, the defenses that the "sixth step" policy was not applied to Ms. Geller and that, if applied, it was cost-justified, must be rejected. The only other defense, that the discharge of Ms. Geller in favor of a younger teacher, was not motivated by the policy but by the superior competence of the latter candidate, was rejected by the jury's findings.

This leads us to defendants' final contention, that the court erred in instructing the jury as to the part age must play in determining whether they violated ADEA in discharging Ms. Geller. In order to make out a case under ADEA, Ms. Geller was not required to show that age discrimination was the *sole* cause of her discharge. Where an employer acts out of mixed motives in discharging or refusing to hire an employee, the plaintiff must show that age was a causative or determinative factor, one that made a difference in deciding whether the plaintiff should be employed. * * *

* * *

We next turn to Ms. Geller's contention that the district court erred in denying her equitable relief beyond the damages awarded by the jury. * * *

* * *

Judge Blumenfeld viewed reinstatement as inappropriate because he interpreted the jury's decision granting damages equal to one year's salary at Bugbee School as a factual conclusion that Ms. Geller was deprived of only one year's employment by the defendants' discriminatory action. We agree with this conclusion. Ms. Geller had never formally been hired as a permanent teacher during the time she was working but had merely been told to get started. Permanent reinstatement therefore is unwarranted.

On the other hand, we disagree with the trial judge's refusal to consider Ms. Geller's request for lost pension benefits on the ground that "[d]amages for lost pension benefits are one component of the overall damages suffered by a plaintiff, which a jury may assess in ADEA actions."

*   *   *

The judgment appealed from by the defendants is affirmed. The district court's order denying equitable relief to the plaintiff is affirmed except as to the denial of pension benefits which is reversed to the extent indicated.

Notes

Although **Geller** deals with age discrimination, it has implications for other types of discrimination litigation. The significance of the discriminatory impact of system practices, the necessity for legally sound school-system policy, and the importance of adequate and appropriate statistics are demonstrated in this decision.

Courts have generally held that those teaching beyond a specified retirement age do so on a year-to-year basis. In addressing this issue, the South Dakota Supreme Court in *Monnier* v. *Todd County Independent School District,* 245 N.W.2d 503 (S.D. 1976) has contended that

> after a school district has adopted a mandatory retirement policy, teachers within that district who attain the age of retirement specified in the policy are no longer entitled to the benefits of the continuing contract law. By its very terms the concept of mandatory retirement is inconsistent with the concept of continuing contract rights. . . . (P. 505)

VII. Teacher Bargaining

A wide range of practices exists among the fifty states pertaining to school employee-employer relations. These practices vary from states that either have no statutory provisions or prohibit collective bargaining to those that mandate bargaining and allow teachers to strike. Although the majority of states have statutory provisions addressing issues surrounding school employee-employer relations, several states rely on the authority of case law, and a handful of states rely on attorney general opinions.

The statutes of the approximately 60 percent of states having provisions pertaining to school employee-employer relations vary considerably. Some, for instance, leave teacher negotiation or bargaining rights to the discretion of local school boards while others provide bargaining rights that compare favorably with those held by employees in the private sector. The range of issues addressed in the various statutes include whether or not there are exclusive bargaining rights for one teacher group, who may be included in the bargaining unit, dues checkoff, the establishment of agency shops, "service fees," the scope of bargaining, impasse procedures, and strike provisions.

Approximately half of the states have statutes providing for good-faith bargaining between local school boards and bargaining groups. A handful of states have statutes requiring that a school board "meet and confer" with representatives of educator organizations or authorize local boards to deal with educator organizations' representatives.

Some state statutes either exclude supervisory personnel from collective bargaining or require them to be in a unit separate from teachers. Yet other states allow supervisory personnel to be included in the teacher bargaining unit, although those statutes often allow principals and other supervisory personnel to form separate bargaining units if they so desire. The vast majority of states with collective-bargaining provisions allow for exclusive bargaining rights for those groups having such rights.

The right of public school teachers to strike is a highly controversial subject. Not all school employee-employer statutory provisions address the issue of strikes. However, in several states (Hawaii, Montana, Maine, New Hampshire, Oregon, Pennsylvania, Vermont) statutory provisions or judicial opinions allow teachers to strike under certain conditions. Statutes in approximately half of the states specifically prohibit strikes by teachers, and in some instances penalties for striking are specified.

A. Dismissal of Striking Teachers

Hortonville Joint School District No. 1 v. Hortonville Education Association

Supreme Court of the United States, 1976
426 U.S. 482

MR. CHIEF JUSTICE BURGER delivered the opinion of the Court.

We granted certiorari in this case to determine whether School Board members vested by state law with the power to employ and dismiss teachers could, consistent with the Due Process Clause of the Fourteenth Amendment, dismiss teachers engaged in a strike prohibited by state law.

The petitioners are a Wisconsin school district, the seven members of its School Board, and three administrative employees of the district. Respondents are teachers suing on behalf of all teachers in the district and the Hortonville Education Association (HEA), the collective-bargaining agent for the district's teachers.

During the 1972–1973 school year Hortonville teachers worked under a master collective-bargaining agreement; negotiations were conducted for renewal of the contract, but no agreement was reached for the 1973–1974 school year. The teachers continued to work while negotiations proceeded during the year without reaching agreement. On March 18, 1974, the members of the teachers' union went on strike, in direct violation of Wisconsin law. On March 20, the district superintendent sent all teachers a letter inviting them to return to work; a few did so. On March 23, he sent another letter, asking the 86 teachers still on strike to return, and reminding them that strikes by public employees were illegal; none of these teachers returned to work. After conducting classes with substitute teachers on March 26 and 27, the Board decided to conduct disciplinary hearings for each of the teachers on strike. Individual notices were sent to each teacher setting hearings for April 1, 2, and 3.

On April 1, most of the striking teachers appeared before the Board with counsel. Their attorney indicated that the teachers did not want individual hearings, but preferred to be treated as a group. Although counsel agreed that the teachers were on strike, he raised several procedural objections to the hearings. He also argued that the Board was not sufficiently impartial to exercise discipline over the striking teachers and that the Due Process Clause of the Fourteenth Amendment required an independent, unbiased decisionmaker. An offer of proof was tendered to demonstrate that the strike had been provoked by the Board's failure to meet teachers' demands, and respondents' counsel asked to cross-examine Board members individually. The Board rejected the request, but permitted counsel to make the offer of proof, aimed at showing that the Board's contract offers were unsatisfactory, that the Board used coercive and illegal bargaining tactics, and that teachers in the district had been locked out by the Board.

* * *

The sole issue in this case is whether the Due Process Clause of the Fourteenth Amendment prohibits this School Board from making the decision to dismiss teachers admittedly engaged in a strike and persistently refusing to return to their duties. The Wisconsin Supreme Court held that state law prohibited the strike and that termination of the striking teachers' employment was within the Board's statutory authority. * * * We are, of course, bound to accept the interpretation of Wisconsin law by the highest court of the State. * * * The only decision remaining for the Board therefore involved the exercise of its discretion as to what should be done to carry out the duties the law placed on the Board.

Respondents argue, and the Wisconsin Supreme Court held, that the choice presented for the Board's decision is analogous to that involved in revocation of parole in *Morrissey* v. *Brewer*, * * * that the decision could be made only by an impartial decisionmaker, and that the Board was not impartial. In *Morrissey* the Court considered a challenge to state procedures employed in revoking the parole of state prisoners. There we noted that the parole revocation decision involved two steps: first, an inquiry whether the parolee had in fact violated the conditions of his parole; second, determining whether the violations found were serious enough to justify revocation of parole and the consequent deprivation of the parolee's conditional liberty. * * * Nothing in this case is analogous to the first step in *Morrissey*, since the teachers admitted to being on strike. But respondents argue that the School Board's decision in this case is, for constitutional purposes, the same as the second aspect of the decision to revoke parole. The Board cannot make a "reasonable" decision on this issue, the Wisconsin Supreme Court held and respondents argue, because its members are biased in some fashion that the due process guarantees of the Fourteenth Amendment prohibit.

* * * A school board is not to be equated with the parole officer as an arresting officer; the school board is more like the parole board, for it has ultimate plenary authority to make its decisions derived from the state legislature. General language about due process in a holding concerning revocation of parole is not a reliable basis for dealing with the School Board's power as an employer to dismiss teachers for cause. We must focus more clearly on, first, the nature of the bias respondents attribute to the Board, and, second, the nature of the interests at stake in this case.

Respondents' argument rests in part on doctrines that have no application to this case. They seem to argue that the Board members had some personal or official stake in the decision whether the teachers should be dismissed, * * * and that the Board has manifested some personal bitterness toward the teachers, aroused by teacher criticism of the Board during the strike. * * * Even assuming that those cases state the governing standards when the decisionmaker is a public employer dealing with employees, the teachers did not show, and the Wisconsin courts did not find, that the Board members had the kind of personal or financial stake in the decision that might create a conflict of interest, and there is nothing in the record to support charges of personal animosity. The Wisconsin Supreme Court was careful "not to suggest . . . that the board members were anything but dedicated public servants, trying to provide the district with quality education . . . within its limited budget." * * *

That court's analysis would seem to be confirmed by the Board's repeated invitations for striking teachers to return to work, the final invitation being contained in the letter that notified them of their discharge.

The only other factor suggested to support the claim of bias is that the School Board was involved in the negotiations that preceded and precipitated the striking teachers' discharge. Participation in those negotiations was a statutory duty of the Board. The Wisconsin Supreme Court held that this involvement, without more, disqualified the Board from deciding whether the teachers should be dismissed. * * * Mere familiarity with the facts of a case gained by an agency in the performance of its statutory role does not, however, disqualify a decisionmaker. * * * Nor is a decisionmaker disqualified simply because he has taken a position, even in public, on a policy issue related to the dispute, in the absence of a showing that he is not "capable of judging a particular controversy fairly on the basis of its own circumstances." * * *

Respondents' claim and the Wisconsin Supreme Court's holding reduce to the argument that the Board was biased because it negotiated with the teachers on behalf of the school district without reaching agreement and learned about the reasons for the strike in the course of negotiating. From those premises the Wisconsin court concluded that the Board lost its statutory power to determine that the strike and persistent refusal to terminate it amounted to conduct serious enough to warrant discharge of the strikers. Wisconsin statutes vest in the Board the power to discharge its employees, a power of every employer, whether it has negotiated with the employees before discharge or not. The Fourteenth Amendment permits a court to strip the Board of the otherwise remarkable power the Wisconsin Legislature has given it only if the Board's prior involvement in negotiating with the teachers means that it cannot act consistently with due process.

Due process, as this Court has repeatedly held, is a term that "negates any concept of inflexible procedures universally applicable to every imaginable situation." * * * Determining what process is due in a given setting requires the Court to take into account the individual's stake in the decision at issue as well as the State's interest in a particular procedure for making it. * * * Our assessment of the interests of the parties in this case leads to the conclusion that * * * the Board's prior role as negotiator does not disqualify it to decide that the public interest in maintaining uninterrupted classroom work required that teachers striking in violation of state law be discharged.

The teachers' interest in these proceedings is, of course, self-evident. They wished to avoid termination of their employment, obviously an important interest, but one that must be examined in light of several factors. Since the teachers admitted that they were engaged in a work stoppage, there was no possibility of an erroneous factual determination on this critical threshold issue. Moreover, what the teachers claim as a property right was the expectation that the jobs they had left to go and remain on strike in violation of law would remain open to them. The Wisconsin court accepted at least the essence of that claim in defining the property right under state law, and we do not quarrel with its conclusion. * * *

* * * The Board's decision whether to dismiss striking teachers involves broad considerations, and does not in the main turn on the Board's view of the "seriousness" of the teachers' conduct or the factors they urge mitigated their violation of state law. It was not an adjudicative decision, for the Board had an obligation to make a decision based on its own answer to an important question of policy: What choice among the alternative responses to the teachers' strike will best serve the interests of the school system, the interests of the parents and children who depend on the system, and the interests of the citizens whose taxes support it? The Board's decision was only incidentally a disciplinary decision; it had significant governmental and public policy dimensions as well. * * *

State law vests the governmental, or policymaking function exclusively in the School Board and the State has two interests in keeping it there. First, the Board is the body with overall responsibility for the governance of the school district; it must cope with the myriad day-to-day problems of a modern public school system including the severe consequences of a teachers' strike; by virtue of electing them the constituents have declared the Board members qualified to deal with these problems, and they are accountable to the voters for the manner in which they perform. Second, the state legislature has given to the Board the power to employ and dismiss teachers, as a part of the balance it has struck in the area of municipal labor relations; altering those statutory powers as a matter of federal due process clearly changes that balance. Permitting the Board to make the decision at issue here preserves its control over school district affairs, leaves the balance of power in labor relations where the state legislature struck it, and assures that the decision whether to dismiss the teachers will be made by the body responsible for that decision under state law.

Respondents have failed to demonstrate that the decision to terminate their employment was infected by the sort of bias that we have held to disqualify other decisionmakers as a matter of federal due process. A showing that the Board was "involved" in the events preceding this decision, in light of the important interest in leaving with the Board the power given by the state legislature, is not enough to overcome the presumption of honesty and integrity in policymakers with decisionmaking power. * * * Accordingly, we hold that the Due Process Clause of the Fourteenth Amendment did not guarantee respondents that the decision to terminate their employment would be made or reviewed by a body other than the School Board.

The judgment of the Wisconsin Supreme Court is reversed, and the case is remanded for further proceedings not inconsistent with this opinion.

Reversed and remanded.

B. Compulsory Union Dues

Abood v. Detroit Board of Education

Supreme Court of the United States, 1977
431 U.S. 209

MR. JUSTICE STEWART delivered the opinion of the Court.

The State of Michigan has enacted legislation authorizing a system for union representation of local governmental employees. A union and a local government employer are specifically permitted to agree to an "agency shop" arrangement, whereby every employee represented by a union—even though not a union member—must pay to the union, as a condition of employment, a service fee equal in amount to union dues. The issue before us is whether this arrangement violates the constitutional rights of government employees who object to public-sector unions as such or to various union activities financed by the compulsory service fees.

After a secret ballot election, the Detroit Federation of Teachers (Union) was certified in 1967 pursuant to Michigan law as the exclusive representative of teachers employed by the Detroit Board of Education (Board). The Union and the Board thereafter concluded a collective-bargaining agreement effective from July 1, 1969, to July 1, 1971. Among the agreement's provisions was an "agency shop" clause, requiring every teacher who had not become a Union member within 60 days of hire (or within 60 days of January 26, 1970, the effective date of the clause) to pay the Union a service charge equal to the regular dues required of Union members. A teacher who failed to meet this obligation was subject to discharge. Nothing in the agreement, however, required any teacher to join the Union, espouse the cause of unionism, or participate in any other way in Union affairs.

* * *

The designation of a union as exclusive representative carries with it great responsibilities. The tasks of negotiating and administering a collective-bargaining agreement and representing the interests of employees in settling disputes and processing grievances are continuing and difficult ones. They often entail expenditure of much time and money. * * * The services of lawyers, expert negotiators, economists, and a research staff, as well as general administrative personnel, may be required. Moreover, in carrying out these duties, the union is obliged "fairly and equitably to represent all employees . . . , union and non-union," within the relevant unit. * * * A union-shop arrangement has been thought to distribute fairly the cost of these activities among those who benefit, and it counteracts the incentive that employees might otherwise have to become "free riders"—to refuse to contribute to the union while obtaining benefits of union representation that necessarily accrue to all employees. * * *

To compel employees financially to support their collective-bargaining representative has an impact upon their First Amendment interests. An employee may very well have ideological objections to a wide variety of activities undertaken by the union in its role as exclusive representative. His moral or religious views about the desirability of abortion may not square with the union's policy in negotiating a medical benefits plan. One individual might disagree with a union policy of negotiating limits on the right to strike, believing that to be the road to serfdom for the working class, while another might have economic or political objections to unionism itself. An employee might object to the union's wage policy because it violates guidelines designed to limit inflation, or might object to the union's seeking a clause in the collective-bargaining agreement proscribing racial discrimination. The examples could be multiplied. To be required to help finance the union as a collective bargaining agent might well be thought, therefore, to interfere in some way with an employee's freedom to associate for the advancement of ideas, or to refrain from doing so, as he sees fit. * * *

The National Labor Relations Act leaves regulation of the labor relations of state and local governments to the States. See 29 U.S.C. § 152 (2). Michigan has chosen to establish for local government units a regulatory scheme which, although not identical in every respect to the NLRA or the Railway Labor Act, is broadly modeled after federal law. * * * Under Michigan law employees of local government units enjoy rights parallel to those protected under federal legislation: the rights to self-organization and to bargain collectively. * * *

* * *

Finally, decisionmaking by a public employer is above all a political process. The officials who represent the public employer are ultimately responsible to the electorate, which for this purpose can be viewed as comprising three overlapping classes of voters—taxpayers, users of particular government services, and government employees. Through exercise of their political influence as part of the electorate, the employees have the opportunity to affect the decisions of government representatives who sit on the other side of the bargaining table. Whether these representatives accede to a union's demands will depend upon a blend of political ingredients, including community sentiment about unionism generally and the involved union in particular, the degree of taxpayer resistance, and the views of voters as to the importance of the service involved and the relation between the demands and the quality of service. It is surely arguable, however, that permitting public employees to unionize and a union to bargain as their exclusive representative gives the employees more influence in the decisionmaking process than is possessed by employees similarly organized in the private sector.

The distinctive nature of public-sector bargaining has led to widespread discussion about the extent to which the law governing labor relations in the private sector provides an appropriate model. To take but one example, there has been considerable debate about the desirability of prohibiting public employee unions from striking, a step that the State of Michigan itself has taken, Mich. Comp. Law § 423.202 (1970). But although Michigan has not adopted the federal model of labor relations in every respect, it has determined that labor stability will be served by a system of exclusive representation and the permissive use of an agency shop in public employment. * * * The only remaining constitutional inquiry evoked by the appellants' argument, therefore, is whether a public employee has a weightier First Amendment interest than a private employee in not being compelled to contribute to the costs of exclusive union representation. We think he does not.

Public employees are not basically different from private employees; on the whole, they have the same sort of skills, the same needs, and seek the same advantages. "The uniqueness of public employment is *not in the employees* nor in the work performed; the uniqueness is in the special character of the employer." * * * The very real differences between exclusive-agent collective bargaining in the public and private sectors are not such as to work any greater infringement upon the First Amendment interests of public employees. A public employee who believes that a union representing him is urging a course that is unwise as a matter of public policy is not barred from expressing his viewpoint. Besides voting in accordance with his convictions, every public employee is largely free to express his views, in public or private, orally or in writing. With some exceptions not pertinent here, public employees are free to participate in the full range of political activities open to other citizens. * * *

There can be no quarrel with the truism that because public employee unions attempt to influence governmental policymaking, their activities—and the views of members who disagree with them—may be properly termed political. But that characterization does not raise the ideas and beliefs of public employees onto a higher plane than the ideas and beliefs of private employees. It is no doubt true that a central purpose of the First Amendment " 'was to protect the free discussion of governmental affairs.' " * * * But our cases have never suggested that expression about philosophical, social, artistic, economic, literary, or ethical matters—to take a nonexhaustive list of labels—is not entitled to full First Amendment protection. Union members in both the public and private sectors may find that a variety of union activities conflict with their beliefs. * * * Nothing in the First Amendment or our cases discussing its meaning makes the question whether the adjective "political" can properly be attached to those beliefs the critical constitutional inquiry.

The differences between public- and private-sector collective bargaining simply does not translate into differences in First Amendment rights. Even those commentators most acutely aware of the distinctive nature of public-sector bargaining and most seriously concerned with its policy implications agree that "[t]he union security issue in the public sector . . . is fundamentally the same issue . . . as in the private sector . . . No special dimension results from the fact that a union represents public rather than private employees." * * *

* * *

Our decisions establish with unmistakable clarity that the freedom of an individual to associate for the purpose of advancing beliefs and ideas is protected by the First and Fourteenth Amendments. * * * Equally clear is the proposition that a government may not require an individual to relinquish rights guaranteed him by the First Amendment as a condition of public employment. * * * The appellants argue that they fall within the protection of these cases because they have been prohibited, not from actively associating, but rather from refusing to associate. They specifically argue that they may constitutionally prevent the Union's spending a part of their required service fees to contribute to political candidates and to express political views unrelated to its duties as exclusive bargaining representative. We have concluded that this argument is a meritorious one.

* * *

The fact that the appellants are compelled to make, rather than prohibited from making, contributions for political purposes works no less an infringement of their constitutional rights. For at the heart of the First Amendment is the notion that an individual should be free to believe as he will, and that in a free society one's beliefs should be shaped by his mind and his conscience rather than coerced by the State. * * *

These principles prohibit a State from compelling any individual to affirm his belief in God * * * or to associate with a political party

* * * as a condition of retaining public employment. They are no less applicable to the case at bar, and they thus prohibit the appellees from requiring any of the appellants to contribute to the support of an ideological cause he may oppose as a condition of holding a job as a public school teacher.

We do not hold that a union cannot constitutionally spend funds for the expression of political views, on behalf of political candidates, or toward the advancement of other ideological causes not germane to its duties as collective-bargaining representative. Rather, the Constitution requires only that such expenditures be financed from charges, dues or assessments paid by employees who do not object to advancing those ideas and who are not coerced into doing so against their will by the threat of loss of governmental employment.

There will, of course, be difficult problems in drawing lines between collective-bargaining activities, for which contributions may be compelled, and ideological activities unrelated to collective bargaining, for which such compulsion is prohibited. * * * The process of establishing a written collective-bargaining agreement prescribing the terms and conditions of public employment may require not merely concord at the bargaining table, but subsequent approval by other public authorities; related budgetary and appropriations decisions might be seen as an integral part of the bargaining process. We have no occasion in this case, however, to try to define such a dividing line. * * *

* * *

The judgment is vacated, and the case is remanded for further proceedings not inconsistent with this opinion.

It is so ordered.

VIII. Political Activities*

Not many states have addressed the issue of whether restrictions should be placed on the political activities of public school teachers. Although several states have statutes covering the political candidacy of public school employees, most of the statutory provisions are far from comprehensive.† Only a handful of states, California, Ohio, Oregon, and Pennsylvania, have comprehensive provisions.

*Material for this section was obtained from an unpublished doctoral dissertation by Betty C. Hull, "A Legal Study of the Political Activities of Public School Employees: Their Candidacy for Public Offices and their Campaigning for Other Political Candidates and Issues," University of Georgia, Athens, 1980.

†As of 1980, California, Florida, Georgia, Illinois, Indiana, Maine, Massachusetts, New Jersey, Ohio, Oregon, Pennsylvania, South Carolina, and Tennessee had statutory provisions concerning the political candidacy of public school employees.

Four significant legal issues are involved when a public school employee becomes a candidate for public office or campaigns for other political candidates and issues. These issues are (1) the school employee's First Amendment right of freedom of expression and association, (2) incompatibility of office provisions, (3) conflict-of-interest provisions, and (4) nepotism provisions.

Although a public school employee has the First Amendment right to run for public office, a distinction must be made between the employee's right to run for public office and the right to continue school employment while holding a public office. Well-settled case law has established that a public school employee may not simultaneously hold a public office and his or her school employment if this is against (1) incompatibility-of-office provisions, (2) conflict-of-interest provisions, or (3) provisions providing for the tripartite separation of the divisions of government. Courts have consistently held that these provisions represent a compelling state need that justifies infringements upon the school employee's political rights.

Under state incompatibility-of-office and conflict-of-interest provisions, courts have established that public school employees may not maintain their employment while holding office on (1) their employing board of education or (2) any governmental body, or while holding an office that has supervisory powers over their employing school district. However, in the absence of statutory prohibitions, public school employees may serve on a board of education that is not their employing board.

Whether public school employees may maintain their employment and serve in the state legislature depends on the conflict-of-interest statute covering the state's legislators. In those states that prohibit legislators from having a direct or indirect interest in any contract dependent upon funds appropriated while they serve in the legislature, school employees may not be able to continue school employment. However, in states that do not have this type of statutory provision, courts have held that the school employee may serve in the legislature but that it is reasonable for the board of education to require the employee to take an unpaid leave of absence while so serving. Under incompatibility-of-office provisions, courts have held that there is no incompatibility between local school employment and serving in the state legislature. However, some courts have held that it is incompatible for employees of the state university system to serve simultaneously in the legislature and hold their university jobs.

Under state nepotism provisions, a school employee's continued employment may be in jeopardy when a relative is elected to his or her employing board of education. Or the board member's continuation in office may be in jeopardy if he or she has relatives who are employed by the school board. Some state courts, under general nepotism statutes, do not strictly apply nepotism provisions to certificated school personnel. These courts have applied the rationale that state certification requirements and teacher tenure acts prevent nepotism practices in the hiring of school employees. On the other hand, where an education statute addresses nepotism issues on the part of members of a board of education, the courts strictly apply the language of such a statute.

Courts have generally upheld board of education political-leave policies that require school employees to take unpaid leaves of absence while running for and holding public offices. However, such a policy was not upheld by the United States Supreme Court in *Dougherty County Board of Education* v. *White,* 439 U.S. 32 (1978). This case turned on a racial issue revealing that school systems in states covered by the Voting Rights Act of 1965 would generally be required to have prior clearance by the district court in Washington or the United States attorney general's office before adopting rules on employee political leave. A later decision in *White* v. *Dougherty County Board of Education,* 579 F. Supp. 1480 (1984), aff'd 470 U.S. ___, 105 S.Ct. 1824 (1985), however, held that the board's neutral personnel-leave policy was acceptable since the current policy neither constrained employee political activity nor acted as a burden on the electoral process.

Public school employees have the First Amendment right to campaign for other political candidates and issues; however, this right is not absolute. Courts have held that these types of activities (1) may not take place during working hours, (2) may not take place in the classroom, (3) may not interfere with the school employee's job performance, and (4) are not permissible if the employee uses his or her position of employment to influence the outcome of a political election. Further, courts have held that these activities can be restricted if they result in material disruption of the normal administrative operations of the school system.

school desegregation

INTRODUCTION

A Supreme Court decision in 1896 established the "separate but equal" doctrine regarding public facilities and services used by blacks. This decision, *Plessy* v. *Ferguson,* established a legal basis for segregated public facilities and services, including public education. Where there were no state statutory and/or constitutional provisions pertaining to segregation, **Plessy** enabled custom to be affirmed by also providing a legal basis for dual school systems in which black and white students were segregated. Although generally associated with the southern states, dual school systems were operated in several nonsouthern states. Under the dual school system, black students in a community attended all-black schools, which were staffed by blacks, and white students attended schools exclusively for whites. Little or no intercourse took place between the schools serving blacks and those attended by whites. Such de jure segregation, which had its most rigid codification and practice in the southern public schools, had the force of the law behind it since it was mandated by state constitutional and/or statutory provisions and official local school policies.

A 1954 United States Supreme Court decision, ***Brown*** **v.** ***Board of***

Education, reversed the *Plessy* doctrine as it pertained to public schools by declaring that in the field of education the doctrine of "separate but equal" had no place. This landmark reversal by the Supreme Court held de jure public school segregation to be unconstitutional. Since this decision, courts have had a veritable stream of cases brought before them in which they have had to determine whether alleged segregative policies in southern schools, nonsouthern schools, and private schools were unconstitutional.

I. Historical Perspective

A. Separate but Equal Doctrine

Plessy v. Ferguson

Supreme Court of the United States, 1896
163 U.S. 537

MR. JUSTICE BROWN, after stating the case, delivered the opinion of the court.

This case turns upon the constitutionality of an act of the General Assembly of the State of Louisiana, passed in 1890, providing for separate railway carriages for the white and colored races. * * *

The first section of the statute enacts "that all railway companies carrying passengers in their coaches in this State, shall provide equal but separate accommodations for the white, and colored races, by providing two or more passenger coaches for each passenger train, or by dividing the passenger coaches by a partition so as to secure separate accommodations: *Provided,* That this section shall not be construed to apply to street railroads. No person or persons, shall be admitted to occupy seats in coaches, other than, the ones, assigned, to them on account of the race they belong to."

By the second section it was enacted "that the officers of such passenger trains shall have the power and are hereby required to assign each passenger to the coach or compartment used for the race to which such passenger belongs; any passenger insisting on going into a coach or compartment to which by race he does not belong, shall be liable to a fine of twenty-five dollars, or in lieu thereof to imprisonment for a period of not more than twenty days in the parish prison, and any officer of any railroad insisting on assigning a passenger to a coach or compartment other than the one set aside for the race to which said passenger belongs, shall be liable to a fine of twenty-five dollars, or in lieu thereof to imprisonment for a period of not more than twenty days in the parish prison; and should any passenger refuse to occupy the coach or compartment to which he or she is assigned by the officer of such railway, said officer shall have power to refuse to carry such passenger on his train, and for such refusal neither he nor the railway company which he represents shall be liable for damages in any of the courts of this State."

The third section provides penalties for the refusal or neglect of the officers, directors, conductors and employes of railway companies to comply with the act, with a proviso that "nothing in this act shall be construed as applying to nurses attending children of the other race." The fourth section is immaterial.

The information filed in the criminal District Court charged in substance that Plessy, being a passenger between two stations within the State of Louisiana, was assigned by officers of the company to the coach used for the race to which he belonged, but he insisted upon going into a coach used by the race to which he did not belong. Neither in the information nor the plea was his particular race or color averred.

The petition for the writ of prohibition averred that petitioner was seven eighths Caucasian and one eighth African blood; that the mixture of colored blood was not discernible in him, and that he was entitled to every right, privilege and immunity secured to citizens of the United States of the white race; and that, upon such theory, he took possession of a vacant seat in a coach where passengers of the white race were accommodated, and was ordered by the conductor to vacate said coach and take a seat in another assigned to persons of the colored race, and having refused to comply with such demand he was forcibly ejected with the aid of a police officer, and imprisoned in the parish jail to answer a charge of having violated the above act.

The constitutionality of this act is attacked upon the ground that it conflicts both with the Thirteenth Amendment of the Constitution, abolishing slavery, and the Fourteenth Amendment, which prohibits certain restrictive legislation on the part of the States.

1. That it does not conflict with the Thirteenth Amendment, which abolished slavery and involuntary servitude, except as a punishment for crime, is too clear for argument. Slavery implies involuntary servitude—a state of bondage; the ownership of mankind as a chattel, or at least the control of the labor and services of one man for the benefit of another, and the absence of a legal right to the disposal of his own person, property and services. * * *

* * *

A statute which implies merely a legal distinction between white and colored races—a distinction which is founded in the color of the two races, and which must always exist so long as white men are distinguished from the other race by color—has no tendency to destroy the legal quality of the two races, or reestablish a state of involuntary servitude. Indeed, we do not understand that the Thirteenth Amendment is strenuously relied upon by the plaintiff in error in this connection.

2. By the Fourteenth Amendment, all persons born or naturalized in the United States, and subject to the jurisdiction thereof, are made citizens of the United States and of the State wherein they reside; and the States are forbidden from making or enforcing any law which shall abridge the privileges or immunities of citizens of the United States, or shall deprive any person or life, liberty or property without due process of law, or deny to any person within their jurisdiction the equal protection of the laws.

The proper construction of this amendment was first called to the attention of this court in the *Slaughter-house cases,* 16 Wall. 36, which involved, however, not a question of race, but one of exclusive privileges. The case did not call for any expression of opinion as to the exact rights it was intended to secure to the colored race, but it was said generally that its main purpose was to establish the citizenship of the negro; to give definitions of citizenship of the United States and of the States, and to protect from the hostile legislation of the States the privileges and immunities of citizens of the United States, as distinguished from those of citizens of the States.

The object of the amendment was undoubtedly to enforce the absolute equality of the two races before the law, but in the nature of things it could not have been intended to abolish distinctions based upon color, or to enforce social, as distinguished from political equality, or a commingling of the two races upon terms unsatisfactory to either. Laws permitting, and even requiring, their separation in places where they are liable to be brought into contact do not necessarily imply the inferiority of either race to the other, and have been generally, if not universally, recognized as within the competency of the state legislatures in the exercise of their police power. The most common instance of this is connected with the establishment of separate schools for white and colored children, which has been held to be a valid exercise of the legislative power even by courts of States where the political rights of the colored race have been longest and most earnestly enforced.

One of the earliest of these cases is that of *Roberts* v. *City of Boston,* 5 Cush. 198, in which the Supreme Judicial Court of Massachusetts held that the general school committee of Boston had power to make provision for the instruction of colored children in separate schools established exclusively for them, and to prohibit their attendance upon the other schools. * * * It was held that the powers of the committee extended to the establishment of separate schools for children of different ages, sexes and colors, and that they might also establish special schools for poor and neglected children, who have become too old to attend the primary school, and yet have not acquired the rudiments of learning, to enable them to enter the ordinary schools. Similar laws have been enacted by Congress under its general power of legislation over the District of Columbia, * * * as well as by the legislatures of many of the States, and have been generally, if not uniformly, sustained by the courts. * * *

Laws forbidding the intermarriage of the two races may be said in a technical sense to interfere with the freedom of contract, and yet have been universally recognized as within the police power of the State. * * *

The distinction between laws interfering with the political equality of the negro and those requiring the separation of the two races in schools, theatres and railway carriages has been frequently drawn by this court. Thus in *Strauder* v. *West Virginia*, 100 U.S. 303, it was held that a law of West Virginia limiting white male persons, 21 years of age and citizens of the State, the right to sit upon juries, was a discrimination which implied a legal inferiority in civil society, which lessened the security of the right of the colored race, and was a step toward reducing them to a condition of servility. Indeed, the right of the colored man that, in the selection of jurors to pass upon his life, liberty and property, there shall be no exclusion of his race, and no discrimination against them because of color, has been asserted in a number of cases. * * *

* * *

So far, then, as a conflict with the Fourteenth Amendment is concerned, the case reduces itself to the question of whether the statute of Louisiana is a reasonable regulation, and with respect to this there must necessarily be a large discretion on the part of the legislature. In determining the question of reasonableness it is at liberty to act with reference to the established usages, customs and traditions of the people, and with a view to the promotion of their comfort, and the preservation of the public peace and good order. Gauged by this standard, we cannot say that a law which authorized or even requires the separation of the two races in public conveyances is unreasonable, or more obnoxious to the Fourteenth Amendment than the acts of Congress requiring separate schools for colored children in the District of Columbia, the constitutionality of which does not seem to have been questioned, or the corresponding acts of state legislatures.

We consider the underlying fallacy of the plaintiff's argument to consist in the assumption that the enforced separation of the two races stamps the colored race with a badge of inferiority. If this be so, it is not by reason of anything found in the act, but solely because the colored race chooses to put that construction upon it. The argument necessarily assumes that if, as had been more than once the case, and is not unlikely to be so again, the colored race should become the dominant power in the state legislature, and should enact a law in precisely similar terms, it would thereby relegate the white race to an inferior position. We imagine that the white race, at least, would not acquiesce in this assumption. The argument also assumes that social prejudices may be overcome by legislation, and that equal rights cannot be secured to the negro except by an enforced commingling of the two races. We cannot accept this proposition. If the two races are to meet upon terms of social equity, it must be the result of natural affinities, a mutual appreciation of each other's merits and a voluntary consent of individuals. * * * Legislation is powerless to eradicate racial instincts or to abolish distinctions based upon physical differences, and the attempt to do so can only result in accentuating the difficulties of the present situation. If the civil and political rights of both races be equal one cannot be inferior to the other civilly or politically. If one race be inferior to the other socially, the Constitution of the United States cannot put them upon the same plane.

It is true that the question of the proportion of colored blood necessary to constitute a colored person, as distinguished from a white person, is one upon which there is a difference of opinion in the different States, some holding that any visible admixture of black blood stamps the person as belonging to the colored race, * * * others that it depends upon the preponderance of blood, * * * and still others that the predominance of white blood must only be in the proportion of three fourths. * * * But these are questions to be determined under the laws of each State and are not properly put in issue in this case. Under the allegations of his petition it may undoubtedly become a question of importance whether, under the laws of Louisiana, the petitioner belongs to the white or colored race.

The judgment of the court below is, therefore,

Affirmed.

MR. JUSTICE HARLAN dissenting.

* * *

* * * [W]e have before us a state enactment that compels, under penalties, the separation of the two races in railroad passenger coaches, and makes it a crime for a citizen of either race to enter a coach that has been assigned to citizens of the other race.

* * *

However apparent the injustice of such legislation may be, we have only to consider whether it is consistent with the Constitution of the United States.

* * *

In respect of civil rights, common to all citizens, the Constitution of the United States does not, I think, permit any public authority to know the race of those entitled to be protected in the enjoyment of such rights. Every true man has pride of race, and under appropriate circumstances when the rights of others, his equals before the law, are not to be affected, it is his privilege to express such pride and to take such action based upon it as to him seems proper. But I deny that any legislative body or judicial tribunal may have regard to the race of citizens when the civil rights of those citizens are involved. Indeed, such legislation, as that here in question, is inconsistent not only with that equality of rights which pertains to citizenship, National and State, but with the personal liberty enjoyed by every one within the United States.

The Thirteenth Amendment does not permit the withholding or the deprivation of any right necessarily inhering in freedom. It not only struck down the institution of slavery as previously existing in the United States, but it prevents the imposition of any burdens or disabilities that constitute badges of slavery or servitude. It decreed universal civil freedom in this country. This court has so adjudged. But that amendment having been found inadequate to the protection of the rights of those who had been in slavery, it was followed by the Fourteenth Amendment, which added greatly to the dignity and glory of American citizenship, and to the security of personal liberty, by declaring that "all persons born or naturalized in the United States, and subject to the jurisdiction thereof, are citizens of the United States and of the State wherein they reside," and that "no State shall make or enforce any law which shall abridge the privileges or immunities of citizens of the United States; nor shall any State deprive any person of life, liberty or property without due process of law, nor deny to any person within its jurisdiction the equal protection of the laws." These two amendments, if enforced according to their true intent and meaning, will protect all the civil rights that pertain to freedom and citizenship. Finally, and to the end that no citizen should be denied, on account of his race, the privilege of participating in the political control of his country, it was declared by the Fifteenth Amendment that "the right of the citizens of the United States to vote shall not be denied or abridged by the United States or by any State on account of race, color or previous condition of servitude."

These notable additions to the fundamental law were welcomed by the friends of liberty throughout the world. They removed the race line from our governmental systems. They had, as this court has said, a common purpose, namely, to secure "to a race recently emancipated, a race that through many generations have been held in slavery, all the civil rights that the superior race enjoy." They declared, in legal effect, this court has further said, "that the law in the States shall be the same for the black as for the white; that all persons, whether colored or white, shall stand equal before the laws of the States, and, in regard to the colored race, for whose protection the amendment was primarily designed, that no discrimination shall be made against them by law because of their color." We also said: "The words of the amendment, it is true, are prohibitory, but they contain a necessary implication of a positive immunity, or right, most valuable to the colored race—the right to exemption from unfriendly legislation against them distinctively as colored—exemption from legal discriminations, implying inferiority in civil society, lessening the security of their enjoyment of the rights which others enjoy, and discriminations which are steps towards reducing them to the condition of a subject race." It was, consequently, adjudged that a state law that excluded citizens of the colored race from juries, because of their race and however well qualified in other respects to discharge the duties of jurymen, was repugnant to the Fourteenth Amendment. * * *

* * *

It was said in argument that the statute of Louisiana does not discriminate against either race, but prescribes a rule applicable alike to white and colored citizens. But this argument does not meet the difficulty. Every one knows that the statute in question had its origins in the purpose, not so much to exclude white persons from railroad cars occupied by blacks, as to exclude colored people from coaches occupied by or assigned to white persons. Railroad corporations of Louisiana did not make discrimination among whites in the matter of accommodation for travellers. The thing to accomplish was, under the guise of giving equal accommodation for whites and blacks, to compel the latter to keep to themselves while travelling in railroad passenger coaches. No one would be so wanting in candor as to assert the contrary. The fundamental objection, therefore, to the statute is that it interferes with the personal freedom of citizens. * * * If a white man and a black man choose to occupy the same public conveyance on a public highway, it is their right to do so, and no government proceeding alone on grounds of race can prevent it without infringing the personal liberty of each.

* * *

The white race deems itself to be the dominant race in this country. And so it is, in prestige, in achievements, in education, in wealth and power. So, I doubt not, it will continue to be for all time, if it remains true to its great heritage and holds fast to the principles of constitutional liberty. But in view of the Constitution, in the eye of the law, there is in this country no superior, dominant, ruling class of citizens. There is no caste here. Our Constitution is color-blind, and neither knows nor tolerates classes among citizens. In respect of civil rights, all citizens are equal before the law. The humblest is the peer of the most powerful. The law regards man as man, and takes no account of his surroundings or of his color when his civil rights as guaranteed by the supreme law of the land are involved. It is, therefore, to be regretted that this high tribunal, the final expositor of the fundamental law of the land, has reached the conclusion that it is competent for a State to regulate the enjoyment by citizens of their civil rights solely upon the basis of race.

In my opinion, the judgment this day rendered will, in time, prove to be quite as pernicious as the decision made by this tribunal in the *Dred Scott case*. It was adjudged in that case that the descendants of Africans who were imported into this country and sold as slaves were not included nor intended to be included under the word "citizens" in the Constitution, and could not claim any of the rights and privileges which that instrument provided for and ensured to citizens of the United States; that at the time of the adoption of the Constitution they were "considered as a subordinate and inferior class of beings, who had been subjugated by the dominant race, and, whether emancipated or not, yet remained subject to their authority, and had no rights or privileges but such as those who held the power and the government might choose to grant them." * * * The recent amendments of the Constitution, it was supposed, had eradicated these principles from our institutions. But it seems that we have yet, in some of the States, a dominant race—a superior class of citizens, which assumes to regulate the enjoyment of civil rights, common to all citizens, upon the basis of race. The present decision, it may well be apprehended, will not only stimulate aggressions, more or less brutal and irritating, upon the admitted rights of colored citizens, but will encourage the belief that it is possible, by means of state enactments, to defeat the beneficent purposes which the people of the United States had in view when they adopted the recent amendments of the Constitution, by one of which the blacks of this country were made citizens of the United States and of the States in which they respectively reside, and whose privileges and immunities, as citizens, the States are forbidden to abridge. Sixty millions of whites are in no danger from the presence here of eight millions of blacks. The destinies of the two races, in this country, are indissolubly linked together, and the interests of both require that the common government of all shall not permit the seeds of race hate to be planted under the sanction of law. What can more certainly arouse race hate, what more certainly create and perpetuate a feeling of distrust between these races, than state enactments, which, in fact, proceed on the ground that colored citizens are so inferior and degraded that they cannot be allowed to sit in public coaches occupied by white citizens? That, as all will admit, is the real meaning of such legislation as was enacted in Louisiana.

* * *

There is a race so different from our own that we do not permit those belonging to it to become citizens of the United States. Persons belonging to it are, with few exceptions, absolutely excluded from our country. I allude to the Chinese race. But by the statute in question, a Chinaman can ride in the same passenger coach with white citizens of the United States, while citizens of the black race in Louisiana, many of whom, perhaps, risked their lives for the preservation of the Union, who are entitled, by law, to participate in the political control of the State and nation, who are not excluded, by law or by reason of their race, from public stations of any kind, and who have all the legal rights that belong to white citizens, are yet declared to be criminals, liable to imprisonment, if they ride in a public coach occupied by citizens of the white race. * * *

* * *

I do not deem it necessary to review the decisions of state courts to which reference was made in argument. Some, and the most important, of them are wholly inapplicable, because rendered prior to the adoption of the last amendment of the Constitution, when colored people had very few rights which the dominant race felt obliged to respect. Others were made at a time when public opinion, in many localities, was dominated by the institution of slavery; when it would not have been safe to do justice to the black man; and when, so far as the rights of blacks were concerned, race prejudice was, practically, the supreme law of the land. Those decisions cannot be guides in the era introduced by the recent amendments of the supreme law, which established universal civil freedom, gave citizenship to all born or naturalized in the United States and residing here, obliterated the race line from our systems of governments, National and State, and placed our free institutions upon the broad and sure foundation of the equality of all men before the law.

* * *

For the reasons stated, I am constrained to withhold my assent from the opinion and judgment of the majority.

Notes and Questions

Justice Harlan's dissenting opinion has proven to be prophetic. As we shall see, it is an example of how a dissent's rationale, in time, may be adopted as a majority view.

What did the "equal" in "separate but equal" mean? Did it mean that black facilities and services would be equal to those provided whites, or did it mean services and facilities afforded blacks should be equal? Could "equal" have had any other meaning than the latter one, since at the time of the decision whites dominated political, economic and social life?

Given the racial attitudes of that day, some argue that a contrary decision in *Plessy* would have been widely flouted, thereby weakening the status of the Court as an institution. Do you think it possible that the Court would take such factors into consideration in rendering a decision?

The Court drew a distinction between "social" and "political" equality. Is the key to this distinction the involvement of state action? Do you agree that the Constitution should protect only "political" equality?

It was not until 1927 that the Court specifically extended the *Plessy* doctrine to public education. See *Gong Lum* v. *Rice,* 275 U.S. 78 (1927).

B. De Jure Public School Segregation Unconstitutional (*Brown I*)

Several United States Supreme Court decisions dealing with higher education segregative practices successfully eroded the *Plessy* doctrine before it received a mortal blow from *Brown* v. *Board of Education.* In one of these cases a black law-school applicant challenged a policy under which he had to attend an out-of-state law school because his home state did not have a "separate" law school for blacks. The Court held that such an arrangement did not meet the "separate but equal" doctrine. See *Missouri ex rel. Gaines* v. *Canada,* 305 U.S. 337 (1938). In another decision, *Sweatt* v. *Painter,* 339 U.S. 629 (1950), the Court contended that "separate" law schools in Texas were not "equal" to those attended by whites. In its decision the Court not only compared tangible factors between the black and white law schools, but also such intangible factors as prestige, faculty reputation, and experience of the administration.

Decisions such as *Gaines, Sweatt,* and others set the stage for a challenge to the de jure segregative practices in the primary and secondary public schools. This challenge was presented in *Brown,* and the Court declared that segregation in public education was a denial of the Fourteenth Amendment's guarantee of the equal protection of the laws.

Brown v. Board of Education of Topeka

Supreme Court of the United States, 1954
347 U.S. 483

MR. CHIEF JUSTICE WARREN delivered the opinion of the Court.

These cases come to us from the States of Kansas, South Carolina, Virginia, and Delaware. They are premised on different facts and different local conditions, but a common legal question justifies their consideration together in this consolidated opinion.

In each of the cases, minors of the Negro race, through their legal representatives, seek the aid of the courts in obtaining admission to the public schools of their community on a nonsegregated basis. In each instance, they had been denied admission to schools attended by white children under laws requiring or permitting segregation according to race. This segregation was alleged to deprive the plaintiffs of the equal protection of the laws under the Fourteenth Amendment. In each of the cases other than the Delaware case, a three-judge federal district court denied relief to the plaintiffs on the so-called "separate but equal" doctrine announced by this Court in *Plessy* v. *Ferguson,* 163 U.S. 537. Under that doctrine, equality of treatment is accorded when the races are provided substantially equal facilities, even though these facilities be separate. In the Delaware case, the Supreme Court of Delaware adhered to that doctrine, but ordered that the plaintiffs be admitted to the white schools because of their superiority to the Negro schools.

The plaintiffs contend that segregated public schools are not "equal" and cannot be made "equal," and that hence they are deprived of the equal protection of the laws. Because of the obvious importance of the question presented, the Court took jurisdiction. Argument was heard in the 1952 Term, and reargument was heard this Term on certain questions propounded by the Court.

Reargument was largely devoted to the circumstances surrounding the adoption of the Fourteenth Amendment in 1868. It covered exhaustively consideration of the Amendment in Congress, ratification by the states, then existing practices in racial segregation, and the views of proponents and opponents of the Amendment. This discussion and our own investigation convince us that, although the sources cast some light, it is not enough to resolve the problem with which we are faced. At best, they are inconclusive. The most avid proponents of the post-War Amendments undoubtedly intended them to remove all legal distinctions among "all persons born or naturalized in the United States." Their opponents, just as certainly, were antagonistic to both the letter and the spirit of the Amendments and wished them to have the most limited effect. What others in Congress and the state legislatures had in mind cannot be determined with any degree of certainty.

An additional reason for the inconclusive nature of the Amendment's history, with respect to segregated schools, is the status of public education at that time. In the South, the movement toward free common schools, supported by general taxation, had not yet taken hold. Education of white children was largely in the hands of private groups. Education of Negroes was almost nonexistent, and practically all of the race were illiterate. In fact, any education of Negroes was forbidden by law in some states. Today, in contrast, many Negroes have achieved outstanding success in the arts and sciences as well as in the business and professional world. It is true that public school education at the time of the Amendment had advanced further in the North, but the effect of the Amendment on Northern States was generally ignored in the congressional debates. Even in the North, the conditions of public education did not approximate those existing today. The curriculum was usually rudimentary; ungraded schools were common in rural areas; the school term was but three months a year in many states; and compulsory school attendance was virtually unknown. As a consequence, it is not surprising that there should be so little in the history of the Fourteenth Amendment relating to its intended effect on public education.

In the first cases in this Court construing the Fourteenth Amendment, decided shortly after its adoption, the Court interpreted it as proscribing all state-imposed discriminations against the Negro race. The doctrine of "separate but equal" did not make its appearance in this Court until 1896 in the case of *Plessy* v. *Ferguson, supra,* involving not education but transportation. American courts have since labored with the doctrine for over half a century. In this Court, there have been six cases involving the "separate but equal" doctrine in the field of public education. In *Cumming* v. *County Board of Education,* 175 U.S. 528, and *Gong Lum* v. *Rice,* 275 U.S. 78, the validity of the doctrine itself was not challenged. In more recent cases, all on the graduate school level, inequality was found in that specific benefits enjoyed by white students were denied to Negro students of the same educational qualifications. *Missouri ex rel. Gaines* v. *Canada,* 305 U.S. 337; *Sipuel* v. *Oklahoma,* 332 U.S. 631; *Sweatt* v. *Painter,* 339 U.S. 629; *McLaurin* v. *Oklahoma State Regents,* 339 U.S. 637. In none of these cases was it necessary to re-examine the doctrine to grant relief to the Negro plaintiff. And in *Sweatt* v. *Painter, supra,* the Court expressly reserved decision on the question whether *Plessy* v. *Ferguson* should be held inapplicable to public education.

In the instant cases, that question is directly presented. Here, unlike *Sweatt* v. *Painter,* there are findings below that the Negro and white schools involved have been equalized, or are being equalized, with respect to buildings, curricula, qualifications and salaries of teachers, and other "tangible" factors. Our decision, therefore, cannot turn on merely a comparison of these tangible factors in the Negro and white schools involved in each of the cases. We must look instead to the effect of segregation itself on public education.

In approaching this problem, we cannot turn the clock back to 1868 when the Amendment was adopted, or even to 1896 when *Plessy* v. *Ferguson* was written. We must consider public education in the light of its full development and its present place in American life throughout the Nation. Only in this way can it be determined if segregation in public schools deprives these plaintiffs of the equal protection of the laws.

Today, education is perhaps the most important function of state and local governments. Compulsory school attendance laws and the great expenditures for education both demonstrate our recognition of the importance of education to our democratic society. It is required in the performance of our most basic public responsibilities, even service in the armed forces. It is the very foundation of good citizenship. Today it is a principal instrument in awakening the child to cultural values, in preparing him for later professional training, and in helping him to adjust normally to his environment. In these days, it is doubtful that any child may reasonably be expected to succeed in life if he is denied the opportunity of an education. Such an opportunity, where the state has undertaken to provide it, is a right which must be made available to all on equal terms.

We come then to the question presented: Does segregation of children in public schools solely on the basis of race, even though the physical facilities and other "tangible" factors may be equal, deprive the children of the minority group of equal educational opportunities? We believe that it does.

In *Sweatt* v. *Painter, supra,* in finding that a segregated law school for Negroes could not provide them equal educational opportunities, this Court relied in large part on "those qualities which are incapable of objective measurement but which make for greatness in a law school." In *McLaurin* v. *Oklahoma State Regents, supra,* the Court, in requiring that a Negro admitted to a white graduate school be treated like all other students, again resorted to intangible considerations: ". . . his ability to study, to engage in discussions and exchange views with other students, and, in general, to learn his profession." Such considerations apply with added force to children in grade school and high schools. To separate them from others of similar age qualifications solely because of their race generates a feeling of inferiority as to their status in the community that may affect their hearts and minds in a way unlikely ever to be undone. The effect of this separation on their educational opportunities was well stated by a finding in the Kansas case by a court which nevertheless felt compelled to rule against the Negro plaintiffs:

> "Segregation of white and colored children in public schools has a detrimental effect upon the colored children. The impact is greater when it has the sanction of the law; for the policy of separating the races is usually interpreted as denoting the inferiority of the negro group. A sense of inferiority affects the motivation of a child to learn. Segregation with the sanction of law, therefore, has a tendency to [retard] the educational and mental development of negro children and to deprive them of some of the benefits they would receive in a racial[ly] integrated school system."

Whatever may have been the extent of psychological knowledge at the time of *Plessy* v. *Ferguson,* this finding is amply supported by modern authority. Any language in *Plessy* v. *Ferguson* contrary to this finding is rejected.

We conclude that in the field of public education the doctrine of "separate but equal" has no place. Separate educational facilities are inherently unequal. Therefore, we hold that the plaintiffs and others similarly situated for whom the actions have been brought are, by reason of the segregation complained of, deprived of the equal protection of the laws guaranteed by the Fourteenth Amendment. This disposition makes unnecessary any discussion whether such segregation also violates the Due Process Clause of the Fourteenth Amendment.

Because these are class actions, because of the wide applicability of this decision, and because of the great variety of local conditions, the formulation of decrees in these cases presents problems of considerable complexity. On reargument, the consideration of appropriate relief was necessarily subordinated to the primary question—the constitutionality of segregation in public education. We have now announced that such segregation is a denial of the equal protection of the laws. ∗ ∗ ∗

Notes and Questions

Brown may be one of the most significant decisions rendered by the United States Supreme Court. By declaring de jure segregation in the schools unconstitutional, the decision had reverberations far beyond the public schools. It was a catalyst that forced Americans to examine many forms of government-condoned separation of the races.

It should be emphasized that the consolidated opinion in *Brown* addressed de jure segregation in the public schools. Constitutional and statutory provisions in South Carolina, Virginia, and Delaware and statutory provisions in Kansas required the segregation of black and white students. Consequently, *Brown* applied only to those states having government-imposed segregation at the time of the decision. It did not have applicability to de facto segregated public schools outside the South.

The decision was widely criticized by those opposed to desegregation and applauded by those who were for it. Criticism on legalistic grounds focused on the fact that the Court relied on sociological evidence to establish the negative effect of segregation on black students rather than relying on precedent. This raises the question of what factors the Court should take into consideration when attempting to determine whether or not a person has received "equal protection of the laws" guaranteed by the Fourteenth Amendment to the Constitution.

Proponents of "judicial activism" argued that since the executive and legislative branches were apparently unwilling to address this issue, it was the duty of the judiciary to ensure that all persons, in this instance blacks, receive their constitutional rights. Opponents of the decision contended that nine appointed judges, as opposed to elected officials, should not have the power to institute such fundamental social change. Which view do you hold?

C. Implementation (*Brown II*)

Brown discussed the broad issue of public school segregation and declared a de jure segregation to be unconstitutional. However, the decision did not provide a remedy for those whom it affected. As the Court stated:

> Because these are class actions, because of the wide applicability of this decision, and because of the great variety of local conditions, the formulation of decrees in these cases presents problems of considerable complexity. (P. 495)

Therefore, the Court addressed this question in a separate opinion in *Brown II*.

Brown v. Board of Education of Topeka

Supreme Court of the United States, 1955
349 U.S. 294

MR. CHIEF JUSTICE WARREN delivered the opinion of the Court.

These cases were decided on May 17, 1954. The opinions of that date, declaring the fundamental principle that racial discrimination in public education is unconstitutional, are incorporated herein by reference. All provisions of federal, state, or local law requiring or permitting such discrimination must yield to this principle. There remains for consideration the manner in which relief is to be accorded.

Because these cases arose under different local conditions and their disposition will involve a variety of local problems, we requested further argument on the question of relief. * * *

These presentations were informative and helpful to the Court in its consideration of the complexities arising from the transition to a system of public education freed of racial discrimination. The presentations also demonstrated that substantial steps to eliminate racial discrimination in public schools have already been taken, not only in some of the communities in which these cases arose, but in some of the states appearing as *amici curiae*, and in other states as well. Substantial progress has been made in the District of Columbia and in the communities in Kansas and Delaware involved in this litigation. The defendants in the cases coming to us from

South Carolina and Virginia are awaiting the decision of this Court concerning relief.

Full implementation of these constitutional principles may require solution of varied local school problems. School authorities have the primary responsibility for elucidating, assessing, and solving these problems; courts will have to consider whether the action of school authorities constitutes good faith implementation of the governing constitutional principles. Because of their proximity to local conditions and the possible need for further hearings, the courts which originally heard these cases can best perform this judicial appraisal. Accordingly, we believe it appropriate to remand the cases to those courts.

In fashioning and effectuating the decrees, the courts will be guided by equitable principles. Traditionally, equity has been characterized by a practical flexibility in shaping its remedies and by a facility for adjusting and reconciling public and private needs. These cases call for the exercise of these traditional attributes of equity power. At stake is the personal interest of the plaintiffs in admission to public schools as soon as practicable on a nondiscriminatory basis. To effectuate this interest may call for elimination of a variety of obstacles in making the transition to school systems operated in accordance with the constitutional principles set forth in our May 17, 1954, decision. Courts of equity may properly take into account the public interest in the elimination of such obstacles in a systematic and effective manner. But it should go without saying that the vitality of these constitutional principles cannot be allowed to yield simply because of disagreement with them.

While giving weight to these public and private considerations, the courts will require that the defendants make a prompt and reasonable start toward full compliance with our May 17, 1954, ruling. Once such a start has been made, the courts may find that additional time is necessary to carry out the ruling in an effective manner. The burden rests upon the defendants to establish that such time is necessary in the public interest and is consistent with good faith compliance at the earliest practicable date. To that end, the courts may consider problems related to administration, arising from the physical condition of the school plant, the school transportation system, personnel, revision of school districts and attendance areas into compact units to achieve a system of determining admission to the public schools on a nonracial basis, and revision of local laws and regulations which may be necessary in solving the foregoing problems. They will also consider the adequacy of any plans the defendants may propose to meet these problems and to effectuate a transition to a racially nondiscriminatory school system. During this period of transition, the courts will retain jurisdiction of these cases.

The judgments below, except that in the Delaware case, are accordingly reversed and the cases are remanded to the District Courts to take such proceedings and enter such orders and decrees consistent with this opinion as are necessary and proper to admit to public schools on a racially nondiscriminatory basis with all deliberate speed the parties to these cases. The judgment in the Delaware case—ordering the immediate admission of plaintiffs to schools previously attended only by white children—is affirmed on the basis of the principles stated in our May 17, 1954, opinion, but the case is remanded to the Supreme Court of Delaware for such further proceedings as that Court may deem necessary in light of this opinion.

It is so ordered.

Notes and Questions

Did **Brown II** temper the original decision by employing such an imprecise standard as "all deliberate speed"? In this regard Justice Frankfurter suggested: "Nothing could be worse from my point of view than for this court to make an abstract declaration that segregation is bad and then to have it evaded by tricks." Would the establishment of a specific time frame, for instance, have been enforceable?

In addition to not setting a time frame, why do you believe the Court did not offer specific desegregation guidelines to the lower courts that were effecting desegregation? Do **Brown I** and **Brown II** provide sufficient instructions and guidance from the Supreme Court to the lower federal courts for the latter to have effected desegregation adequately? Since the Court did not provide a test for compliance with the desegregation ruling, what criteria would one use to determine if a school system was in compliance with **Brown I?**

II. Desegregation in the South

Under the **Brown II** formula local school authorities were given the primary responsibility for fashioning desegregation plans. Lower-level federal courts were to determine whether such plans constituted good faith implementation of the principles enunciated in **Brown I.** However, the Court's abstract doctrine, lack of clear guidance, and imprecise time frame, especially in those areas of the South where there was considerable animosity to the decision, all contributed to attempts at delay if not outright noncompliance with **Brown I.**

Consequently, lower federal courts in the South were inundated with school desegregation cases. Some of these cases represented resistance in complying with **Brown I** on the part of local school systems, yet in other instances local authorities were thwarted in their attempt to desegregate by state-level action. An example of this latter problem, which gained nationwide notoriety at the time, is the events in Little Rock, Arkansas. Here the local school system had made good-faith efforts to desegregate; however, the governor ordered the national guard to prevent black students from entering the school to which they had been assigned. Under the circumstances, the local authorities sought a postponement of the desegregation plan by citing preservation of the public peace. In addressing this issue, the Supreme Court, in *Cooper* v. *Aaron,* 358 U.S. 1 (1958), declared that while the Court was sympathetic to the authorities' good-faith efforts that had been hindered by state action, desegregation of the schools could not be postponed.

In Virginia that state's compulsory-education laws were repealed, and school attendance was made a matter of local option. Prince Edward County closed its schools, and private schools for whites only were operated in their place with state and county assistance. The Supreme Court rejected such a course in *Griffin* v. *County School Board of Prince Edward County,* 377 U.S. 218 (1964) by instructing the local district court to require the authorities to levy taxes, thereby raising funds to reopen and operate a nondiscriminatory public school system such as those in other Virginia counties.

A so-called freedom-of-choice plan was another method school systems employed to comply with the necessity to desegregate. Under such a plan parents had the choice of determining which school their children would attend, with the result that there was often little or no actual desegregation within a school system.

A. Freedom of Choice

Green v. County School Board of New Kent County

Supreme Court of the United States, 1968
391 U.S. 430

MR. JUSTICE BRENNAN delivered the opinion of the Court.

The question for decision is whether, under all the circumstances here, respondent School Board's adoption of a "freedom-of-choice" plan which allows a pupil to choose his own public school constitutes adequate compliance with the Board's responsibility "to achieve a system of determining admission to the public schools on a non-racial basis. . . ." *Brown* v. *Board of Education,* 349 U.S. 294, 300–301 (*Brown II*).

Petitioners brought this action in March 1965 seeking injunctive relief against respondent's continued maintenance of an alleged racially segregated school system. New Kent County is a rural county in Eastern

Virginia. About one-half of its population of some 4,500 are Negroes. There is no residential segregation in the county; persons of both races reside throughout. The school system has only two schools, the New Kent school on the east side of the county and the George W. Watkins school on the west side. In a memorandum filed May 17, 1966, the District Court found that the "school system serves approximately 1,300 pupils, of which 740 are Negro and 550 are White. The School Board operates one white combined elementary and high school [New Kent], and one Negro combined elementary and high school [George W. Watkins]. There are no attendance zones. Each school serves the entire county." The record indicates that 21 school buses—11 serving the Watkins school and 10 serving the New Kent school—travel overlapping routes throughout the county to transport pupils to and from the two schools.

The segregated system was initially established and maintained under the compulsion of Virginia constitutional and statutory provisions mandating racial segregation in public education. * * * These provisions were held to violate the Federal Constitution in *Davis* v. *County School Board of Education of Prince Edward County,* decided with *Brown* v. *Board of Education,* 347 U.S. 483, 487 (*Brown I*). The respondent School Board continued the segregated operation of the system after the *Brown* decisions, presumably on the authority of several statutes enacted by Virginia in resistance to those decisions. Some of these statutes were held to be unconstitutional on their face or as applied. One statute, the Pupil Placement Act, Va. Code § 22–232.1 *et seq.* (1964), not repealed until 1966, divested local boards of authority to assign children to particular schools and placed that authority in a State Pupil Placement Board. Under that Act children were each year automatically reassigned to the school previously attended unless upon their application the State Board assigned them to another school; students seeking enrollment for the first time were also assigned at the discretion of the State Board. To September 1964, no Negro pupil had applied for admission to the New Kent school under this statute and no white pupil had applied for admission to the Watkins school.

The School Board initially sought dismissal of this suit on the ground that petitioners had failed to apply to the State Board for assignment to New Kent school. However on August 2, 1965, five months after the suit was brought, respondent School Board, in order to remain eligible for federal financial aid, adopted a "freedom-of-choice" plan for desegregating the schools. Under that plan, each pupil, except for those entering the first and eighth grades, may annually choose between the New Kent and Watkins schools and pupils not making a choice are assigned to the school previously attended; first and eighth grade pupils must affirmatively choose a school. * * *

The pattern of separate "white" and "Negro" schools in the New

Kent County school system established under compulsion of state laws is precisely the pattern of segregation to which *Brown I* and *Brown II* were particularly addressed, and which *Brown I* declared unconstitutionally denied Negro school children equal protection of the laws. Racial identification of the system's schools was complete, extending not just to the composition of student bodies at the two schools but to every facet of school operations—faculty, staff, transportation, extracurricular activities and facilities. In short, the State, acting through the local school board and school officials, organized and operated a dual system, part "white" and part "Negro."

It was such dual systems that 14 years ago *Brown I* held unconstitutional and a year later *Brown II* held must be abolished; school boards operating such school systems were *required* by *Brown II* "to effectuate a transition to a racially nondiscriminatory school system." 349 U.S., at 301. It is of course true that for the time immediately after *Brown II* the concern was with making an initial break in a long-established pattern of excluding Negro children from schools attended by white children. The principal focus was on obtaining for those Negro children courageous enough to break with tradition a place in the "white" schools. See, *e.g.*, *Cooper* v. *Aaron*, 358 U.S. 1. Under *Brown II* that immediate goal was only the first step, however. The transition to a unitary, nonracial system of public education was and is the ultimate end to be brought about; it was because of the "complexities arising from the transition to a system of public education freed of racial discrimination" that we provided for "all deliberate speed" in the implementation of the principles of *Brown I.* * * * Thus we recognized the task would necessarily involve solution of "varied local school problems." * * * In referring to the "personal interest of the plaintiffs in admission to public schools as soon as practicable on a nondiscriminatory basis," we also noted that "[t]o effectuate this interest may call for elimination of a variety of obstacles in making the transition. . . ." * * * Yet we emphasized that the constitutional rights of Negro children required school officials to bear the burden of establishing that additional time to carry out the ruling in an effective manner "is necessary in the public interest and is consistent with good faith compliance at the earliest practicable date." * * * We charged the district court in their review of particular situations to

"consider problems related to administration, arising from the physical condition of the school plant, the school transportation system, personnel, revision of school districts and attendance areas into compact units to achieve a system of determining admission to the public schools on a nonracial basis, and revision of local laws and regulations which may be necessary in solving the foregoing problems. They will also consider the adequacy of any plans the defendants may propose to meet these problems and to effectuate a transition to a racially nondiscriminatory school system." * * *

It is against this background that 13 years after *Brown II* commanded the abolition of dual systems we must measure the effectiveness of respondent School Board's "freedom-of-choice" plan to achieve that end. The School Board contends that it has fully discharged its obligation by adopting a plan by which every student, regardless of race, may "freely" choose the school he will attend. The Board attempts to cast the issue in its broadest form by arguing that its "freedom-of-choice" plan may be faulted only by reading the Fourteenth Amendment as universally requiring "compulsory integration," a reading it insists the wording of the Amendment will not support. But that argument ignores the thrust of *Brown II*. In the light of the command of that case, what is involved here is the question whether the Board has achieved the "racially nondiscriminatory school system" *Brown II* held must be effectuated in order to remedy the established unconstitutional deficiencies of its segregated system. In the context of the state-imposed segregated pattern of long standing, the fact that in 1965 the Board opened the doors of the former "white" school to Negro children and of the "Negro" school to white children merely begins, not ends, our inquiry whether the Board has taken steps adequate to abolish its dual, segregated system. *Brown II* was a call for the dismantling of well-entrenched dual systems tempered by an awareness that complex and multifaceted problems would arise which would require time and flexibility for a successful resolution. School boards such as the respondent then operating state-compelled dual systems were nevertheless clearly charged with the affirmative duty to take whatever steps might be necessary to convert to a unitary system in which racial discrimination would be eliminated root and branch. * * * The constitutional rights of Negro school children articulated in *Brown I* permit no less than this; and it was to this end that *Brown II* commanded school boards to bend their efforts.

In determining whether respondent School Board met that command by adopting its "freedom-of-choice" plan, it is relevant that this first step did not come until some 11 years after *Brown I* was decided and 10 years after *Brown II* directed the making of a "prompt and reasonable start." This deliberate perpetuation of the unconstitutional dual system can only have compounded the harm of such a system. Such delays are no longer tolerable, for "the governing constitutional principles no longer bear the imprint of newly enunciated doctrine." * * * Moreover, a plan that at this late date fails to provide meaningful assurance of prompt and effective disestablishment of a dual system is also intolerable. "The time for mere 'deliberate speed' has run out," *Griffin* v. *County School Board*, 377 U.S. 218, 234; "the context in which we must interpret and apply this language [of *Brown II*] to plans for desegregation has been significantly altered." * * * The burden on a school board today is to come forward with a plan that promises realistically to work, and promises realistically to work *now*.

The obligation of the district courts, as it always has been, is to assess the effectiveness of a proposed plan in achieving desegregation. There is no universal answer to complex problems of desegregation; there is obviously no one plan that will do the job in every case. The matter must be assessed in light of the circumstances present and the options available in each instance. It is incumbent upon the school board to establish that its proposed plan promises meaningful and immediate progress toward disestablishing state-imposed segregation. It is incumbent upon the district court to weigh that claim in light of the facts at hand and in light of any alternatives which may be shown as feasible and more promising in their effectiveness. Where the court finds the board to be acting in good faith and the proposed plan to have real prospects for dismantling the state-imposed dual system "at the earliest practicable date," then the plan may be said to provide effective relief. Of course, the availability to the board of other more promising courses of action may indicate a lack of good faith; and at the least it places a heavy burden upon the board to explain its preference for an apparently less effective method. Moreover, whatever plan is adopted will require evaluation in practice, and the court should retain jurisdiction until it is clear that state-imposed segregation has been completely removed. * * *

We do not hold that "freedom of choice" can have no place in such a plan. We do not hold that a "freedom-of-choice" plan might of itself be unconstitutional, although that argument has been urged upon us. Rather all we decide today is that in desegregating a dual system a plan utilizing "freedom of choice" is not an end in itself. * * * Although the general experience under "freedom of choice" to date has been such as to indicate its ineffectiveness as a tool of desegregation, there may well be instances in which it can serve as an effective device. Where it offers real promise of aiding a desegregation program to effectuate conversion of a state-imposed dual system to a unitary, nonracial system there might be no objection to allowing such a device to prove itself in operation. On the other hand, if there are reasonably available other ways, such for illustration as zoning, promising speedier and more effective conversion to a unitary, nonracial school system, "freedom of choice" must be held unacceptable.

The New Kent School Board's "freedom-of-choice" plan cannot be accepted as a sufficient step to "effectuate a transition" to a unitary system. In three years of operation not a single white child has chosen to attend Watkins school and although 115 Negro children enrolled in New Kent school in 1967 (up from 35 in 1965 and 111 in 1966) 85% of the Negro children in the system still attend the all-Negro Watkins school. In other words, the school system remains a dual system. Rather than further the dismantling of the dual system, the plan has operated simply to burden children and their parents with a responsibility which *Brown II* placed squarely on the School Board. The Board must be required to formulate a new plan and, in light of other courses which appear open to the Board, such as zoning, fashion steps which promise realistically to convert promptly to a system without a "white" school and a "Negro" school, but just schools.

It is so ordered.

Notes and Questions

Does the opinion in *Green* suggest that in the future a school system must engage in affirmative action in order to desegregate schools? Do you think the school board's failure to take any steps to eliminate segregation for eleven years after *Brown I* influenced the Court's decision?

In a per curiam opinion one year after *Green,* the Court declared that with respect to continued operation of racially segregated schools, the standard of "all deliberate speed" was no longer constitutionally permissible and that school districts must immediately terminate dual school systems based on race or color. See *Alexander* v. *Holmes County Board of Education,* 396 U.S. 19 (1969).

B. Defining the Scope of the Duty to Eliminate
the Dual School System

Swann v. Charlotte-Mecklenburg Board of Education

Supreme Court of the United States, 1971
402 U.S. 1

MR. CHIEF JUSTICE BURGER delivered the opinion of the Court.

* * *

This case and those argued with it arose in States having a long history of maintaining two sets of schools in a single school system deliberately operated to carry out a governmental policy to separate pupils in schools solely on the basis of race. That was what *Brown* v. *Board of Education* was all about. These cases present us with the problem of defining in more precise terms than heretofore the scope of the duty of school authorities and district courts in implementing *Brown I* and the mandate to eliminate dual systems and establish unitary systems at once. Meanwhile district courts and courts of appeals have struggled in hundreds of cases with a multitude and variety of problems under this Court's general directive. Understandably, in an area of evolving remedies, those courts had to improvise and experiment without detailed or specific guidelines. This Court, in *Brown I*, appropriately dealt with the large constitutional principles; other federal courts had to grapple with the flinty, intractable realities of day-to-day implementation of those constitutional commands. Their efforts, of necessity, embraced a process of "trial and error," and our effort to formulate guidelines must take into account their experience.

The Charlotte-Mecklenburg school system, the 43d largest in the Nation, encompasses the city of Charlotte and surrounding Mecklenburg County, North Carolina. The area is large—550 square miles—spanning roughly 22 miles east-west and 36 miles north-south. During the 1968–1969 school year the system served more than 84,000 pupils in 107 schools. Approximately 71% of the pupils were found to be white and 29% Negro. As of June 1969 there were approximately 24,000 Negro students in the system, of whom 21,000 attended schools within the city of Charlotte. Two-thirds of those 21,000—approximately 14,000 Negro students—attended 21 schools which were either totally Negro or more than 99% Negro.

* * *

In April 1969 the District Court ordered the school board to come forward with a plan for both faculty and student desegregation. Proposed plans were accepted by the court in June and August 1969 on an interim basis only, and the board was ordered to file a third plan by November 1969. In November the board moved for an extension of time until February 1970, but when that was denied the board submitted a partially completed plan. In December 1969 the District Court held that the Board's submission was unacceptable and appointed an expert in education administration, Dr. John Finger, to prepare a desegregation plan. Thereafter in February 1970, the District Court was presented with two alternative pupil assignment plans—the finalized "board plan" and the "Finger plan."

The Board Plan. As finally submitted, the school board plan closed seven schools and reassigned their pupils. It restructured school attendance zones to achieve greater racial balance but maintained existing grade structures and rejected techniques such as pairing and clustering as part of a desegregation effort. The plan created a single athletic league, eliminated the previously racial basis of the school bus system, provided racially mixed faculties and administrative staffs, and modified its free-transfer plan into an optional majority-to-minority transfer system.

The board plan proposed substantial assignment of Negroes to nine of the system's 10 high schools, producing 17% to 36% Negro population in each. The projected Negro attendance at the 10th school, Independence, was 2%. The proposed attendance zones for the high schools were typically shaped like wedges of a pie, extending outward from the center of the city to the suburban and rural areas of the county in order to afford residents of the center city area access to outlying schools.

As for junior high schools, the board rezoned the 21 school areas so that in 20 the Negro attendance would range from 0% to 38%. The other school, located in the heart of the Negro residential area, was left with an enrollment of 90% Negro.

The board plan with respect to elementary schools relied entirely upon gerry-mandering of geographic zones. More than half of the Negro elementary pupils were left in nine schools that were 86% to 100% Negro; approximately half of the white elementary pupils were assigned to schools 86% to 100% white.

The Finger Plan. The plan submitted by the court-appointed expert, Dr. Finger, adopted the school board zoning plan for senior high schools with one modification: it required that an additional 300 Negro students be transported from the Negro residential area of the city to the nearly all-white Independence High School.

The Finger plan for the junior high schools employed much of the rezoning plan of the board, combined with the creation of nine "satellite" zones. Under the satellite plan, inner-city Negro students were assigned by attendance zones to nine outlying predominantly white junior high schools, thereby substantially desegregating every junior high school in the system.

The Finger plan departed from the board plan chiefly in its handling of the system's 76 elementary schools. Rather than relying solely upon geographic zoning, Dr. Finger proposed use of zoning, pairing, and grouping techniques, with the result that student bodies throughout the system would range from 9% to 38% Negro. * * * Under the Finger plan, nine inner-city Negro schools were grouped in this manner with 24 suburban white schools.

On February 5, 1970, the District Court adopted the board plan, as modified by Dr. Finger, for the junior and senior high schools. The court rejected the board elementary school plan and adopted the Finger plan as presented. * * *

On appeal the Court of Appeals affirmed the District Court's order as to faculty desegregation and the secondary school plans, but vacated the order respecting elementary schools. * * *

* * *

Nearly 17 years ago this Court held, in explicit terms, that state-imposed segregation by race in public schools denies equal protection of the laws. At no time has the Court deviated in the slightest degree from that holding or its constitutional underpinnings. * * *

* * *

Over the 16 years since *Brown II*, many difficulties were encountered in implementation of the basic constitutional requirement that the State not discriminate between public school children on the basis of their race. Nothing in our national experience prior to 1955 prepared anyone for dealing with changes and adjustments of the magnitude and complexity encountered since then. Deliberate resistance of some to the Court's mandates has impeded the good-faith efforts of others to bring school systems into compliance. The detail and nature of these dilatory tactics have been noted frequently by this Court and other courts.

* * *

The problems encountered by the district courts and courts of appeals make plain that we should now try to amplify guidelines, however incomplete and imperfect, for the assistance of school authorities and courts. The failure of local authorities to meet their constitutional obligations aggravated the massive problem of converting from the state-enforced discrimination of racially separate school systems. This process has been rendered more difficult by changes since 1954 in the structure and patterns of communities, the growth of student population, movement of families, and other changes, some of which had marked impact on school planning, sometimes neutralizing or negating remedial action before it was fully implemented. Rural areas accustomed for half a century to the consolidated school systems implemented by bus transportation could make adjustments more readily than metropolitan areas with dense and shifting population, numerous schools, congested and complex traffic patterns.

* * *

This allocation of responsibility once made, the Court attempted from time to time to provide some guidelines for the exercise of the district judge's discretion and for the reviewing function of the courts of appeals. However, a school desegregation case does not differ fundamentally from other cases involving the framing of equitable remedies to repair the denial of a constitutional right. The task is to correct, by a balancing of the individual and collective interests, the condition that offends the Constitution.

In seeking to define even in broad and general terms how far this remedial power extends it is important to remember that judicial powers may be exercised only on the basis of a constitutional violation. Remedial judicial authority does not put judges automatically in the shoes of school authorities whose powers are plenary. Judicial authority enters only when local authority defaults.

* * *

We turn now to the problem of defining with more particularity the responsibilities of school authorities in desegregating a state-enforced dual school system in light of the Equal Protection Clause. Although the several related cases before us are primarily concerned with problems of student assignment, it may be helpful to begin with a brief discussion of other aspects of the process.

In *Green,* we pointed out that existing policy and practice with regard to faculty, staff, transportation, extracurricular activities, and facilities were among the most important indicia of a segregated system. 391 U.S., at 435. Independent of student assignment, where it is possible to identify a "white school" or a "Negro school" simply by reference to the racial composition of teachers and staff, the quality of school buildings and equipment, or the organization of sports activities, a *prima facie* case of violation of substantive constitutional rights under the Equal Protection Clause is shown.

When a system has been dual in these respects, the first remedial responsibility of school authorities is to eliminate invidious racial distinctions. With respect to such matters as transportation, supporting personnel, and extracurricular activities, no more than this may be necessary. Similar corrective action must be taken with regard to the maintenance of buildings and the distribution of equipment. In these areas, normal administrative practice should produce schools of like quality, facilities, and staffs. Something more must be said, however, as to faculty assignment and new school construction.

* * *

In *United States* v. *Montgomery County Board of Education,* 395 U.S. 225 (1969), the District Court set as a goal a plan of faculty assignment in each school with a ratio of white to Negro faculty members substantially the same throughout the system. * * *

The District Court in *Montgomery* then proceeded to set an initial ratio for the whole system of at least two Negro teachers out of each 12 in any given school. The Court of Appeals modified the order by eliminating what it regarded as "fixed mathematical" ratios of faculty and substituted an initial requirement of *"substantially or approximately"* a five-to-one ratio. With respect to the future, the Court of Appeals held that the numerical ratio should be eliminated and that compliance should not be tested solely by the achievement of specified proportions. * * *

We reversed the Court of Appeals and restored the District Court's order in its entirety. * * * The principles of *Montgomery* have been properly followed by the District Court and the Court of Appeals in this case.

The construction of new schools and the closing of old ones are two of the most important functions of local school authorities and also two of the most complex. They must decide questions of location and capacity in light of population growth, finances, land values, site availability, through an almost endless list of factors to be considered. The result of this will be a decision which, when combined with one technique or another of student assignment, will determine the racial composition of the student body in each school in the system. Over the long run, the consequences of the choices will be far reaching. People gravitate toward school facilities, just as schools are located in response to the needs of people. The location of schools may thus influence the patterns of residential development of a metropolitan area and have important impact on composition of inner-city neighborhoods.

In the past, choices in this respect have been used as a potent weapon for creating or maintaining a state-segregated school system. In addition to the classic pattern of building schools specifically intended for Negro or white students, school authorities have sometimes, since *Brown*, closed schools which appeared likely to become racially mixed through changes in neighborhood residential patterns. This was sometimes accompanied by building new schools in the areas of white suburban expansion farthest from Negro population centers in order to maintain the separation of the races with a minimum departure from the formal principles of "neigborhood zoning." Such a policy does more than simply influence the short-run composition of the student body of a new school. It may well promote segregated residential patterns which, when combined with "neighborhood zoning," further lock the school system into the mold of separation of the races. Upon a proper showing a district court may consider this in fashioning a remedy.

In ascertaining the existence of legally imposed school segregation, the existence of a pattern of school construction and abandonment is thus a factor of great weight. In devising remedies where legally imposed segregation has been established, it is the responsibility of local authorities and district courts to see to it that future school construction and abandonment are not used and do not serve to perpetuate or re-establish the dual system. * * *

The central issue in this case is that of student assignment, and there are essentially four problem areas:

* * *

[1] Racial Balances or Racial Quotas.

* * *

Our objective in dealing with the issues presented by these cases is to see that school authorities exclude no pupil of a racial minority from any school, directly or indirectly, on account of race; it does not and cannot embrace all the problems of racial prejudice, even when those problems contribute to disproportionate racial concentrations in some schools.

In this case it is urged that the District Court has imposed a racial balance requirement of 71%–29% on individual schools. * * *

The District Judge went on to acknowledge that variation "from that norm may be unavoidable." This contains intimations that the "norm" is a fixed mathematical racial balance reflecting the pupil constituency of the system. If we were to read the holding of the District Court to require, as a matter of substantive constitutional right, any particular degree of racial balance or mixing, that approach would be disapproved and we would be obliged to reverse. The constitutional command to desegregate schools does not mean that every school in every community must always reflect the racial composition of the school system as a whole.

As the voluminous record in this case shows, the predicate for the District Court's use of the 71%–29% ratio was twofold: first, its express finding, approved by the Court of Appeals and not challenged here, that a dual school system had been maintained by the school authorities at least until 1969; second, its finding, also approved by the Court of Appeals, that the school board had totally defaulted in its acknowledged duty to come forward with an acceptable plan of its own, notwithstanding the patient efforts of the District Judge who, on at least three occasions, urged the board to submit plans. As the statement of facts shows, these findings are abundantly supported by the record. It was because of this total failure of the school board that the District Court was obliged to turn to other qualified sources, and Dr. Finger was designated to assist the District Court to do what the board should have done.

We see therefore that the use made of mathematical ratios was no more than a starting point in the process of shaping a remedy, rather than an inflexible requirement. From that starting point the District Court proceeded to frame a decree that was within its discretionary powers, as an equitable remedy for the particular circumstances. As we said in *Green*, a school authority's remedial plan or a district court's remedial decree is to be judged by its effectiveness. Awareness of the racial composition of the whole school system is likely to be a useful starting point in shaping a remedy to correct past constitutional violations. In sum, the very limited use made of mathematical ratios was within the equitable remedial discretion of the District Court.

[2] One-race Schools.

The record in this case reveals the familiar phenomenon that in metropolitan areas minority groups are often found concentrated in one part of the city. In some circumstances certain schools may remain all or largely of one race until new schools can be provided or neighborhood patterns change. Schools all or predominately of one race in a district of mixed population will require close scrutiny to determine that school assignments are not part of state-enforced segregation.

In light of the above, it should be clear that the existence of some small number of one-race, or virtually one-race, schools within a district is not in and of itself the mark of a system that still practices segregation by law. The district judge or school authorities should make every effort to achieve the greatest possible degree of actual desegregation and will thus necessarily be concerned with the elimination of one-race schools. No *per se* rule can adequately embrace all the difficulties of reconciling the competing interests involved; but in a system with a history of segregation the need for remedial criteria of sufficient specificity to assure a school authority's compliance with its constitutional duty warrants a presumption against schools that are substantially disproportionate in their racial composition. Where the school authority's proposed plan for conversion from a dual to a unitary system contemplates the continued existence of some schools that are all or predominately of one race, they have the burden of showing that such school assignments are genuinely nondiscriminatory. The court should scrutinize such schools, and the burden upon the school authorities will be to satisfy the court that their racial composition is not the result of present or past discriminatory action on their part.

An optional majority-to-minority transfer provision has long been recognized as a useful part of every desegregation plan. Provision for optional transfer of those in the majority racial group of a particular school to other schools where they will be in the minority is an indispensable remedy for those students willing to transfer to other schools in order to lessen the impact on them of the state-imposed stigma of segregation. In order to be effective, such a transfer arrangement must grant the transferring student free transportation and space must be made available in the school to which he desires to move. * * * The court orders in this and the companion *Davis* case now provide such an option.

[3] *Remedial Altering of Attendance Zones.*

The maps submitted in these cases graphically demonstrate that one of the principal tools employed by school planners and by courts to break up the dual school system has been a frank—and sometimes drastic—gerrymandering of school districts and attendance zones. An additional step was pairing, "clustering," or "grouping" of schools with attendance assignments made deliberately to accomplish the transfer of Negro students out of formerly segregated Negro schools and transfer of white students to formerly all-Negro schools. More often than not, these zones are neither compact nor contiguous; indeed, they may be on opposite ends of the city. As an interim corrective measure, this cannot be said to be beyond the broad remedial powers of a court.

Absent a constitutional violation there would be no basis for judicially ordering assignment of students on a racial basis. All things being equal, with no history of discrimination, it might well be desirable to assign pupils to schools nearest their homes. But all things are not equal in a system that has been deliberately constructed and maintained to enforce racial segregation. The remedy for such segregation may be administratively awkward, inconvenient, and even bizarre in some situations and may impose burdens on some; but all awkwardness and inconvenience cannot be avoided in the interim period when remedial adjustments are being made to eliminate the dual school systems.

No fixed or even substantially fixed guidelines can be established as to how far a court can go, but it must be recognized that there are limits. The objective is to dismantle the dual school system. "Racially neutral" assignment plans proposed by school authorities to a district court may be inadequate; such plans may fail to counteract the continuing effects of past school segregation resulting from discriminatory location of school sites or distortion of school size in order to achieve or maintain an artificial racial separation. When school authorities present a district court with a "loaded game board," affirmative action in the form of remedial altering of attendance zones is proper to achieve truly nondiscriminatory assignments. In short, an assignment plan is not acceptable simply because it appears to be neutral.

* * *

We hold that the pairing and grouping of noncontiguous school zones is a permissible tool and such action is to be considered in light of the objectives sought. * * * Maps do not tell the whole story since noncontiguous school zones may be more accessible to each other in terms of critical travel time, because of traffic patterns and good highways, than schools geographically closer together. Conditions in different localities will vary so widely that no rigid rules can be laid down to govern all situations.

[4] *Transportation of Students.*

The scope of permissible transportation of students as an implement of a remedial decree has never been defined by this Court and by the very nature of the problem it cannot be defined with precision. No rigid guidelines as to student transportation can be given for application to the infinite variety of problems presented in thousands of situations. Bus transportation has been an integral part of the public education system for years, and was perhaps the single most important factor in the transition from the one-room schoolhouse to the consolidated school. Eighteen million of the Nation's public school children, approximately 39%, were transported to their schools by bus in 1969–1970 in all parts of the country.

The importance of bus transportation as a normal and accepted tool of educational policy is readily discernible in this and the companion case, *Davis, supra.* The Charlotte school authorities did not purport to assign students on the basis of geographically drawn zones until 1965 and then they allowed almost unlimited transfer privileges. The District Court's conclusion that assignment of children to the school nearest their home serving their grade would not produce an effective dismantling of the dual system is supported by the record.

Thus the remedial techniques used in the District Court's order were within that court's power to provide equitable relief; implementation of the decree is well within the capacity of the school authority.

The decree provided that buses used to implement the plan would operate on direct routes. Students would be picked up at schools near their homes and transported to the schools they were to attend. The trips for elementary school pupils average about seven miles and the District Court found that they would take "not over 35 minutes at the most." This system compares favorably with the transportation plan previously operated in Charlotte under which each day 23,600 students on all grade levels were transported an average of 15 miles one way for an average trip requiring over an hour. In these circumstances, we find no basis for holding that the local school authorities may not be required to employ bus transportation as one tool of school desegregation. Desegregation plans cannot be limited to the walk-in school.

An objection to transportation of students may have validity when the time or distance of travel is so great as to either risk the health of the children or significantly impinge on the educational process. * * * It hardly needs stating that the limits on time of travel will vary with many factors, but probably with none more than the age of the students. The reconciliation of competing values in a desegregation case is, of course, a difficult task with many sensitive facets but fundamentally no more so than remedial measures courts of equity have traditionally employed.

The Court of Appeals, searching for a term to define the equitable remedial power of the district courts, used the term "reasonableness." In *Green, supra,* this Court used the term "feasible" and by implication, "workable," "effective," and "realistic" in the mandate to develop "a plan that promises realistically to work, and . . . to work *now*." On the facts of this case, we are unable to conclude that the order of the District Court is not reasonable, feasible or workable. However, in seeking to define the scope of remedial power or the limits on remedial power of courts in an area as sensitive as we deal with here, words are poor instruments to convey the sense of basic fairness inherent in equity. Substance, not semantics, must govern, and we have sought to suggest the nature of limitations without frustrating the appropriate scope of equity.

At some point, these school authorities and others like them should have achieved full compliance with this Court's decision in *Brown I*. The systems would then be "unitary" in the sense required by our decisions in *Green* and *Alexander*.

It does not follow that the communities served by such systems will remain demographically stable, for in a growing, mobile society, few will do so. Neither school authorities nor district courts are constitutionally required to make year-by-year adjustments of the racial composition of student bodies once the affirmative duty to desegregate has been accomplished and racial discrimination through official action is eliminated from the system. This does not mean that federal courts are without power to deal with future problems; but in the absence of a showing that either the school authorities or some other agency of the State has deliberately attempted to fix or alter demographic patterns to affect the racial composition of the schools, futher intervention by a district court should not be necessary.

* * *

Notes and Questions

Swann represented another example of the Supreme Court's continued effort to render decisions that unequivocally reflected its desire to eliminate the dual school system. The unanimous decision contended that the dismantling of the dual school system could be accomplished by assigning teachers so as to achieve a particular degree of faculty desegregation; ensuring that future school construction and abandonment would not perpetuate or reestablish a dual system; scrutinizing one-race schools to ensure that the racial composition did not result from present or past discriminatory action; altering attendance zones and employing pairing and grouping of noncontiguous zones to counteract past segregation; and although not requiring it, employing bus transportation as a constitutionally permissible method of dismantling the dual system. Would the path to eliminating de jure segregation have been smoother if *Brown I* had contained such guidelines?

III. Desegregation in Nonsouthern States

Continued and successful desegregation efforts in the southern states clearly revealed the lack of similar efforts in many nonsouthern states where public school racial segregation existed. The legitimate question was often raised of why one section of the country was required to desegregate its schools while obviously segregated school systems continued to operate in the northern and western portions of the United States. From a legal standpoint a partial answer to this question lies in the Supreme Court's reliance on the distinction between de jure and de facto segregation.

As we have noted, the presence of constitutional and/or statutory provisions and local policies mandating segregated schools in the southern states made it possible to address this form of state-sanctioned de jure segregation. Segregated school systems existed outside the South, and although such segregation was not always based on officially stated state or local policy, in some areas it had been. Several nonsouthern states had statutes authorizing separate but equal public schools, and although eventually repealed, such statutes remained on the books in New York until 1938, in Wyoming until 1954, and in Indiana until 1959. The presence of such statutes established persistent patterns of segregated schools that were not always easily changed.

Segregation outside the South existed for other reasons. In some instances long-standing "customs" were present at the local level, which also contributed to racial attitudes and resultant segregated schools. Perhaps the most significant force, however, contributing to segregated schools outside the South resulted from housing patterns, which in some areas found blacks living in all-black neighborhoods and black students attending all-black neighborhood schools. Such de facto segregation was often based on housing patterns that allegedly were not the result of direct state action. Since the Supreme Court had not considered de facto segregation violative of the **Brown I** edict, nonsouthern public schools that were segregated on that basis were not immediately challenged in the courts. However, in time, segregative practices of nonsouthern school systems were examined by the judiciary. One of the contentions made against segregated nonsouthern school systems was that they had engaged in a form of de jure segregation, perhaps not as blatant as in the South but nevertheless resulting in impermissible racial discrimination.

A. Nonsouthern Segregation

Keyes v. School District No. 1

Supreme Court of the United States, 1973
413 U.S. 189

MR. JUSTICE BRENNAN delivered the opinion of the Court.

This school desegregation case concerns the Denver, Colorado, school system. That system has never been operated under a constitutional or statutory provision that mandated or permitted racial segregation in public education. Rather, the gravamen of this action, brought in

June 1969 in the District Court for the District of Colorado by parents of
Denver schoolchildren, is that respondent School Board alone, by use of
various techniques such as the manipulation of student attendance zones,
schoolsite selection and a neighborhood school policy, created or maintained racially or ethnically (or both racially and ethnically) segregated
schools throughout the school district, entitling petitioners to a decree
directing desegregation of the entire school district.

The boundaries of the school district are coterminous with the boundaries of the city and county of Denver. There were in 1969, 119 schools
with 96,580 pupils in the school system. * * * The District Court
found that by the construction of a new, relatively small elementary
school, Barrett, in the middle of the Negro community west of Park Hill,
by the gerrymandering of student attendance zones, by the use of so-
called "optional zones," and by the excessive use of mobile classroom
units, among other things, the respondent School Board had engaged
over almost a decade after 1960 in an unconstitutional policy of deliberate
racial segregation with respect to the Park Hill schools. The court therefore ordered the Board to desegregate those schools through the implementation of the three rescinded resolutions. * * *

Segregation in Denver schools is not limited, however, to the schools
in the Park Hill area, and not satisfied with their success in obtaining
relief for Park Hill, petitioners pressed their prayer that the District Court
order desegregation of all segregated schools in the city of Denver, particularly the heavily segregated schools in the core city area. But that
court concluded that its finding of a purposeful and systematic program
of racial segregation affecting thousands of students in the Park Hill area
did not, in itself, impose on the School Board the affirmative duty to
eliminate segregation throughout the school district. Instead, the court
fractionated the district and held that the petitioners had to make a fresh
showing of *de jure* segregation in each area of the city for which they
sought relief. Moreover, the District Court held that its finding of intentional segregation in Park Hill was not in any sense material to the question of segregative intent in other areas of the city. * * *

* * *

Before turning to the primary question we decide today, a word
must be said about the District Court's method of defining a "segregated"
school. Denver is a tri-ethnic, as distinguished from a bi-racial, community. The overall racial and ethnic composition of the Denver public
schools is 66% Anglo, 14% Negro, and 20% Hispano. * * * What is
or is not a segregated school will necessarily depend on the facts of each
particular case. In addition to the racial and ethnic composition of a
school's student body, other factors, such as the racial and ethnic composition of faculty and staff and the community and administration attitudes

toward the school, must be taken into consideration. The District Court has recognized these specific factors as elements of the definition of a "segregated" school, * * * and we may therefore infer that the court will consider them again on remand.

We conclude, however, that the District Court erred in separating Negroes and Hispanos for purposes of defining a "segregated" school. We have held that Hispanos constitute an identifiable class for purposes of the Fourteenth Amendment. * * * Indeed, the District Court recognized this in classifying predominantly Hispano schools as "segregated" schools in their own right. But there is also much evidence that in the Southwest Hispanos and Negroes have a great many things in common. The United States Commission on Civil Rights has recently published two Reports on Hispano education in the Southwest. Focusing on students in the States of Arizona, California, Colorado, New Mexico, and Texas, the Commission concluded that Hispanos suffer from the same educational inequities as Negroes and American Indians. In fact, the District Court itself recognized that "[o]ne of the things which the Hispano has in common with the Negro is economic and cultural deprivation and discrimination." * * *

In our view, the only other question that requires our decision at this time is * * * whether the District Court and the Court of Appeals applied an incorrect legal standard in addressing petitioners' contention that respondent School Board engaged in an unconstitutional policy of deliberate segregation in the core city schools. Our conclusion is that those courts did not apply the correct standard in addressing that contention.

Petitioners apparently concede for the purpose of this case that in the case of a school system like Denver's, where no statutory dual system has ever existed, plaintiffs must prove not only that segregated schooling exists but also that it was brought about or maintained by intentional state action. Petitioners proved that for almost a decade after 1960 respondent School Board had engaged in an unconstitutional policy of deliberate racial segregation in the Park Hill schools. Indeed, the District Court found that "[b]etween 1960 and 1969 the Board's policies with respect to these northeast Denver schools show an undeviating purpose to isolate Negro students" in segregated schools "while preserving the Anglo character of [other] schools." * * * This finding did not relate to any unsubstantial or trivial fragment of the school system. On the contrary, respondent School Board was found guilty of following a deliberate segregation policy at schools attended, in 1969, by 37.69% of Denver's total Negro school population, including one-fourth of the Negro elementary pupils, over two-thirds of the Negro junior high pupils, and over two-fifths of the Negro high school pupils. In addition, there was uncontroverted evidence that teachers and staff had for years been assigned on the basis of a minority teacher to a minority school throughout the school system. Respondent argues, however, that a finding of state-imposed segregation as to a substantial portion of the school system can be viewed in isolation from the rest of the district, and that even if state-imposed segregation does exist in a substantial part of the Denver school system, it does not follow that the District Court could predicate on that fact a finding that the entire school system is a dual system. We do not agree. We have never suggested that plaintiffs in school desegregation cases must bear the burden of proving the element of *de jure* segregation as to each and every school or each and every student within the school system. Rather, we have held that where plaintiffs prove that a current condition of segregated schooling exists within a school district where a dual system was compelled or authorized by statute at the time of our decision in *Brown* v. *Board of Education,* 347 U.S. 483 (1954) (*Brown I*), the State automatically assumes an affirmative duty "to effectuate a transition to a racially nondiscriminatory school system," *Brown* v. *Board of Education,* 349 U.S. 294, 301 (1955) (*Brown II*), see also *Green* v. *County School Board,* 391 U.S. 430, 437–438 (1968), that is, to eliminate from the public schools within their school system "all vestiges of state-imposed segregation." *Swann* v. *Charlotte-Mecklenburg Board of Education,* 402 U.S. 1, 15 (1971).

This is not a case, however, where a statutory dual system has ever existed. Nevertheless, where plaintiffs prove that the school authorities have carried out a systematic program of segregation affecting a substantial portion of the students, schools, teachers, and facilities within the school system, it is only common sense to conclude that there exists a predicate for a finding of the existence of a dual school system. Several considerations support this conclusion. First, it is obvious that a practice of concentrating Negroes in certain schools by structuring attendance zones or designating "feeder" schools on the basis of race has the reciprocal effect of keeping other nearby schools predominantly white. Similarly, the practice of building a school—such as the Barrett Elementary School in this case—to a certain size and in a certain location, "with conscious knowledge that it would be a segregated school" * * * has a substantial reciprocal effect on the racial composition of other nearby schools. So also, the use of mobile classrooms, the drafting of student transfer policies, the transportation of students, and the assignment of faculty and staff, on racially identifiable bases, have the clear effect of earmarking schools according to their racial composition, and this, in turn, together with the elements of student assignment and school construction, may have a profound reciprocal effect on the racial composition of residential neighborhoods within a metropolitan area, thereby causing further racial concentration within the schools. * * *

In short, common sense dictates the conclusion that racially inspired school board actions have an impact beyond the particular schools that are the subjects of those actions. This is not to say, of course, that there can never be a case in which the geographical structure of, or the natural boundaries within, a school district may have the effect of dividing the district into separate, identifiable and unrelated units. Such a determination is essentially a question of fact to be resolved by the trial court in the first instance, but such cases must be rare. In the absence of such a determination, proof of state-imposed segregation in a substantial portion of the district will suffice to support a finding by the trial court of the existence of a dual system. Of course, where that finding is made, as in cases involving statutory dual systems, the school authorities have an affirmative duty "to effectuate a transition to a racially nondiscriminatory school system." *Brown II, supra,* at 301.

* * *

On the question of segregative intent, petitioners presented evidence tending to show that the Board, through its actions over a period of years, intentionally created and maintained the segregated character of the core city schools. Respondents countered this evidence by arguing that the segregation in these schools is the result of a racially neutral "neighborhood school policy" and that the acts of which petitioners complain are explicable within the bounds of that policy. Accepting the School Board's explanation, the District Court and the Court of Appeals agreed that a finding of *de jure* segregation as to the core city schools was not permissible since petitioners had failed to prove "(1) a racially discriminatory purpose and (2) a causal relationship between the acts complained of and the racial imbalance admittedly existing in those schools." * * * This assessment of petitioners' proof was clearly incorrect.

Although petitioners had already proved the existence of intentional school segregation in the Park Hill schools, this crucial finding was totally ignored when attention turned to the core city schools. Plainly, a finding of intentional segregation as to a portion of a school system is not devoid of probative value in assessing the school authorities' intent with respect to other parts of the same school system. On the contrary, where, as here, the case involves one school board, a finding of intentional segregation on its part in one portion of a school system is highly relevant to the issue of the board's intent with respect to other segregated schools in the system. This is merely an application of the well-settled evidentiary principle that "the prior doing of other similar acts, whether clearly a part of a scheme or not, is useful as reducing the possibility that the act in question was done with innocent intent." * * *

Applying these principles in the special context of school desegregation cases, we hold that a finding of intentionally segregative school board actions in a meaningful portion of a school system, as in this case, creates a presumption that other segregated schooling within the system is not adventitious. It establishes, in other words, a prima facie case of unlawful segregative design on the part of school authorities, and shifts to those authorities the burden of proving that other segregated schools within the system are not also the result of intentionally segregative actions. This is true even if it is determined that different areas of the school district should be viewed independently of each other because, even in that situation, there is high probability that where school authorities have effectuated an intentionally segregative policy in a meaningful portion of the school system, similar impermissible considerations have motivated their actions in other areas of the system. We emphasize that the differentiating factor between *de jure* segregation and so-called *de facto* segregation to which we referred in *Swann* is *purpose* or *intent* to segregate. Where school authorities have been found to have practiced purposeful segregation in part of a school system, they may be expected to oppose system-wide desegregation, as did the respondents in this case, on the ground that their purposefully segregative actions were isolated and individual events, thus leaving plaintiffs with the burden of proving otherwise. But at that point where an intentionally segregative policy is practiced in a meaningful segment of a school system, as in this case, the school authorities cannot be heard to argue that plaintiffs have proved only "isolated and individual" unlawfully segregative actions. In that circumstance, it is both fair and reasonable to require that the school authorities bear the burden of showing that their actions as to other segregated schools within the system were not also motivated by segregative intent.

* * *

In discharging that burden, it is not enough, of course, that the school authorities rely upon some allegedly logical, racially neutral explanation for their actions. Their burden is to adduce proof sufficient to support a finding that segregative intent was not among the factors that motivated their actions. The courts below attributed much significance to the fact that many of the Board's actions in the core city area antedated our decision in *Brown*. We reject any suggestion that remoteness in time has any relevance to the issue of intent. If the actions of school authorities were to any degree motivated by segregative intent and the segregation resulting from those actions continues to exist, the fact of remoteness in time certainly does not make those actions any less "intentional."

* * *

The respondent School Board invoked at trial its "neighborhood school policy" as explaining racial and ethnic concentrations within the core city schools, arguing that since the core city area population had long been Negro and Hispano, the concentrations were necessarily the result of residential patterns and not of purposefully segregative policies. We have no occasion to consider in this case whether a "neighborhood school policy" of itself will justify racial or ethnic concentrations in the absence of a finding that school authorities have committed acts constituting *de jure* segregation. It is enough that we hold that the mere assertion of such a policy is not dispositive where, as in this case, the school authorities have been found to have practiced *de jure* segregation in a meaningful portion of the school system by techniques that indicate that the "neighborhood school" concept has not been maintained free of manipulation. * * *

* * *

The judgment of the Court of Appeals is modified to vacate instead of reverse the parts of the Final Decree that concern the core city schools, and the case is remanded to the District Court for further proceedings consistent with this opinion.

It is so ordered.

MR. JUSTICE DOUGLAS.

While I join the opinion of the Court, I agree with my Brother Powell that there is, for the purposes of the Equal Protection Clause of the Fourteenth Amendment as applied to the school cases, no difference between *de facto* and *de jure* segregation. The school board is a state agency and the lines that it draws, the locations it selects for school sites, the allocation it makes of students, the budgets it prepares are state action for Fourteenth Amendment purposes.

* * *

I think it is time to state that there is no constitutional difference between *de jure* and *de facto* segregation, for each is the product of state actions or policies. If a "neighborhood" or "geographical" unit has been created along racial lines by reason of the play of restrictive covenants that restrict certain areas to "the elite," leaving the "undesirables" to move elsewhere, there is state action in the constitutional sense because the force of law is placed behind those covenants.

There is state action in the constitutional sense when public funds are dispersed by urban development agencies to build racial ghettoes.

Where the school district is racially mixed and the races are segregated in separate schools, where black teachers are assigned almost exclusively to black schools, where the school board closed existing schools located in fringe areas and built new schools in black areas and in distant white areas, where the school board continued the "neighborhood" school policy at the elementary level, these actions constitute state action. They are of a kind quite distinct from the classical *de jure* type of school segregation. Yet calling them *de facto* is a misnomer, as they are only more subtle types of state action that create or maintain a wholly or partially segregated school system. * * *

When a State forces, aids, or abets, or helps create a racial "neighborhood," it is a travesty of justice to treat that neighborhood as sacrosanct in the sense that its creation is free from the taint of state action.

* * *

MR. JUSTICE POWELL concurring in part and dissenting in part.

I concur in the remand of this case for further proceedings in the District Court, but on grounds that differ from those relied upon by the Court.

This is the first school desegregation case to reach the Court which involves a major city outside the South. It comes from Denver, Colorado, a city and a State which have not operated public schools under constitutional or statutory provisions which mandated or permitted racial segregation. Nor has it been argued that any other legislative actions (such as zoning and housing laws) contributed to the segregation which is at issue. The Court has inquired only to what extent the Denver public school authorities may have contributed to the school segregation which is acknowledged to exist in Denver.

* * *

The situation in Denver is generally comparable to that in other large cities across the country in which there is a substantial minority population and where desegregation has not been ordered by the federal courts. There is segregation in the schools of many of these cities fully as pervasive as that in southern cities prior to the desegregation decrees of the past decade and a half. The focus of the school desegregation problem has now shifted from the South to the country as a whole. Unwilling and footdragging as the process was in most places, substantial progress toward achieving integration has been made in Southern States. No comparable progress has been made in many nonsouthern cities with large minority populations primarily because of the *de facto/de jure* distinction nurtured by the courts and accepted complacently by many of the same voices which denounced the evils of segregated schools in the South. But if our national concern is for those who attend such schools, rather than for perpetuating a legalism rooted in history rather than present reality, we must recognize that the evil of operating separate schools is no less in Denver than in Atlanta.

In my view we should abandon a distinction which long since has outlived its time, and formulate constitutional principles of national rather than merely regional application. When *Brown* v. *Board of Education,* 347 U.S. 483 (1954) (*Brown I*), was decided, the distinction between *de jure* and *de facto* segregation was consistent with the limited constitutional rationale of that case. The situation confronting the Court, largely confined to the Southern States, was officially imposed racial segregation in the schools extending back for many years and usually embodied in constitutional and statutory provisions.

The great contribution of *Brown I* was its holding in unmistakable terms that the Fourteenth Amendment forbids state-compelled or state-authorized segregation of public schools. 347 U.S., at 488, 493–495. Although some of the language was more expansive, the holding in *Brown I* was essentially negative: It was impermissible under the Constitution for the States, or their instrumentalities, to force children to attend segregated schools. The forbidden action was *de jure,* and the opinion in *Brown I* was construed—for some years and by many courts—as requiring only state neutrality, allowing "freedom of choice" as to schools to be attended so long as the State itself assured that the choice was genuinely free of official restraint.

But the doctrine of *Brown I,* as amplified by *Brown II,* * * * did not retain its original meaning. In a series of decisions extending from 1954 to 1971 the concept of state neutrality was transformed into the present constitutional doctrine requiring affirmative state action to desegregate school systems. The keystone case was *Green* v. *County School Board* * * * where school boards were declared to have "the affirmative duty to take whatever steps might be necessary to convert to a unitary system in which racial discrimination would be eliminated root and branch." * * * The Court properly identified the freedom-of-choice program there as a subterfuge, and the language in *Green* imposing an affirmative duty to convert to a unitary system was appropriate on the facts before the Court. There was, however, reason to question to what extent this duty would apply in the vastly different factual setting of a large city with extensive areas of residential segregation, presenting problems and calling for solutions quite different from those in the rural setting of New Kent County, Virginia.

But the doubt as to whether the affirmative-duty concept would flower into a new constitutional principle of general application was laid to rest by *Swann* v. *Charlotte-Mecklenburg Board of Education,* * * * in which the duty articulated in *Green* was applied to the urban school system of metropolitan Charlotte, North Carolina. * * *

* * *

Whereas *Brown I* rightly decreed the elimination of state-imposed segregation in that particular section of the country where it did exist, *Swann* imposed obligations on southern school districts to eliminate conditions which are not regionally unique but are similar both in origin and effect to conditions in the rest of the country. As the remedial obligations of *Swann* extend far beyond the elimination of the outgrowths of the state-imposed segregation outlawed in *Brown,* the rationale of *Swann* points inevitably toward a uniform, constitutional approach to our national problem of school segregation.

The Court's decision today, while adhering to the *de jure/de facto* distinction, will require the application of the *Green/Swann* doctrine of "affirmative duty" to the Denver School Board despite the absence of any history of state-mandated school segregation. The only evidence of a constitutional violation was found in various decisions of the School Board. I concur in the Court's position that the public school authorities are the responsible agency of the State, and that if the affirmative-duty doctrine is sound constitutional law for Charlotte, it is equally so for Denver. I would not, however, perpetuate the *de jure/de facto* distinction nor would I leave to petitioners the initial tortuous effort of identifying "segregation acts" and deducing "segregative intent." I would hold, quite simply, that where segregated public schools exist within a school district to a substantial degree, there is a prima facie case that the duly constituted public authorities (I will usually refer to them collectively as the "school board") are sufficiently responsible to warrant imposing upon them a nationally applicable burden to demonstrate they nevertheless are operating a genuinely integrated school system.

*   *   *

* * * In *Brown II,* the Court identified the "fundamental principle" enunciated in *Brown I* as being the unconstitutionality of "racial discrimination in public education" * * * and spoke of "the personal interest of the plaintiffs in admission to public schools as soon as practicable on a nondiscriminatory basis." * * * Although this and similar language is ambiguous as to the specific constitutional right, it means—as a minimum—that one has the right not to be compelled by state action to attend a segregated school system. In the evolutionary process since 1954, decisions of this Court have added a significant gloss to this original right. Although nowhere expressly articulated in these terms, I would now define it as the right, derived from the Equal Protection Clause, to expect that once the State has assumed responsibility for education, local school boards will operate *integrated school systems* within their respective districts. This means that school authorities, consistent with the generally accepted educational goal of attaining quality education for all pupils, must make and implement their customary decisions with a view toward enhancing integrated school opportunities.

The term "integrated school system" presupposes, of course, a total absence of any laws, regulations, or policies supportive of the type of "legalized" segregation condemned in *Brown*. A system would be integrated in accord with constitutional standards if the responsible authorities had taken appropriate steps to (i) integrate faculties and administration; (ii) scrupulously assure equality of facilities, instruction, and curriculum opportunities throughout the district; (iii) utilize their authority to draw attendance zones to promote integration; and (iv) locate new schools, close old ones, and determine the size and grade categories with this same objective in mind. Where school authorities decide to undertake the transportation of students, this also must be with integrative opportunities in mind.

The foregoing prescription is not intended to be either definitive or all-inclusive, but rather an indication of the contour characteristics of an *integrated school system* in which all citizens and pupils may justifiably be confident that racial discrimination is neither practiced nor tolerated. An integrated school system does not mean—and indeed could not mean in view of the residential patterns of most of our major metropolitan areas— that *every school* must in fact be an integrated unit. A school which happens to be all or predominantly white or all or predominantly black is not a "segregated" school in an unconstitutional sense if the system itself is a genuinely integrated one.

Having school boards operate an integrated school system provides the best assurance of meeting the constitutional requirement that racial discrimination, subtle or otherwise, will find no place in the decisions of public school officials. Courts judging past school board actions with a view to their *general integrative effect* will be best able to assure an absence of such discrimination while avoiding the murky, subjective judgments inherent in the Court's search for "segregative intent." Any test resting on so nebulous and elusive an element as a school board's segregative "intent" provides inadequate assurance that minority children will not be short-changed in the decisions of those entrusted with the nondiscriminatory operation of our public schools.

Public schools are creatures of the State, and whether the segregation is state-created or state-assisted or merely state-perpetuated should be irrelevant to constitutional principle. The school board exercises pervasive and continuing responsibility over the long-range planning as well as the daily operations of the public school system. It sets policies on attendance zones, faculty employment and assignments, school construction, closings and consolidations, and myriad other matters. School board decisions obviously are not the sole cause of segregated school conditions. But if, after such detailed and complete public supervision, substantial school segregation still persists, the presumption is strong that the school board, by its acts or omission, is in some part responsible. Where state action and supervision are so pervasive and where, after years of such action, segregated schools continue to exist within the district to a substantial degree, this Court is justified in finding a prima facie case of a constitutional violation. The burden then must fall on the school board to demonstrate it is operating an "integrated school system."

It makes little sense to find prima facie violations and the consequent affirmative duty to desegregate solely in those States with state-imposed segregation at the time of the *Brown* decision. The history of state-imposed segregation is more widespread in our country than the *de jure/de facto* distinction has traditionally cared to recognize. * * *

* * *

The Court today does move for the first time toward breaking down past sectional disparities, but it clings tenuously to its distinction. It searches for *de jure* action in what the Denver School Board has done or failed to do, and even here the Court does not rely upon the results or effects of the Board's conduct but feels compelled to find segregative intent. * * *

* * *

The issue in these cases will not be whether segregated education exists. This will be conceded in most of them. * * *

* * *

MR. JUSTICE REHNQUIST, dissenting.

* * *

Underlying the Court's entire opinion is its apparent thesis that a district judge is at least permitted to find that if a single attendance zone between two individual schools in the large metropolitan district is found by him to have been "gerrymandered," the school district is guilty of operating a "dual" school system, and is apparently a candidate for what is in practice a federal receivership. * * *

* * *

The drastic extension of *Brown* which *Green* represented was barely, if at all, explicated in the latter opinion. To require that a genuinely "dual" system be disestablished, in the sense that the assignment of a child to a particular school is not made to depend on his race, is one thing. To require that school boards affirmatively undertake to achieve racial mixing in schools where such mixing is not achieved in sufficient degree by neutrally drawn boundary lines is quite obviously something else.

The Court's own language in *Green* makes it unmistakably clear that this significant extension of *Brown's* prohibition against discrimination, and the conversion of that prohibition into an affirmative duty to integrate, was made in the context of a school system which had for a number of years rigidly excluded Negroes from attending the same schools as were attended by whites. Whatever may be the soundness of that decision in the context of a genuinely "dual" system, where segregation of the races had once been mandated by law, I can see no constitutional justification for it in a situation such as that which the record shows to have obtained in Denver.

* * *

The Court has taken a long leap in this area of constitutional law in equating the district-wide consequences of gerrymandering individual attendance zones in a district where separation of the races was never required by law with statutes or ordinances in other jurisdictions which did so require. It then adds to this potpourri a confusing enunciation of evidentiary rules in order to make it more likely that the trial court will on remand reach the result which the Court apparently wants it to reach. Since I believe neither of these steps is justified by prior decisions of this Court, I dissent.

Notes and Questions

Although admonished by Justices Powell and Douglas to abandon the distinction between de jure and de facto segregation in its decisions, the Court relied on the distinction in its decision in **Keyes.** Does **Keyes** represent a broadening of the concept of de jure segregation?

Subsequent Court decisions reveal a continued reliance on the de jure/de facto distinction. In decisions involving Columbus and Dayton, Ohio, the Court upheld lower court-ordered desegregation measures on the basis that both school systems had operated racially segregated dual school systems at the time of **Brown I.** The majority of the Court maintained that since the schools were intentionally segregated in 1954, the boards of education had an "affirmative duty" not to engage in actions that would impede the desegregation process. In these cases, the Court declared that the respective boards of education took actions which assured the continuance of racial separation in the schools. See *Columbus Board of Education* v. *Penick*, 443 U.S. 449 (1979), a seven-to-two decision, and *Dayton Board of Education* v. *Brinkman*, 443 U.S. 526 (1979), a five-to-four decision. Do these decisions suggest a further broadening of the concept of de jure segregation?

Although commentators disagree on the significance of Supreme Court denials of certiorari, examination of two such denials reveals the Court's continuing strong stance on effecting desegregation. In *Tasby* v. *Estes*, 572 F.2d 1010 (5th Cir. 1978), cert. denied 444, U.S. 437 (1980), the Court refused to review the Fifth Circuit's overturning of a district court order substituting certain educational remedies and neighborhood schools in Dallas for systemwide busing based on black-white student population ratios. Additionally the appellate court required mandatory pupil reassignment unless "the natural boundaries and traffic considerations preclude either the pairing and clustering of schools or the use of transportation to eliminate the large number of one race schools still existing." In *Kelley* v. *Metropolitan County Board of Education of Nashville and Davidson County*, 687 F.2d 814 (6th Cir. 1982), cert. denied, 459 U.S. 1183 (1983), the Court denied certiorari to the Sixth Circuit's decision that the Nashville School Board had a continuing obligation to ensure that modifications in desegregation remedies reflected current black-white student population ratios.

B. Interdistrict Integration

Milliken v. Bradley

Supreme Court of the United States, 1974
418 U.S. 717

MR. CHIEF JUSTICE BURGER delivered the opinion of the Court.

We granted certiorari in these consolidated cases to determine whether a federal court may impose a multidistrict, areawide remedy to a single-district *de jure* segregation problem absent any finding that the other included school districts have failed to operate unitary school systems within their districts, absent any claim or finding that the boundary lines of any affected school district were established with the purpose of fostering racial segregation in public schools, absent any finding that the included districts committed acts which effected segregation within the other districts, and absent a meaningful opportunity for the included neighboring school districts to present evidence or be heard on the propriety of a multidistrict remedy or on the question of constitutional violations by those neighboring districts.

* * *

The District Court found that the Detroit Board of Education created and maintained optional attendance zones within Detroit neighborhoods undergoing racial transition and between high school attendance areas of opposite predominant racial compositions. These zones, the court found, had the "natural, probable, foreseeable and actual effect" of allowing white pupils to escape identifiably Negro schools. Similarly, the District Court found that Detroit school attendance zones had been drawn along north-south boardary lines despite the Detroit Board's awareness that drawing boundary lines in an east-west direction would result in significantly greater desegregation. Again, the District Court concluded, the natural and actual effect of these acts was the creation and perpetuation of school segregation within Detroit.

The Distric Court found that in the operation of its school transportation program, which was designed to relieve overcrowding, the Detroit Board had admittedly bused Negro Detroit pupils to predominantly Negro schools which were beyond or away from closer white schools with available space. * * *

With respect to the Detroit Board of Education's practices in school construction, the District Court found that Detroit school construction generally tended to have a segregative effect with the great majority of schools being built in either overwhelmingly all-Negro or all-white neighborhoods so that the new schools opened as predominantly one-race schools. Thus, of the 14 schools opened for use in 1970–1971, 11 opened over 90% Negro and one opened less than 10% Negro.

The District Court also found that the State of Michigan had committed several constitutional violations with respect to the exercise of its general responsibility for, and supervision of, public education. The State, for example, was found to have failed, until the 1971 Session of Michigan Legislature, to provide authorization or funds for the transportation of pupils within Detroit regardless of their poverty or distance from the school to which they were assigned; during this same period the State provided many neighboring, mostly white, suburban districts the full range of state-supported transportation.

The District Court found that the State, through Act 48 acted to "impede, delay and minimize racial integration in Detroit schools." The first sentence of § 12 of Act 48 was designed to delay the April 7, 1970, desegregation plan originally adopted by the Detroit Board. The remainder of § 12 sought to prescribe for each school in the eight districts criteria of "free choice" and "neighborhood schools," which, the District Court found, "had as their purpose and effect the maintenance of segregation." * * *

The District Court also held that the acts of the Detroit Board of Education, as a subordinate entity of the State, were attributable to the State of Michigan, thus creating a vicarious liability on the part of the State. Under Michigan law, Mich. Comp. Laws § 388.851 (1970), for example, school building construction plans had to be approved by the State Board of Education, and, prior to 1962, the State Board had specific statutory authority to supervise schoolsite selection. The proofs concerning the effect of Detroit's school construction program were, therefore, found to be largely applicable to show state responsibility for the segregative results.

Turning to the question of an appropriate remedy for these several constitutional violations, the District Court deferred a pending motion by intervening parent defendants to join as additional parties defendant the 85 outlying school districts in the three-county Detroit metropolitan area on the ground that effective relief could not be achieved without their presence. The District Court concluded that this motion to join was "premature," since it "has to do with relief" and no reasonably specific desegregation plan was before the court. * * * Accordingly, the District Court proceeded to order the Detroit Board of Education to submit desegregation plans limited to the segregation problems found to be existing within the city of Detroit. At the same time, however, the state defendants were directed to submit desegregation plans encompassing the three-county metropolitan area despite the fact that the 85 outlying school districts of these three counties were not parties to the action and despite the fact that there had been no claim that these outlying districts had committed constitutional violations. * * *

* * *

On June 12, 1973, a divided Court of Appeals, sitting en banc, affirmed in part, vacated in part, and remanded for further proceedings. * * * The Court of Appeals held, first, that the record supported the District Court's findings and conclusions on the constitutional violations committed by the Detroit Board * * * and by the state defendants * * * . It stated that the acts of racial discrimination shown in the record are "causally related to the substantial amount of segregation found in the Detroit school system," * * * and that "the District Court was therefore authorized and required to take effective measures to desegregate the Detroit Public School System." * * *

The Court of Appeals also agreed with the District Court that "any less comprehensive a solution than a metropolitan area plan would result in an all black school system immediately surrounded by practically all white suburban school systems, with an overwhelmingly white majority population in the total metropolitan area." * * * The court went on to state that it could "not see how such segregation can be any less harmful to the minority students than if the same result were accomplished within one school district." * * *

Accordingly, the Court of Appeals concluded that "the only feasible desegregation plan involves the crossing of the boundary lines between the Detroit School District and adjacent or nearby school districts for the limited purpose of providing an effective desegregation plan." * * * It reasoned that such a plan would be appropriate because of the State's violations, and could be implemented because of the State's authority to control local school districts.   *   *   *   An interdistrict remedy was thus held to be "within the equity powers of the District Court."   *   *   *

*   *   *

Viewing the record as a whole, it seems clear that the District Court and the Court of Appeals shifted the primary focus from a Detroit remedy to the metropolitan area only because of their conclusion that total desegregation of Detroit would not produce the racial balance which they perceived as desirable. Both courts proceeded on an assumption that the Detroit schools could not be fully desegregated—in their view of what constituted desegregation—unless the racial composition of the student body of each school substantially reflected the racial composition of the population of the metropolitan area as a whole. The metropolitan area was then defined as Detroit plus 53 of the outlying school districts.   *   *   *

Here the District Court's approach to what constituted "actual desegregation" raised the fundamental question, not presented in *Swann*, as to the circumstances in which a federal court may order desegregation relief that embraces more than a single school district. The court's analytical starting point was its conclusion that school district lines are no more than arbitrary lines on a map drawn "for political convenience." Boundary lines may be bridged where there has been a constitutional violation calling for interdistrict relief, but the notion that school district lines may be casually ignored or treated as a mere administrative convenience is contrary to the history of public education in our country. No single tradition in public education is more deeply rooted than local control over the operation of schools; local autonomy has long been thought essential both to the maintenance of community concern and support for public schools and to quality of the educational process.   *   *   *   [L]ocal control over the educational process affords citizens an opportunity to participate in decisionmaking, permits the structuring of school programs to fit local needs, and encourages "experimentation, innovation, and a healthy competition for educational excellence."

The Michigan educational structure involved in this case, in common with most States, provides for a large measure of local control, and a review of the scope and character of these local powers indicates the extent to which the interdistrict remedy approved by the two courts could disrupt and alter the structure of public education in Michigan. The metropolitan remedy would require, in effect, consolidation of 54 independent school districts historically administered as separate units into a vast new super school district.   *   *   *   Entirely apart from the logistical and other serious problems attending large-scale transportation of students, the consolidation would give rise to an array of other problems in financing and operating this new school system. Some of the more obvious questions would be: What would be the status and authority of the present popularly elected school boards? Would the children of Detroit be within the jurisdiction and operating control of a school board elected by the parents and residents of other districts? What board or boards would levy taxes for school operations in these 54 districts constituting the consolidated metropolitan area? What provisions could be made for assuring substantial equality in tax levies among the 54 districts, if this were deemed requisite? What provisions would be made for financing? Would the validity of long-term bonds be jeopardized unless approved by all of the component districts as well as the State? What body would determine that portion of the curricula now left to the discretion of local school boards? Who would establish attendance zones, purchase school equipment, locate and construct new schools, and indeed attend to all the myriad day-to-day decisions that are necessary to school operations affecting potentially more than three-quarters of a million pupils? * * *

It may be suggested that all of these vital operational problems are yet to be resolved by the District Court, and that this is the purpose of the Court of Appeals' proposed remand. But it is obvious from the scope of the interdistrict remedy itself that absent a complete restructuring of the laws of Michigan relating to school districts the District Court will become first, a *de facto* "legislative authority" to resolve these complex questions, and then the "school superintendent" for the entire area. This is a task which few, if any, judges are qualified to perform and one which would deprive the people of control of schools through their elected representatives.

Of course, no state law is above the Constitution. School district lines and the present laws with respect to local control, are not sacrosanct and if they conflict with the Fourteenth Amendment federal courts have a duty to prescribe appropriate remedies. * * * But our prior holdings have been confined to violations and remedies within a single school district. We therefore turn to address, for the first time, the validity of a remedy mandating cross-district or inter-district consolidation to remedy a condition of segregation found to exist in only one district.

The controlling principle consistently expounded in our holdings is that the scope of the remedy is determined by the nature and extent of the constitutional violation. *Swann,* 402 U.S., at 16. Before the boundaries of separate and autonomous school districts may be set aside by consolidating the separate units for remedial purposes or by imposing a cross-district remedy, it must first be shown that there has been a constitutional violation within one district that produces a significant segregative effect in another district. Specifically, it must be shown that racially discriminatory acts of the state or local school districts, or of a single school district have been a substantial cause of interdistrict segregation. Thus an interdistrict remedy might be in order where the racially discriminatory acts of one or more school districts caused racial segregation in an adjacent district, or where district lines have been deliberately drawn on the basis of race. In such circumstances an interdistrict remedy would be appropriate to eliminate the interdistrict segregation directly caused by the constitutional violation. Conversely, without an interdistrict violation and interdistrict effect, there is no constitutional wrong calling for an interdistrict remedy.

The record before us, voluminous as it is, contains evidence of *de jure* segregated conditions only in the Detroit schools; indeed, that was the theory on which the litigation was initially based and on which the District Court took evidence. * * * With no showing of significant violation by the 53 outlying school districts and no evidence of any interdistrict violation or effect, the court went beyond the original theory of the case as framed by the pleading and mandated a metropolitan area remedy. To approve the remedy ordered by the court would impose on the outlying districts, not shown to have committed any constitutional violation, a wholly impermissible remedy based on a standard not hinted at in *Brown I* and *II* or any holding of this Court.

In dissent, MR. JUSTICE WHITE and MR. JUSTICE MARSHALL undertake to demonstrate that agencies having statewide authority participated in maintaining the dual school system found to exist in Detroit. They are apparently of the view that once such participation is shown, the District Court should have a relatively free hand to reconstruct school districts outside of Detroit in fashioning relief. Our assumption, *arguendo,* * * * that state agencies did participate in the maintenance of the Detroit system, should make it clear that it is not on this point that we part company. The difference between us arises instead from established doctrine laid down by our cases. *Brown, supra; Green, supra; Swann, supra; Scotland Neck, supra;* and *Emporia, supra,* each addressed the issue of constitutional wrong in terms of an established geographic and administrative school system populated by both Negro and white children. In such a context, terms such as "unitary" and "dual" systems, and "racially identifiable schools," have meaning, and the necessary federal authority to remedy the constitutional wrong is firmly established. But the remedy is necessarily designed, as all remedies are, to restore the victims of discriminatory conduct to the position they would have occupied in the absence of such conduct. Disparate treatment of white and Negro students occurred within the Detroit school system, and not elsewhere, and on this record the remedy must be limited to that system. * * *

The constitutional right of the Negro respondents residing in Detroit is to attend a unitary school system in that district. Unless petitioners drew the district lines in a discriminatory fashion, or arranged for white students residing in the Detroit District to attend schools in Oakland and Macomb Counties, they were under no constitutional duty to make provisions for Negro students to do so. The view of the dissenters, that the existence of a dual system in *Detroit* can be made the basis for a decree requiring cross-district transportation of pupils, cannot be supported on the grounds that it represents merely the devising of a suitably flexible remedy for the violation of rights already established by our prior decisions. It can be supported only by drastic expansion of the constitutional right itself, an expansion without any support in either constitutional principle or precedent.

* * *

We conclude that the relief ordered by the District Court and affirmed by the Court of Appeals was based upon an erroneous standard and was unsupported by record evidence that acts of the outlying districts effected the discrimination found to exist in the schools of Detroit. Accordingly, the judgment of the Court of Appeals is reversed and the case is remanded for further proceedings consistent with this opinion leading to prompt formulation of a decree directed to eliminating the segregation found to exist in Detroit city schools, a remedy which has been delayed since 1970.

Reversed and remanded.

* * *

MR. JUSTICE DOUGLAS; dissenting.

The Court of Appeals has acted responsibly in these cases and we should affirm its judgment * * * .

We have before us today no plan for integration. The only orders entered so far are interlocutory. No new principles of law are presented here. Metropolitan treatment of metropolitan problems is commonplace. If this were a sewage problem or a water problem, or an energy problem, there can be no doubt that Michigan would stay well within federal constitutional bounds if she sought a metropolitan remedy. * * * The State controls the boundaries of school districts. The state supervised school site selection. The construction was done through municipal bonds approved by several state agencies. Education in Michigan is a state project with very little completely local control. * * *

* * *

As I indicated in *Keyes* * * * there is so far as the school cases go no constitutional difference between *de facto* and *de jure* segregation. Each school board performs state action for Fourteenth Amendment purposes when it draws the lines that confine it to a given area, when it builds schools at particular sites, or when it allocates students. The creation of the school districts in Metropolitan Detroit either maintained existing segregation or caused additional segregation. Restrictive covenants maintained by state action or inaction build black ghettos. It is state action when public funds are dispensed by housing agencies to build racial ghettos. Where a community is racially mixed and school authorities segregate schools, or assign black teachers to black schools or close schools in fringe areas and build new schools in black areas and in more distant white areas, the State creates and nurtures a segregated school system, just as surely as did those States involved in *Brown* v. *Board of Education,* * * * when they maintained dual school systems.

     * * * The issue is not whether there should be racial balance but whether the State's use of various devices that end up with black schools and white schools brought the Equal Protection Clause into effect. Given the State's control over the educational system in Michigan, the fact that the black schools are in one district and the white schools are in another is not controlling—either constitutionally or equitably. No specific plan has yet been adopted. We are still at an interlocutory state of a long drawn-out judicial effort at school desegregation. It is conceivable that ghettos develop on their own without any hint of state action. But since Michigan by one device or another has over the years created black school districts and white school districts, the task of equity is to provide a unitary system for the affected area where, as here, the State washes its hands of its own creations.

MR. JUSTICE WHITE, with whom MR. JUSTICE DOUGLAS, MR. JUSTICE BRENNAN, and MR. JUSTICE MARSHALL join, dissenting.

* * *

     Regretfully, and for several reasons, I can join neither the Court's judgment nor its opinion. The core of my disagreement is that deliberate acts of segregation and their consequences will go unremedied, not because a remedy would be infeasible or unreasonable in terms of the usual criteria governing school desegregation cases, but because an effective remedy would cause what the Court considers to be undue administrative inconvenience to the State. The result is that the State of Michigan, the entity at which the Fourteenth Amendment is directed, has successfully insulated itself from its duty to provide effective desegregation remedies by vesting sufficient power over its public schools in its local school districts. If this is the case in Michigan, it will be the case in most States.

     There are undoubted practical as well as legal limits to the remedial powers of federal courts in school desegregation cases. The Court has made it clear that the achievement of any particular degree of racial balance in the school system is not required by the Constitution; nor may it be the primary focus of a court in devising an acceptable remedy for *de jure* segregation. A variety of procedures and techniques are available to a district court engrossed in fashioning remedies in a case such as this; but the courts must keep in mind that they are dealing with the process of *educating* the young, including the very young. The task is not to devise a system of pains and penalties to punish constitutional violations brought to light. Rather, it is to desegregate an *educational* system in which the races have been kept apart, without, at the same time, losing sight of the central *educational* function of the schools.

Viewed in this light, remedies calling for school zoning, pairing, and pupil assignments, become more and more suspect as they require that school children spend more and more time in buses going to and from school and that more and more educational dollars be diverted to transportation systems. Manifestly, these considerations are of immediate and urgent concern when the issue is the desegregation of a city school system where residential patterns are predominantly segregated and the respective areas occupied by blacks and whites are heavily populated and geographically extensive. Thus, if one postulates a metropolitan school system covering a sufficiently large area, with the population evenly divided between whites and Negroes and with the races occupying identifiable residential areas, there will be very real practical limits on the extent to which racially identifiable schools can be eliminated within the school district. It is also apparent that the larger the proportion of Negroes in the area, the more difficult it would be to avoid having a substantial number of all-black or nearly all-black schools.

The Detroit school district is both large and heavily populated. * * * If "racial balance" were achieved in every school in the district, each school would be approximately 64% Negro. A remedy confined to the district could achieve no more desegregation. * * *

* * *

I am * * * mystified how the Court can ignore the legal reality that the constitutional violations, even if occurring locally, were committed by governmental entities for which the State is responsible and that it is the State that must respond to the command of the Fourteenth Amendment. An interdistrict remedy for the infringements that occurred in this case is well within the confines and powers of the State, which is the governmental entity ultimately responsible for desegregating its schools. * * *

* * *

The Court draws the remedial line at the Detroit School District boundary, even though the Fourteenth Amendment is addressed to the State and even though the *State* denies equal protection of the laws when its public agencies, acting in its behalf, invidiously discriminate. * * * I cannot understand, nor does the majority satisfactorily explain, why a federal court may not order an appropriate interdistrict remedy, if this is necessary or more effective to accomplish this constitutionally mandated task. * * *

* * *

MR. JUSTICE MARSHALL, with whom MR. JUSTICE DOUG-LAS, MR. JUSTICE BRENNAN, and MR. JUSTICE WHITE join, dissenting.

* * *

The great irony of the Court's opinion and, in my view, its most serious analytical flaw may be gleaned from its concluding sentence, in which the Court remands for "prompt formulation of a decree directed to eliminating the segregation found to exist in Detroit city schools, a remedy which has been delayed since 1970." * * * The majority, however, seems to have forgotten the district Court's explicit finding that a Detroit only decree, the only remedy permitted under today's decision, "would not accomplish desegregation."

Nowhere in the Court's opinion does the majority confront, let alone respond to, the District Court's conclusion that a remedy limited to the city of Detroit would not effectively desegregate the Detroit city schools. * * *

* * *

Desegregation is not and was never expected to be an easy task. Racial attitudes ingrained in our Nation's childhood and adolescence are not quickly thrown aside in its middle years. But just as the inconvenience of some cannot be allowed to stand in the way of the rights of others, so public opposition, no matter how strident, cannot be permitted to divert this Court from the enforcement of the constitutional principles at issue in this case. Today's holding, I fear, is more a reflection of a perceived public mood that we have gone far enough in enforcing the Constitution's guarantee of equal justice than it is the product of neutral principles of law. In the short run, it may seem to be the easier course to allow our great metropolitan areas to be divided up each into two cities—one white, the other black—but it is a course, I predict, our people will ultimately regret. I dissent.

Notes and Questions

Milliken was a five-to-four decision. Would suburbanite parents have complied with the Metropolitan Plan if the Court had upheld it? Would black parents have allowed their children to be bussed to the suburbs?

Is the following an accurate description of the attitude of many white suburbanites living adjacent to cities having a large minority concentration? Their preference for suburban life stemmed from the perception that an absence of congestion, lack of crime, and "good" schools all contributed to the "good life." A move to an often "lily-white" suburb was considered to be a partial fulfillment of the American dream, whereby a person may improve his or her lot by sheer hard work and dedication. Central to this fulfillment was the sending of children to "good" neighborhood schools, which in many instances attempted to emulate the better private schools. Would persons having such attitudes allow their children to be bussed, often long distances, into predominantly black inner-city schools? If not, could a court-mandated metropolitan plan have been enforced?

Is there an assumption that black parents agree with plans whereby their children would be bussed into the suburbs for schooling? Does evidence exist that sustains such an assumption? One noted black educator and chairman of the Atlanta Board of Education for many years, Dr. Benjamin Mays, for instance, agreed with the Supreme Court's affirmation of a lower-court decision not to order a metropolitan solution for Atlanta. See *Armour* v. *Nix,* 446 U.S. 930 (1980).

On remand, the district court approved a desegregation plan that included educational components in the areas of reading, inservice teacher training, testing, and counseling. Costs were to be borne by both the Detroit School Board and the state. The Supreme Court upheld the lower court's action, and stated that such a remedy was reasonable in the light of past acts of de jure segregation. See *Milliken* v. *Bradley,* 433 U.S. 267 (1977) (*Milliken II*).

school finance reform

INTRODUCTION

Court decisions involving racial segregation in the public schools over the last several decades revealed that the judiciary would deal with issues that other branches of government were unwilling to be concerned with or were reluctant to recognize. Consequently, many persons who perceived that they were being denied rights owing to governmental action or inaction increasingly employed the courts in an attempt to redress alleged grievances. One such group of persons brought the issue of equality of educational opportunity before the courts. Their contention was that many state methods of financing public education were unconstitutional because they violated the equal protection clause for certain classes of people.

    Reliance on local revenue to support a large portion of the total public school budget, it was alleged, was unfair because of the disparity in taxable wealth among local school systems.* Since the property tax is

*Nationally, through 1984, local revenue made up approximately 44 percent of the total revenue for elementary and secondary schools, while state revenue made up approximately 49 percent and federal revenue 6 percent. Across the country local support for public elementary and secondary education ranged from a high of approximately 90 percent to a low of approximately 10 percent. Hawaii is the only state having no official local support for education.

the most commonly used local school tax, many school finance experts have defined school system wealth as the ratio of taxable property divided by the number of students. Consequently, a "wealthy" school system would achieve such status by having much valuable taxable property, such as factories, utilities, or natural resources and few children to educate. Conversely, a "poor" school system would have little valuable property and many children to educate. A school system composed largely of trailer parks, where each trailer contained several school-age children, would be an example of a poor system. School-district wealth is not based on income wealth; consequently, there may or may not be a relationship in poor or wealthy school systems with the income wealth of its inhabitants.

Those who contend that a state's method of financing the public schools is unfair often argue that wealthy school systems can raise large amounts of money with lower tax rates than can poor systems. Allowing this situation under a state-authorized method of financing public education, it is alleged, is unfair to both taxpayers and the recipients of school services in poor systems. For example, assume that the wealthiest school system in a state has a taxable assessed valuation per student (usually expressed on the basis of average daily attendance or membership) of $200,000 and the poorest school system has a taxable assessed valuation per student of $10,000. A levy of one mill (one-tenth of one percent, also expressed as a tax rate of $1 per $1,000 of property value) would raise $200 per student in the wealthiest system and only $10 per student in the poorest school system. Since education is a responsibility of the state, school finance reformers allege that a state's allowing a school-financing system in which such disparities operate in favor of wealthy school systems denies equality of educational opportunity to those students in poorer school systems.

Widely diverse school finance issues have been raised since the earliest court cases. These issues include the effects of municipal overburden, the higher costs of urban education, the greater concentrations of disadvantaged children in urban schools, and the necessity in some states to raise local funds by referenda. However, the issue that has received the greatest court attention addressed the alleged inequality of educational opportunity resulting from statewide school finance systems that make educational funding a function of district property wealth. Courth attention to this issue will be the subject of the remainder of this chapter.

I. Early Decisions

In one of the earliest decisions, *McInnis* v. *Shapiro*, 293 F. Supp. 327 (Ill. 1968), aff'd sub nom. *McInnis* v. *Ogilvie*, 394 U.S. 322 (1969), the Illinois method of financing public education was described by plaintiffs as being particularly inequitable, since it permitted wide variations in expenditures per student and did not apportion funds according to the educational needs of students. In rejecting this contention, the court declared that the controversy was essentially nonjusticiable because of a lack of judicially manageable standards. The court contended that equal expenditures per student were inappropriate as a standard and that courts were ill-equipped to devise an equitable financing plan for the public schools. A virtually indistinguishable case, *Burruss* v. *Wilkerson*, 310 F. Supp. 572 (Va. 1969), aff'd mem., 397 U.S. 44 (1970), essentially reached the same conclusion as *McInnis*.

Questions raised in these early cases revealed the lack of empirical data necessary to have a clear and accurate understanding of the effects of a state's finance system. Additionally, these cases revealed other methodological shortcomings, such as the lack of consensus over the goals of schooling and especially what constituted a "basic" education, an absence of meaningful cost-effectiveness analysis, a clear definition of educational need, and the inexactitude of measurement technology. Courts, it soon became evident, had great difficulty in dealing with broad generalizations or abstractions concerning education, requiring, instead, quantifiable evidence.

II. Fiscal Neutrality

Lack of success in *McInnis* and *Burruss* did not dissuade others interested in school finance reform from continuing a legal assault on interdistrict resource inequality. A California case, *Serrano* v. *Priest,* 5 Cal. 3d 584, 487 P.2d 1241, 96 Cal. Rptr. 601 (1971) (*Serrano I*), provided the court with a judicially manageable standard, which had been missing in *McInnis* and *Burruss*. In this case the plaintiffs attempted to demonstrate that the California method of financing public education allowed substantial disparities among the various school districts in the amount of revenue available for education, thereby denying students equal protection of the laws under both the United States and California constitutions.

Furthermore, plaintiffs alleged that under this system parents were required to pay taxes at a higher rate than taxpayers in many other districts in order to provide the same or lesser educational opportunities for their children. In its decision, the California Supreme Court established that education was a constitutionally protected fundamental interest and that "wealth" was a "suspect classification." When a fundamental interest or suspect classification is involved, the court contended, the state must establish not only that it has a compelling interest that justifies the law, but that the distinctions drawn by the law are necessary to further its purpose. Employing this line of reasoning places the so-called burden of proof on the state. Perhaps most important in this decision was the standard established by the court to determine whether or not a school finance plan was constitutional. Under this standard, which the court called fiscal neutrality, the quality of a child's education could not be based on the wealth of the child's local school district but rather had to be based on the wealth of the state as a whole. This provided the court with a judicially manageable standard, in contrast to the "needs" standard in *McInnis,* since the court merely had to reject the present financing plan as unconstitutional, thereby placing the burden of adopting a constitutionally acceptable finance plan with the state.*

III. Rodriguez

Suits were filed in both state and federal courts in over three dozen states after the California *Serrano I* decision. In many of these suits plaintiffs were successful in their request that the court endorse the fiscal neutrality standard adopted in *Serrano I* to remedy wealth disparity. One of these cases, **San Antonio Independent School District v. Rodriguez,** provided the United States Supreme Court with an opportunity to address this issue.

San Antonio Independent School District v. Rodriguez

Supreme Court of the United States, 1973
411 U.S. 1

MR. JUSTICE POWELL delivered the opinion of the Court.

This suit attacking the Texas system of financing public education was initiated by Mexican-American parents whose children attend the elementary and secondary schools in the Edgewood Independent School District, an urban school district in San Antonio, Texas. They brought a class action on behalf of schoolchildren throughout the State who are members of minority groups or who are poor and reside in school districts having a low property tax base. * * * The complaint was filed in the summer of 1968 and a three-judge court was impaneled in January 1969. In December 1971 the panel rendered its judgment in a *per curiam* opinion holding the Texas school finance system unconstitutional under the Equal Protection Clause of the Fourteenth Amendment. The State appealed, and we noted probable jurisdiction to consider the far-reaching constitutional questions presented. * * * For the reasons stated in this opinion, we reverse the decision of the District Court.

*A subsequent decision by the California Supreme Court in *Serrano II,* 18 Cal. 3d 728, 557 P. 2d 929, 135 Cal. Rptr. 345 (1976) again affirmed the trial court's finding that the California school finance system was unconstitutional under the equal protection provision of the state constitution.

The first Texas State Constitution, promulgated upon Texas' entry into the Union in 1845, provided for the establishment of a system of free schools. Early in its history, Texas adopted a dual approach to the financing of its schools, relying on mutual participation by the local school districts and the State. * * *

Until recent times, Texas was a predominantly rural State and its population and property wealth were spread relatively evenly across the State. Sizable differences in the value of assessable property between local school districts became increasingly evident as the State became more industrialized and as rural-to-urban population shifts became more pronounced. The location of commercial and industrial property began to play a significant role in determining the amount of tax resources available to each school district. These growing disparities in population and taxable property between districts were responsible in part for increasingly notable differences in levels of local expenditure for education.

* * *

Recognizing the need for increased state funding to help offset disparities in local spending and to meet Texas' changing educational requirements, the state legislature in the late 1940's undertook a thorough evaluation of public education with an eye toward major reform. * * * [It established] the Texas Minimum Foundation School Program. Today, this Program accounts for approximately half of the total educational expenditures in Texas.

The Program calls for state and local contributions to a fund earmarked specifically for teacher salaries, operating expenses, and transportation costs. The State, supplying funds from its general revenues, finances approximately 80% of the Program, and the school districts are responsible—as a unit—for providing the remaining 20%. The districts' share, known as the Local Fund Assignment, is apportioned among the school districts under a formula designed to reflect each district's relative taxpaying ability. * * *

* * *

The school district in which appellees reside, the Edgewood Independent School District, has been compared throughout this litigation with the Alamo Heights Independent School District. This comparison between the least and most affluent districts in the San Antonio area serves to illustrate the manner in which the dual system of finance operates and to indicate the extent to which substantial disparities exist despite the State's impressive progress in recent years. Edgewood is one of seven public school districts in the metropolitan area. Approximately 22,000 students are enrolled in its 25 elementary and secondary schools. The district is situated in the core-city sector of San Antonio in a residential neighborhood that has little commercial or industrial property. The residents are predominantly of Mexican-American descent: approximately 90% of the student population is Mexican-American and over 6% is Negro. The average assessed property value per pupil is $5,960—the lowest in the metropolitan area—and the median family income ($4,686) is also the lowest. At an equalized tax rate of $1.05 per $100 of assessed property—the highest in the metropolitan area—the district contributed $26 to the education of each child for the 1967–1968 school year above its Local Fund Assignment for the Minimum Foundation Program. The Foundation Program contributed $222 per pupil for a state-local total of $248. Federal funds added another $108 for a total of $356 per pupil.

Alamo Heights is the most affluent school district in San Antonio. Its six schools, housing approximately 5,000 students, are situated in a residential community quite unlike the Edgewood District. The school population is predominantly "Anglo," having only 18% Mexican-Americans and less than 1% Negroes. The assessed property value per pupil exceeds $49,000, and the median family income is $8,001. In 1967–1968 the local tax rate of $.85 per $100 of valuation yielded $333 per pupil over and above its contribution to the Foundation Program. Coupled with the $225 provided from that Program, the district was able to supply $558 per student. Supplemented by a $36 per-pupil grant from federal sources, Alamo Heights spent $594 per pupil.

Although the 1967–1968 school year figures provide the only complete statistical breakdown for each category of aid, more recent partial statistics indicate that the previously noted trend of increasing state aid has been significant. For the 1970–1971 school year, the Foundation School Program allotment of Edgewood was $356 per pupil. * * * Alamo Heights enjoyed a similar increase under the Foundation Program, netting $491 per pupil in 1970–1971. These recent figures also reveal the extent to which these two districts' allotments were funded from their own required contributions to the Local Fund Assignment. Alamo Heights, because of its relative wealth, was required to contribute out of its local property tax collections approximately $100 per pupil, or about 20% of its Foundation grant. Edgewood, on the other hand, paid only $8.46 per pupil, which is about 2.4% of its grant. It appears then that, at least as to these two districts, the Local Fund Assignment does reflect a rough approximation of the relative taxpaying potential of each.

Despite these recent increases, substantial interdistrict disparities in school expenditures found by the District Court to prevail in San Antonio and in varying degrees throughout the State still exist. And it was these disparities, largely attributable to differences in the amounts of money collected through local property taxation, that led the District Court to conclude that Texas' dual system of public school financing violated the Equal Protection Clause. * * *

* * *

* * * We must decide, first, whether the Texas system of financing public education operates to the disadvantage of some suspect class or impinges upon a fundamental right explicitly or implicitly protected by the Constitution, thereby requiring strict judicial scrutiny. If so, the judgment of the District Court should be affirmed. If not, the Texas scheme must still be examined to determine whether it rationally furthers some legitimate, articulated state purpose and therefore does not constitute an invidious discrimination in violation of the Equal Protection Clause of the Fourteenth Amendment.

* * *

The wealth discrimination discovered by the District Court in this case, and by several other courts that have recently struck down school-financing laws in other states, is quite unlike any of the forms of wealth discrimination heretofore reviewed by this Court. * * *

The case comes to us with no definitive description of the classifying facts or delineation of the disfavored class. Examination of the District Court's opinion and of appellees' complaint, briefs, and contentions at oral arguments suggests, however, at least three ways in which the discrimination claimed here might be described. The Texas system of school financing might be regarded as discriminating (1) against "poor" persons whose incomes fall below some identifiable level of poverty or who might be characterized as functionally "indigent," or (2) against those who are relatively poorer than others, or (3) against all those who, irrespective of their personal incomes, happen to reside in relatively poorer school districts. Our task must be to ascertain whether, in fact, the Texas system has been shown to discriminate on any of these possible bases and, if so, whether the resulting classification may be regarded as suspect.

The precedents of this Court provide the proper starting point. The individuals, or groups of individuals, who constituted the class discriminated against in our prior cases shared two distinguishing characteristics: because of their impecunity they were completely unable to pay for some desired benefit, and as a consequence, they sustained an absolute deprivation of a meaningful opportunity to enjoy that benefit. * * *

* * *

Only appellees' first possible basis for describing the class disadvantaged by the Texas school-financing system—discrimination against a class of definably "poor" persons—might arguably meet the criteria established in these prior cases. Even a cursory examination, however, demonstrates that neither of the two distinguishing characteristics of wealth classifications can be found here. First, in support of their charge that the system discriminates against the "poor," appellees have made no effort to demonstrate that it operates to the peculiar disadvantage of any class fairly definable as indigent, or as composed of persons whose incomes are beneath any designated poverty level. Indeed, there is reason to believe that the poorest families are not necessarily clustered in the poorest property districts. A recent and exhaustive study of school districts in Connecticut concluded that "[i]t is clearly incorrect . . . to contend that the 'poor' live in 'poor' districts. . . . Thus, the major factual assumption of *Serrano*—that the educational financing system discriminates against the "poor"—is simply false in Connecticut." Defining "poor" families as those below the Bureau of the Census "poverty level," the Connecticut study found, not surprisingly, that the poor were clustered around commercial and industrial areas—those same areas that provide the most attractive sources of property tax income for school districts. Whether a similar pattern would be discovered in Texas is not known, but there is no basis on the record in this case for assuming that the poorest people—defined by reference to any level of absolute impecunity—are concentrated in the poorest districts.

Second, neither appellees nor the District Court addressed the fact that, unlike each of the foregoing cases, lack of personal resources had not occasioned an absolute deprivation of the desired benefit. The argument here is not that the children in districts having relatively low assessable property values are receiving no public education; rather, it is that they are receiving a poorer quality education than that available to children in districts having more assessable wealth. Apart from the unsettled and disputed question whether the quality of education may be determined by the amount of money expended for it, a sufficient answer to appellees' argument is that, at least where wealth is involved, the Equal Protection Clause does not require absolute equality or precisely equal advantages. * * *

For these two reasons—the absence of any evidence that the financing system discriminates against any definable category of "poor" people or that it results in the absolute deprivation of education—the disadvantaged class is not susceptible of identification in traditional terms.

As suggested above, appellees and the District Court may have embraced a second or third approach, the second of which might be characterized as a theory of relative comparative discrimination based on family income. Appellees sought to prove that a direct correlation exists between the wealth of families within each district and the expenditures therein for education. That is, along a continuum, the poorer the family the lower the dollar amount of education received by the family's children.

* * *

This brings us, then, to the third way in which the classification scheme might be defined—*district* wealth discrimination. Since the only correlation indicated by the evidence is between district property wealth and expenditures, it may be argued that discrimination might be found without regard to the individual income characteristics of district residents. * * *

However described, it is clear that appellees' suit asks this Court to extend its most exacting scrutiny to review a system that allegedly discriminates against a large, diverse, and amorphous class, unified only by the common factor of residence in its districts that happen to have less taxable wealth than other districts. The system of alleged discrimination and the class it defines have none of the traditional indicia of suspectness: the class is not saddled with such disabilities, or subjected to such a history of purposeful unequal treatment, or relegated to such a position of political powerlessness as to command extraordinary protection from the majoritarian political process.

We thus conclude that the Texas system does not operate to the peculiar disadvantage of any suspect class. But in recognition of the fact that this Court has never heretofore held that wealth discrimination alone provides an adequate basis for invoking strict scrutiny, appellees have not relied solely on this contention. They also assert that the State's system impermissibly interferes with the exercise of a "fundamental" right and that accordingly the prior decisions of this Court require the application of the strict standard of judicial review. * * * It is this question—whether education is a fundamental right, in the sense that it is among the rights and liberties protected by the Constitution—which has so consumed the attention of courts and commentators in recent years.

* * *

Nothing this Court holds today in any way detracts from our historic dedication to public education. We are in complete agreement with the conclusion of the three-judge panel below that "the grave significance of education both to the individual and to our society" cannot be doubted. But the importance of a service performed by the State does not determine whether it must be regarded as fundamental for purposes of examination under the Equal Protection Clause. * * *

* * *

* * * It is not the province of this Court to create substantive constitutional rights in the name of guaranteeing equal protection of the laws. Thus, the key to discovering whether education is "fundamental" is not to be found in comparisons of the relative societal significance of education as opposed to subsistence or housing. Nor is it to be found by weighing whether education is as important as the right to travel. Rather,

the answer lies in assessing whether there is a right to education explicitly or implicitly guaranteed by the Constitution. * * *

Education, of course, is not among the rights afforded explicit protection under our Federal Constitution. Nor do we find any basis for saying it is implicitly so protected. As we have said, the undisputed importance of education will not alone cause this Court to depart from the usual standard for reviewing a State's social and economic legislation. It is appellees' contention, however, that education is distinguishable from other services and benefits provided by the State because it bears a peculiarly close relationship to other rights and liberties accorded protection under the Constitution. Specifically, they insist that education is itself a fundamental personal right because it is essential to the effective exercise of First Amendment freedoms and to intelligent utilization of the right to vote. In asserting a nexus between speech and education, appellees urge that the right to speak is meaningless unless the speaker is capable of articulating his thoughts intelligently and persuasively. The "marketplace of ideas" is an empty forum for those lacking basic communicative tools. Likewise, they argue that the corollary right to receive information becomes little more than a hollow privilege when the recipient has not been taught to read, assimilate, and utilize available knowledge.

* * *

Even if it were conceded that some identifiable quantum of education is a constitutionally protected prerequisite to the meaningful exercise of either right, we have no indication that the present levels of educational expenditures in Texas provides an education that falls short. Whatever merit appellees' argument might have if a State's financing system occasioned an absolute denial of educational opportunities to any of its children, that argument provides no basis for finding an interference with fundamental rights where only relative differences in spending levels are involved and where—as is true in the present case—no charge fairly could be made that the system fails to provide each child with an opportunity to acquire the basic minimal skills necessary for the enjoyment of the rights of speech and of full participation in the political process.

Furthermore, the logical limitations on appellees' nexus theory are difficult to perceive. How, for instance, is education to be distinguished from the significant personal interests in the basics of decent food and shelter? Empirical examination might well buttress an assumption that the ill-fed, ill-clothed, and ill-housed are among the most ineffective participants in the political process, and that they derive the least enjoyment from the benefits of the First Amendment. * * *

* * *

Thus, we stand on familiar ground when we continue to acknowledge that the Justices of this Court lack both the expertise and the familiarity with local problems so necessary to the making of wise decisions with respect to the raising and disposition of public revenues. Yet, we are urged to direct the States either to alter drastically the present system or to throw out the property tax altogether in favor of some other form of taxation. No scheme of taxation, whether the tax is imposed on property, income, or purchases of goods and services, has yet been devised which is free of all discriminatory impact. In such a complex arena in which no perfect alternatives exist, the Court does well not to impose too rigorous a standard of scrutiny lest all local fiscal schemes become subjects of criticism under the Equal Protection Clause.

In addition to matters of fiscal policy, this case also involves the most persistent and difficult questions of educational policy, another area in which this Court's lack of specialized knowledge and experience counsels against premature interference with the informed judgments made at the state and local levels. Education, perhaps even more than welfare assistance, presents a myriad of "intractable economic, social, and even philosophical problems." * * * The very complexity of the problems of financing and managing a statewide public school system suggests that "there will be more than one constitutionally permissible method of solving them," and that, within the limits of rationality, "the legislature's efforts to tackle the problems" should be entitled to respect. * * * On even the most basic questions in this area the scholars and educational experts are divided. Indeed, one of the major sources of controversy concerns the extent to which there is a demonstrable correlation between educational expenditures and the quality of education—an assumed correlation underlying virtually every legal conclusion drawn by the District Court in this case. Related to the questioned relationship between cost and quality is the equally unsettled controversy as to the proper goals of a system of public education. And the question regarding the most effective relationship between state boards of education and local school boards, in terms of their respective responsibilities and degrees of control, is now undergoing searching re-examination. The ultimate wisdom as to these and related problems of education is not likely to be divined for all time even by the scholars who now so earnestly debate the issues. In such circumstances, the judiciary is well advised to refrain from imposing on the States inflexible constitutional restraints that could circumscribe or handicap the continued research and experimentation so vital to finding even partial solutions to educational problems and to keeping abreast of ever-changing conditions.

* * *

The foregoing considerations buttress our conclusion that Texas' system of public school finance is an inappropriate candidate for strict judicial scrutiny. * * *

* * *

Appellees further urge that the Texas system is unconstitutionally arbitrary because it allows the availability of local taxable resources to turn on "happenstance." They see no justification for a system that allows, as they contend, the quality of education to fluctuate on the basis of the fortuitous positioning of the boundary lines of political subdivisions and the location of valuable commercial and industrial property. But any scheme of local taxation—indeed the very existence of identifiable local governmental units—requires the establishment of jurisdictional boundaries that are inevitably arbitrary. It is equally inevitable that some localities are going to be blessed with more taxable assets than others. Nor is local wealth a static quantity. Changes in the level of taxable wealth within any district may result from any number of events, some of which local residents can and do influence. For instance, commercial and industrial enterprises may be encouraged to locate within a district by various actions—public and private.

Moreover, if local taxation for local expenditures were an unconstitutional method of providing for education then it might be an equally impermissible means of providing for other necessary services customarily financed largely from local property taxes, including local police and fire protection, public health and hospitals, and public utility facilities of various kinds. We perceive no justification for such a severe denigration of local property taxation and control as would follow from appellees' contentions. It has simply never been within the constitutional prerogative of this Court to nullify statewide measures for financing public services merely because the burdens or benefits thereof fall unevenly depending upon the relative wealth of the political subdivisions in which citizens live.

* * * One also must remember that the system here challenged is not peculiar to Texas or to any other State. In its essential characteristics, the Texas plan for financing public education reflects what many educators for a half century have thought was an enlightened approach to a problem for which there is no perfect solution. We are unwilling to assume for ourselves a level of wisdom superior to that of legislators, scholars, and educational authorities in 50 States, especially where the alternatives proposed are only recently conceived and nowhere yet tested. * * *

* * *

* * * The consideration and initiation of fundamental reforms with respect to state taxation and education are matters reserved for the legislative processes of the various States, and we do no violence to the values of federalism and separation of powers by staying our hand. We hardly need add that this Court's action today is not to be viewed as placing its judicial imprimatur on the status quo. The need is apparent for reform in tax systems which may well have relied too long and too heavily on the local property tax. And certainly innovative thinking as to public education, its methods, and its funding is necessary to assure both a higher level of quality and greater uniformity of opportunity. These matters merit the continued attention of the scholars who already have contributed much by their challenges. But the ultimate solutions must come from the lawmakers and from the democratic pressures of those who elect them.

Reversed.

MR. JUSTICE STEWART, concurring.

The method of financing public schools in Texas, as in almost every other State, has resulted in a system of public education that can fairly be described as chaotic and unjust. It does not follow, however, and I cannot find, that this system violates the Constitution of the United States. I join the opinion and judgment of the Court because I am convinced that any other course would mark an extraordinary departure from principled adjudication under the Equal Protection Clause of the Fourteenth Amendment. * * *

* * *

MR. JUSTICE WHITE, with whom MR. JUSTICE DOUGLAS and MR. JUSTICE BRENNAN join, dissenting.

* * *

I cannot disagree with the proposition that local control and local decisionmaking play an important part in our democratic system of government. * * * Much may be left to local option, and this case would be quite different if it were true that the Texas system, while insuring minimum educational expenditures in every district through state funding, extended a meaningful option to all local districts to increase their per-pupil expenditures and so to improve their children's education to the extent that increased funding would achieve that goal. The system would then arguably provide a rational and sensible method of achieving the stated aim of preserving an area for local initiative and decision.

The difficulty with the Texas system, however, is that it provides a meaningful option to Alamo Heights and like school districts but almost none to Edgewood and those other districts with a low per-pupil real estate tax base. In these latter districts, no matter how desirous parents are of supporting their schools with greater revenues, it is impossible to do so through the use of the real estate property tax. In these districts, the Texas system utterly fails to extend a realistic choice to parents because the property tax, which is the only revenue-raising mechanism extended to school districts, is practically and legally unavailable. * * *

* * *

* * * If the State aims at maximizing local initiative and local choice, by permitting school districts to resort to the real property tax if they choose to do so, it utterly fails in achieving its purpose in districts with property tax bases so low that there is little if any opportunity for interested parents, rich or poor, to augment school district revenues. Requiring the State to establish only that unequal treatment is in furtherance of a permissible goal, without also requiring the State to show that the means chosen to effectuate that goal are rationally related to its achievement, makes equal protection analysis no more than an empty gesture. In my view, the parents and children in Edgewood, and in like districts, suffer from an invidious discrimination violative of the Equal Protection Clause.

This does not, of course, mean that local control may not be a legitimate goal of a school-financing system. Nor does it mean that the State must guarantee each district an equal per-pupil revenue from the state school-financing system. Nor does it mean, as the majority appears to believe, that, by affirming the decision below, this Court would be "imposing on the States inflexible constitutional restraints that could circumscribe or handicap the continued research and experimentation so vital to finding even partial solutions to educational problems and to keeping abreast of ever-changing conditions." On the contrary, it would merely mean that the State must fashion a financing scheme which provides a rational basis for the maximization of local control, if local control is to remain a goal of the system, and not a scheme with "different treatment be[ing] accorded to persons placed by a statute into different classes on the basis of criteria wholly unrelated to the objective of that statute." * * *

* * *

MR. JUSTICE MARSHALL, with whom MR. JUSTICE DOUGLAS concurs, dissenting.

The Court today decides, in effect, that a State may constitutionally vary the quality of education which it offers its children in accordance with the amount of taxable wealth located in the school districts within which they reside. The majority's decision represents an abrupt departure from the mainstream of recent state and federal court decisions concerning the unconstitutionality of state educational financing schemes dependent upon taxable local wealth. More unfortunately, though, the majority's holding can only be seen as a retreat from our historic commitment to equality of educational opportunity and as unsupportable acquiescence in a system which deprives children in their earliest years of the chance to reach their full potential as citizens. The Court does this despite the absence of any substantial justification for a scheme which arbitrarily channels educational resources in accordance with the fortuity of the amount of taxable wealth within each district.

In my judgment, the right of every American to an equal start in life, so far as the provision of a state service as important as education is concerned, is far too vital to permit state discrimination on grounds as tenuous as those presented by this record. Nor can I accept the notion that it is sufficient to remit these appellees to the vagaries of the political process which, contrary to the majority's suggestion, has proved singularly unsuited to the task of providing a remedy for this discrimination. I, for one, am unsatisfied with the hope of an ultimate "political" solution sometime in the indefinite future while, in the meantime, countless children unjustifiably receive inferior educations that "may affect their hearts and minds in a way unlikely ever to be undone." * * *

The Court acknowledges that "substantial interdistrict disparities in school expenditures" exist in Texas, * * * and that these disparities are "largely attributable to differences in the amounts of money collected through local property taxation." * * * But instead of closely examining the seriousness of these disparities and the invidiousness of the Texas financing scheme, the Court undertakes an elaborate exploration of the efforts Texas has purportedly made to close the gaps between its districts in terms of level district wealth and resulting educational funding. Yet, however praiseworthy Texas' equalizing efforts, the issue in this case is not whether Texas is doing its best to ameliorate the worst features of a discriminatory scheme but, rather, whether the scheme itself is in fact unconstitutionally discriminatory in the face of the Fourteenth Amendment's guarantee of equal protection of the laws. When the Texas financing scheme is taken as a whole, I do not think it can be doubted that it produces a discriminatory impact on substantial numbers of the school-age children in the State of Texas.

* * *

* * * I must once more voice my disagreement with the Court's rigidified approach to equal protection analysis. * * * The Court seeks to establish today that equal protection cases fall into one of two neat categories which dictate the appropriate standard of review—strict scrutiny or mere rationality. But this Court's decisions in the field of equal protection defy such easy categorization. A principled reading of what this Court has done reveals that it has applied a spectrum of standards in reviewing discrimination allegedly violative of the Equal Protection Clause. This spectrum clearly comprehends variations in the degree of care with which the Court will scrutinize particular classifications, depend-

ing, I believe, on the constitutional and societal importance of the interest adversely affected and the recognized invidiousness of the basis upon which the particular classification is drawn. * * *

I therefore cannot accept the majority's labored efforts to demonstrate that fundamental interests which call for strict scrutiny of the challenged classification, encompass only established rights which we are somehow bound to recognize from the text of the Constitution itself. To be sure, some interests which the Court has deemed to be fundamental for purposes of equal protection analysis are themselves constitutionally protected rights. * * *

I would like to know where the Constitution guarantees the right to procreate, *Skinner* v. *Oklahoma,* 316 U.S. 535, 541 (1942), or the right to vote in state elections, *e.g., Reynolds* v. *Sims,* 377 U.S. 533 (1964), or the right to an appeal from a criminal conviction, *e.g., Griffin* v. *Illinois,* 351 U.S. 12 (1956). These are instances in which, due to the importance of the interests at stake, the Court has displayed a strong concern with the existence of discriminatory state treatment. But the Court has never said or indicated that these are interests which independently enjoy full-blown constitutional protection.

* * *

The study introduced in the District Court showed a direct inverse relationship between equalized taxable district property wealth and district tax effort with the result that the property-poor districts making the highest tax effort obtained the lowest per-pupil yield. * * * Since the funds received through the Minimum Foundation School Program are to be used only for minimum professional salaries, transportation costs, and operating expenses, it is not hard to see the lack of local choice—with respect to higher teacher salaries to attract more and better teachers, physical facilities, library books, and facilities, special courses, or participation in special state and federal matching funds programs—under which a property-poor district such as Edgewood is forced to labor. In fact, because of the difference in taxable local property wealth, Edgewood would have to tax itself almost nine times as heavily to obtain the same yield as Alamo Heights. At present, then, local control is a myth for many of the local school districts in Texas. As one district court has observed, "rather than reposing in each school district the economic power to fix its own level of per-pupil expenditure, the State has so arranged the structure as to guarantee that some districts will spend low (with high taxes) while others will spend high (with low taxes)." * * *

* * *

In conclusion, it is essential to recognize that an end to the wide variations in taxable district property wealth inherent in the Texas financing scheme would entail none of the untoward consequences suggested by the Court or by the appellants.

First, affirmance of the District Court's decisions would hardly sound the death knell for local control of education. It would mean neither centralized decisionmaking nor federal court intervention in the operation of public schools. Clearly, this suit has nothing to do with local decisionmaking with respect to educational policy or even educational spending. It involves only a narrow aspect of local control—namely, local control over the raising of educational funds. In fact, in striking down interdistrict disparities in taxable local wealth, the District Court took the course which is most likely to make true local control over educational decisionmaking a reality for *all* Texas school districts.

Nor does the District Court's decision even necessarily eliminate local control of educational funding. The District Court struck down nothing more than the continued interdistrict wealth discrimination inherent in the present property tax. Both centralized and decentralized plans for educational funding not involving such interdistrict discrimination have been put forward. The choice among these or other alternatives would remain with the State, not with the federal courts. * * *

* * *

The Court seeks solace for its action today in the possibility of legislative reform. The Court's suggestions of legislative redress and experimentation will doubtless be of great comfort to the schoolchildren of Texas' disadvantaged districts, but considering the vested interests of wealthy school districts in the preservation of the status quo, they are worth little more. The possibility of legislative action is, in all events, no answer to this Court's duty under the Constitution to eliminate unjustified state discrimination. In this case we have been presented with an instance of such discrimination, in a particularly invidious form, against an individual interest of large constitutional and practical importance. To support the demonstrated discrimination in the provision of educational opportunity the State has offered a justification which, on analysis, takes on at best an ephemeral character. Thus, I believe that the wide disparities in taxable district property wealth inherent in the local property tax element of the Texas financing scheme render that scheme violative of the Equal Protection Clause.

* * *

Notes and Questions

Rodriguez was a five-to-four decision. Joining Justice Powell in the majority opinion were Chief Justice Burger and Justices Stewart, Blackmun, and Rehnquist. In addition to upholding the constitutionality of the

Texas method of financing public schools, the Court held that education was not a fundamental interest requiring strict scrutiny under the Equal Protection Clause. The Court also concluded that school finance reform should flow from state legislative processes.

Some observers have contended that, if the Court had mandated equality of educational opportunity for public school students, floodgates would have opened resulting in judicial attacks on statewide inequality in other government services, such as police and fire protection, recreational facilities, and health care. Do you agree with this contention? Does the fact that most state constitutions contain language committing the state to a responsibility for providing education negate this contention?

Despite the *Rodriguez* outcome, plaintiffs in Louisiana attempted to distinguish between practices in Louisiana and Texas in a suit alleging that the equal protection clause of the Fourteenth Amendment was violated by the Louisiana school finance system. Nevertheless, a federal district court found the issues indistinguishable from *Rodriguez* and dismissed the case. See *Scarnato* v. *Parker,* 415 F. Supp. 272 (La. 1976), aff'd, 430 U.S. 960 (1977).

IV. Post-*Rodriguez* Litigation

Proponents of the school-finance-reform movement viewed the *Rodriguez* decision as essentially eliminating the federal courts as a viable battleground. Consequently, their attention turned to the state courts. In addition to relying on state equal protection grounds, litigation was brought under state constitutional provisions requiring public education to be "uniform," "adequate," or "thorough and efficient." The result has been much judicial activity among the states. However, largely because of the differences among states in the constitutional language or the specific statutory provisions that were challenged, state court holdings have not been uniform.

Supreme courts of nine states (Arizona, Colorado, Georgia, Idaho, Maryland, Michigan, New York, Ohio, and Oregon) have concluded that state methods of financing public education are not constitutionally deficient. However, most of these courts emphasized that their decisions did not represent an acceptance of the existence of substantial equity or adequacy under school finance statutes but, rather, that language in state constitutions did not justify judicial involvement in changing existing shortcomings. See list of cases on pages 367–68.

To varying degrees, the nine state supreme court decisions upholding school-finance systems involved suits that were based on principles set forth in *Serrano*. Cases in Arizona, Idaho, and Oregon, in particular, were filed shortly after the initial *Serrano* decision and were closely patterned after the doctrines of the California decision.

Several cases involved tangential school-finance issues. In the New York litigation, New York City intervened on behalf of plaintiffs, adding a "municipal overburden" issue to the case. Several new issues were raised in Ohio. These included (1) the contention that voter control over tax levies should not have been permissible in a state that required a thorough and efficient educational program and (2) the argument that property-poor school districts tended to be income poor in that state and, therefore, constituted a more clearly identifiable suspect classification. Ohio plaintiffs also claimed that fiscal capacity should not be represented solely by property value per student. In Maryland plaintiffs also attempted to base their case, in part, on a correlation between income and property wealth. Additionally, they sought to convince the court that a constitutional requirement of a "thorough and efficient" education should be construed as disallowing wide expenditure variations, even those resulting from factors other than local wealth disparity.

With the exception of the Arizona case, these decisions all addressed the issue of whether education is a fundamental interest. Their conclusions that education is not a fundamental interest appear to have dealt a blow to the potential of other legal rationales for holding school-finance systems unconstitutional.

State supreme courts in six states (Arkansas, California, Connecticut, New Jersey, Washington, and Wyoming) have ruled that statutes governing state and local financing of public education were unconstitutional. In one other state, West Virginia, a lower-court decision upholding the finance system was overturned and remanded by the supreme court for further consideration of the constitutionality of the plan; the lower court then ruled against the school finance system. Although no decision rejected all features of a state's school finance legislation, each of these states was ordered to restructure the basic formula for the distribution of state funds or for the receipt of local revenues for education in order to eliminate or reduce local wealth disparity as a factor influencing expenditure variation among school districts.

Litigation continues in some of these states, generally as a consequence of dissatisfaction on the part of original plaintiffs or new parties with the quantity or quality of reforms enacted by legislatures in response to court orders. To date, no court has retreated from its initial requirement that inequities be corrected. Standards for alleviating disparities, after being promulgated by courts, have not been relaxed in subsequent orders. However, second- and third-generation decisions have in some instances declined to expand the scope or impact of earlier rulings, especially if new claims were brought by plaintiffs. See list of cases on pages 366–67.

Doctrines established in *Serrano* played an important role in invalidating school finance methods, although reliance on *Serrano* was more clearly evident in some holdings than in others. Each of the decisions in the seven states employed a set of rationales that did not precisely match that of any other state.

Decisions in the seven states reveal that, as a general rule, courts have sought to avoid direct involvement in fashioning remedies to existing inequities. Courts have clearly demonstrated a reluctance to participate in supervising the process of change so closely as to make themselves susceptible to charges of formulating public policy and implementing details of such policies through autocratic judicial decrees.

Horton v. Meskill

Supreme Court of Connecticut, 1977
172 Conn. 615, 376 A.2d 359

HOUSE, Chief Justice.

* * *

The cases were brought seeking (1) a declaratory judgment that the system of financing public elementary and secondary education in this state, at least as it affects the town of Canton, violates the Connecticut and the United States constitutions; (2) an order in equity directing the defendants to cease implementing the present financing system, at least as it affects the town of Canton, except as necessary to provide an orderly transition to a constitutional system for financing public schools; (3) an order that the court retain jurisdiction to assure a transition with all deliberate speed to a constitutional system of financing public education.
* * *
In essence, each action sought by declaratory judgment a judicial determination as to whether the Connecticut educational finance system, at least as it existed at the time of trial (1974), violates constitutional equal rights and equal protection guarantees and is constitutionally mandated "appropriate legislation"; Conn. Const. Art. VIII § 1; to provide free public elementary and secondary schools in the state. The questions presented are not only of great importance but of considerable complexity, and it is of small comfort to note that members of the judiciary throughout the country are also being faced with the same or similar complex questions. * * *

* * *

Without attempting to recite in detail the lengthy finding of facts, we note certain findings which are of special significance. The public schools in Canton, like those of all other towns in the state, are financed primarily by two means: funds raised by the town by assessment on property within the town and funds distributed by the state pursuant to legislation providing for a flat grant depending on the average number of pupils attending school daily. This grant is usually referred to as the ADM (average daily membership) grant. General Statutes §10–262. The ADM grant paid during 1973–74 was $215 per pupil and has since been increased to $250 per pupil. It has been the principal source of the state's contribution to local public school education for about three decades though, by statute, the state provides for various other grant payments to each town or district for public and nonpublic school programs and activities. * * *

In Connecticut, the percentage contribution of the local, state, and federal governments has been approximately 70 percent local, 20 to 25 percent state, and 5 percent or less federal. * * * Funds raised by local governments for local public school education come principally from one source—the local property tax. For the year 1972–73, 80.1 percent of the state aid for local public school operating expenses was distributed as a flat grant that was not based upon the ability of the towns to finance education * * *

* * *

Because local property taxes are the principal source of revenue for local public schools, a significant measure of the ability of the various towns to finance local education is the dollar amount of taxable property per pupil in each town which can be figured by dividing the grand list of a town by the numbers of pupils. For the 1972–73 school year, wide disparities existed in the effective yield per pupil ranging from approximately $20,000 per pupil to approximately $170,000 per pupil. During that year, the state average was $53,639. In Canton, it was $38,415.

* * *

The tax effort of a town to finance education may be measured by determining the net school mill rate which is that part of the net mill rate which a town spends on education. * * *

* * *

In sum, taxpayers in property-poor towns such as Canton pay higher tax rates for education than taxpayers in property-rich towns. The higher tax rates generate tax revenues in comparatively small amounts and property-poor towns cannot afford to spend for the education of their pupils, on a per pupil basis, the same amounts that property-rich towns do. These facts were affirmed by a conclusion of the governor's commission on tax reform: "In short, many towns can tax far less and spend much more; and those less fortunate towns can never catch up in school expenditure because taxes are already as high as homeowners can tolerate. . . . This dual inequity—a family can pay more and get less for its children—is the fundamental issue of school finance." * * *

The wide disparities that exist in the amount spent on education by the various towns result primarily from the wide disparities that exist in the taxable wealth of the various towns; the present system of financing education in Connecticut ensures that, regardless of the educational needs or wants of children, more educational dollars will be allotted to children who live in property-rich towns than to children who live in property-poor towns.

* * *

The *Rodriguez* case is very relevant to the appeal before us. The equal protection clauses of both the United States and Connecticut constitutions having a like meaning, the decisions of the United States Supreme Court defining federal constitutional rights are, at the least, persuasive authority, although we fully recognize the primary independent vitality of the provisions of our own constitution. Paraphrasing the language of the California Supreme Court in *People* v. *Longwill*, 14 Cal. 3d 943, 951 n.4, 123 Cal. Rptr. 297, 538 P.2d 753: In the area of fundamental civil liberties—which includes all protections of the declaration of rights contained in article first of the Connecticut constitution—we sit as a court of last resort, subject only to the qualification that our interpretations may not restrict the guarantees accorded the national citizenry under the federal charter. In such constitutional adjudication, our first referent is Connecticut law and the full panoply of rights Connecticut residents have come to expect as their due. Accordingly, decisions of the United States Supreme Court defining fundamental rights are persuasive authority to be afforded respectful consideration, but they are to be followed by Connecticut courts only when they provide no less individual protection than is guaranteed by Connecticut law.

* * *

In our consideration of the merits of the present appeals, we have not found material aid in the many decisions from the courts of other jurisdictions since most of them depend upon the controlling and differing provisions of the constitutions in the particular jurisdictions. Nor have we found the *Rodriguez* test for fundamentality of the right to an education of particular help—although under that test it cannot be questioned but that in the light of the Connecticut constitutional recognition of the right to education * * * it is, in Connecticut, a "fundamental" right.

As other courts have recognized, educational equalization cases are "in significant aspects sui generis" and not subject to analysis by accepted conventional tests or the application of mechanical standards. The wealth discrimination found among school districts differs materially from the usual equal protection case where a fairly defined indigent class suffers discrimination to its peculiar disadvantage. The discrimination is relative rather than absolute. * * *

We find our thinking to be substantially in accord with the decisions of the New Jersey Supreme Court in *Robinson* v. *Cahill,* 62 N.J. 473, 303 A.2d 273, and the California Supreme Court in *Serrano* v. *Priest,* 18 Cal. 3d 728, 135 Cal. Rptr. 345, 557 P.2d 929 (*Serrano II*), and whether we apply the "fundamentality" test adopted by *Rodriguez* or the pre-*Rodriguez* test under our state constitution (as the California Supreme Court did in *Serrano II*) or the "arbitrary" test applied by the New Jersey Supreme Court in *Robinson* v. *Cahill,* supra, 62 N.J. 492, 303 A.2d 273, we must conclude that in Connecticut the right to education is so basic and fundamental that any infringement of that right must be strictly scrutinized.

* * *

The present-day problem arises from the circumstance that over the years there has arisen a great disparity in the ability of local communities to finance local education, which has given rise to a consequent significant disparity in the quality of education available to the youth of the state. It was well stated in the memorandum of decision of the trial court, which noted that the "present method [of financing education in the state] is the result of legislation in which the state delegates to municipalities of disparate financial capability the state's duty of raising funds for operating public schools within that municipality. That legislation gives no consideration to the financial capability of the municipality to raise funds sufficient to discharge another duty delegated to the municipality by the state, that of educating the children within that municipality. The evidence in this case is that, as a result of this duty-delegating to Canton without regard to Canton's financial capabilities, pupils in Canton receive an education that is in a substantial degree lower in both breadth and quality than that received by pupils in municipalities with a greater financial capability, even though there is no difference between the constitutional duty of the state to the children in Canton and the constitutional duty of the state to the children in other towns."

* * *

While the development of an appropriate legislative plan is not without its complexities, the problem is not insoluble. Nor do we share the alarm expressed in the dissenting opinion at what it concludes are "the implications of the decision" as requiring total state financing of education, loss of local administrative control over educational decisions and the requirement that education in all towns "be brought up to the Darien standard" which, if it occurred, the trial court found would require an increase of $313,000,000 over the amounts being currently expended. To the contrary, as we have noted, the trial court expressly found that none of these consequences would of necessity follow the adoption by the state of a financing program designed to achieve a substantial degree of equality of educational opportunity and permit all towns to exercise a meaningful choice as to educational services to be offered to students, that the property tax is still a viable means of producing income for education, and that there is no reason why local control needs to be diminished in any degree merely because some system other than the one presently in effect is adopted. We find no reason to reject the validity of these findings. Obviously, absolute equality or precisely equal advantages are not required and cannot be attained except in the most relative sense. Logically, the state may recognize differences in educational costs based on relevant economic and educational factors and on course offerings of special interest in diverse communities. None of the basic alternative plans to equalize the ability of various towns to finance education requires that all towns spend the same amount for the education of each pupil. The very uncertainty of the extent of the nexus between dollar input and quality of educational opportunity requires allowance for variances as do individual and group disadvantages and local conditions.

* * *

Notes and Questions

Horton demonstrates that relief regarding wealth disparity may be obtained in a state court although there was an opposite ruling in a similar situation by the United States Supreme Court in *Rodriguez.* This decision reveals that a state supreme court may grant greater protections to its citizenry under a state equal protection constitutional provision than is available under the federal Fourteenth Amendment provision. It also discloses that a state supreme court may establish education as a "fundamental" right. As we have seen, such a determination places the burden of proof on the defendant.

Does the *Horton* court provide a satisfactory test to determine what type of state finance plan would be an acceptable "constitutional system for financing public schools"?

State courts have upheld plaintiffs' position regarding the inequity of wealth differentials in a number of decisions. These include:

Arkansas

Dupree v. Alma School District No. 30, 279 Ark. 340, 651 S.W.2d 90 (1983)

California

Serrano v. Priest, 5 Cal.3d 584, 487 P.2d 1241 (1971) (*Serrano I*); 18 Cal.3d 728, 557 P.2d 929 (1976), cert. den., 432 U.S. 907 (1977) (*Serrano II*); No.1554 (Los Angeles County Superior Court) (1983)

Connecticut

Horton v. *Meskill*, 195 Conn. 24, 486 A.2d 1099 (1985), 172 Conn. 615, 376 A.2d 359 (1977), affirming 31 Conn. Supp. 377, 332 A.2d 113 (Hartford County Superior Court) (1974)

New Jersey

Robinson v. *Cahill*, 118 N.J. Super. 223, 287 A.2d 187 (1972), aff'd, 62 N.J. 473, 303 A.2d 273, cert. den. sub. nom., *Dickey* v. *Robinson*, 414 U.S. 976 (1973), 63 N.J. 196, 306 A.2d 65 (1973), 67 N.J. 35, 335 A.2d 6 (1975), 67 N.J. 333, 339 A.2d 193 (1975) (*Robinson I*); 69 N.J. 449, 355 A.2d 129 (1976), 70 N.J. 155, 358 A.2d 457 (1976) (*Robinson II*)

Abbott v. *Burke*, 195 N.J. Super. 59 (1984)

Washington

Northshore School District No. 417 v. *Kinnear*, 84 Wash.2d 685, 530 P.2d 178 (1974)

Seattle School District No. 1 v. *State of Washington*, 90 Wash.2d 476, 585 P.2d 71 (1978)

West Virginia

Pauley v. *Kelley*, 255 S.E.2d 859 (1979)

Wyoming

Washaki County School District No. 1 v. *Herschler*, 606 P.2d 310 (1980), reh'g den., 606 P.2d 340 (1980), cert. den., 449 U.S. 824 (1980)

State courts upholding challenged school finance schemes include:

Arizona

Shofstall v. *Hollins*, 110 Ariz. 88, 515 P.2d 590 (1973)

Colorado

Lujan v. *Colorado State Board of Education*, 649 P.2d 1005 (1982)

Georgia

McDaniel v. *Thomas*, 248 Ga. 632, 285 S.E.2d 156 (1981)

Idaho

Thompson v. *Engelking*, 96 Ida. 793, 537 P.2d 635 (1975)

Maryland

Hornbeck v. *Somerset County Board of Education*, 295 Md. 597, 458 A.2d 758 (1983)

Michigan

Milliken v. *Green,* 389 Mich. 1, 203 N.W.2d 457 (1972), vacated, 390 Mich. 389, 212 N.W.2d 711 (1973)

East Jackson Public Schools v. *Michigan,* 133 Mich. App. 132, 348 N.W.2d 303 (1984)

New York

Board of Education, Levittown Union Free School District v. *Nyquist,* 94 Misc.2d 466, 408 N.Y.S.2d 606 (1978), aff'd, 83 A.D. 217, 443 N.Y.S.2d 843 (1981), rev'd, 439 N.E.2d 359, 453 N.Y.S.2d 643 (1982)

Ohio

Board of Education of the City School District of Cincinnati v. *Walter,* 58 Ohio St.2d 368, 390 N.E.2d 813 (1979), cert. den., 444 U.S. 1015 (1980)

Oregon

Olsen v. *Oregon,* 276 Or. 9, 544 P.2d 139 (1976)

educator
and
school district
liability

INTRODUCTION

Educators are often concerned about the extent, if any, of their liability for damages as a result of their official action or inaction. The many types of concerns educators have in this area include possible liability on the part of the school district, individual board members, administrative personnel, and teachers for the injury or death of a child at school or while under school supervision; liability, if any, of a teacher or administrator for injuring a child while administering corporal punishment; school district, administrator, or teacher liability, if any, for depriving someone of his or her constitutional rights; and liability for malpractice.

The area of law that addresses these concerns is known as tort law. A tort is a civil wrong where one suffers loss as a result of the improper conduct of another. This branch of law is concerned with the compensation of losses suffered by an individual owing to an intentional or negligent act. Some torts may also be criminal, and if so, the person or persons charged may be prosecuted and punished by the state. Tort law is a highly specialized branch of law that is exceedingly complicated. Consequently, the purpose of this chapter is to provide educators with a brief discussion of applicable principles and major issues of general concern.

I. School District Immunity

A. Liability under State Law

In approximately half of the states school districts have governmental or sovereign immunity from liability for torts committed by the school district, school board members or employees. Governmental immunity is grounded in the theory that the state and its agencies are sovereign and cannot be sued without consent. Such a view has its basis in the historic notion that "the king can do no wrong." Additionally, the doctrine seeks to protect the limited resources of government agencies. School districts in particular often have limited funds for other than educational purposes and frequently, therefore, are unable to pay high judgments rendered against them. Employment of the defense of sovereign immunity indicates that unless state courts or the legislature have modified or abrogated the doctrine, school districts cannot be sued for tort actions in a court of law. Many legal scholars, however, have been critical of the doctrine of sovereign immunity since it often leaves an injured party without any means to be compensated for losses. Consequently, governmental immunity has been substantially abrogated or modified in approximately thirty states, resulting in considerable variation regarding liability in those states.

Application of the doctrine of immunity differs from state to state: in most states where sovereign immunity has been preserved statutory law has been modified to allow limited liability, particularly for school-bus accidents. Although the majority of these states allow school districts to purchase liability insurance without waiving their immunity, some states have asserted that the purchase of insurance will constitute a waiver of immunity within the limits of insurance protection.

Individual liability also varies among the states. Generally, school board members or other officials may be held personally liable for the improper performance of so-called ministerial duties; they may not be liable, however, for the performance of discretionary responsibilities. Ministerial functions are defined as those having to do with the execution of policy as opposed to the formulation of policy represented by discretionary actions. If a school official is required to decide or act without established or readily ascertainable standards for guidance, that act is a discretionary function. Protection of discretionary activity follows from a desire to encourage governmental decision making; ministerial decisions, involving a lesser degree of discretion and judgment, require less protection or immunity. In school-related decisions courts have recognized a vital public interest in securing the free and independent judgment of school officials.

Historically, the immunity of school districts did not protect individual school employees from liability in tort. Many states, however, have reconsidered this notion, arguing that the individual school employees are least able to defend themselves in court. In Georgia, for instance, immunity has been extended to school principals and to classroom teachers. See *Hennessy v. Webb*, 245 Ga. 329, 264 S.E.2d 878 (1980) and *Truelove* v. *Wilson*, 159 Ga. App. 906, 285 S.E.2d 556 (1981).

B. Liability under Federal Law

A section of the Civil Rights Act of 1871 provides for liability if a "person" operating under the color of the state violates another person's civil rights. Specifically, the law states:

> Every person who, under color of any statute, ordinance, regulation, custom, or usage, of any State or Territory or the District of Columbia, subjects, or causes to be subjected, any citizen of the United States or other person within the jurisdiction thereof to the deprivation of any rights, privileges, or immunities secured by the Constitution and laws, shall be liable to the party injured in an action at law, suit in equity, or other proper proceeding for redress . . . 42 U.S.C. § 1983.

Although this law had not received much judicial attention for nearly a hundred years, several recent Supreme Court decisions have addressed school district and school officials' liability and the extent, if any, of damages under it. **Wood v. Strickland** addresses the issue of school board member immunity from liability under § 1983, while **Carey v. Piphus** clarifies the elements and prerequisites for recovery of damages under this act.

Wood v. Strickland

Supreme Court of the United States, 1975
420 U.S. 308

MR. JUSTICE WHITE delivered the opinion of the Court.

Respondents Peggy Strickland and Virginia Crain brought this lawsuit against petitioners, who were members of the school board at the time in question, two school administrators, and the Special School District of Mena, Ark., purporting to assert a cause of action under 42 U.S.C. § 1983, and claiming that their federal constitutional rights to due process were infringed under color of state law by their expulsion from the Mena Public High School on the grounds of their violation of a school regulation prohibiting the use or possession of intoxicating beverages at school or school activities. The complaint as amended prayed for compensatory and punitive damages against all petitioners, injunctive relief allowing respondents to resume attendance, preventing petitioners from imposing any sanctions as a result of the expulsion, and restraining enforcement of the challenged regulation, declaratory relief as to the constitutional invalidity of the regulation, and expunction of any record of their expulsion. * * *

I

The violation of the school regulation prohibiting the use or possession of intoxicating beverages at school or school activities with which respondents were charged concerned their "spiking" of the punch served at a meeting of an extra-curricular school organization attended by parents and students. At the time in question, respondents were 16 years old and were in the 10th grade. The relevant facts begin with their discovery that the punch had not been prepared for the meeting as previously planned. The girls then agreed to "spike" it. Since the county in which the school is located is "dry," respondents and a third girl drove across the state border into Oklahoma and purchased two 12-ounce bottles of "Right Time," a malt liquor. They then bought six 10-ounce bottles of a soft drink, and after having mixed the contents of the eight bottles in an empty milk carton, returned to school. Prior to the meeting, the girls experienced second thoughts about the wisdom of their prank, but by then they were caught up in the force of events and the intervention of other girls prevented them from disposing of the illicit punch. The punch was served at the meeting, without apparent effect.

Ten days later, the teacher in charge of the extracurricular group and meeting, Mrs. Curtis Powell, having heard something about the "spiking," questioned the girls about it. Although first denying any knowledge, the girls admitted their involvement after the teacher said that she would handle the punishment herself. The next day, however, she told the girls that the incident was becoming increasingly the subject of talk in the school and that the principal, P. T. Waller, would probably hear about it. She told them that her job was in jeopardy but that she would not force them to admit to Waller what they had done. If they did not go to him then, however, she would not be able to help them if the incident became "distorted." The three girls then went to Waller and admitted their role in the affair. He suspended them from school for a maximum two-week period, subject to the decision of the school board. Waller also told them that the board would meet that night, that the girls could tell their parents about the meeting, but that the parents should not contact any members of the board.

Neither the girls nor their parents attended the school board meeting that night. Both Mrs. Powell and Waller, after making their reports concerning the incident, recommended leniency. At this point, a telephone call was received by S. L. Inlow, then the superintendent of schools, from Mrs. Powell's husband, also a teacher at the high school, who reported that he had heard that the third girl involved had been in a fight that evening at a basketball game. Inlow informed the meeting of the news, although he did not mention the name of the girl involved. Mrs. Powell and Waller then withdrew their recommendations of leniency, and the board voted to expel the girls from school for the remainder of the semester, a period of approximately three months.

The board subsequently agreed to hold another meeting on the matter, and one was held approximately two weeks after the first meeting. The girls, their parents, and their counsel attended this session. The board began with a reading of a written statement of facts as it had found them. The girls admitted mixing the malt liquor into the punch with the intent of "spiking" it, but asked the board to forgo its rule punishing such violations by such substantial suspensions. Neither Mrs. Powell nor Waller was present at this meeting. The board voted not to change its policy and, as before, to expel the girls for the remainder of the semester.

II

* * *

Petitioners as members of the school board assert here, as they did below, an absolute immunity from liability under § 1983 and at the very least seek to reinstate the judgment of the District Court. If they are correct and the District Court's dimissal should be sustained, we need go no further in this case. Moreover, the immunity question involves the construction of a federal statute, and our practice is to deal with possibly dispositive statutory issues before reaching questions turning on the construction of the Constitution. * * * We essentially sustain the position of the Court of Appeals with respect to the immunity issue.

The nature of the immunity from awards of damages under § 1983 available to school administrators and school board members is not a question which the lower federal courts have answered with a single voice. There is general agreement on the existence of a "good faith" immunity, but the courts have either emphasized different factors as elements of good faith or have not given specific content to the good-faith standard.

* * *

Common-law tradition, recognized in our prior decisions, and strong public-policy reasons also lead to a construction of § 1983 extending a qualified good-faith immunity to school board members from liability for damages under that section. Although there have been different emphases and formulations of the common-law immunity of public school officials in cases of student expulsion or suspension, state courts have generally recognized that such officers should be protected from tort liability under state law for all good-faith, nonmalicious action taken to fulfill their official duties.

* * *

Liability for damages for every action which is found subsequently to have been violative of a student's constitutional rights and to have caused compensable injury would unfairly impose upon the school decisionmaker the burden of mistakes made in good faith in the course of exercising his discretion within the scope of his official duties. School board members, among other duties, must judge whether there have been violations of school regulations and, if so, the appropriate sanctions for the violations. Denying any measure of immunity in these circumstances "would contribute not to principled and fearless decisionmaking but to intimidation." * * * The imposition of monetary costs for mistakes which were not unreasonable in the light of all the circumstances would undoubtedly deter even the most conscientious school decisionmaker from exercising his judgment independently, forcefully, and in a manner best serving the long-term interest of the school and the students. The most capable candidates for school board positions might be deterred from seeking office if heavy burdens upon their private resources from monetary liability were a likely prospect during their tenure.

These considerations have undoubtedly played a prime role in the development by state courts of a qualified immunity protecting school officials from liability for damages in lawsuits claiming improper suspensions or expulsions. But at the same time, the judgment implicit in this common-law development is that absolute immunity would not be justified since it would not sufficiently increase the ability of school officials to exercise their discretion in a forthright manner to warrant the absence of a remedy for students subjected to intentional or otherwise inexcusable deprivations.

* * *

The disagreement between the Court of Appeals and the District Court over the immunity standard in this case has been put in terms of an "objective" versus a "subjective" test of good faith. As we see it, the appropriate standard necessarily contains elements of both. The official himself must be acting sincerely and with a belief that he is doing right, but an act violating a student's constitutional rights can be no more justified by ignorance or disregard of settled, indisputable law on the part of one entrusted with supervision of students' daily lives than by the presence of actual malice. To be entitled to a special exemption from the categorical remedial language of § 1983 in a case in which his action violated a student's constitutional rights, a school board member, who has voluntarily undertaken the task of supervising the operation of the school and the activities of the students, must be held to a standard of conduct based not only on permissible intentions, but also on knowledge of the basic, unquestioned constitutional rights of his charges. Such a standard imposes neither an unfair burden upon a person assuming a responsible public office requiring a high degree of intelligence and judgment for the proper fulfillment of its duties, nor an unwarranted burden in light of the value which civil rights have in our legal system. Any lesser standard would deny much of the promise of § 1983. Therefore, in the specific context of school discipline, we hold that a school board member is not immune from liability for damages under § 1983 if he knew or reasonably should have known that the action he took within his sphere of official responsibility would violate the constitutional rights of the student affected, or if he took the action with the malicious intention to cause a deprivation of constitutional rights or other injury to the student. * * * A compensatory award will be appropriate only if the school board member has acted with such an impermissible motivation or with such disregard of the student's clearly established constitutional rights that his action cannot reasonably be characterized as being in good faith.

III

* * *

Given the fact that there *was* evidence supporting the charge against respondents, the contrary judgment of the Court of Appeals is improvident. It is not the role of the federal courts to set aside decisions of school administrators which the court may view as lacking a basis in wisdom or compassion. Public high school students do have substantive and procedural rights while at school. * * * But § 1983 does not extend the right to relitigate in federal court evidentiary questions arising in school disciplinary proceedings or the proper construction of school regulations. The system of public education that has evolved in this Nation relies necessarily upon the discretion and judgment of school administrators and school board members, and § 1983 was not intended to be a vehicle for federal-court corrections of errors in the exercise of that discretion which do not rise to the level of violations of specific constitutional guarantees. * * *

IV

* * *

The judgment of the Court of Appeals is vacated and the case remanded for further proceedings consistent with this opinion.

So ordered.

MR. JUSTICE POWELL, with whom THE CHIEF JUSTICE, MR. JUSTICE BLACKMUN, and MR. JUSTICE REHNQUIST join, concurring in part and dissenting in part.

I join in Parts I, III, and IV of the Court's opinion, and agree that the judgment of the Court of Appeals should be vacated and the case remanded. I dissent from Part II which appears to impose a higher standard of care upon public school officials, sued under § 1983, than that heretofore required of any other official.

* * * It would impose personal liability on a school official who acted sincerely and in the utmost good faith, but who was found—after the fact—to have acted in "ignorance . . . of settled, indisputable law." * * * Or, as the Court also puts it, the school official must be held to a standard of conduct based not only on good faith "but also on knowledge of the basic, unquestioned constitutional rights of his charges." * * * Moreover, ignorance of the law is explicitly equated with "actual malice." * * * This harsh standard, requiring knowledge of what is characterized as "settled, indisputable law," leaves little substance to the doctrine of qualified immunity. The Court's decision appears to rest on an unwarranted assumption as to what lay school officials know or can know about the law and constitutional rights. These officials will now act at the peril of some judge or jury subsequently finding that a good-faith belief as to the applicable law was mistaken and hence actionable.

The Court states the standard of required knowledge in two cryptic phrases: "settled, indisputable law" and "unquestioned constitutional rights." Presumably these are intended to mean the same thing, although the meaning of neither phrase is likely to be self-evident to constitutional law scholars—much less the average school board member. One need only look to the decisions of this Court—to our reversals, our recognition of evolving concepts, and our five-to-four splits—to recognize the hazard of even informed prophecy as to what are "unquestioned constitutional rights." * * *

* * *

There are some 20,000 school boards, each with five or more members, and thousands of school superintendents and school principals.

Most of the school board members are popularly elected, drawn from the citizenry at large, and possess no unique competency in divining the law. Few cities and counties provide any compensation for service on school boards, and often it is difficult to persuade qualified persons to assume the burdens of this important function in our society. Moreover, even if counsel's advice constitutes a defense, it may safely be assumed that few school boards and school officials have ready access to counsel or indeed have deemed it necessary to consult counsel on the countless decisions that necessarily must be made in the operation of our public schools.

In view of today's decision significantly enhancing the possibility of personal liability, one must wonder whether qualified persons will continue in the desired numbers to volunteer for service in public education.

Notes and Questions

Although **Wood** specifically addresses school board member liability, the decision has implications for other school employees. Would the reasoning of the Court also apply to such school officials as superintendents and building-level administrators?

The majority opinion in **Wood** declared that ignorance of constitutional law pertaining to school discipline is no excuse. Do you agree, as the dissenters suggest, that the **Wood** standard is a "harsh" one that will place a board member's actions "at the peril of some judge or jury subsequently finding that a good-faith belief as to the applicable law was mistaken . . ."?

Subsequent Supreme Court decisions have continued to address the issue of governmental immunity under § 1983. *Monell* v. *Department of Social Services of City of New York*, 436 U.S. 658 (1978), ruled that school districts are considered "persons" subject to suit under § 1983. Additionally, the Court held that

> a local government may not be sued under § 1983 for an injury inflicted solely by its employees or agents. Instead, it is when execution of a government's policy or custom, whether made by its lawmakers or by those whose edicts or acts may fairly be said to represent official policy, inflicts the injury that the government as an entity is responsible under § 1983. . . . (P. 694)

Monell reversed an earlier Court decision, *Monroe* v. *Pape*, 365 U.S. 167 (1961), which had held governmental bodies absolutely immune from liability under § 1983. Another decision, *Owen* v. *City of Independence*, 445 U.S. 622 (1980), which addressed the discharge of a police chief, held that

> there is no tradition of immunity for municipal corporations, and neither history nor policy support a construction of § 1983 that would justify the qualified immunity. . . . [T]he municipality may not assert the good faith of its officers or agents as a defense to liability under § 1983. (P. 638)

Potential areas of liability were expanded by the Court when it ruled that violations of federal statutory law as well as violations of constitutional provisions could be addressed under § 1983. See *Maine* v. *Thiboutot*, 448 U.S. 1 (1980). Additionally, the Court has ruled that state administrative remedies do not have to be exhausted before § 1983 claims are addressed in federal courts. See *Patsy* v. *Board of Regents of Florida*, 457 U.S. 496 (1982).

Carey v. Piphus

Supreme Court of the United States, 1978
435 U.S. 247

MR. JUSTICE POWELL delivered the opinion of the Court.

In this case, brought under 42 U.S.C. § 1983, we consider the elements and prerequisites for recovery of damages by students who were suspended from public elementary and secondary schools without procedural due process. The Court of Appeals for the Seventh Circuit held that the students are entitled to recover substantial nonpunitive damages even if their suspensions were justified, and even if they do not prove that any other actual injury was caused by the denial of procedural due process. We disagree, and hold that in the absence of proof of actual injury, the students are entitled to recover only nominal damages.

Respondent Jarius Piphus was a freshman at Chicago Vocational High School during the 1973–74 school year. On January 23, 1974, during school hours, the school principal saw Piphus and another student standing outdoors on school property passing back and forth what the principal described as an irregularly shaped cigarette. The principal approached the students unnoticed and smelled what he believed was the strong odor of burning marihuana. He also saw Piphus try to pass a packet of cigarette papers to the other student. When the students became aware of the principal's presence, they threw the cigarette into a nearby hedge.

The principal took the students to the school's disciplinary office and directed the assistant principal to impose the "usual" 20-day suspension for violation of the school rule against the use of drugs. The students protested that they had not been smoking marihuana, but to no avail. Piphus was allowed to remain at school, although not in class, for the remainder of the school day while the assistant principal tried, without success, to reach his mother.

A suspension notice was sent to Piphus' mother, and a few days later two meetings were arranged among Piphus, his mother, his sister, school officials, and representatives from a legal aid clinic. The purpose of the meetings was not to determine whether Piphus had been smoking marihuana, but rather to explain the reasons for the suspension. Following an unfruitful exchange of views, Piphus and his mother, as guardian *ad litem*, filed suit against petitioners in Federal District Court under 42 U.S.C. § 1983 * * * , charging that Piphus had been suspended without due process of law in violation of the Fourteenth Amendment. The complaint sought declaratory and injunctive relief, together with actual and punitive damages in the amount of $3,000. Piphus was readmitted to school under a temporary restraining order after eight days of his suspension.

Respondent Silas Brisco was in the sixth grade at Clara Barton Elementary School in Chicago during the 1973–74 school year. On September 11, 1973, Brisco came to school wearing one small earring. The previous school year the school principal had issued a rule against the wearing of earrings by male students because he believed that this practice denoted membership in certain street gangs and increased the likelihood that gang members would terrorize other students. Brisco was reminded of this rule, but he refused to remove the earring asserting that it was a symbol of black pride, not of gang membership.

The assistant principal talked to Brisco's mother, advising her that her son would be suspended for 20 days if he did not remove the earring. Brisco's mother supported her son's position, and a 20-day suspension was imposed. Brisco and his mother, as guardian *ad litem*, filed suit in Federal District Court under 42 U.S.C. § 1983 * * * , charging that Brisco had been suspended without due process of law in violation of the Fourteenth Amendment. The complaint sought declaratory and injunctive relief, together with actual and punitive damages in the amount of $5,000. Brisco was readmitted to school during the pendency of proceedings for a preliminary injunction after 17 days of his suspension.

* * *

Title 42 U.S.C. § 1983, Rev. Stat. § 1979, derived from § 1 of the Civil Rights Act of 1871, 17 Stat. 13, provides:

> "Every person who, under color of any statute, ordinance, regulation, custom, or usage, of any State or Territory, subjects, or causes to be subjected, any citizen of the United States or other person within the jurisdiction thereof to the deprivation of any rights, privileges, or immunities secured by the Constitution and laws, shall be liable to the party injured in an action at law, suit in equity, or other proper proceeding for redress."

The legislative history of § 1983 * * * demonstrates that it was intended to "[create] a species of tort liability" in favor of persons who are deprived of "rights, privileges, or immunities secured" to them by the Constitution. * * *

* * *

Insofar as petioners contend that the basic purpose of a § 1983 damages award should be to compensate persons for injuries caused by the deprivation of constitutional rights, they have the better of the argument. Rights, constitutional and otherwise, do not exist in a vacuum. Their purpose is to protect persons from injuries to particular interests, and their contours are shaped by the interests they protect.

Our legal system's concept of damages reflects this view of legal rights. "The cardinal principal of damages in Anglo-American law is that of *compensation* for the injury caused to plaintiff by defendant's breach of duty." * * * The Court implicitly has recognized the applicability of this principle to actions under § 1983 by stating that damages are available under that section for actions "found . . . to have been violative of . . . constitutional rights *and to have caused compensable injury.* . . . " *Wood* v. *Strickland,* 420 U.S., at 319 (emphasis supplied). * * *

The Members of the Congress that enacted § 1983 did not address directly the question of damages, but the principle that damages are designed to compensate persons for injuries caused by the deprivation of rights hardly could have been foreign to the many lawyers in Congress in 1871. Two other sections of the Civil Rights Act of 1871 appear to incoporate this principle, and no reason suggests itself for reading § 1983 differently. To the extent that Congress intended that awards under § 1983 should deter the deprivation of constitutional rights, there is no evidence that it meant to establish a deterrent more formidable than that inherent in the award of compensatory damages. * * *

It is less difficult to conclude that damages awards under § 1983 should be governed by the principle of compensation than it is to apply this principle to concrete cases. But over the centuries the common law of torts has developed a set of rules to implement the principle that a person should be compensated fairly for injuries caused by the violation of his legal rights. These rules, defining the elements of damages and the prerequisites for their recovery, provide the appropriate starting point for the inquiry under § 1983 as well.

It is not clear, however, that common-law tort rules of damages will provide a complete solution to the damages issue in every § 1983 case. In some cases, the interests protected by a particular branch of the common law of torts may parallel closely the interests protected by a particular constitutional right. In such cases, it may be appropriate to apply the tort rules of damages directly to the § 1983 action. * * * In other cases, the interests protected by a particular constitutional right may not also be

protected by an analogous branch of the common law of torts. * * *
In those cases, the task will be the more difficult one of adapting common-law rules of damages to provide fair compensation for injuries caused by the deprivation of a constitutional right.

Although this task of adaptation will be one of some delicacy—as this case demonstrates—it must be undertaken. The purpose of § 1983 would be defeated if injuries caused by the deprivation of constitutional rights went uncompensated simply because the common law does not recognize an analogous cause of action. * * * In order to further the purpose of § 1983, the rules governing compensation for injuries caused by the deprivation of constitutional rights should be tailored to the interests protected by the particular right in question—just as the common-law rules of damages themselves were defined by the interests protected in the various branches of tort law. * * *

* * *

Even if respondents' suspensions were justified, and even if they did not suffer any other actual injury, the fact remains that they were deprived of their right to procedural due process. "It is enough to invoke the procedural safeguards of the Fourteenth Amendment that a significant property interest is at stake, whatever the ultimate outcome of a hearing. . . ." * * *

Common-law courts traditionally have vindicated deprivations of certain "absolute" rights that are not shown to have caused actual injury through the award of a nominal sum of money. By making the deprivation of such rights actionable for nominal damages without proof of actual injury, the law recognizes the importance to organized society that those rights be scrupulously observed; but at the same time, it remains true to the principle that substantial damages should be awarded only to compensate actual injury or, in the case of exemplary or punitive damages, to deter or punish malicious deprivations of rights.

Because the right to procedural due process is "absolute" in the sense that it does not depend upon the merits of a claimant's substantive assertions, and because of the importance to organized society that procedural due process be observed, * * * we believe that the denial of procedural due process should be actionable for nominal damages without proof of actual injury. We therefore hold that if, upon remand, the District Court determines that respondents' suspensions were justified, respondents nevertheless will be entitled to recover nominal damages not to exceed one dollar from petitioners.

The judgment of the Court of Appeals is reversed, and the case is remanded for further proceedings consistent with this opinion.

It is so ordered.

II. Educator Liability

A. Intentional Torts

The most common intentional torts with which educators become involved are assault and battery. Battery is the unpermitted and unprivileged contact with another's person, such as striking someone. Actual harm is not necessary in order to bring suit. However, ordinary contact allowed by social usage is not actionable. Assault is the placing of someone in apprehension of immediate harmful or offensive contact. Shaking a fist at someone or holding a weapon in a hostile manner are examples of an assault. Although courts have allowed wide latitude, a teacher may be charged with assault and battery as a result of disciplining a student. A teacher could be held liable if he or she administered punishment while angry or in a brutal, cruel, or excessive manner. Other factors taken into consideration to determine liability would be where on the body the child was struck, the child's age, the child's mental capacity, and the nature of the child's offense. A teacher may use only sufficient force for self-protection when in an altercation with a student or when attempting to restrain a student.

B. Negligence

An educator may be liable if an injury to a student, for instance, can be shown to have resulted from the educator's negligence. Liability for negligence may accrue if it can be shown that the alleged negligent party should have anticipated the possible harmful results of his or her actions or inactions. It differs from the intentional torts in the sense that there is no conscious desire to injure someone. A commonly employed test to determine negligence in a particular factual situation is whether a reasonable and prudent degree of care has been exercised. When this test is used, the question often asked is whether the person accused of negligence acted as a reasonable and prudent person would have acted in a similar situation under similar circumstances.

Several elements must be present to have a valid cause of action for negligence: (1) a legal duty to conform to a standard of conduct for the protection of others, (2) a failure to exercise an appropriate standard of care, (3) a causal connection often referred to as "proximate cause" between the conduct and the resultant injury, and (4) actual loss or damage as a result of the injury.

1. Duty of Care

There is a duty of care not to harm or injure another person with whom a common-law or statutory relationship exists. The common law, for instance, has established a teacher-student relationship that imposes a duty of care on the part of the teacher. The common-law liability may be reduced by statutory provision, as has been done in Illinois. There liability is imposed only for willful or wanton misconduct.

2. Standard of Care

For the most part the standard of care a teacher must exercise to avoid liability is defined as that of the "reasonable and prudent" person. It is that degree of care a reasonable and prudent teacher, charged with like duties, would exercise under similar circumstances. This standard is not absolute, and many factors are taken into consideration when determining liability. The standard of care varies according to such factors as the age of the student, the child's mental capacity, and the environment and circumstances under which an injury took place. The amount of care due school children increases with the immaturity of the child; therefore, it is expected that greater care will be given while supervising extremely young children.

A higher degree of care should also be exercised in such potentially dangerous classroom situations as a "shop" class or a chemistry laboratory than in an English class or a library. Particular circumstances surrounding an injury must also be taken into consideration. If a teacher suffered a disability prior to a student's injury, for instance, the disability would have to be taken into consideration. A teacher is not necessarily liable for all injuries sustained by students, since it would be impossible for a teacher to foresee every possible situation where student injury could result. However, whenever a school-related injury occurs, the question of whether it could have been foreseen will be raised. Because many factors impinge on liability for alleged negligence, dissimilar court judgments are often rendered regarding seemingly similar factual situations.

3. Proximate Cause

A causal connection must exist between a teacher's conduct and the resultant injury for an action in neglience to prevail. The teacher's negligence must be a substantial cause of the injury to a student. Liability may be mitigated, however, if it can be shown that the cause of injury was the result of an intervening act or if responsibility can be legitimately shifted. Misconduct by a student, for instance, could be advanced as an intervening act. Alleging failure to maintain a safe playground could be an example of a legitimate shift of responsibility from a teacher to those responsible for properly maintaining the playground.

4. Actual Loss or Injury

Proof of damage is an essential element in a negligence action. Damages to assuage one's feelings generally cannot be recovered in a negligence action where there has been no actual loss. Damages may be apportioned if more than one person has been adjudged to have been negligent.

C. Defenses for Negligence

In seeking to avoid liability for an allegedly negligent act, a teacher may attempt to demonstrate that the elements necessary to establish negligence discussed above were not present. However, other defenses may be applicable. The more common defenses include contributory negligence and assumption of risk.

Contributory negligence may be available as a defense if it can be demonstrated that the injured party failed to exercise the required degree of care necessary to ensure safety. This defense is not always available to teachers since courts generally consider children unable to act with the same standard of care as adults. Because of their youth students are often careless and do not act in a responsible manner; therefore, it may be difficult to convince a court that they were contributorially negligent.

Assumption of risk may be available as a defense when the injured party knew of the possible danger and either by agreement or actions voluntarily accepted the possibility of harm. Participants in athletic contests or spectators assume the normal risks associated with these activities by voluntarily placing themselves in a potentially harmful environment.

III. Duties of Supervision

Variations in the required common-law or the statutory standard of duty and care among the states make it difficult to generalize about the extent of educators' tort liability in certain situations. Further compounding the difficulty in generalizing about tort liability is that seemingly similar factual situations giving rise to an alleged tort may contain sufficient nuance to produce different court holdings. The following brief descriptions of court decisions are offered as illustrations. Caution should be exercised in generalizing from them since only a partial description of the factual situation is provided, and the duty and standard of care varies among the jurisdictions.

A. Before and after School

In the absence of statutory requirements, courts generally do not find a duty on the part of schools to supervise students on their way to and from school except when they are on school buses. There is no duty, for instance, in the absence of legislation, to provide a school safety patrol. In a case where a seven-year-old child was killed while crossing a road in front of his school, a Louisiana appellate court, *Johnson* v. *Ouachita Parish Police Jury*, 377 So.2d 397 (La. App. Ct. 1979), held that the public school did not have a legal duty to provide safety patrols or adult school-crossing guards.

A duty of care may be established, however, if procedures for supervision are implemented and communicated to parents. Where a school had established procedures for supervision of students leaving school in the afternoons and had informed parents that rules were in force, the Colorado Court of Appeals determined that such a duty did exist. See *Justus* v. *Jefferson County School District R-1,* 683 P.2d 805 (Colo. App. 1984).

Adequate supervision must be afforded students for a reasonable time as they congregate and wait for school to begin in the morning. In a New Jersey decision, *Titus* v. *Lindberg,* 49 N.J. 66, 228 A.2d 65 (1967), a principal was held liable for an injury to a student that occurred before school. In this instance the injury resulted from a paper clip that was propelled by a student waiting for transportation to another school. It was customary for students to arrive at school about 8:00 A.M., although classrooms did not officially open until 8:15 A.M. This incident occurred at approximately 8:05 A.M. The court offered several reasons for its holding that the principal's negligent supervision was a proximate cause of the injury: his failure to announce rules concerning playground supervision before school, to assign teachers to supervision, and personally to provide adequate supervision.

In another Louisiana decision, *Richard* v. *St. Landry Parish School Board,* 344 So.2d 1116 (La. Ct. App. 1977), a teacher was not held liable for an injury to a third grade student that occurred while unsupervised students were cleaning the classroom after school. While engaged at this task, one of the students went through the teacher's desk and found a knife, which subsequently was used to inflict injury. In its opinion, the court emphasized that the students had been forbidden to go near the desk and, furthermore, the teacher had not placed the knife in the student's hand.

In a California decision, *Bartell* v. *Palos Verdes Peninsula School District,* 83 Cal. App.3d 492, 147 Cal. Rptr. 898 (1978), the school district was not held liable for an injury occuring after school hours. In this instance a twelve-year-old boy was fatally injured while playing a skateboard version of crack-the-whip after school hours. The court maintained that school districts and their employees are placed under a general duty to supervise the conduct of children on school grounds during school sessions, school activities, recesses, and lunch periods. Furthermore, the court stated:

> To require virtual round-the-clock supervision or prison-tight security for school premises, as plaintiffs suggest, would impose a financial burden which manifestly would impinge on the very educational purpose for which the school exists. While it is common knowledge that children often heedlessly engage in games or activities which are dangerous or harmful to their health, at some point the obligation of the public entity to answer for the malfeasance or misfeasance of others, whether children or parents, reaches its outer limits. Public entities labor under budgetary constraints which peculiarly affect their obligation of care. * * * (P. 500)

B. During School Hours

Generally, the standard of care owed to pupils by a teacher during school hours is that care which a reasonable and prudent teacher would observe in comparable circumstances.

A court in Louisiana ruled that a school board was not liable for injuries to a student by a rock thrown on school property. The court held that adequate supervision had been provided for the students and that reasonable supervision did not require constant supervision of every child on the playground. See *Hampton* v. *Orleans Parish School Board*, 422 So.2d 202 (La. App. 1982).

Although a state statute may require a teacher to "keep good order" in the classroom, this implies the use of reasonable force and does not authorize the teacher's use of excessive force. A Florida court, in *Williams* v. *Cotton*, 346 So.2d 1039 (Fla. App. Ct. 1977), held that a teacher, in attempting to restore order to his classroom, could not exceed the bounds of a reasonable and prudent person by using such excessive force that it injures a student.

Schools must provide proper supervision during times when students are out of class, such as recess, passing through the halls, or lunch hour. The California Supreme Court, in *Dailey* v. *Los Angeles Unified School District*, 2 Cal.3d 741, 470 P.2d 360, 87 Cal. Rptr. 376 (1970), contended that school authorities were negligent in the supervision provided at a noon recess. In this case two high school students engaged in "slap fighting," a form of boxing employing open hands, which resulted in the death of one of the students. The court maintained that since adolescent high school students are not adults, they should not be expected to exhibit the degree of discretion and judgment associated with mature adults. Therefore, the court contended it was negligent not to have a comprehensive schedule of supervising assignments and proper instructions for subordinates as to what was expected of them while they were supervising.

A physical education teacher was found to have a duty of properly instructing students before a vertical jumping exercise was attempted. After she failed to provide sufficient instruction, a child suffered injury when she ran into a wall while performing the exercise. Although the court felt that the facts of the case should be ascertained in a jury trial, it was noted that proper instruction could have prevented the injury. See *Dibortolo* v. *Metropolitan School District of Washington Township*, 440 N.E.2d 506 (Ind. App. 1982).

Schools may be liable for injury to a student who leaves school without school or parental permission. In one such case, *Hoyem* v. *Manhatten Beach City School District*, 22 Cal.3d 508, 585 P.2d 851, 150 Cal. Rptr. 1 (1978), the California Supreme Court held that the school district could be held liable for injuries suffered by a ten-year-old truant student who was hit by a motorcycle. The court contended that the school district would not be liable for injury sustained by a truant under all circumstances; however, the school district would be legally responsible if the district's supervisory procedures to thwart truancy fell below that degree of care which reasonably prudent persons would exercise.

C. Off-Campus Activities

Required participation in off-campus activities, such as a field trip or excursion, or interscholastic activities, such as athletics or debate, places the school in the same position of duty to use care to prevent injury as if students were on campus.

In Florida, for instance, a teacher and principal were found to be negligent in failing to supervise school club activities. When a student was injured during a hazing incident, the court ruled that the school had violated a duty of supervision that had been established by school board policy when the club advisor was appointed. The court felt that the incident would not have occurred if the advisor had been present. See *Rupp* v. *Bryant*, 417 So.2d 658 (Fla. 1982).

A school district was found negligent in failing to provide adequate supervision at a required attendance by students of a downtown showing of a controversial movie entitled *King*. Students were bused to the theater accompanied by chaperones. Obscene racial comments were made by both white and black students during the showing. Upon leaving the balcony for the lobby, a student was pushed, her wrist slashed, and her purse taken. The Minnesota Supreme Court in *Raleigh* v. *Independent School District No. 625*, 275 N.W.2d 572 (Minn. 1979), upheld the awarding of damages against the school for failure to provide sufficient precautions in the light of having knowledge about racial tensions.

IV. Parental Consent

Written parental consent for participation in extracurricular activities, such as athletic competition or travel related to a school activity, is often required by school district policy. The importance of having parental consent for travel to an off-campus activity is obvious. One can only imagine the difficulty, and increased legal complications, in having to inform parents of an off-campus injury to their child when those parents had no knowledge of an away-from-school activity or had not given consent for their child to participate. Parental consent forms may contain language purporting to release the school from liability in the event of an injury. It is questionable whether such a signed form would offer those supervising the school activity any immunity from suit in the event of negligence. Parental consent not only would be a surrendering of the independent claim of the child but would also be considered by many courts to be counter to public policy because it was the intentional waiving of a suit to recover damages for subsequent negligent supervision.

V. Malpractice

Suits alleging "educational malpractice" have been brought in several states. Plaintiffs in these suits generally allege that the school district has been negligent because it has issued a certificate or diploma, yet the student does not have the basic academic skills necessary for such tasks as understanding and completing a job application. In one of the first suits of this kind, *Peter W.* v. *San Francisco Unified School District*, 60 Cal. App.3d 814, 131 Cal. Rptr. 854 (1976), plaintiff's position was not upheld. The California court contended that failure of educational achievement is not an injury within the meaning of tort law. Additionally, the court stated:

> . . . Few of our institutions, if any, have aroused the controversies, or incurred the public dissatisfaction, which have attended the operation of the public schools during the last few decades. Rightly or wrongly, but widely, they are charged with outright failure in the achievement of their educational objectives; according to some critics, they bear responsibility for many of the social and moral problems of our society at large. Their public plight in these respects is attested in the daily media, in bitter governing board elections, in wholesale rejections of school bond proposals, and in survey upon survey. To hold them to an actionable "duty of care," in the discharge of their academic functions, would expose them to the tort claims—real or imagined—of disaffected students and parents in countless numbers. They are already beset by social and financial problems which have gone to major litigation, but for which no permanent solution has yet appeared. . . . The ultimate consequences, in terms of public time and money, would burden them—and society—beyond calculation. (P. 825)

In another decision, *Donohue* v. *Copiague Union Free School District*, 47 N.Y.2d 440, 391 N.E.2d 1352, 418 N.Y.S.2d 375 (1979), New York's Court of Appeals also disallowed a cause of action against a school district that sought monetary damages for educational malpractice. The plaintiff alleged that notwithstanding his receipt of a certificate of graduation, he lacked "the rudimentary ability to comprehend written English on a level sufficient to enable him to complete applications for employment." In its decision the court held that

> the Constitution places the obligation of *maintaining and supporting* a system of public schools upon the *Legislature*. To be sure, this general directive was never intended to impose a duty flowing directly from a local school district to individual pupils to ensure that each pupil receives a minimum level of education, the breach of which duty would entitle a pupil to compensatory damages. . . . (P. 443)

Recent educational-malpractice litigation has addressed claims for monetary damages resulting from misdiagnoses of learning abilities or of special educational needs. In 1982 the Maryland Supreme Court considered a claim based on a complaint that a school system had negligently evaluated a first-grade student and had consequently caused him to be taught first-grade materials for a second year while he was physically placed in second grade. Charges were also made that certain educators had furnished false information concerning the child's learning problems, had altered school records to cover their actions, and had demeaned the child. In reviewing earlier malpractice claims the court concluded that an award of monetary damages represents an inappropriate remedy for errors in the educational process. It noted, however, that the parents could take later legal action against the educators who had demonstrated alleged outrageous conduct. See *Hunter* v. *Board of Education of Montgomery County*, 292 Md. 481, 439 A.2d 582 (1982).

A Michigan appellate court also considered monetary claims resulting from misdiagnosis of a language impairment. Although the child had been treated for a period of time based on the diagnosis, the court held the speech therapist and the school system to be immune from liability. Since the evaluation and treatment of speech problems were a part of the regular functions of a school system, the court ruled that school personnel should not be held liable in tort for honest mistakes. See *Brosnan* v. *Livonia Public Schools*, 123 Mich. App. 377, 333 N.W.2d 288 (1983). A Montana decision, however, supported the monetary claims of foster parents of a child who had been improperly placed in a program for the educable mentally retarded. Since the child had been placed in the program despite scores showing that the placement was inappropriate, the court ruled that this case was not like other educational-malpractice claims. This situation involved misplacement despite accurate knowledge of ability scores, not misdiagnosis of a handicap. See *B.M.* v. *Montana*, 649 P.2d 425 (Mont. 1982).

VI. Insurance

Although it is important for educators to be aware of their potential liability for failure to act in a reasonable and prudent manner in preventing injury, the fear of significant monetary loss has been lessened by the availability of liability insurance. Many educators have such coverage as a part of their membership in a professional organization. Individual liability-insurance policies are also available. Although a strong case for liability may be made against them, particularly impecunious, uninsured educators are often unlikely candidates for suit.

Questions

What is the status of school district immunity in your state? What are the advantages and disadvantages of school district immunity?

What is the common law or statutory duty and standard of care in your state for tortious liability of individual school board members? administrators? teachers?

appendix a

analyzing
a court decision

Significant information may be extracted from court decisions by employing an orderly process such as a case analysis, sometimes referred to as "briefing" a case. General categories of information included in a case analysis are the title and citation of the case, the level or type of court hearing the case, the relevant facts involved in the case, the disputed issue or issues in the case, the holding or holdings of the court, the legal doctrine(s) or legal principle(s) underlying the decision, and the significance of the decision regarding future actions of individuals or institutions.

TITLE AND CITATION

The title of the decision contains the name of the litigants. A judicial citation contains the volume number and page number of the reporter system(s) in which the decision appears as well as the year in which the decision was issued. A complete citation includes reference to all reporter systems, official or unofficial, in which the decision appears. These are referred to as parallel citations. See appendix B for a fuller explanation of the citation process.

LEVEL OR TYPE OF COURT

Noting the level or type of court hearing the case is important because it indicates the federal or state jurisdiction immediately affected by the decision. For example, decisions by the United States Supreme Court or states' highest courts represent the final authority on issues within the courts' respective jurisdictions.

FACTS

Facts include the actual circumstances, events, or occurrences involved in the case. Disputed facts must be resolved at the trial level. Appellate courts do not decide questions of fact. Their decision is based on the facts given. If these are insufficient, the case may be remanded to the lower court for further proceedings to determine additional facts.

ISSUE

An issue is a disputed point or question of law upon which a legal action is based. One or more issues may be present in a single case. Issues are of two types, procedural and substantive. Procedural issues involve specific disputed questions of law, and these issues are the basis for an appeal to a higher court. They may include whether a particular legal motion should have been granted or denied, whether certain information was admissible, or whether injunctive relief should have been granted. Substantive issues, on the other hand, involve broader questions of legal rights and principles, such as liberty and property interests. Substantive issues are generally of greater importance to the nonlawyer/student of school law.

HOLDING

The court's decision consists of a holding or holdings in regard to the question or questions before it and usually includes an opinion stating the reasons for the particular holding(s). Written opinions normally include an analysis of the arguments and supporting legal precedent presented by each side and the court's examination of the arguments, precedents, statutes, and facts applicable to the decision.

Concurring or dissenting opinions written by individual judges are frequently included in court decisions. In these opinions judges may discuss reasons for agreeing or disagreeing with the action of the court, elaborate on the issues considered by the court, or introduce additional principles or concepts not considered in the majority opinion. Concurring and dissenting opinions are often quite beneficial in analyzing the decision of the court.

In addition, decisions often include dicta, additional statements of opinion by the court or an individual judge concerning a question or point of law that arises during the hearing of a case. Since these comments may not be vital to the formulation of the holding, they are not binding as precedent. However, dicta may indicate the persuasion of a particular court or judge.

In some instances, if specific legal relief is required or if the appellate court wishes the trial court to reexamine the case in the light of the appellate court's legal reasoning, a case may be remanded to the trial court.

LEGAL DOCTRINE

Court decisions generally are based on a particular legal doctrine or principle. Analysis of a decision includes identifying the doctrine or principle and determining how it is affected by the decision. For example, a student should attempt to ascertain whether a decision may establish, distinguish, extend, affirm, modify, overturn, or reverse a legal doctrine.

SIGNIFICANCE

A concise statement of the implications of the decision with regard to future actions by individuals and institutions completes the analysis. Naturally, certain decisions possess greater significance for educational practices than do others.

A court decision's significance is determined to a large degree by its generalizability to a particular judicial jurisdiction. For example, courts in different jurisdictions may disagree on particular issues when no precedent has been established by a higher court. Consequently, an authoritative decision in one jurisdiction may not be applicable to actions within other jurisdictions. In fact, courts in other jurisdictions may reach opposite decisions.

appendix b

an introduction to research in school law

There are several sources with which an educator may begin legal research. These may be divided into three broad categories—primary sources, secondary sources, and finding aids. Primary sources of law represent some form of binding or highly persuasive authority. State and federal statutes and constitutional provisions, along with court decisions interpreting them, are the most important primary sources of law. Secondary-source materials provide interpretive references regarding primary sources of law. Textbooks and casebooks, periodicals and law reviews, dissertations, legal encyclopedias, and legal dictionaries are examples of secondary materials. In addition, finding aids facilitate the location of primary sources of law related to a particular topic of interest. These include digests of the case law, citators, and various indexing materials.

Thorough legal research involves a systematic examination of an appropriate portion of the voluminous legal literature. This examination may be facilitated by the use of numerous research aids. While the aids are quite effective in locating relevant materials, a word of caution may be appropriate. A limitation to most legal research aids is the perspective of an aid's publisher. Many publications in the legal field are prepared primarily for use by attorneys and may not necessarily address the needs of the educational researcher.

Legal issues may be divided into substantive and procedural ones. Procedural issues address the various rules of form in legal proceedings, whereas substantive issues are concerned with legal rights and principles. Procedural questions are generally of greater interest to attorneys than to educators; therefore, the location of substantive legal information is emphasized in this discussion of legal research.

ELEMENTS OF SCHOOL LAW RESEARCH

Primary Sources of Law

Statutes

Federal statutes are officially compiled according to topic in the *United States Code* (U.S.C.). Unofficial annotated editions of the federal statutes are available in the *United States Code Annotated* (U.S.C.A.) and *United States Code Service* (U.S.C.S.). Annotated versions include supplemental historical notes, editorial comments, and a digest of interpretive court decisions related to each provision. When applicable, rules and regulations designed to assist in the implementation of federal statutes are published in the *Federal Register* (Fed. Reg.), the *Code of Federal Regulations* (C.F.R.), and *A Compilation of Federal Education Laws,* which is prepared for the use of the House Committee on Education and Labor and the Senate Committee of Human Resources. Official state codes and unofficial annotated versions generally group related statutes into chapters, which are indexed to facilitate search within the volumes. Laws related to the schools are often included in chapters entitled "Education" or "Schools and School Districts." Both official codes and related annotated publications are kept up to date by the use of paperback pocket supplements. Unofficial annotated codes often provide faster and more convenient supplementation as well as additional analytical and interpretive material. Local ordinances are not generally compiled in a standardized code; however, some counties and larger cities may publish local ordinances.

Constitutions

Provisions of federal and state constitutions may be located in several sources. The *United States Code* contains the official text of the Constitution of the United States. Annotated versions appear in the *United States Code Annotated* and *United States Code Service.* Similarly, state constitutions are generally set forth in official state codes. Annotated state constitutions are available for many states.

Court Decisions

Disputes between parties and the interpretation of statutory and constitutional provisions are resolved in court decisions. Lawsuits are initiated in trial courts, which examine the formal written statements of the parties and hear the parties' oral arguments as well as the testimony of witnesses. Trial court decisions may be appealed to higher courts. These appellate courts do not repeat the trial proceedings; rather, the courts review the written record of lower courts' decisions. They may affirm, reverse, vacate, or modify the judgment of the lower courts or order that a case be tried again.

Most trial-court decisions are not reported for general distribution. Therefore, copies of trial-court decisions usually must be obtained from the court issuing the decision. However, decisions of most appellate courts and certain trial courts are available in official and unofficial reporters. Reporters are published in a series of numbered bound volumes. Preliminary paperback booklets containing the most recent decisions available, referred to as advance sheets, are issued periodically as supplements to the bound volumes. These advance sheets are compiled to form the subsequent bound volumes of the reporters. Unofficial reporters are useful because of greater speed of publication through more extensive use of advance sheets. In addition, they include special research aids as well as other supplementary materials.

United States Supreme Court
Decisions of the United States Supreme Court are officially reported in the *United States Reports* (U.S.). Supreme Court decisions also appear in two privately published unofficial reporters called the *Supreme Court Reporter* (S.Ct.) and the *United States Supreme Court Reports, Lawyers' Edition* (L.Ed.). Although unofficial reporters include features unique to their particular series, text of the Court's decisions is identical in these reporters.

Each decision of the Supreme Court is reported by the Court in a separate pamphlet shortly after the decision is announced. These slip opinions are the first official text of the Court's decisions. Slip opinions are later paginated and compiled into advance sheets.

Supreme Court decisions also appear in two unofficial looseleaf publications. *United States Law Week* (U.S.L.W.) and the *Supreme Court Bulletin* (S.Ct.Bull.) report Supreme Court decisions immediately after they are issued by the Court. These publications provide the researcher timely access to reported decisions of the Supreme Court.

Lower Federal Courts

Decisions of the lower federal courts may be found in two publications. Decisions of the United States Courts of Appeals are published in the *Federal Reporter* (F.), now in its second series, *Federal Reporter, Second Series* (F.2d). Selected decisions of the United States District Courts are contained in the *Federal Supplement* (F.Supp.). *Federal Rules Decisions* (F.R.D.) includes various lower-federal-court decisions addressing procedural issues. In addition to these publications, a selection of annotated federal court decisions addressing particular areas of legal questions is offered in *American Law Reports—Federal* (A.L.R.).

State Courts

Decisions of state courts are published in two main sources. In many states official reporters are published by the courts. Where such reporters are available, they provide the authoritative texts of the reported decisions. Generally, only decisions of the state's highest court are officially reported; however, several states also report decisions of lower appellate courts. Slip opinions and advance sheets are not always incorporated within state courts' reporting systems.

The National Reporter System provides the most comprehensive system of unofficial reports of state court decisions. Within the National Reporter System, which also includes the *Supreme Court Reporter, Federal Reporter,* and *Federal Supplement,* the nation is divided into geographic regions for the purpose of reporting state court decisions. Reporters for each of the seven regions are published periodically containing state supreme court decisions and many state appellate court decisions within the region.* These regional reporters are supplemented by the *California Reporter* (Cal. Rptr.) and *New York Supplement* (N.Y.S.), including selected decisions of the lower courts in those two states. Some states have ceased official publication of court decisions and adopted the appropriate regional reporter as the state's official reporter.

Selected significant state court decisions are also published in *American Law Reports* (A.L.R.). These unofficial reports include analytical annotations to each decision, which discuss the various points of law presented in the case.

Judicial Citation

In order to locate reported court decisions contained in the diverse official and unofficial reporters, a shorthand method of reference is provided by a system of judicial citation. A citation of a reported court decision

*The seven regions and their states are: *Atlantic* (A. or A.2d)—Conn., Del., Maine, Md., N.H., N.J., Pa., R.I., Vt.; *Northeastern* (N.E. or N.E.2d)—Ill., Ind., Mass., N.Y., Ohio; *Southeastern*—(S.E. or S.E.2d)—Ga., N.C., S.C., Va., W. Va; *Southern* (So. or So.2d)—Ala., Fla., La., Miss.; *Southwestern* (S.W. or S.W.2d)—Ark., Ky., Mo., Tenn., Tex.; *Northwestern* (N.W. or N.W.2d)—Iowa, Mich., Minn., Nebr., N.D., S.D., Wis.; *Pacific* (P. or P.2d)—Alaska, Ariz., Calif., Colo., Hawaii, Idaho, Kans., Mont., Nev., N.M., Okla., Oreg., Utah, Wash., Wyo.

reveals specific information regarding where the decision is reported. For example, a researcher investigating the subject of student-hair regulations and the law might determine that the decision in *Karr v. Schmidt*, 460 F.2d 609 (5th Cir. 1972), is applicable. In this instance the title of the case, *Karr v. Schmidt*, indicates that Karr and Schmidt are the parties involved in the action. In case titles *versus* is abbreviated by a lower-case *v.* When legal action is initiated in the court of original jurisdiction, the plaintiff's name is listed first. However, upon appeal of the case, the names of the parties may switch positions or be altered should the parties to the action change. Following the case title is a reference to the volume number, the title of the reporter, and the page number at which the decision appears. *Karr v. Schmidt*, for instance, is reported in volume number 460 of the *Federal Reporter, Second Series,* (F.2d), beginning on page 609. This particular format is consistent throughout all case citations. The initial number designates the volume number of the reporter; then the title of the reporter and the series are indicated, followed by the page number on which the text of the decision begins. Within parentheses following the information regarding the reporter is the year in which the decision was issued and in some instances the court issuing the decision. In 1972 the United States Court of Appeals for the Fifth Circuit issued the decision in *Karr v. Schmidt*.

As a second example, consider *Wood v. Mount Lebanon School District*, 342 F. Supp. 1293 (W.D.Pa. 1972). Here the decision in the case of *Wood v. Mount Lebanon School District* is reported in volume 342 of the *Federal Supplement* at page 1293. A federal district court for the western district of Pennsylvania rendered the decision in 1972.

When decisions appear in more than one reporter, parallel, also known as dual, citations are often used to indicate other sources in which the decision is reported. When parallel citations are used, the official reporter, or authoritative text of the decision, is cited first. For example, the citation to the well-known Bible reading and prayer decision of the United States Supreme Court may appear as *Abington School District v. Schempp*, 374 U.S. 203, 83 S.Ct. 1560, 10 L.Ed.2d 844 (1963). This parellel citation reveals that the decision is officially reported in volume 374 of the *United States Reports* at page 203, and also appears in volume 83 of the *Supreme Court Reporter* at page 1560, and in the second series of the *United States Supreme Court Reports, Lawyers' Edition,* at page 844 of volume 10. The decision was issued by the Court in 1963. Consider a decision of the California Supreme Court, cited as *Morrison v. State Board of Education*, 1 Cal.3d 214, 461 P.2d 375, 82 Cal. Rptr. 175 (1969). In 1969, the California Supreme Court issued a decision in the case, which was officially reported by the court in the first volume of the *California Reports, Third Series* at page 214. Two unofficial reporters of the National Reporter System contain the decision as well: volume 461 of the *Pacific Reporter, Second Series* at page 375 and volume 82 of the *California Reporter* at page 175.

Explanatory words or phrases often appear in citations in explanation of the prior or subsequent history of a case. For example, in *State* v. *Young*, 234 Ga. 488, 216 S.E.2nd 586 (1975), cert. denied, 423 U.S. 1039 (1975), a decision of the Georgia Supreme Court, issued in 1975, is reported in volume 234 of the *Georgia Reports* at page 488 and volume 216 of the *Southeastern Reporter, Second Series,* at page 586. In that same year the United States Supreme Court denied certiorari (declined to review the case). This action by the Court is reported on page 1039 of volume 423 of the *United States Reports*. In *Alabama Civil Liberties Union* v. *Wallace*, 331 F.Supp. 966 (M.D. Ala. 1971), aff'd, 456 F.2d 1069 (5th Cir. 1972), a 1971 decision by a federal district court for the middle district of Alabama is reported in the *Federal Supplement* at page 966 of volume 331. Action in which the United States Court of Appeals for the Fifth Circuit affirmed the lower court's decision the following year is reported in volume 456 of the *Federal Reporter, Second Series* at page 1069.

In addition to court decisions, many other sources of legal literature are subject to similar uniform rules of citation. However, a treatment of all of these areas is beyond the scope of this discussion. For a generally accepted reference to rules of citation for all forms of legal literature, the researcher is directed to *A Uniform System of Citation,* published by the Harvard Law Review Association.

Board of Education Policies and Regulations

At the state and local levels the educational system is subject to policies and procedures implemented by the appropriate boards of education. State board of education policies are generally arranged according to subject matter and available in a form providing convenient access and rapid updating. While local board policies are most likely available in printed form, access to them may be somewhat less convenient for the researcher.

Attorney General Opinions

States' legal counsels are frequently requested to issue advisory opinions concerning proposed legislative or administrative action or questions related to present constitutional and statutory provisions. While these opinions are only advisory, they are often helpful in the study of legal topics. Reports of attorneys general are published by many states.

Secondary Sources of Legal Literature

Textbooks and Casebooks

Available textbooks in the field of school law vary from general texts to brief monographs presenting discussion of a specific area of school law. While some textbooks offer in-depth analysis of legal issues, others contain no endeavors at such scholarly analysis, but provide convenient manuals to introduce the reader to particular issues in school law. Many textbooks contain tables of cases, bibliographies, or other reference materials that may serve as useful research aids. Casebooks contain edited versions of decisions with particular significance. These works often provide supplementary, explanatory, and interpretive material. Although textbooks and casebooks provide valuable information, they are somewhat limited in that they may become dated as the law changes and interpretive court decisions are rendered.

Periodical and Law Review Articles

Expositive articles of interest may be found in the legal and educational literature. Law reviews and bar journals are indexed in the *Index to Legal Periodicals*. *Shephard's Law Review Citations*, a compilation of citations to articles in over one hundred law reviews and legal periodicals, enables the researcher to determine where articles appearing in these publications in recent decades have been cited in subsequent articles and in federal or state court decisions. *The Journal of Law and Education* is a specialized journal containing articles related to school law issues. Educational periodical articles related to legal topics may be located by utilizing the *Education Index, Current Index to Journals in Education*, and *Educational Administration Abstracts*.

Dissertations

Unpublished doctoral research often provides comprehensive treatment of particular topics regarding education and the law. Pertinent dissertations may be identified by examining *Dissertation Abstracts International* and the *Comprehensive Dissertation Index, 1861–1972, 1973–1982*, and subsequent yearly editions.

Encyclopedias

Corpus Juris Secundum and *American Jurisprudence 2d*, the two major legal encyclopedias of national scope, include narrative discussion of a wide variety of legal topics. Each series of encyclopedias includes volumes providing a general index and topical indexes (such as Schools and School Districts) of the subject matter. In addition, several state encyclopedias are published following the same basic format as the national publications.

Since the copious extended footnotes contain numerous case references, these encyclopedias are often quite helpful in locating pertinent court decisions. However, the encyclopedias may not always be as helpful as they might first appear. Although periodic supplements are published, it is difficult for works of this nature to reflect accurately the rapidly changing law. Suffering from the same limitations as many other encyclopedic efforts, the works are often criticized for a lack of scholarly analysis and a tendency toward oversimplification and generalization regarding complex legal issues.

Legally significant words and phrases are listed alphabetically in an encyclopedic collection entitled *Words and Phrases*. Each word or phrase is followed by brief summaries of judicial decisions in which it has been interpreted or defined, as well as citations to the decisions. Annual supplements are issued to keep *Words and Phrases* up to date.

Other Secondary Materials

Additional aids may be helpful in employing the various research procedures. For example, *A Uniform Code of Citation*, commonly referred to as the Bluebook, provides a generally accepted standard for the rules of citation and style. This reference enables the researcher to report research effectively and may answer questions related to the shorthand system of legal citation. Legal terms and abbreviations may be clarified by the use of a reputable legal dictionary, such as *Black's Law Dictionary, Revised Fifth Edition.*

Finding Aids

Various methods may be employed to locate pertinent court decisions. Each of the various sources possesses particular strengths and limitations, but may be used effectively in reviewing the existing case law. It is not likely that a particular method of case finding will prove most effective in all situations. Consideration of the individual research problem, the tools available, and the researcher's personal preference will probably determine which sources are employed in the search for applicable case law.

Case Digests

The *American Digest System* provides an exhaustive compilation of case references, appearing under alphabetically arranged topic headings (such as Schools and School Districts). The system is divided into decennial digests, each addressing a ten-year period. *The Ninth Decennial Digest* deals with the years 1976–1986. Cases reported since 1986 are included in the *General Digest, Seventh Series.* The system's current component is kept up to date by the use of paperback supplements issued monthly.

In addition to the *American Digest System*, digests devoted to the geographic regions covered by most of the regional reporters and many of the individual states are available. There are also digests dealing solely with federal court decisions, as well as a digest covering decisions of the United States Supreme Court.

Specialty Law Digest: Education Cases, first published in 1982 and annually thereafter, indexes all published decisions of state and federal courts on educational issues. Monthly updates include scholarly analyses of several topical issues and a state-by-state survey of that month's significant litigation.

Looseleaf Services

Several looseleaf services are published that aid in locating pertinent court decisions. A bimonthly publication of the National Organization on Legal Problems of Education, the *NOLPE School Law Reporter,* contains brief summaries and citations to judicial decisions related to school law. Among the looseleaf services available, the *School Law Reporter* provides the most comprehensive source of school law cases. Decisions addressing school law issues are also cited and summarized in the *School Law Bulletin* and *Education Court Digest. United States Law Week* and the *Supreme Court Reporter* provide rapid access to recent United States Supreme Court decisions. Both of these publications also include information concerning Court proceedings, calendars, cases docketed, and general Court news. In addition, *United States Law Week* includes a section entitled *General Law,* summarizing significant weekly developments in all legal areas, including judicial, legislative, and administrative actions at both the state and federal levels.

Annotated Codes and Reporters

Annotated constitutions and statutory codes are useful sources for ascertaining applicable case law. Citations and summaries of interpretive court decisions are usually included in the analytical annotations to the particular provisions.

American Law Reports and *American Law Reports—Federal* report a small selection of significant cases, each annotated by an editorial discussion of the point of law dealt with in the case. Appropriate tables of cases, word indexes, and digests are published in conjunction with these, facilitating the location of decisions and annotations. Related cases are cited within the analytical annotations.

Secondary Materials

Secondary materials previously discussed may be helpful as sources of case citations. Textbooks, periodical and law review articles, dissertations, and encyclopedias often include numerous references to court decisions within their text and footnotes. In addition, summaries of recent school law cases are published in issues of the *Journal of Law and Education.* The *School Law Yearbook,* published annually by the National Organization of

Legal Problems of Education, also contains numerous references to decisions addressing a diverse selection of school law issues.

Shephard's Citations

A court decision's current status may be determined by using an appropriate volume of *Shephard's Citations*. It is possible to ascertain whether a decision has been affirmed, reversed, overrruled, vacated, distinguished, or otherwise modified by subsequent court action through the use of this comprehensive system of case citators. A series of bound volumes, paperback supplements, and advance sheets covers state and federal decisions reported in an official or unofficial reporter. Volumes are devoted to United States Supreme Court decisions, United States Courts of Appeals decisions, United States District Court decisions, the various regional reporters in the national reporter system, and the individual states. Every volume of *Shephard's Citations* follows a similar format utilizing a system of symbols, which is described in the preliminary pages of each volume.

Besides verifying the current status of court decisions, *Shephard's Citations* provides a method by which parallel citations may be determined, the judicial history of a case may be traced and citations to all subsequent proceedings in a case located. In addition, the citators indicate all subsequent decisions in which a case in question is cited and reveal other research leads, such as periodical and law review articles, attorney general opinions, and annotated reports in which the case is cited.

A system of *Shephard's Citations,* similar to the case citators, is also available to verify the current status of constitutional and statutory provisions. Volumes are devoted to the federal Constitution and statutes and to similar provisions of the individual states, with limited reference to local ordinances contained in the various state volumes. Though use of these citators is considerably more complex than the case citators, similar information is revealed. Subsequent legislative action or court interpretation regarding particular provisions is cited. The legislative and judicial history of a provision may be ascertained to determine whether it has been altered or otherwise affected by such action or interpretation.

Computer-Assisted Services

There are several commercially-available, computer-assisted systems for legal research. Presently, these services include, *Lexis, Westlaw,* and *Auto-Cite.* Primary advantages of using these services include: eliminating the need for direct access to a law library; availability of a wider selection of law materials than most law libraries contain; availability of decisions from most reporter systems; up-to-date shepardizing; access to major law reviews; capability of parallel citations; and specific topic or subject matter search.

A Final Note

A legal researcher may be confident of the fruits of his or her labors when a systematic use of research tools continues to reveal references which have previously been identified. Depending upon the particular problem or issue being examined, it may not be necessary or practical to employ all of the available research procedures that have been discussed.

appendix c

the constitution
of the united states
# of america—edited

PREAMBLE

We the People of the United States, in Order to form a more perfect Union, establish Justice, insure domestic Tranquility, provide for the common defence, promote the general Welfare, and secure the Blessings of Liberty to ourselves and our Posterity, do ordain and establish this Constitution for the United States of America.

ARTICLE I

Section 1. All legislative Powers herein granted shall be vested in a Congress of the United States, which shall consist of a Senate and House of Representatives.

* * *

Section 8. The Congress shall have Power To lay and collect Taxes, Duties, Imposts and Excises, to pay the Debts and provide for the common Defence and general Welfare of the United States; * * *

To constitute Tribunals inferior to the supreme Court; * * *

* * *

Section 10. No state shall * * * pass any * * * Law impairing the Obligation of Contracts, * * *

* * *

ARTICLE II

Section 1. The executive Power shall be vested in a President of the United States of America. * * *

* * *

ARTICLE III

Section 1. The judicial Power of the United States, shall be vested in one supreme Court, and in such inferior Courts as the Congress may from time to time ordain and establish. The Judges, both of the supreme and inferior Courts, shall hold their Offices during good Behavior, and shall, at stated Times, receive for their Services a Compensation, which shall not be diminished during their Continuance in Office.

Section 2. The judicial Power shall extend to all Cases, in Law and Equity, arising under this Constitution, the Laws of the United States, * * *

In all Cases affecting Ambassadors, other public Ministers and Consuls, and those in which a State shall be a Party, the supreme Court shall have original Jurisdiction. In all the other Cases before mentioned, the supreme Court shall have appellate Jurisdiction, both as to Law and Fact, with such Exceptions, and under such Regulations as the Congress shall make.

* * *

ARTICLE IV

Section 1. Full Faith and Credit shall be given in each State to the public Acts, Records, and judicial Proceedings of every other State. And the Congress may by general Laws prescribe the Manner in which such Acts, Records and Proceedings shall be proved, and the Effect thereof.

Section 2. The Citizens of each State shall be entitled to all Privileges and Immunities of Citizens in the several States. * * *

* * *

ARTICLE V

The Congress, whenever two-thirds of both Houses shall deem it necessary, shall propose Amendments to this constitution, or, on the Application of the Legislatures of two-thirds of the several States, shall call a Convention for proposing Amendments, which, in either Case, shall be valid to all Intents and Purposes, as part of this Constitution, when ratified by the Legislatures of three-fourths of the several States, or by Conventions in three-fourths thereof, as the one or the other Mode of Ratification may be proposed by Congress; Provided that no Amendment which may be made prior to the Year One thousand eight hundred and eight shall in any Manner affect the first and fourth Clauses in the Ninth Section of the first Article; and that no State, without its Consent, shall be deprived of its equal Suffrage in the Senate.

ARTICLE VI

* * *

This Constitution, and the Laws of the United States which shall be made in Pursuance thereof; and all Treaties made, or which shall be made, under the Authority of the United States, shall be the supreme Law of the Land; and the Judges in every State shall be bound thereby, any Thing in the Constitution or Laws of any State to the Contrary notwithstanding.

The Senators and Representatives before mentioned, and the Members of the several State Legislatures, and all executive and judicial Officers, both of the United States and of the several States, shall be bound by Oath or Affirmation, to support this Constitution; but no religious

Test shall ever be required as a Qualification to any Office or public Trust under the United States.

* * *

AMENDMENT I [1791]

Congress shall make no law respecting an establishment of religion, or prohibiting the free exercise thereof; or abridging the freedom of speech, or of the press; or the right of the people peaceably to assemble, and to petition the Government for a redress of grievances.

* * *

AMENDMENT IV [1791]

The right of the people to be secure in their persons, houses, papers, and effects, against unreasonable searches and seizures, shall not be violated, and no Warrants shall issue, but upon probable cause, supported by Oath or affirmation, and particularly describing the place to be searched, and the persons or things to be seized.

AMENDMENT V [1791]

No person shall * * * be subject for the same offense to be twice put in jeopardy of life or limb; nor shall be compelled in any criminal case to be a witness against himself, nor be deprived of life, liberty, or property, without due process of law; nor shall private property be taken for public use without just compensation.

AMENDMENT VI [1791]

In all criminal prosecutions, the accused shall enjoy the right to a speedy and public trial, by an impartial jury of the State and district wherein the crime shall have been committed, which district shall have been previously ascertained by law, and to be informed of the nature and cause of the accusation: to be confronted with the witnesses against him; to have compulsory process for obtaining witnesses in his favor, and to have the Assistance of Counsel for his defence.

AMENDMENT VII [1791]

In Suits at common law, where the value in controversy shall exceed twenty dollars, the right of trial by jury shall be preserved, and no fact tried by a jury, shall be otherwise reexamined in any Court of the United States, than according to the rules of the common law.

AMENDMENT VIII [1791]

Excessive bail shall not be required, nor excessive fines imposed, nor cruel and unusual punishments inflicted.

AMENDMENT IX [1791]

The enumeration in the Constitution, of certain rights, shall not be construed to deny or disparage others retained by the people.

AMENDMENT X [1791]

The powers not delegated to the United States by the Constitution, nor prohibited by it to the States, are reserved to the States respectively, or to the people.

AMENDMENT XI [1798]

The Judicial power of the United States shall not be construed to extend to any suit in law or equity, commenced or prosecuted against one of the United States by Citizens of another State, or by Citizens or Subjects of any Foreign State.

* * *

AMENDMENT XIII [1865]

Section 1. Neither slavery nor involuntary servitude, except as a punishment for crime whereof the party shall have been duly convicted, shall exist within the United States, or any place subject to their jurisdiction.

Section 2. Congress shall have power to enforce this article by appropriate legislation.

AMENDMENT XIV [1868]

Section 1. All persons born or naturalized in the United States, and subject to the jurisdiction thereof, are citizens of the United States and of the State wherein they reside. No State shall make or enforce any law which shall abridge the privileges or immunities of citizens of the United States; nor shall any State deprive any person of life, liberty, or property, without due process of law; nor deny to any person within its jurisdiction the equal protection of the laws.

* * *

AMENDMENT XV [1870]

Section 1. The right of citizens of the United States to vote shall not be denied or abridged by the United States or by any State on account of race, color, or previous condition of servitude.

Section 2. The Congress shall have power to enforce this article by appropriate legislation.

AMENDMENT XVI [1913]

The Congress shall have power to lay and collect taxes on incomes, from whatever source derived, without apportionment among the several States, and without regard to any census or enumeration.

* * *

AMENDMENT XIX [1920]

Section 1. The right of citizens of the United States to vote shall not be denied or abridged by the United States or by any State on account of sex.

Section 2. Congress shall have power to enforce this article by appropriate legislation.

* * *

AMENDMENT XXIV [1964]

Section 1. The right of citizens of the United States to vote in any primary or other election for President or Vice President, for electors for President or Vice President, or for Senator or Representative in Congress, shall not be denied or abridged by the United States or any State by reason of failure to pay any poll tax or other tax.

Section 2. The Congress shall have power to enforce this article by appropriate legislation.

* * *

AMENDMENT XXVI [1971]

Section 1. The right of citizens of the United States, who are eighteen years of age or older, to vote shall not be denied or abridged by the United States or by any State on account of age.

Section 2. The Congress shall have power to enforce this article by appropriate legislation.

appendix d

statutory material

Family Educational Rights and Privacy Act of 1974—P.L. 93-380

IMPLEMENTING REGULATIONS—45 CFR 99 (EDITED)

PART 99—PRIVACY RIGHTS OF PARENTS AND STUDENTS

* * *

Subpart A—General

§99.1 Applicability of Part.

(a) This part applies to all educational agencies or institutions to which funds are made available under any Federal [program for which the U.S. Commissioner of Education has administrative responsibility, as specified by law or by delegation of authority pursuant to law.]

　(b) This part does not apply to an educational agency or institution solely because students attending that non-monetary agency or institution receive benefits under one or more of the Federal programs referenced in paragraph (a) of this section, if no funds under those programs are made available to the agency or institution itself.

* * *

(d) Except as otherwise specifically provided, this part applies to education records of students who are or have been in attendance at the educational agency or institution which maintains the records.

* * *

§99.3 Definitions.

As used in this Part:

* * *

"Directory information" includes the following information relating to a student: the student's name, address, telephone number, date and place of birth, major field of study, participation in officially recognized activities and sports, weight and height of members of athletic teams, dates of attendance, degrees and awards received, the most recent previous educational agency or institution attended by the student, and other similar information.

* * *

§99.4 Student Rights.

(a) For the purposes of this part, whenever a student has attained eighteen years of age, or is attending an institution of postsecondary education, the rights accorded to and the consent required of the parent of the student shall thereafter only be accorded to and required of the eligible student.

* * *

§99.5 Formulation of Institutional Policy and Procedures.

(a) Each educational agency or institution shall * * * formulate and adopt a policy of—

(1) Informing parents of students or eligible students of their rights under § 99.6;

(2) Permitting parents of students or eligible students to inspect and review the education records of the student in accordance with § 99.11, including at least:

(i) A statement of the procedure to be followed by a parent or an eligible student who requests to inspect and review the education records of the student;

(ii) With an understanding that it may not deny access to an education record, a description of the circumstances in which the agency or institution feels it has a legitimate cause to deny a request for a copy of such records;

(iii) A schedule of fees for copies, and

(iv) A listing of the types and locations of education records maintained by the educational agency or institution and the titles and addresses of the officials responsible for those records;

(3) Not disclosing personally identifiable information from the education records of a student without the prior written consent of the parent of the student or the eligible student, except as otherwise permitted by §§ 99.31 and 99.37; the policy shall include, at least:

(i) A statement of whether the educational agency or institution will disclose personally identifiable information from the education records of a student under § 99.31(a)(1) and, if so, a specification of the criteria for determining which parties are "school officials" and what the educational agency or institution considers to be a "legitimate educational interest," and

(ii) a specification of the personally identifiable information to be designated as directory information under § 99.37;

(4) Maintaining the record of disclosures of personally identifiable information from the education records of a student required to be maintained by § 99.32, and permitting a parent or an eligible student to inspect that record;

(5) Providing a parent of the student or an eligible student with an opportunity to seek the correction of education records of the student through a request to amend the records or a hearing under Subpart C, and permitting the parent of a student or an eligible student to place a statement in the education records of the student as provided in § 99.21 (c);

(b) The policy required to be adopted by paragraph (a) of this section shall be in writing and copies shall be made available upon request to parents of students and to eligible students.

§99.6 Annual Notification of Rights.

(a) Each educational agency or institution shall give parents of students in attendance or eligible students in attendance at the agency or institution annual notice by such means as are reasonably likely to inform them of the following:

(1) Their rights under section 438 of the Act, the regulations in this part, and the policy adopted under § 99.5; the notice shall also inform

parents of students or eligible students of the location where copies of the policy may be obtained; and

(2) The right to file complaints under § 99.63 concerning alleged failures by the educational agency or institution to comply with the requirements of section 438 of the Act and this part.

(b) Agencies and institutions of elementary and secondary education shall provide for the need to effectively notify parents of students identified as having a primary or home language other than English.

§99.7 Limitations on Waivers.

(a) Subject to the limitations in this section and § 99.12, a parent of a student or a student may waive any of his or her rights under section 438 of the Act or this part. A waiver shall not be valid unless in writing and signed by the parent or student, as appropriate.

(b) An educational agency or institution may not require that a parent of a student or student waive his or her rights under section 438 of the Act or this part. This paragraph does not preclude an educational agency or institution from requesting such a waiver.

(c) An individual who is an applicant for admission to an institution of post-secondary education or is a student in attendance at an institution of post-secondary education may waive his or her right to inspect and review confidential letters and confidential statements of recommendation described in § 99.12(a)(3) except that the waiver may apply to confidential letters and statements only if: (1) The applicant or student is, upon request, notified of the names of all individuals providing the letters or statements; (2) the letters or statements are used only for the purpose for which they were originally intended, and (3) such waiver is not required by the agency or institution as a condition of admission to or receipt of any other service or benefit from the agency or institution.

(d) All waivers under paragraph (c) of this section must be executed by the individual, regardless of age, rather than by the parent of the individual.

(e) A waiver under this section may be made with respect to specified classes of: (1) Education records, and (2) persons or institutions.

(2) A revocation under this paragraph must be in writing.

(3) If a parent of a student executes a waiver under this section, that waiver may be revoked by the student at any time after he or she becomes an eligible student.

§99.8 Fees.

(a) An educational agency or institution may charge a fee for copies of education records which are made for the parents of students, students, and eligible students under section 438 of the Act and this part; *Provided,*

That the fee does not effectively prevent the parents and students from exercising their right to inspect and review those records.

(b) An educational agency or institution may not charge a fee to search for or to retrieve the education records of a student.

Subpart B—Inspection and Review of Education Records

§99.11 Right to Inspect and Review Education Records.

(a) Each educational agency or institution, except as may be provided by § 99.12, shall permit the parent of a student or an eligible student who is or has been in attendance at the agency or institution, to inspect and review the education records of the student. The agency or institution shall comply with a request within a reasonable period of time, but in no case more than 45 days after the request has been made.

(b) The right to inspect and review education records under paragraph (a) of this section includes:

(1) The right to a response from the educational agency or institution to reasonable requests for explanations and interpretations of the records; and

(2) The right to obtain copies of the records from the educational agency or institution where failure of the agency or institution to provide the copies would effectively prevent a parent or eligible student from exercising the right to inspect and review the education records.

(c) An educational agency or institution may presume that either parent of the student has authority to inspect and review the education records of the student unless the agency or institution has been provided with evidence that there is a legally binding instrument, or a State law or court order governing such matters as divorce, separation or custody, which provides to the contrary.

* * *

Subpart C—Amendment of Education Records

§99.20 Request to Amend Education Records.

(a) The parent of a student or an eligible student who believes that information contained in the education records of the student is inaccurate or misleading or violates the privacy or other rights of the student may request that the educational agency or institution which maintains the records amend them.

(b) The educational agency or institution shall decide whether to amend the education records of the student in accordance with the request within a reasonable period of time of receipt of the request.

(c) If the educational agency or institution decides to refuse to amend the education records of the student in accordance with the request it shall so inform the parent of the student or the eligible student of the refusal, and advise the parent or the eligible student of the right to a hearing under § 99.21.

§99.21 Right to a Hearing.

(a) An educational agency or institution shall, on request, provide an opportunity for a hearing in order to challenge the content of a student's education records to insure that information is the education records of the student is not inaccurate, misleading or otherwise in violation of the privacy or other rights of students. The hearing shall be conducted in accordance with §99.22.

(b) If, as a result of the hearing, the educational agency or institution decides that the information is inaccurate, misleading or otherwise in violation of the privacy or other rights of students, it shall amend the education records of the student accordingly and so inform the parent of the student or the eligible student in writing.

(c) If, as a result of the hearing, the educational agency or institution decides that the information is not inaccurate, misleading or otherwise in violation of the privacy or other rights of students, it shall inform the parent or eligible student of the right to place in the education records of the student a statement commenting upon the information in the education records and/or setting forth any reasons for disagreeing with the decision of the agency or institution.

(d) Any explanation placed in the education records of the student under paragraph (c) of this section shall:

(1) Be maintained by the educational agency or institution as part of the education records of the student as long as the record or contested portion thereof is maintained by the agency or institution, and

(2) If the education records of the student or the contested portion thereof is disclosed by the educational agency or institution to any party, the explanation shall also be disclosed to that party.

§99.22 Conduct of the Hearing.

The hearing required to be held by §99.21 (a) shall be conducted according to procedures which shall include at least the following elements:

(a) The hearing shall be held within a reasonable period of time after the educational agency or institution has received the request, and the parent of the student or the eligible student shall be given notice of the date, place and time reasonably in advance of the hearing;

(b) The hearing may be conducted by any party, including an official of the educational agency or institution, who does not have a direct interest in the outcome of the hearing;

(c) The parent of the student or the eligible student shall be afforded a full and fair opportunity to present evidence relevant to the issues raised under §99.21, and may be assisted or represented by individuals of his or her choice at his or her own expense, including an attorney;

(d) The educational agency or institution shall make its decision in writing within a reasonable period of time after the conclusion of the hearing; and

(c) The decision of the agency or institution shall be based solely upon the evidence presented at the hearing and shall include a summary of the evidence and the reasons for the decision.

Subpart D—Disclosure of Personally Identifiable Information From Education Records

§99.30 Prior Consent for Disclosure Required.

(a) (1) An educational agency or institution shall obtain the written consent of the parent of a student or the eligible student before disclosing personally identifiable information from the education records of a student, other than directory information, except as provided in §99.31.

(2) Consent is not required under this section where the disclosure is to (i) the parent of a student who is not an eligible student, or (ii) the student himself or herself.

(b) Whenever written consent is required, an educational agency or institution may presume that the parent of the student or the eligible student giving consent has the authority to do so unless the agency or institution has been provided with evidence that there is a legally binding instrument, or a State law or court order governing such matters as divorce, separation or custody, which provides to the contrary.

(c) The written consent required by paragraph (a) of this section must be signed and dated by the parent of the student or the eligible student giving the consent and shall include:

(1) A specification of the records to be disclosed,

(2) The purpose or purposes of the disclosure, and

(3) The party or class of parties to whom the disclosure may be made.

(d) When a disclosure is made pursuant to paragraph (a) of this section, the educational agency or institution shall, upon request, provide a copy of the record which is disclosed to the parent of the student, and to the student who is not an eligible student if so requested by the student's parents.

§99.31 Prior Consent for Disclosure not Required.

(a) An educational agency or institution may disclose personally identifiable information from the education records of a student without the written consent of the parent of the student or the eligible student if the disclosure is—

(1) To other school officials, including teachers, within the educational institution or local educational agency who have been determined by the agency or institution to have legitimate educational interests;

(2) To officials of another school or school system in which the student seeks or intends to enroll, subject to the requirements set forth in §99.34;

(3) Subject to the conditions set forth in §99.35, to authorized representatives of:

(i) The Comptroller General of the United States,

(ii) The Secretary,

(iii) The Commissioner, the Director of the National Institute of Education, or the Assistant Secretary for Education, or

(iv) State educational authorities;

(4) In connection with financial aid for which a student has applied or which a student has received; *Provided,* That personally identifiable information from the education records of the student may be disclosed only as may be necessary for such purposes as:

(i) To determine the eligibility of the student for financial aid,

(ii) To determine the amount of the financial aid, or

(iii) To determine the conditions which will be imposed regarding the financial aid; or

(iv) To enforce the terms or conditions of the financial aid;

(5) To State and local officials or authorities to whom information is specifically required to be reported or disclosed pursuant to State statute adopted prior to November 19, 1974. This subparagraph applies only to statutes which require that specific information be disclosed to State or local officials and does not apply to statutes which permit but do not require disclosure. Nothing in this paragraph shall prevent a State from further limiting the number or type of State or local officials to whom disclosures are made under this subparagraph;

(6) To organizations conducting studies for, or on behalf of, educational agencies or institutions for the purpose of developing, validating, or administering predictive tests, administering student aid programs, and improving instructions; *Provided,* That the studies are conducted in a manner which will not permit the personal identification of students and their parents by individuals other than representatives of the organization and the information will be destroyed when no longer needed for the purposes for which the study was conducted; the term "organizations"

includes, but is not limited to, Federal, State and local agencies, and independent organizations;

(7) To accrediting organizations in order to carry out their accrediting functions;

(8) To parents of a dependent student, as defined in section 152 of the Internal Revenue Code of 1954;

(9) To comply with a judicial order or lawfully issued subpoena; *Provided,* That the educational agency or institution makes a reasonable effort to notify the parent of the student or the eligible student of the order or subpoena in advance of compliance therewith; and

(10) To appropriate parties in a health or safety emergency subject to the conditions set forth in §99.36.

(b) This section shall not be construed to require or preclude disclosure of any personally identifiable information from the education records of a student by an educational agency or institution to the parties set forth in paragraph (a) of this section.

§99.32 Record of Requests and Disclosures Required to be Maintained.

(a) An educational agency or institution shall for each request for and each disclosure of personally identifiable information from the education records of a student, maintain a record kept with the education records of the student which indicates:

(1) The parties who have requested or obtained personally identifiable information from the education records of the student, and

(2) The legitimate interests these parties had in requesting or obtaining the information.

(b) Paragraph (a) of this section does not apply:

(i) To requests by or disclosure to a parent of a student or an eligible student;

(ii) To requests by or disclosures to school officials under §99.31 (a)(1);

(iii) If there is written consent of a parent of a student or an eligible student, or

(iv) To requests for or disclosure of directory information under §99.37.

(c) The record of requests and disclosures may be inspected,

(1) By the parent of the student or the eligible student,

(2) By the school official and his or her assistants who are responsible for the custody of the records, and

(3) For the purpose of auditing the recordkeeping procedures of the educational agency or institution by the parties authorized in, and under the conditions set forth in §99.31 (a) (1) and (3).

* * *

§99.34 Conditions for Disclosure to Officials of Other Schools and School Systems.

(a) An educational agency or institution transferring the education records of a student pursuant to §99.31(a)(2) shall:

(1) Make a reasonable attempt to notify the parent of the student or the eligible student of the transfer of the records at the last known address of the parent or eligible student, except:

(i) When the transfer of the records is initiated by the parent or eligible student at the sending agency or institution, or

(ii) When the agency or institution includes a notice in its policies and procedures formulated under §99.5 that it forwards education records on request to a school in which a student seeks or intends to enroll; the agency or institution does not have to provide any further notice of the transfer;

(2) Provide the parent of the student or the eligible student, upon request, with a copy of the education records which have been transferred; and

(3) Provide the parent of the student or the eligible student, upon request, with an opportunity for a hearing under Subpart C of this part.

(b) If a student is enrolled in more than one school, or receives services from more than one school, the schools may disclose information from the education records of the student to each other without obtaining the written consent of the parent of the student or the eligible student; *Provided,* That the disclosure meets the requirements of paragraph (a) of this section.

§99.35 Disclosure to Certain Federal and State Officials for Federal Program Purposes.

(a) Nothing in section 438 of the Act or this part shall preclude authorized representatives of officials listed in §99.31(a)(3) from having access to student and other records which may be necessary in connection with the audit and evaluation of Federally supported education programs, or in connection with the enforcement of or compliance with the Federal legal requirements which relate to these programs.

(b) Except when the consent of the parent of a student or an eligible student has been obtained under §99.30 or when the collection of personally identifiable information is specifically authorized by Federal law, any data collected by officials listed in §99.31(a)(3) shall be protected in a manner which will not permit the personal identification of students and their parents by other than those officials, and personally identifiable data shall be destroyed when no longer needed for such audit, evaluation or enforcement of or compliance with Federal legal requirements.

§99.36 Conditions for Disclosure in Health and Safety Emergencies.

(a) An educational agency or institution may disclose personally identifiable information from the education records of a student to appropriate parties in connection with an emergency if knowledge of the information is necessary to protect the health or safety of the student or other individuals.

(b) The factors to be taken into account in determining whether personally identifiable information from the education records of a student may be disclosed under this section shall include the following:

(1) The seriousness of the threat to the health or safety of the student or other individuals;

(2) The need for the information to meet the emergency;

(3) Whether the parties to whom the information is disclosed are in a position to deal with the emergency; and

(4) The extent to which time is of the essence in dealing with the emergency.

(c) Paragraph (a) of this section shall be strictly construed.

§99.37 Conditions for Disclosure of Directory Information.

(a) An educational agency or institution may disclose personally identifiable information from the education records of a student who is in attendance at the institution or agency if that information has been designated as directory information (as defined in §99.3) under paragraph (c) of this section.

(b) An educational agency or institution may disclose directory information from the education records of an individual who is no longer in attendance at the agency or institution without following the procedures under paragraph (c) of this section.

(c) An educational agency or institution which wishes to designate directory information shall give public notice of the following:

(1) The categories of personally identifiable information which the institution has designated as directory information;

(2) The right of the parent of the student or the eligible student to refuse to permit the designation of any or all of the categories of personally identifiable information with respect to that student as directory information; and

(3) The period of time within which the parent of the student or the eligible student must inform the agency or institution in writing that such personally identifiable information is not to be designated as directory information with respect to that student.

Title IX of the Education Amendments of 1972–P.L. 92–318

IMPLEMENTING REGULATIONS—45 CFR 86 (EDITED)

PART 86—NONDISCRIMINATION ON THE BASIS OF SEX IN EDUCATION PROGRAMS AND ACTIVITIES RECEIVING OR BENEFITING FROM FEDERAL FINANCIAL ASSISTANCE

* * *

Subpart A—Introduction

§86.1 Purpose and Effective Date.

The purpose of this part is to effectuate title IX of the Education Amendments of 1972, as amended by Pub. L. 93-568, 88 Stat. 1855 (except sections 904 and 906 of those Amendments) which is designed to eliminate (with certain exceptions) discrimination on the basis of sex in any education program or activity receiving Federal financial assistance, whether or not such program or activity is offered or sponsored by an educational institution as defined in this part. This part is also intended to effectuate section 844 of the Education Amendments of 1974, Pub. L. 93-380, 88 Stat. 484. The effective date of this part shall be July 21, 1975.

§86.3 Remedial and Affirmative Action and Self-evaluation.

(a) *Remedial action.* If the Director finds that a recipient has discriminated against persons on the basis of sex in an education program or activity, such recipient shall take such remedial action as the Director deems necessary to overcome the effects of such discrimination.

(b) *Affirmative action.* In the absence of a finding of discrimination on the basis of sex in an education program or activity, a recipient may take affirmative action to overcome the effects of conditions which resulted in limited participation therein by persons of a particular sex. Nothing herein shall be interpreted to alter any affirmative action obligations which a recipient may have under Executive Order 11246.

* * *

§86.7 Effect of Employment Opportunities.

The obligation to comply with this part is not obviated or alleviated because employment opportunities in any occupation or profession are or may be more limited for members of one sex than for members of the other sex.

§86.8 Designation of Responsible Employee and Adoption of Grievance Procedures.

(a) *Designation of responsible employee.* Each recipient shall designate at least one employee to coordinate its efforts to comply with and carry out its responsibilities under this part, including any investigation of any complaint communicated to such recipient alleging its noncompliance with this part or alleging any actions which would be prohibited by this part. The recipient shall notify all its students and employees of the name, office address and telephone number of the employee or employees appointed pursuant to this paragraph.

(b) *Complaint procedure of recipient.* A recipient shall adopt and publish grievance procedures providing for prompt and equitable resolution of student and employee complaints alleging any action which would be prohibited by this part.

§86.9 Dissemination of Policy.

(a) *Notification of policy.* (1) Each recipient shall implement specific and continuing steps to notify applicants for admission and employment, students and parents of elementary and secondary school students, employees, sources of referral of applicants for admission and employment, and all unions or professional organizations holding collective bargaining or professional agreements with the recipient, that it does not discriminate on the basis of sex in the educational programs or activities which it operates, and that is required by title IX and this part not to discriminate in such a manner. Such notification shall contain such information, and be made in such manner, as the Director finds necessary to apprise such persons of the protections against discrimination assured them by title IX and this part, but shall state at least that the requirements not to discriminate in education programs and activities extends to employment therein, and to admission thereto unless Subpart C does not apply to the recipient, and that inquiries concerning the application of title IX and this part to such recipient may be referred to the employee designated pursuant to §86.8, or to the Director.

* * *

(b) *Publications.* (1) Each recipient shall prominently include a statement of the policy described in paragraph (a) of this section in each announcement, bulletin, catalog, or application form which it makes available to any person of a type, described in paragraph (a) of this section, or which is otherwise used in connection with the recruitment of students or employees.

(2) A recipient shall not use or distribute a publication of the type described in this paragraph which suggests, by text or illustration, that such recipient treats applicants, students, or employees differently on the basis of sex except as such treatment is permitted by this part.

(c) *Distribution.* Each recipient shall distribute without discrimination on the basis of sex each publication described in paragraph (b) of this section, and shall apprise each of its admission and employment recruitment representatives of the policy of nondiscrimination described in paragraph (a) of this section, and require such representatives to adhere to such policy.

Subpart B—Coverage

§86.11 Application.

Except as provided in this subpart, this Part 86 applies to every recipient and to each education program or activity operated by such recipient which receives or benefits from Federal financial assistance.

§86.12 Educational Institutions Controlled by Religious Organizations.

(a) *Application.* This part does not apply to an educational institution which is controlled by a religious organization to the extent application of this part would not be consistent with the religious tenets of such organization.

(b) *Exemption.* An educational institution which wishes to claim the exemption set forth in paragraph (a) of this section, shall do so by submitting in writing to the Director a statement by the highest ranking official of the institution, identifying the provisions of this part which conflict with a specific tenet of the religious organization.

§86.14 Membership Practices of Certain Organizations.

(a) *Social Fraternities and sororities.* This part does not apply to the membership practices of social fraternities and sororities which are exempt from taxation under section 501(a) of the Internal Revenue Code of 1954, the active membership of which consists primarily of students in attendance at institutions of higher education.

(b) *YMCA, YWCA, Girl Scouts, Boy Scouts and Camp Fire Girls.* This part does not apply to the membership practices of the Young Men's

Christian Association, the Young Women's Christian Association, the Girl Scouts, the Boy Scouts and Camp Fire Girls.

(c) *Voluntary youth service organizations.* This part does not apply to the membership practices of voluntary youth service organizations which are exempt from taxation under section 501(a) of the Internal Revenue Code of 1954 and the membership of which has been traditionally limited to members of one sex and principally to persons of less than nineteen years of age.

* * *

Subpart C—Discrimination on the Basis of Sex in Admission and Recruitment Prohibited

§86.21 Admission.

(a) *General.* No person shall, on the basis of sex, be denied admission, or be subjected to discrimination in admission, by any recipient to which this subpart applies. * * *

(b) *Specific prohibitions.* (1) In determining whether a person satisfies any policy or criterion for admission, or in making any offer of admission, a recipient to which this Subpart applies shall not:

(i) Give preference to one person over another on the basis of sex, by ranking applicants separately on such basis, or otherwise;

(ii) Apply numerical limitations upon the number or proportion of persons of either sex who may be admitted; or

(iii) Otherwise treat one individual differently from another on the basis of sex.

(2) A recipient shall not administer or operate any test or other criterion for admission which has a disproportionately adverse effect on persons on the basis of sex unless the use of such test or criterion is shown to predict validly success in the education program or activity in question and alternative tests or criteria which do not have such a disproportionately adverse effect are shown to be unavailable.

(c) *Prohibitions relating to marital or parental status.* In determining whether a person satisfies any policy or criterion for admission, or in making any offer of admission, a recipient to which this subpart applies:

(1) Shall not apply any rule concerning the actual or potential parental, family, or marital status of a student or applicant which treats persons differently on the basis of sex,

(2) Shall not discriminate against or exclude any person on the basis of pregnancy, childbirth, termination of pregnancy, or recovery therefrom, or establish or follow any rule or practice which so discriminates or excludes;

(3) Shall treat disabilities related to pregnancy, childbirth, termination

of pregnancy, or recovery therefrom in the same manner and under the same policies as any other temporary disability or physical condition; and

(4) Shall not make pre-admission inquiry as to the marital status of an applicant for admission, including whether such applicant is "Miss" or "Mrs." A recipient may make pre-admission inquiry as to the sex of an applicant for admission, but only if such inquiry is made equally of such applicants of both sexes and if the results of such inquiry are not used in connection with discrimination prohibited by this part.

Subpart D—Discrimination on the Basis of Sex in Education Programs and Activities Prohibited

§86.31 Education Programs and Activities.

(a) *General.* Except as provided elsewhere in this part, no person shall, on the basis of sex, be excluded from participation in, be denied the benefits of, or be subjected to discrimination under any academic, extracurricular, research, occupational training, or other education program or activity operated by a recipient which receives of benefits from Federal financial assistance. This subpart does not apply to actions of a recipient in connection with admission of its students to an education program or activity of (1) a recipient to which Subpart C does not apply, or (2) an entity, not a recipient, to which Subpart C would not apply if the entity were a recipient.

(b) *Specific prohibitions.* Except as provided in this subpart, in providing any aid, benefit, or service to a student, a recipient shall not, on the basis of sex:

(1) Treat one person differently from another in determining whether such person satisfies any requirements or condition for the provision of such aid, benefit, or service;

(2) Provide different aid, benefits, or services or provide aid, benefits, or services in a different manner;

(3) Deny any person any such aid, benefit, or service;

(4) Subject any person to separate or different rules of behavior, sanctions, or other treatment;

(5) Discriminate against any person in the application of any rules of appearance;

(6) Apply any rule concerning the domicile or residence of a student or applicant, including eligibility for instate fees and tuition;

(7) Aid or perpetuate discrimination against any person by providing significant assistance to any agency, organization, or person which discriminates on the basis of sex in providing any aid, benefit or service to students or employees;

(8) Otherwise limit any person in the enjoyment of any right, privilege, advantage, or opportunity.

* * *

§86.33 Comparable Facilities.

A recipient may provide separate toilet, locker room, and shower facilities on the basis of sex, but such facilities provided for students of one sex shall be comparable to such facilities provided for students of the other sex.

§86.34 Access to Course Offerings.

A recipient shall not provide any course or otherwise carry out any of its education program or activity separately on the basis of sex, or require or refuse participation therein by any of its students on such basis, including health, physical education, industrial, business, vocational, technical, home economics, music, and adult education courses.

(a) With respect to classes and activities in physical education at the elementary school level, the recipient shall comply fully with this section as expeditiously as possible but in no event later than one year from the effective date of this regulation. With respect to physical education classes and activities at the secondary and post-secondary levels, the recipient shall comply fully with this section as expeditiously as possible but in no event later than three years from the effective date of this regulation.

(b) This section does not prohibit grouping of students in physical education classes and activities by ability as assessed by objective standards of individual performance developed and applied without regard to sex.

(c) This section does not prohibit separation of students by sex within physical education classes or activities during participation in wrestling, boxing, rugby, ice hockey, football, basketball and other sports the purpose or major activity of which involves bodily contact.

(d) Where use of a single standard of measuring skill or progress in a physical education class has an adverse effect on members of one sex, the recipient shall use appropriate standards which do not have such effect.

(3) Portions of classes in elementary and secondary schools which deal exclusively with human sexuality may be conducted in separate sessions for boys and girls.

(f) Recipients may make requirements based on vocal range or quality which may result in a chorus or choruses of one or predominantly one sex.

§86.35 Access to Schools Operated by L.E.A.s.

A recipient which is a local educational agency shall not, on the basis of sex, exclude any person from admission to:

(a) Any institution of vocational education operated by such recipient; or

(b) Any other school or educational unit operated by such recipient, unless such recipient otherwise makes available to such person, pursuant to the same policies and criteria of admission, courses, services, and facilities comparable to each course, service, and facility offered in or through such schools.

§86.36 Counseling and Use of Appraisal and Counseling Materials.

(a) *Counseling.* A recipient shall not discriminate against any person on the basis of sex in the counseling or guidance of students or applicants for admission.

(b) *Use of appraisal and counseling materials.* A recipient which uses testing or other materials for appraising or counseling students shall not use different materials for students on the basis of their sex or use materials which permit or require different treatment of students on such basis unless such different materials cover the same occupations and interest areas and the use of such different materials is shown to be essential to eliminate sex bias. Recipients shall develop and use internal procedures for ensuring that such materials do not discriminate on the basis of sex. Where the use of a counseling test or other instrument results in a substantially disproportionate number of members of one sex in any particular course of study or classification, the recipient shall take such action as is necessary to assure itself that such disproportion is not the result of discrimination in the instrument or its application.

(c) *Disproportion in classes.* Where a recipient finds that a particular class contains a substantially disproportionate number of individuals of one sex, the recipient shall take such action as is necessary to assure itself that such disproportion is not the result of discrimination on the basis of sex in counseling or appraisal materials or by counselors.

* * *

§86.38 Employment Assistance to Students.

(a) *Assistance by recipient in making available outside employment.* A recipient which assists any agency, organization or person in making employment available to any of its students:

(1) Shall assure itself that such employment is made available without discrimination on the basis of sex; and

(2) Shall not render such services to any agency, organization, or person which discriminates on the basis of sex in its employment practices.

(b) *Employment of students by recipients.* A recipient which employs any of its students shall not do so in a manner which violates Subpart E of this part.

§86.39 Health and Insurance Benefits and Services.

In providing a medical, hospital, accident, or life insurance benefit, service, policy, or plan to any of its students, a recipient shall not discriminate on the basis of sex, or provide such benefit, service, policy, or plan in a manner which would violate Subpart E of this part if it were provided to employees of the recipient. This section shall not prohibit a recipient from providing any benefit or service which may be used by a different proportion of students of one sex than of the other, including family planning services. However, any recipient which provides full coverage health service shall provide gynecological care.

* * *

§86.42 Textbooks and Curricular Material.

Nothing in this regulation shall be interpreted as requiring or prohibiting or abridging in any way the use of particular textbooks or curricular materials.

* * *

*THE EQUAL ACCESS ACT**

Denial of Equal Access Prohibited

SEC. 802 (a) It shall be unlawful for any public secondary school which receives Federal financial assistance and which has a limited open forum to deny equal access or a fair opportunity to, or discriminate against, any students who wish to conduct a meeting within that limited open forum on the basis of the religious, political, philosophical, or other content of the speech at such meetings.

(b) A public secondary school has a limited open forum whenever such school grants an offering to or opportunity for one or more noncurriculum related students groups to meet on school premises during non-instructional time.

(c) Schools shall be deemed to offer a fair opportunity to students who wish to conduct a meeting within its limited open forum if such school uniformly provides that—

*Title VIII of the Education for Economic Security Act, Public Law 98-377 (1984).

(1) the meeting is voluntary and student-initiated;

(2) there is no sponsorship of the meeting by the school, the government, or its agents or employees;

(3) employees or agents of the school or government are present at religious meetings only in a nonparticipatory capacity;

(4) the meeting does not materially and substantially interfere with the orderly conduct of educational activities within the school; and

(5) nonschool persons may not direct, conduct, control, or regularly attend activities of student groups.

(d) Nothing in this title shall be construed to authorize the United States or any State or political subdivision thereof—

(1) to influence the form or content of any prayer or other religious activity;

(2) to require any person to participate in prayer or other religious activity;

(3) to expend public funds beyond the incidental cost of providing the space for student-initiated meetings;

(4) to compel any school agent or employee to attend a school meeting if the content of the speech at the meeting is contrary to the beliefs of the agent or employee;

(5) to sanction meetings that are otherwise unlawful;

(6) to limit the rights of groups of students which are not of a specified numerical size; or

(7) to abridge the constitutional rights of any person.

(e) Notwithstanding the availability of any other remedy under the Constitution or the laws of the United States, nothing in this title shall be construed to authorize the United States to deny or withhold Federal financial assistance to any school.

(f) Nothing in this title shall be construed to limit the authority of the school, its agents or employees, to maintain order and discipline on school premises, to protect the well-being of students and faculty, and to assure that attendance of students at meetings is voluntary.

Definitions

SEC. 803. As used in this title—

(1) The term "secondary school" means a public school which provides secondary education as determined by State law.

(2) The term "sponsorship" includes the act of promoting, leading, or participating in a meeting. The assignment of a teacher, administrator, or other school employee to a meeting for custodial purposes does not constitute sponsorship of the meeting.

(3) The term "meeting" includes those activities of student

groups which are permitted under a school's limited open forum and are not directly related to the school curriculum.

(4) The term "noninstructional time" means time set aside by the school before actual classroom instruction begins or after actual classroom instruction ends.

* * *

Section 504 of the Rehabilitation Act of 1973—P.L. 93-112

IMPLEMENTING REGULATIONS—45 CFR 84 (EDITED)

PART 84—NONDISCRIMINATION ON THE BASIS OF HANDICAP IN PROGRAMS AND ACTIVITIES RECEIVING OR BENEFITING FROM FEDERAL FINANCIAL ASSISTANCE

* * *

Subpart A—General Provisions

§ 84.1 Purpose.

The purpose of this part is to effectuate section 504 of the Rehabilitation Act of 1973, which is designed to eliminate discrimination on the basis of handicap in any program or activity receiving Federal financial assistance.

* * *

§ 84.4 Discrimination Prohibited.

(a) *General.* No qualified handicapped person shall, on the basis of handicap, be excluded from participation in, be denied the benefits of, or otherwise be subjected to discrimination under any program or activity which receives or benefits from Federal financial assistance.

* * *

(2) For purposes of this part, aids, benefits, and services, to be equally effective, are not required to produce the identical result or level of achievement for handicapped and nonhandicapped persons, but must afford handicapped persons equal opportunity to obtain the same result, to gain the same benefit, or to reach the same level of achievement, in the most integrated setting appropriate to the person's needs.

(3) Despite the existence of separate or different programs or activities provided in accordance with this part, a recipient may not deny a

qualified handicapped person the opportunity to participate in such programs or activities that are not separate or different.

(4) A recipient may not, directly or through contractual or other arrangements, utilize criteria or methods of administration (i) that have the effect of subjecting qualified handicapped persons to discrimination on the basis of handicap, (ii) that have the purpose or effect of defeating or substantially impairing accomplishment of the objectives of the recipient's program with respect to handicapped persons, or (iii) that perpetuate the discrimination of another recipient if both recipients are subject to common administrative control or are agencies of the same State.

(5) In determining the site or location of a facility, an applicant for assistance or a recipient may not make selections (i) that have the effect of excluding handicapped persons from, denying them the benefits of, or otherwise subjecting them to discrimination under any program or activity that receives or benefits from Federal financial assistance or (ii) that have the purpose or effect of defeating or substantially impairing the accomplishment of the objectives of the program or activity with respect to handicapped persons.

* * *

§ 84.5 Assurances Required.

(a) *Assurances.* An applicant for Federal financial assistance for a program or activity to which this part applies shall submit an assurance, on a form specified by the Director, that the program will be operated in compliance with this part. An applicant may incorporate these assurances by reference in subsequent applications to the Department.

§ 84.6 Remedial Action, Voluntary Action, and Self-evaluation.

(a) *Remedial action.* (1) If the Director finds that a recipient has discriminated against persons on the basis of handicap in violation of section 504 or this part, the recipient shall take such remedial action as the Director deems necessary to overcome the effects of the discrimination.

(2) Where a recipient is found to have discriminated against persons on the basis of handicap in violation of section 504 or this part and where another recipient exercises control over the recipient that has discriminated, the Director, where appropriate, may require either or both recipients to take remedial action.

(3) The Director may, where necessary to overcome the effects of discrimination in violation of section 504 or this part, require a recipient to take remedial action (i) with respect to handicapped persons who are no longer participants in the recipient's program but who were partici-

pants in the program when such discrimination occurred or (ii) with respect to handicapped persons who would have been participants in the program had the discrimination not occurred.

(b) *Voluntary action.* A recipient may take steps, in addition to any action that is required by this part, to overcome the effects of conditions that resulted in limited participation in the recipient's program or activity by qualified handicapped persons.

* * *

§ 84.7 Designation of Responsible Employee and Adoption of Grievance Procedures.

(a) *Designation of responsible employee.* A recipient that employs fifteen or more persons shall designate at least one person to coordinate its efforts to comply with this part.

(b) *Adoption of grievance procedure.* A recipient that employs fifteen or more persons shall adopt grievance procedures that incorporate appropriate due process standards and that provide for the prompt and equitable resolution of complaints alleging any action prohibited by this part. Such procedures need not be established with respect to complaints from applicants for employment or from applicants for admission to postsecondary educational institutions.

§ 84.8 Notice.

(a) A recipient that employs fifteen or more persons shall take appropriate initial and continuing steps to notify participants, beneficiaries, applicants, and employees, including those with impaired vision or hearing, and unions or professional organizations holding collective bargaining or professional agreements with the recipient that it does not discriminate on the basis of handicap in violation of section 504 and this part. The notification shall state, where appropriate, that the recipient does not discriminate in admission or access to, or treatment or employment in, its programs and activities. The notification shall include an identification of the responsible employee designated pursuant to § 84.7(a). A recipient shall make the initial notification required by this paragraph within 90 days of the effective date of this part. Methods of initial and continuing notification may include the posting of notices, publication in newspapers and magazines, placement of notices in recipients' publication, and distribution of memoranda or other written communications.

(b) If a recipient publishes or uses recruitment materials or publications containing general information that it makes available to participants, beneficiaries, applicants, or employees, it shall include in those materials or publications a statement of the policy described in paragraph

(a) of this section. A recipient may meet the requirement of this paragraph either by including appropriate inserts in existing materials and publications or by revising and reprinting the materials and publications.

* * *

Subpart C—Program Accessibility

§ 84.21 Discrimination Prohibited.

No qualified handicapped person shall, because a recipient's facilities are inaccessible to or unusable by handicapped persons, be denied the benefits of, be excluded from participation in, or otherwise be subjected to discrimination under any program or activity to which this part applies.

§ 84.22 Existing Facilities.

(a) *Program accessibility.* A recipient shall operate each program or activity to which this part applies so that the program or activity, when viewed in its entirety, is readily accessible to handicapped persons. This paragraph does not require a recipient to make each of its existing facilities or every part of a facility accessible to and usable by handicapped persons.

* * *

Subpart D—Preschool, Elementary, and Secondary Education

§ 84.31 Application of this Subpart.

Subpart D applies to preschool, elementary, secondary, and adult education programs and activities that receive or benefit from Federal financial assistance and to recipients that operate, or that receive or benefit from Federal financial assistance for the operation of, such programs or activities.

§ 84.32 Location and Notification.

A recipient that operates a public elementary or secondary education program shall annually:

(a) Undertake to identify and locate every qualified handicapped person residing in the recipient's jurisdiction who is not receiving a public education; and

(b) Take appropriate steps to notify handicapped persons and their parents or guardians of the recipient's duty under this subpart.

§ 84.33 Free Appropriate Public Education

(a) *General.* A recipient that operates a public elementary or secondary education program shall provide a free appropriate public education to each qualified handicapped person who is in the recipient's jurisdiction, regardless of the nature or severity of the person's handicap.

(b) *Appropriate education.* (1) For the purpose of this subpart, the provision of an appropriate education is the provision of regular or special education and related aids and services that (i) are designed to meet individual educational needs of handicapped persons as adequately as the needs of nonhandicapped persons are met and (ii) are based upon adherence to procedures that satisfy the requirements of §§ 84.34, 84.35, and 84.36.

(2) Implementation of an individualized education program developed in accordance with the Education of the Handicapped Act is one means of meeting the standard established in paragraph (b) (1) (i) of this section.

(3) A recipient may place a handicapped person in or refer such person to a program other than the one that it operates as its means of carrying out the requirements of this subpart. If so, the recipient remains responsible for ensuring that the requirements of this subpart are met with respect to any handicapped person so placed or referred.

(c) *Free education*—(1) *General.* For the purpose of this section, the provision of a free education is the provision of educational and related services without cost to the handicapped person or to his or her parents or guardian, except for those fees that are imposed on non-handicapped persons or their parents or guardian. It may consist either of the provision of free services or, if a recipient places a handicapped person in or refers such person to a program not operated by the recipient as its means of carrying out the requirements of this subpart, of payment for the costs of the program. Funds available from any public or private agency may be used to meet the requirements of this subpart. Nothing in this section shall be construed to relieve an insurer or similar third party from an otherwise valid obligation to provide or pay for services provided to a handicapped person.

(2) *Transportation.* If a recipient places a handicapped person in or refers such person to a program not operated by the recipient as its means of carrying out the requirements of this subpart, the recipient shall ensure that adequate transportation to and from the program is provided at no greater cost than would be incurred by the person or his or her parents or guardian if the persons were placed in the program operated by the recipient.

(3) *Residential placement.* If placement in a public or private residential program is necessary to provide a free appropriate public education to a handicapped person because of his or her handicap, the program, including non-medical care and room and board, shall be provided at no cost to the person or his or her parents or guardian.

(4) *Placement of handicapped persons by parents.* If a recipient has made available, in conformance with the requirements of this section and § 84.34, a free appropriate public education to a handicapped person and the person's parents or guardian choose to place the person in a private school, the recipient is not required to pay for the person's education in the private school. Disagreements between a parent or guardian and a recipient regarding whether the recipient has made such a program available or otherwise regarding the question of financial responsibility are subject to the due process procedures of § 84.36.

(d) *Compliance.* A recipient may not exclude any qualified handicapped person from a public elementary or secondary education after the effective date of this part. A recipient that is not, on the effective date of this regulation, in full compliance with the other requirements of the preceding paragraphs of this section shall meet such requirements at the earliest practicable time and in no event later than September 1, 1978.

§ 84.34 Educational Setting.

(a) *Academic setting.* A recipient to which this subpart applies shall educate, or shall provide for the education of, each qualified handicapped person in its jurisdiction with persons who are not handicapped to the maximum extent appropriate to the needs of the handicapped person. A recipient shall place a handicapped person in the regular educational environment operated by the recipient unless it is demonstrated by the recipient that the education of the person in the regular environment with use of supplementary aids and services cannot be achieved satisfactorily. Whenever a recipient takes a person in a setting other than the regular educational environment pursuant to this paragraph, it shall take into account the proximity of the alternate setting to the person's home.

(b) *Nonacademic settings.* In providing or arranging for the provision of nonacademic and extracurricular services and activities, including meals, recess periods, and the services and activities set forth in § 84.37(a)(2), a recipient shall ensure that handicapped persons participate with nonhandicapped persons in such activities and services to the maximum extent appropriate to the needs of the handicapped person in question.

(c) *Comparable facilities.* If a recipient, in compliance with paragraph (a) of this section, operates a facility that is identifiable as being for handicapped persons, the recipient shall ensure that the facility and the services and activities provided therein are comparable to the other facilities, services, and activities of the recipient.

§ 84.35 Evaluation and Placement.

(a) *Preplacement evaluation.* A recipient that operates a public elementary or secondary education program shall conduct an evaluation in accordance with the requirements of paragraph (b) of this section of any person who, because of handicap, needs or is believed to need special education or related services before taking any action with respect to the initial placement of the person in a regular or special education program and any subsequent significant changes in placement.

(b) *Evaluation procedures.* A recipient to which this subpart applies shall establish standards and procedures for the evaluation and placement of persons who, because of handicap, need or are believed to need special education or related services which ensure that:

(1) Tests and other evaluation materials have been validated for the specific purpose for which they are used and are administered by trained personnel in conformance with the instructions provided by their producer;

(2) Tests and other evaluation materials include those tailored to assess specific areas of educational need and not merely those which are designed to provide a single general intelligence quotient; and

(3) Tests are selected and administered so as best to ensure that, when a test is administered to a student with impaired sensory, manual, or speaking skills, the test results accurately reflect the student's aptitude or achievement level or whatever other factor the test purports to measure, rather than reflecting the student's impaired sensory, manual, or speaking skills (except where those skills are the factors that the test purports to measure).

(c) *Placement procedures.* In interpreting evaluation data and in making placement decisions, a recipient shall (1) draw upon information from a variety of sources, including aptitude and achievement tests, teacher recommendations, physical condition, social or cultural background, and adaptive behavior, (2) establish procedures to ensure that information obtained from all such sources is documented and carefully considered, (3) ensure that the placement decision is made by a group of persons, including persons knowledgeable about the child, the meaning of the evaluation data, and the placement options, and (4) ensure that the placement decision is made in conformity with § 84.34.

(d) *Reevaluation.* A recipient to which this section applies shall establish procedures, in accordance with paragraph (b) of this section, for periodic reevaluation of students who have been provided special education and related services. A reevaluation procedure consistent with the Education for the Handicapped Act is one means of meeting this requirement.

§ 84.36 Procedural Safeguards.

A recipient that operates a public elementary or secondary education program shall establish and implement, with respect to actions regarding the identification, evaluation, or educational placement of persons who, because of handicap, need or are believed to need special instruction or related services, a system of procedural safeguards that includes notice, an opportunity for the parents or guardian of the person to examine relevant records, an impartial hearing with opportunity for participation by the person's parents or guardian and representation by counsel, and a review procedure. Compliance with the procedural safeguards of section 615 of the Education of the Handicapped Act is one means of meeting this requirement.

§ 84.37 Nonacademic Services.

(a) *General.* (1) A recipient to which this subpart applies shall provide nonacademic and extracurricular services and activities in such manner as is necessary to afford handicapped students an equal opportunity for participation in such services and activities.

(2) Nonacademic and extracurricular services and activities may include counseling services, physical recreational athletics, transportation, health services, recreational activities, special interest groups or clubs sponsored by the recipients, referrals to agencies which provide assistance to handicapped persons, and employment of students, including both employment by the recipient and assistance in making available outside employment.

(b) *Counseling services.* A recipient to which this subpart applies that provides personal, academic, or vocational counseling, guidance, or placement services to its students shall provide these services without discrimination on the basis of handicap. The recipient shall ensure that qualified handicapped students are not counseled toward more restrictive career objectives than are nonhandicapped students with similar interests and abilities.

(c) *Physical education and athletics.* (1) In providing physical education courses and athletics and similar programs and activities to any of its students, a recipient to which this subpart applies may not discriminate on the basis of handicap. A recipient that offers physical education courses or that operates or sponsors interscholastic, club, or intramural athletics shall provide to qualified handicapped students equal opportunity for participation in these activities.

(2) A recipient may offer to handicapped students physical education and athletic activities that are separate or different from those offered to nonhandicapped students only if separation or differentiation is consistent with the requirements of § 84.34 and only if no qualified handicapped student is denied the oportunity to compete for teams or to participate in courses that are not separate or different.

§ 84.38 Preschool and Adult Education Programs.

A recipient to which this subpart applies that operates a preschool education or day care program or activity or an adult education program or activity may not, on the basis of handicap, exclude qualified handicapped persons from the program or activity and shall take into account the needs of such persons in determining the aid, benefits, or services to be provided under the program or activity.

§ 84.39 Private Education Programs.

(a) A recipient that operates a private elementary or secondary education program may not, on the basis of handicap, exclude a qualified handicapped person from such program if the person can, with minor adjustments, be provided an appropriate education, as defined in § 84.33(b)(1), within the recipient's program.

(b) A recipient to which this section applies may not charge more for the provision of an appropriate education to handicapped persons than to nonhandicapped persons except to the extent that any additional charge is justified by a substantial increase in cost to the recipient.

* * *

Pregnancy Discrimination Act of 1978–P.L. 95-555

Be it enacted by the Senate and House of Representatives of the United States of America in Congress assembled, That section 701 of the Civil Rights Act of 1964 is amended by adding at the end thereof the following new subsection:

"(k) The Terms 'because of sex' or 'on the basis of sex' include, but are not limited to, because of or on the basis of pregnancy, childbirth, or related medical conditions; and women affected by pregnancy, childbirth, or related medical conditions shall be treated the same for all employment-related purposes, including the receipt of benefits under fringe benefit programs, as other persons not so affected but similar in their ability or inability to work, and nothing in section 703(h) of this title shall be interpreted to permit otherwise. This subsection shall not require an employer to pay for health insurance benefits for abortion, except where the life of the mother would be endangered if the fetus were carried to term, or except where medical complications have arisen from an abortion: *Provided,* That nothing herein shall preclude an employer from providing abortion benefits or otherwise affect bargaining agreements in regard to abortion."

SEC. 2 (a) Except as provided in subsection (b), the amendment made by this Act shall be effective on the date of enactment.

(b) The provisions of the amendment made by the first section of this Act shall not apply to any fringe benefit program or fund, or insurance program which is in effect on the date of enactment of this Act until 180 days after enactment of this Act.

SEC. 3 Until the expiration of a period of one year from the date of enactment of this Act or, if there is an applicable collective-bargaining agreement in effect on the date of enactment of this Act, until the termination of that agreement, no person who, on the date of enactment of this Act is providing either by direct payment or by making contributions to a fringe benefit fund or insurance program, benefits in violation with this Act shall, in order to come into compliance with this Act, reduce the benefits or the compensation provided any employee on the date of enactment of this Act, either directly or by failing to provide sufficient contributions to a fringe benefit fund or insurance program: *Provided,* That where the costs of such benefits on the date of enactment of this Act are apportioned between employers and employees, the payments or contributions required to comply with this Act may be made by employers and employees in the same proportion: *And provided further,* That nothing in this section shall prevent the readjustment of benefits or compensation for reasons unrelated to compliance with this Act.

*Civil Rights–42 U.S.C. § 1981–1983**

§ 1981. Equal Rights Under the Law.

All persons within the jurisdiction of the United States shall have the right in every State and Territory to make and enforce contracts, to sue, be parties, give evidence, and to full and equal benefit of all laws and proceedings for the security of persons and property as is enjoyed by white citizens, and shall be subject to like punishment, pains, penalties, taxes, licenses, and exactions of every kind, and to no other.

§ 1982. Property Rights of Citizens

All citizens of the United States shall have the same right, in every State and Territory, as is enjoyed by white citizens thereof to inherit, purchase, lease, sell, hold, and convey real and personal property.

*Original versions of these statutes were enacted shortly after the Civil War.

§ 1983. Civil Action for Deprivation of Rights

Every person who, under color of any statute, ordinance, regulation, custom or usage, of any State or Territory or the District of Columbia, subjects, or causes to be subjected, any citizen of the United States or other person within the jurisdiction thereof to the deprivation of any rights, privileges, or immunities secured by the Constitution and laws, shall be liable to the party injured in an action at law, suit in equity, or other proper proceeding for redress. * * *

glossary

Action A proceeding in a court of law, often referred to as a suit or lawsuit.

Ad litem A guardian ad litem is one appointed to prosecute or defend a suit on behalf of a party incapacitated by infancy or otherwise.

Advisory opinion An opinion rendered by a court when no actual case is before it. Although some state courts render advisory opinions, the United States Supreme Court and lower federal courts do not.

Affirm To approve or uphold a lower court's judgment.

Amicus curiae A friend of the court. Generally, one who has an indirect interest in a case and offers or is requested to provide information to the court in order to clarify particular matters before the court.

Appeal An application to a higher court to amend a lower court's ruling.

Appellant One who takes an appeal to a higher court. The appellant may have been the plaintiff or defendant in the lower court proceeding.

Appellee The party in an action against whom an appeal has been sought. Sometimes also called the respondent.

Bill A formal written statement or complaint filed in a court.

Case law A body of law created by judicial decisions. By establishing precedents upon which courts rely, the case law provides a primary source of legal authority.

Certiorari A judicial process whereby a case is removed from a lower court to a higher court for review. The record of the proceedings is transmitted to the higher court.

Civil action A court action brought to gain or to recover individual or civil rights or to obtain redress for an alleged noncriminal injustice.

Class action A court action brought by one or more individuals on behalf of themselves and all others who have a similar interest in a particular issue.

Code A systematic compilation of statutes, usually incorporating an indexing procedure to facilitate location of pertinent provisions.

Collateral attack An attempt to challenge the credibility or validity of a judicial proceeding based on related or incidental issues.

Common law A system of law in which authority is not derived expressly from statutes. Rather, traditional legal principles are derived from usage and custom as enunciated by court decisions.

Compensatory damages Damages awarded to reimburse the injured party only for the actual loss incurred. Punitive or exemplary damages are not considered compensatory.

Complaint A formal pleading to a court demanding relief as well as informing the defendant of the grounds of the suit.

Concurring opinion An opinion written by a judge expressing agreement with the majority's holding. However, the concurring judge may disagree with the majority's reasoning or discuss additional principles or points of law.

Conflict of laws An area of law dealing with the clarification of inconsistencies and differences in laws or jurisdictions as they apply to the rights of individuals in particular actions.

Consent decree An agreement by parties to a dispute, and although not properly a judicial sentence, it is in effect an admission by them that the decree is a just determination of their rights based upon the facts of the case.

Constitution The supreme fundamental law of a nation or state. Provisions are included to establish and organize the government and to distribute, limit, and prescribe the manner of the exercise of sovereign powers. In addition, basic principles and rights of the citizenry are enumerated.

Court of record A court whose actions are recorded, possessing the authority to levy sanctions.

Criminal action A court action, brought by the state, against one charged with an offense against the state. This type of action may result in a fine or incarceration of the defendant.

Damages The compensation or indemnity claimed by the plaintiff or allowed by the court for injuries sustained as a result of a wrongful act or negligence of another.

De facto In fact. A state of affairs that must be accepted for all practical purposes, but does not have the sanction of laws behind it. As distinguished from de jure.

De jure By right. A legitimate state of affairs that has the force of law behind it.

De minimis Trifling or insignificant matters, with which a court will not concern itself.

De novo Anew, afresh, a second time. A second trial of a case that has been sent back from a higher court for a new trial.

Decision A conclusion or judgment of a court, as opposed to the reasoning or opinion of the court.

Declaratory judgment Without issuing an order for anything to be done, a court clarifies questions of law, recognizes the rights of the parties, or expresses an opinion.

Decree A court order issued in an equity suit.

Defendant The party against whom an action is brought.

Demurrer An allegation by a defendant admitting that although the facts are correct, a suit is not justified nor do they require an answer by the defendant.

Dictum (obiter dictum) An opinion expressed by a judge in a proceeding that is not necessary in formulating the court's decision. Therefore, it does not establish binding precedent. However, it may indicate the judge's persuasion.

Dismissal A final disposition of a suit by a court by sending it out of court without a trial of the issues.

Dissenting opinion An opinion written by a judge in disagreement with the rationale and/or decision of the majority of judges hearing the case.

Due process of law Implies that the powers of the government are exercised similarly in similar situations in order to protect individuals' rights. Denial of this right is prohibited by the Fifth and Fourteenth Amendments when life, liberty, or property are involved.

En banc A proceeding in which all judges of a court participate in the decision.

Enjoin An individual or institution is required by a court of equity to cease or abstain from a particular action. See Injunction.

Equal protection of the law A guarantee that no person or class of persons shall be denied the same protection of the laws that is enjoyed by other persons or classes in similar circumstances. Denial of this right is prohibited by the Fourteenth Amendment.

Equity law A particular branch of law that differs from the common law. Primarily concerned with providing justice and fair treatment, equity law addresses issues the common law is unable to consider.

Et al. And others. Indicates that unnamed parties are involved in the proceedings.

Exclusionary rule A procedure in search-and-seizure cases seeking to suppress the use of evidence which has been improperly obtained.

Ex parte A proceeding for the benefit of one party only.

Ex post facto After the fact, often thought of in terms of a law making an act illegal after someone has committed the act.

Ex rel. Designates a private individual on whose behalf the state is acting in a legal proceeding.

Finding A conclusion of a court or jury regarding a question of fact.

Governmental immunity (See Sovereign immunity).

Hearing Judicial examination of factual or legal issues.

In loco parentis In place of the parent. Possessing a portion of the parent's rights, duties, and responsibilities.

In re In the matter of. A method of entitling a judicial proceeding in which there are no adversaries.

Injunction An order issued by a court of equity prohibiting a person from commiting a threatened act or continuing to do some act that is injurious to the plaintiff.

Inter alia Among other things.

Ipso facto By the fact itself. As a necessary consequence.

Judgment A decision rendered by a court.

Liability A legal responsibility.

Litigation The formal contesting of a dispute in a court, a lawsuit.

Majority opinion The statement expressing the views of the majority of judges in a court decision.

Malfeasance Commission of an unlawful act.

Mandamus A court order compelling a public official or institution to perform a particular nondiscretionary duty.

Mandate A judicial command, order, or direction.

Minority opinion A statement expressing the views of a judge or a minority of judges in a court decision. This may take the form of separate minority opinions.

Misfeasance Improper performance of a lawful act.

Negligence Failure to exercise ordinary prudence and foresight when such failure results in an injury to another.

Nolens volens Whether willing or unwilling.

Nonfeasance Failure to perform a required duty.

Nuisance Continuous private or public use of property that results in injury, inconvenience, or damage.

Original jurisdiction The jurisdiction of a court to entertain a case at its inception, as contrasted with appellate jurisdiction.

Parens patriae The state as a sovereign—referring to the sovereign power of guardianship over persons such as minors.

Per curiam An opinion rendered by an entire court, as opposed to an opinion of any one of several justices.

Petition A written application to a court for the redress of a wrong or the grant of a privilege or license.

Petitioner One who presents a petition to a court.

Plaintiff One who brings an action or files a complaint in a court.

Plea A formal allegation filed by a defendant in an action in reply to the plaintiff's complaint or charges.

Pleadings Formal documents filed in a court action. They include the plaintiff's complaint and the defendant's reply, indicating that which is alleged by one party and denied or conceded by the other party.

Plenary Full, entire, complete.

Prayer A request by the plaintiff that the court of equity grant the particular relief sought.

Precedent Previously decided authoritative court decisions addressing identical or similar questions of law.

Prima facie At first view, before investigation. A fact presumed to be true unless disproved by some evidence to the contrary.

Pro se In person, in their own behalf.

Quasi As if. Almost as it were, analogous to.

Quid pro quo A consideration, giving one valuable thing for another.

Relief Legal redress or assistance sought in court by the complainant.

Remand To send back. Following an appellate decision a case may be sent back to the court from which it came for further proceedings.

Remedy A court's enforcement of a right or the prevention of the violation of a right.

Res ipsa loquitur The thing speaks for itself.

Res judicata A matter judicially decided.

Respondent The party against whom an appeal is taken in a higher court.

Restrain To enjoin or prohibit.

Sovereign immunity A doctrine providing that a governmental body is immune to suit without the expressed permission of the body itself.

Standing The right to raise an issue in a lawsuit.

Stare decisis To stand by decided cases. The doctrine whereby precedent assumes the authority of established law.

Status quo The existing state of affairs.

Statute An act of the state or federal legislature, a law.

Sui generis Of its own kind or class, unique.

Suit A proceeding in a court of law brought by a plaintiff.

Summary judgment A court's decision to settle a controversy or dispose of a case promptly without conducting full legal proceedings.

Tort A private or civil wrong or injury.

Trial The examination of a civil or criminal case by a competent tribunal. It may be made by a judge or judges, with or without a jury.

Ultra vires Exceeding the power or authority.

Vacate To cancel or rescind a court decision.

Void Without force or binding effect. Absolutely null.

Waive To forego, renounce, or abandon a legal right. By waiver, the right is lost.

Writ A written court order requiring performance of a specific act, such as a writ of injunction or mandamus.